a handbook of arts and crafts

tenth edition

Philip R. Wigg
Professor Emeritus
Bowling Green State University

Jean Hasselschwert
Bowling Green City Schools

McGraw Hill

Boston   Burr Ridge, IL   Dubuque, IA   Madison, WI   New York   San Francisco   St. Louis
Bangkok   Bogotá   Caracas   Lisbon   London   Madrid
Mexico City   Milan   New Delhi   Seoul   Singapore   Sydney   Taipei   Toronto

To the memory of Marietta Wigg
coauthor, colleague, and wife

and

Willard F. Wankelman
coauthor, colleague, and friend

McGraw-Hill Higher Education

A Division of The McGraw-Hill Companies

A HANDBOOK OF ARTS AND CRAFTS

Published by McGraw-Hill, an imprint of The McGraw-Hill Companies, Inc. 1221 Avenue of the Americas, New York, NY, 10020. Copyright © 2001, 1997, 1993, 1989, 1985, 1982, 1974, 1968, by The McGraw-Hill Companies, Inc. All rights reserved. No part of this publication may be reproduced or distributed in any form or by any means, or stored in a database or retrieval system, without the prior written consent of The McGraw-Hill Companies, Inc., including, but not limited to, in any network or other electronic storage or transmission, or broadcast for distance learning. Some ancillaries, including electronic and print components, may not be available to customers outside the United States.

This book is printed on acid-free paper.

1 2 3 4 5 6 7 8 9 0 QPD/QPD 0 9 8 7 6 5 4 3 2 1 0

ISBN 0–07–231727–2

Editorial director: *Phillip A. Butcher*
Sponsoring editor: *Joseph Hanson*
Editorial assistant: *Heather McCabe*
Marketing manager II: *David Patterson*
Project manager: *Susanne Riedell*
Production supervisor: *Rose Hepburn*
Senior designer: *Laurie J. Entringer*
Cover image: *PhotoDisc*
Compositor: *Shepherd Incorporated*
Typeface: *10/12 Times Roman*
Printer: *Quebecor Printing Book Group/Dubuque*

Library of Congress Cataloging-in-Publication Data

Wigg, Philip R.
    A handbook of arts & crafts / Philip R. Wigg, Jean Hasselschwert.—10th ed.
      p. cm.
    ISBN 0–07–231727–2 (softcover : alk. paper)
    Includes bibliographical references and index.
    1. Creative activities and seat work—Handbooks, manuals, etc.   2. Art—Study and teaching
—Handbooks, manuals, etc.   3. Handicraft—Handbooks, manuals, etc.   I. Hasselschwert, Jean.
II. Title.
LB1537.W3   2001
372.5 dc—21   00–031865

www.mhhe.com

brief contents

contents

10 pencil, paint, and ink   166

11 paper and cardboard   196

12 papier-mâché   219

part three resources

preface

As this book has evolved through its previous editions, it has reflected our desire to provide useful and timely assistance for the classroom. At the same time, different theories have been evolving regarding art instruction. Many teachers have developed their own approaches to teaching according to their own diverse circumstances. Probably the greatest leap in teaching techniques, hopefully applicable to all, has been the discipline-based art education (DBAE), which has found many disciples nationwide. We have devoted considerable investigation to this system since our last edition and find some merit in it while, at the same time, feeling some doubt as to its usefulness in every situation. In this edition we pay much more attention to DBAE and encourage art teachers who lack familiarity with it to study its recommended procedures.

Our reviewers have been candid in their critiques of the previous edition and their suggestions have been very helpful. Heading the list of constructive feedback is a request for more emphasis on DBAE, which we have provided. The reviewers detected some negativism in the first chapter. We were not aware of this and have consequently expressed our true attitude toward today's art scene, and that is one of *optimism,* as it has always been, despite some reader interpretations. In addition, we have given the art activities a rigorous screening, added many new ones, and have provided more historical and cultural connections.

Some reviewers have been critical of the length of certain sections. On the other hand, there are those who disagree with this criticism. As it has always been, in writing a book, satisfaction is never guaranteed for all, but we walk the fine line of attempting to satisfy the greatest number. Where dissatisfaction has not been highly persuasive, we have usually left things as they are in fairness to those who approve.

Our reviewers have helped identify those activities that have been the most, and least, successful. In addition, they have kindly provided us with new activities, resources, formulas, and hints. These suggestions will undoubtedly add to the quality of the book.

We therefore render our thanks to our reviewers, thanks which must also be extended to the publisher, who has ably assisted our efforts. We hope that a great number of teachers will find much more information and guidance in this edition.

Margaret Benson
Augusta Technical Institute

William Eickhorst
Missouri Western State College

Becky Faulconer
Asbury College

David McIntyre
University of Texas at El Paso

Amy S. Meekins
Salisbury State University

Michael Tayse
Lorain County Community College

Jim Terrell
Northeastern State University

Thomas M. Brewer
University of Central Florida

Shari Stoddard
Ball State University

Laurel Covington Vogl
Fort Lewis College

foundations
part one

art and teaching

1

Basic concepts
of art instruction

Today there is reason for considerable optimism concerning the position of art in our society. Attendance at art museums is rising, and the better art journals often include examples and some analyses of artists and their works past and present. In addition, art instruction for the young is proliferating, with new ideas emerging on teaching techniques that acquaint students with a broader and more critical attitude toward art. This instruction is creating a greater acceptance of art styles that were anathema to many people only a few years ago. A global cultural understanding of art is developing. Continual archaeological discoveries of great interest have brought the artifacts of previous cultures to life. We hope that this book will lend itself to the increasing interest in art, as reflected in school programs.

The benefits of participation in art are listed in the section, An Introduction to the Art Activities, found later in this book. We think that those benefits warrant support of the arts. One of the authors remembers an inscription on a college art building—*Ars Longa Vita Brevis Est* ("Art Is Long, Life Is Short"). History concurs: Some of the most compelling keys to historical eras are in their art. We hope that our era will pass along a distinguished heritage to future generations.

Discipline-based art instruction (DBAE) as a mode of instruction

Throughout the years, art has been increasingly accepted by public and private schools as a constructive part of their curricula. Theories of instruction have varied, but are beginning to be consolidated. Art is being viewed as a solid, meaningful subject. One theory that has come to the fore is that of discipline-based art education (DBAE). If one subscribes to DBAE, the art product is not totally the objective; one can expect correlations with history and life experiences to be brought forth. The goals are to enable students to discuss art with at least a modest degree of connoisseurship, to be conversant with art of the past and present to such a degree that comparisons and choices can be made, and to glean information on a wide variety of these subjects from such sources. Clearly, art in this context is not a soft subject, nor is it a restful interlude for the teacher. This theory presumes a greater potential in the student than has been considered in the past.

Changing attitudes toward art instruction

Education in the visual arts has had a slow path toward professionalism. Many years ago, there were only a few public school teachers who believed art was a significant educational instrument. Many used art, in a generally regimented manner, as an interlude among other subjects. Most career-minded art students went to professional art schools, and few opportunities existed for the study of art teaching. College art programs were few and far between and most were quite academic. The majority of the courses were art "appreciation." Some colleges maintained an artist-in-residence as an obeisance to culture. High schools that offered art (often only the larger ones) only offered them as minimum-credit courses. At the elementary level, when not ousted by other subjects or financial exigencies, art was frequently a greatly appreciated period of relaxation for the teacher who, in most cases, had little or no background in art. Children were either loosely supervised in their work or subjected to projects that were lacking in creativity.

In the intervening years, the picture has changed for the better. We now have large, well-financed, well-staffed, and well-equipped departments of art in many colleges and universities that rival the professional schools. There are programs of study that cater to those who wish to be career artists or designers and to others who are inclined to teach at the college, high school, or elementary levels.

Most teachers now have had instruction in teaching art as part of their college training. Some schools make use of team teaching, and some teachers travel to several schools. Students training to teach art at any level usually follow a college program that closely parallels that of the professional career-track student. Art teaching trainees are often enlightened by courses in educational psychology, art methods, the exceptional child, public school art, art curriculum, and practice teaching. This experience illustrates and reinforces the fact that the art teacher should be a true professional and that art is an area of serious study.

Discipline-based art education

DBAE teaching procedures

As stated earlier, many of today's art teachers are following the tenets of discipline-based art education (DBAE). This type of instruction supersedes traditional methods by placing greater emphasis on critical observation and analysis. The student is exposed to works of all ages and cultures, usually featuring examples of art that demonstrate material to which the students can relate. The examples should help to illustrate the art heritage of which, in a sense, the student is definitely a part.

Superficially, the DBAE teaching approach is not much different from that which makes use of the venerable lesson plan, but it is more intense; the teacher must determine the objective of a given unit, methods of motivation, learning activities, resource materials, and evaluative techniques. Students (at the appropriate age levels) are encouraged to verbalize their reactions to selected works and gain some knowledge of the history of art through this exposure.

The works studied are displayed through reproductions of some kind; visits to museums, if available, are strongly encouraged. Evaluations of the effectiveness of the study unit and the students' comprehension can be achieved through discussion and as reflected in their art products. DBAE places emphasis on the assessment of student artworks. This can be a challenging proposition for the teacher and could depend on the age levels of the students and the openmindedness and consideration of the teacher. Teachers have demonstrated different ways of determining success; they also make use of their own lesson plans, which meet the objectives of DBAE. Examples of some study units that the authors have come across include "*words* in art" (Warhol, Stuart Davis, Gris, Lichtenstein) and "*spaces* and *places*" (landscapes, interiors, different sites). The techniques, lives, and styles of the artists considered should be explored. Needless to say, the procedures employed in teaching art should be those found to be most effective by the individual teacher.

Assessing student art

In previous editions of this book, we sometimes have taken issue with the grading of some artworks. Our stand on this, as artists, is based on the essential *subjectivity* of art; art has little of the *objectivity* of most other subjects in the school curriculum. Nevertheless, there seems to be a ground swell in favor of grading (evaluation), which is supported by DBAE. There are some precisionist areas of activity (perspective and lettering are examples) in which the possibility is self-evident. In such areas, degrees of dexterity can be judged, but one can rarely expect great displays of comprehension and coordination in the lower grades.

Because of this, we suggest a division of the grades (i.e., primary and intermediate), the transition into the intermediate grade being the point at which grading has a greater validity, providing the teacher the opportunity to discern comparative skills. The determination of this point of transition can be decided, perhaps with a bit of difficulty, by the teacher. Once decided on a intermediate grade, the teacher has the challenge of grading the degree of success in a given activity.

Lesson planning and the advent of DBAE

Regardless of how the students are assessed, the teacher should have some kind of plan for guidance. The sample lesson plan, as outlined in our last edition, was used with some success by a former colleague. Incidentally, this plan preceded the advent of DBAE. Here it is, in abbreviated form:

1. Behavioral objectives
2. Materials
3. Motivation
4. Procedure
5. Assignment
6. Evaluation
   a. Self
   b. Students

It can be seen that this plan has some similarities to the DBAE lesson plan here reproduced. The DBAE plan has been derived from the Getty Center for Education in the Arts' *Discipline-Based Art Education Curricular Sampler*. (This is a very good source of information; see the Appendix for the address.)

The Getty Center for Education in the Arts has displayed great interest in the curricular development of art education. Their publication contains, along with supportive material, many illustrative lessons devised by teachers and art specialists in conformity with DBAE. These lessons, or units, are divided into study segments, such as preliminary discussion, objectives, vocabulary, selected artworks, evaluation of same by students, student art production, and final evaluation or debriefing. Bibliographies are included with each unit. Our highly condensed consideration does not permit us to include suggestions for possibly handling different portions of the unit. As regard the genesis of this work, we are quoting the following portion of its Foreword:

> During the past three and one half years a group of dedicated art and museum
> educators along with an artist, art critic, art historian, and aesthetician have labored
> long and hard to create *Discipline-Based Art Education: A Curriculum Sampler*.
> The sampler seeks to be exactly what the name implies. It contains a wide variety of
> teacher-authored approaches that demonstrate the diversity of how DBAE can be
> taught to students at all grade levels. It does so by providing examples of *teachers
> writing for teachers,* and it contains eight units that illustrate eight different ways in
> which DBAE can be approached. The units are meant to be perused, examined,
> dissected, and shared with other teachers. They are meant to be thought-provoking
> and used as take-off points for art specialists to create curriculum-writing teams to
> design their own versions of discipline-based art curricula.* The Getty Center
> responsible for the quoted publication can be found in the Appendix.

---

* The Getty Center for Education in the Arts, 401 Wilshire Boulevard, Suite 950, Santa Monica, California 90401-1455.

Art and teaching

The art public and the teacher's support group

As beneficiaries of the improvement in the art-teaching climate, we must still contend with some lag in art appreciation among the populace. The average understanding of art has rarely kept pace with art as it has with more practical areas of study. Even after a number of generations of crusading artists and art teachers, the lag is with us despite some improvement. The lag probably results from several notions: (1) art as a subject in the classroom is of lesser significance than other subjects (art and music are courses which are often dropped in cases of financial exigencies); (2) art should be cute, traditional, optimistic, and nonthreatening (passive); the taste of any individual who likes what he or she knows is valid and not worth challenging; and serious and reliable standards of art are suspect; (4) artistic outlooks should not change beyond the expected, not exceeding the experience or thought-level fixation of the viewer; and (5) art is incapable of provoking any deep thoughts or containing any abiding truths.

Presumably these points are contrary to the experience of the art teacher and may create teaching difficulties impinging on the support group, parents, friends, other relatives, with whom the student will come in contact. In such an impasse perhaps the teacher may, in some way, attempt explanations of the purposes and diversity of the art program, i.e., educate the support group.

Creative directions

Understanding art and pursuing art activities can benefit all of us. Opportunities for leisure are rare these days, but those who have any opportunity will find art an absorbing avocation. Many well-known figures, such as Winston Churchill and Lionel Barrymore, others of diverse occupations, have practiced art, finding pleasure and therapy.

Genuine creative thinking in any field is done on an intuitive, intellectual, or abstract level; it is a product of flights of fancy (often of great extremes) frequently unlimited by practical considerations. In science, an area of utilitarianism, there is a difference between the *pure* and the *applied.* The more significantly inclusive ideas appear in pure science, whereas originality in applied science is usually directed toward practical considerations. Many art forms have been born in an atmosphere of uninhibited creativity, while others have been directed at specific goals. As for the latter, the motivation may be religious inspiration or propagandistic or other persuasive origins.

Encouraging creativity

Children, if undisturbed, can create art for the joy of manipulating media and the thrill of discovery; but they may, either consciously or unconsciously, express themselves both positively and negatively (as psychologists have testified). This freedom of expression is stifled by teaching assignments that stress standardization. The use of mimeographed materials and coloring books (color between the lines!) discourages invention and expression. Copying is only rarely of value, except possibly in the upper grades. The use of copying seems to derive from the false idea that art is an imitative or re-creative process.

The allowance of creative freedom in the very low grades can result in either total abstraction or some derivation from nature. The character of such work at that level is always interesting, but hardly should be subject to criticism. Due to the subjective nature of the field, some teaching approaches used with increasing age levels can be invitations to chaos unless some control is applied. The role of the teacher is to understand and weigh spontaneity according to the needs, responsibilities, personalities, and ages of the students.

Art can be a fuel for the investigation of a variety of selected subject units. It should not be a mere reportorial device, but should throw fresh light on the subject by being interpreted. If such subjects are tied to creative art programs, both the art and its subject can be enriched.

Children's responses to art

Enthusiasm, to be perpetuated, must be shared by the teacher. Most students are naturally excited by art exploration. Their works are usually enjoyable and meaningful to them. Young children frequently show a natural gift for expression that is unhampered by the consideration of style or accuracy in the adult sense. This lack of inhibition is the envy of many professional artists! If ideas are fed into their absorbent minds, these ideas reappear in marvelously fresh interpretations. The teacher should have the mental flexibility to see the uniqueness of such work.

Good art instruction can be mutually exciting and educational for student and teacher. The history of art, beginning with that of the earliest peoples, indicates that art is an elemental and necessary activity of mankind. It seems the creators of these early works produced them in a very direct manner, with a natural response to such matters as color, rhythm, and texture. This same response is discernible in the works of young children. When the student's freedom dissipates with age, a quest for greater realism emerges and the student may ask for help. When it is given, it should not be as a manifesto, but as a suggestion that, if acknowledged, can coexist with his or her creative resources.

Art structuring

Later in this book, we list the elements of art and give some attention to how they can be used compositionally in creating an artwork. These design principles are important in accenting certain features and in producing unity in the total work. The art elements (line, shape, value, texture, and color) can certainly be given some focus at a fairly early age, but their incorporation into composition should usually be reserved for a more advanced level when children are capable of weighing, judging, and applying them. Determination of this readiness can be made on an individual basis. Older children, in attempting to express themselves, can be given suggestions on how the art elements are used to clarify their expressive intentions. Too much emphasis on compositional concerns at an early age, however, could result in frustration.

The individuality of the student

Respect for the individual and his or her ideas is an important code of conduct for the teacher who expects genuine and sustained interest from art students. Maintaining a cooperative atmosphere of group discussion ensures a continuous outlet and discipline for creative impulses. A further imperative is recognition; conscientious effort in art generally produces some merit in a work. Recognition of this merit should always be given priority in any comments. The younger the child, the more essential the recognition. To ensure development, pointed criticism may be called for, but always diluted with praise and never including personal prejudice, sarcasm, or ridicule. An interest in art can be completely aborted by a few intemperate words.

Appreciation considered

Appreciation is something of an abstruse term. Artists are not likely to use the term because it sometimes means an attachment to the familiar without much foundation in evaluation. Certainly there can be appreciation for what the artist's efforts have produced, but appreciation for the content of the work should more legitimately be supplanted by such a word as *understanding.* Appreciation can suggest a reverence for and unquestioning acceptance of the verdicts of tradition. This is the antithesis of active inquiry in the ideal classroom atmosphere. As the teacher delves into understanding art, he or she may be led to wonder what constitutes real art; this has always been a hotly debated subject, as is pointed out in the later selections, Definitions of Art and Art, Aesthetics, Art History.

The determination of success

Assessment is a difficult issue in children's art. Standards by which the works of the young could be judged are perilous because those works are unparalleled. Because of the chasm that exists between the minds of the child and the adult, the adult perspective for judgment can be unreliable. Children can be their most severe critics; if they are dissatisfied, their works can be ruthlessly discarded. It may be difficult to ascertain the reason for this rejection. In the very low grades, the most legitimate explanation for failure seems to be nonattendance or a determined refusal to participate. More mature student conflicts are dealt with later in the book.

Consideration given selected art works

The guidance we hope to provide for the classroom teacher can be supplemented and enlarged by a variety of other sources. Students' interest in the unit studied can be stimulated and challenged by facts assembled by the teacher. The art the teacher chooses to illustrate gives evidence of his or her research. Commonplace works of art, such as those frequently displayed in the residence, may be decent art, but probably have been seen so often that responses are jaded. It is better to have something that will attract attention and become a center of discourse or even controversy. Artwork has been always a reflection of the controversial selection raging in the artist's mind, and many works throughout the centuries have aroused controversy among the populace. Displaying art that is less-known and even stylistically strange can produce speculation, keeping interest and creative freedom at a high level. Artists are grateful for speculation about their work and are not amused when snap judgments deriving from cursory glance are overheard. Quick impressions in judging art can be as misleading as in judging personalities. True exposure can change opinions, and every work should be given a fair test.

Enlarging teacher qualifications

If a teacher feels unprepared to lead discussions on any type of art, he or she must do some preliminary homework; some learning can be expected along with the class. The teacher will be required to be the interrogator, asking what the work means to the individuals, what the artist's intentions may have been, why a certain color scheme was employed, and so forth. These types of questions evoke surprising responses from children.

Teachers are no doubt thankful for art resources, many of which are listed in our Appendix. The teacher would probably best begin with books. There are any number of books available, including books on biographies, history, techniques, educational theories, and the fundamentals of art. Our listing, besides books, includes videos, materials, audiovisual resources, periodicals, and Internet sites.

Encouraging cultural awareness

We recommend that the classroom work be augmented by trips to museums, if available. Children are invariably fascinated by the things they see and, again, this exposure should be followed by a debriefing. Many museums supply docents (verbal guides) and audiocassettes. These give information on artists: their styles, their backgrounds, and the period and country in which they worked. It is possible that artists could be invited to the school or their studios could be visited. Most communities have artists within reach, and they are often particularly sensitive to the needs and interests of children. Of course, they like to talk about art and willing to discuss their own work.

The consideration of age levels

We have not, in every case, specified recommended age levels for the activities in this book. Some age level activities may be fairly evident, but others have been left to the teacher, assuming he or she is a qualified judge of student capabilities. Children's motor skills and comprehensive levels do not correlate neatly with chronological age. Some classes may be of mixed maturity, and this may necessitate mixed assignments. Hopefully this can be handled in a way that is not demeaning to any portion of the class. Sometimes teachers fear that certain activities are inadequately challenging or beneath the dignity of their students. Adaptation can be made for the older students, but for the younger, fear not! Many artists envy the direct approach of children, some even deliberately adopting childish styles. Pablo Picasso, perhaps the most influential artist of the twentieth century, frequently turned to simplistic, naive,

Children are invariably fascinated by exotically unfamiliar forms of expression. . . .
© James L Shaffer.

and unsophisticated styles. He also employed art media that might be considered elementary, such as wax crayons and linoleum cutting. Nothing was beneath his interest; after all, it's not what is used, but what is done with it!

Positive and negative suggestions on creative art teaching

The following remarks are intended primarily for the classroom teacher who has little specialized instruction in the methods of teaching art. If the suggestions often seem contradictory, it is because no exact recommendation can be provided for every situation, nor can every situation be anticipated. Effectiveness in art teaching, as in any other form of teaching, eventually focuses on the individual teacher's judgment and taste. These comments should therefore be regarded as suggestions, not admonitions. They are included to suggest some of the effective methods and attitudes that are peculiar to the field of art. Perhaps the most important of these is the reminder that an art class is a workshop of ideas and materials, not a standard lecture recitation situation. In such an environment, overguidance is probably worse than underguidance; rules, formulas, and the tried and true are of little value.

Negative suggestions	Positive suggestions
Provide a subject that has general appeal and encourages discovery.	Allow the child free rein in expression; art may be the means to several goals to the young artist. Some are: 1. A feeling of self-confidence in having control of materials. 2. A means through which self-expression can be fostered more fully than in other media. 3. A way of better understanding the world and one's place in it. 4. The satisfaction (rarely obtained these days) that comes with the expression of the basic creative impulse latent in all of us.
Don't create the impression that art is merely busywork or a time filler. Don't set the wheels in motion and turn your attention to other matters.	Use art as an integral part of the day's activities. Demonstrate an active and sincere interest in the things being done.
Don't be surprised by the ideas that pour out of the efforts of the very young, and don't criticize them, even if they prove embarrassing. The children are merely reflecting the events around them and their reactions to them.	Understand that children create emotionally and intellectually. Their works are illustrative of their deepest feelings and, as such, are deserving of sympathetic understanding, not criticism.
Don't be overly critical of objects drawn until students reach a realistic age level.	Children are only interested in demonstrating the reality of the mind and emotions, not the reality of outward appearances.

Positive suggestions	**Negative suggestions**
Children need a certain degree of privacy; give them a feeling of independence.	Don't hover over children who exhibit anxiety over the outcome of their work.
Children are sensitive people, show equal appreciation and concern for all members of the class.	When using student works as examples, avoid extremes of praise or faultfinding.
Give students of all ages opportunities to have contact with art products. Show universality of taste. Let children develop a long-lasting appreciation of art based on their considered judgments, but see to it that honest consideration is given in every case.	Don't limit the child's art consumption to the styles for which you may happen to have a personal preference.
Relate your art instruction to those things that are part of the child's own experiences.	Don't always expect students to show enthusiasm for subjects that are totally unrelated to their own lives.
Encourage children to show and explain their work to others in the class, thereby creating an atmosphere of mutual interest.	Don't isolate pupils from each other or discourage a certain amount of conversation if it is of a constructive nature.
Maintain certain standards in regard to the care of materials and the cleanliness of work area and person.	Don't let freedom of expression lead to abandonment of good work habits. Use copying only when it is enlightening.
Attach fundamental importance to creativity and individual thinking.	Discourage undue reliance on rules and formulas.
Teach the child to develop taste by making use of good design principles in bulletin boards and other displays. Emphasize the art concepts of the twentieth century wherever possible.	Avoid the use of trite, unimaginative, and outdated pictures and materials in the classroom.
Point out correlations and relationships in artworks and between art and other fields. Help make art a vital part of an awakening process.	Art should not be pigeonholed and isolated from other areas. Its concern is humankind and total existence.
If you have had any experience in art that gives you confidence, do your own art teaching. Elementary art is primarily a matter of guidance and encouragement. You can provide this for your own students better than anyone else if you take the trouble to acquaint yourself with the fundamental art concepts.	Don't relinquish your responsibility in teaching art to another person, unless that person's credentials as an art teacher are clearly superior to your own.
Encourage pictorial ideas based on personal activities.	Expect precise, accurate, drawing only from the more mature individuals.
Lend sympathetic assistance to those who don't know where to go with their work. Children expect and deserve help occasionally; this in art is usually a matter of motivation by talking it over.	Don't expect complete self-reliance from immature children or feel that their ideas will be inexhaustible.

Negative suggestions	Positive suggestions
By all means, avoid the use of ready-made art techniques, such as coloring books, number painting, etc. Such devices slam the door on sensitivity and originality, and make art a lifeless, mechanical routine.	Select units that will encourage teacher participation. They should stimulate interest in visual effects and afford an opportunity for exploration.
One cannot expect identical or even very similar results from the diverse personalities normally encountered in the classrooms. Don't demand conformity.	Treat each child as a unique personality. Encourage the child to reveal himself or herself in the art, and try to understand the child and his or her problems better from this revelation through his or her work.
Don't work on a student's project, unless the student asks to see something demonstrated, and do not, if you draw on the work, make it a formula to copy.	Let children do their own work; give them the immense satisfaction that comes from having been solely responsible for the conception and execution of a piece of work.
Don't discourage conversation and a certain degree of class motion.	Expect and encourage greater informality during the class art period. Real art is a matter of expression and cannot flourish under duress. It depends on a contagion of the spirit and a free exchange of ideas.
Don't create the impression that art is child's play in its entirety, or that creation is always unalloyed fun.	Permit students to grapple with problems occasionally. Let them see that the degree of success is often in direct proportion to the amount of perspiration expended, and that the greatest artworks frequently seem simple only because the artist has had the judgment and patience to reduce things to elementals.
Don't lavish praise on children to the extent that they begin to expect acknowledgment of their genius.	Use constructive criticism. Instead of saying "that's bad," try to find a solid solution or imply that something else might work better.
Don't always confuse results with intentions. Accept results if they turn out well, but point out that there comes a time when end products are not enough.	Be honest with yourself and your students by admitting that the sometimes happy results of the activities can occur accidentally or as the result of the special disciplines of the activities.
Don't try to force gifted or low-ability children into the same mold as the average-ability children. Try to set up special activities for those whose talents are extraordinarily great or small.	Allow children to progress according to their abilities.
Children should not be turned off when they are beginning to respond, nor should they have time for distractions.	Ration the time according to the complexities of the activity.
Don't always expect ideas to flow in a torrent. There are fertile and infertile creative periods in any person.	Use all available visual aids that are of good quality. These will serve as an effective stimulus.

Leading questions

Discussion can stimulate thinking and, on occasion, challenge beliefs. The following questions have been devised to point the way to certain surprising conclusions, although others may emerge! See if the class can see the intentions of these questions by discussing them. This interplay might initially be employed among the teachers.

What is the frequency of your visits to museums and/or art exhibits (most likely *in*frequently)?

How often do you listen to music (most likely *much* more often)?

Do you generally judge a piece of music on its reproduction of natural sounds? On its message? What? Could, or should, art be judged similarly?

Do you think a sunset could be beautiful if there were no one around to view it? Is the beauty within us? What is its source?

Do you prefer movies with happy endings? Does this have anything to do with the overall quality of the film? Should the mood or subject matter of an artwork dictate our evaluation of it?

Do you admire designs in home furnishings or clothing? Can you admire non-functional designs in an artwork? If not, why not?

Do you feel that you have had a special talent in each of your required fields of study? If you could handle these without special talent, could you create art without the special talent that many people think is required? Who is the "king" of rock music? The father of the atom bomb? The father of "modern" art? Are we regrettably uninformed on some subjects?

Do you, or have you, found disagreement with your parents on matters of taste? Could we be imprisoned by our generation?

Doubtless one could think of similarly venturesome questions.

Assessment

The public and their representatives, the state legislature, have demanded accountability. They have devised tests to measure students' progress or lack of progress in many areas. And, actually, the people are correct in wanting to know if their children will have the skills necessary for the future. Assessment or evaluation is necessary. But authentic assessment with real evidence of actual learning that focuses on student learning outcomes would be preferable.

There are many methods of evaluation, some very objective and technical that ignore creativity. Those methods that are totally subjective usually have little validity. As in all things, a solution found somewhere in the middle would be viable. Clearly most important would be the simple question, what are your objectives—what do you want the student to learn. Your objectives must be the basis for evaluation.

With discipline-based art education (DBAE), there are four strands to consider in each lesson:

1. *Production* refers to the tangible visual outcome resulting from the use of various media. It concerns the display of creativity, individuality, expression, and demonstration of principles.
2. *Criticism* refers to the skills and knowledge relative to judgment, interpretation, analysis, and description of an artwork.
3. *Aesthetics* encourages activities that assess the emotional, the feelings and the individuality of a work of art.

4. *Art history* refers to the contribution of art and artists. It helps students understand the historical context of a work. It also helps students recognize significant and recognized masterpieces and the importance art plays in a culture. Skills of remembering, understanding, applying, analyzing, and synthesizing are encouraged.

Evaluation should reflect the objectives of the lesson, be of manageable quantity, and be appropriate for the development of the student.

Teachers must comply with the grading policy of the school district in which they are employed. Within this structure, a teacher can make grading more accurate and help it become more supportive of learning. If the school system has a report card in place, it might be good to have the children translate the terms on the card into their own vocabulary. This will complement the portfolio, and the students will understand exactly what is being assessed.

Portfolios

A portfolio is the time-honored way for assessment in art. It takes time, effort, and a lot of work. However, it includes the student in the assessment process, and the student learns strategies for self-evaluation. Teacher and parents have a visual means to see a student's progress and growth. The portfolio gives the student the opportunity to discuss his or her work with individual peers. It is important to set up discussion guidelines that include questions about the work, positive comments, and statements of encouragement, all of which help the student to clarify his or her thinking and feel good about his or her work.

Younger students   Observation and questioning will be very important with the younger students since their oral responses are a very large part of the assessment process. In the introduction of a new lesson, encourage questions and discussion. On note-taking paper, an overhead, or the chalk board, draw three sections. In the first section, list all the things the students already know about the subject. After stating the problem to be solved or the objectives of the lesson, list all the things the students want to know in the second section. When the activity has been completed, list in the third section what has been learned.

A portion of the classroom wall or bulletin board could be allotted to students so that they could post their best work under their name. All pieces should be dated, and it would be advisable to put statements on the backsides concerning what they had learned, what they liked about their works, how they felt when they looked at their works, and any relations to past art or other cultures. As time goes on students will discuss their work more with each other as they have a better idea of the process, and they become more reflective of their work. When little space remains, the students must pick and choose which ones of their pieces should remain on the wall. Evaluation becomes a natural part of the process. The students must decide through reflection and discussion what is their best work, and why, and leave only that work.

The same process can be used with a tag board portfolio. The difference would be that some time would need to be allotted for reflection, sharing, and discussion, and for entering the production in the portfolio.

In written journals kept by the students, have them describe what they did, and discuss what was difficult, what they liked best, how their work looks different than the example, and the steps they took to make the work. What decisions did they have to make? If they did this again, what would they do differently?

It would be advisable to schedule a personal conference with the student to go over the parts of the portfolio, the journal, and any other materials included for assessment. This is one of the most valuable activities for both the student and the teacher.

Older students   The objectives of a lesson or unit should be posted so that the student can refer to them at any time. The teacher should thoroughly discuss the objectives so that the student understands and feels comfortable with them. Oral discussion is very important, and a written journal or a written statement should be added to the assessment process.

Material collected for the portfolio could include preliminary sketches to show the student's interpretation of the lesson. The student should make notes that are clipped to the work that tell the ideas for the work, the reasons for choosing the idea they did, and what solutions they used to solve problems. How would they describe their work, what did they like best, what would they do differently, and how does this relate to another culture or artist or style? What makes this work different or individual and how does it make the student feel?

Time needs to be set aside to collect and organize the portfolio well before assessment is due since it will take a considerable amount of time to make the assessment. The portfolio should have a table of contents and a sticky note attached to each piece of evidence to explain why it is included—how does it relate to the learning goals, is that relationship obvious, and does each piece make the portfolio better. A peer critique could also be part of the portfolio workshop.

A scoring criteria will need to be constructed for the portfolio. Some things to consider include the following: What will the grades mean? How important will behavior, attitude, and effort be? What would be the meaning of failure? What will be the minimum level of achievement? How long did it take to complete the task? Was there improvement and growth? Were materials and tools used safely? Decide how you feel about grade distribution. What will determine the final grade? Will some of the grading components weigh more heavily than others? Determine the standards to be used. What will you do about borderline cases?

A conference between the teacher and the student to talk about the portfolio is an excellent way to assess more information about the productions and the objectives.

Using the portfolio method of assessment is valuable because it helps the teacher clarify and refine his teaching. The teacher must stay focused on the goals.

Computers are used now to help with the record keeping of assessment. A grade book program is used quite routinely by many teachers to keep track of the progress of each of their students. In the future, computers will play a more prominent role in the process of assessment. The student journal, student statements for each art object, and the art pieces or photo can be placed in the traditional tagboard portfolio. The same materials can be scanned and included with digital photographs and sound bytes on a disk. The computer should streamline the process, with information saved on a 3½″ disk for each student. This way, it is possible to save several years of a student's progress and growth on a small disk.

The role of the classroom teacher in teaching art

"Why should the classroom teacher consider including art in the filled curriculum of today's schools? There are so many other things that need to be done, so many other subjects that seem to take precedence. Very often the classroom teacher has had only a class or two in art or art methods. All those materials are messy, and it might be difficult to organize and control a class involved in an art activity."

If the above sounds familiar, think about this for a moment:

> The arts are not pretty bulletin boards. They are not turkeys and bunny rabbits. They are not frivolous entertainment. The arts are our humanity. They are the languages of civilization through which we express our fears, our anxieties, our hungers, our struggles, our hopes. They are systems of meaning that have *real utility*. This is why schools that provide students with the means and encouragement to explore these realms provide a better education.
>
> —"Strong Arts Strong Schools," Charles Fowler. Extracted from keynote address at ASCD Annual Conference, Chicago © 1994.

> Whether it be the Conference Board of Canada or the local Chamber of Commerce the educational expectations of the business community—the ability to think clearly, critically and logically, the capacity to work together in teams effectively, the practice of self discipline, the enhancement of imagination and creativity, the achievement of self confidence, the capacity to articulate ideas with style and clarity, the commitment to excellence—are the very ones emphasized in these moments of artistic effort.
>
> —"Learning the Arts in an Age of Uncertainty," Walter Pitman. Copyright © Arts Education Council of Ontario, ISBN 0-9684672-0-2.

Howard Gardner's theory of multiple intelligences points out something that good classroom teachers have known for years—that children learn in different ways. His theory lists eight different types of intelligences, including:

1. *Linguistic* Children with this kind of intelligence enjoy writing, reading, telling stories, or doing crossword puzzles.
2. *Logical Mathematical* Children with lots of logical intelligence are interested in patterns, categories, and relationships. They are drawn to arithmetic problems, strategy games, and experiments.
3. *Bodily-Kinesthetic* These children possess knowledge through bodily sensations. They are often athletic, dancers, or good at crafts, such as sewing or woodworking.
4. *Spatial* These children think in images and pictures. They may be fascinated with mazes or jigsaw puzzles, or spend free time drawing, building Legos, or daydreaming.
5. *Musical* Musical children are always singing or drumming to themselves. They are usually quite aware of sounds that others may miss. These children are often discriminating listeners.
6. *Interpersonal* Children who are leaders among their peers, are good at communicating, and seem to understand others' feelings and motives possess interpersonal intelligence.
7. *Intrapersonal* These children may be shy. They are very aware of their own feelings and are self-motivated.
8. *Natural* Children who observe, understand, and organize patterns in the natural environment show expertise in the recognition and classification of plants and animals.

To teach in the average classroom filled with children who have different styles of learning, with children coming from divergent backgrounds, all with different needs, is a very exciting but intimidating thought. There are so many pressures imposed by the state, the community, the local school boards, and the administration to teach the "important" things, it leaves very little time or energy to include the arts. The arts are very often the last thing to be included in the school day. And yet, from reading the evidence of recent studies, we know that including the arts is not only important but vital for building confidence, fostering creativity, and encouraging students to keep exploring and discovering. Art is unique in its ability to develop in students a good attitude toward risk-taking and learning from mistakes. These "mistakes" come from trying creative ideas and often lead to new and better ideas.

"*Let the art specialists take care of teaching art!* After all, they are trained in the theories of teaching art and they know how to work with all those materials."

If the school system is fortunate enough to have an art specialist, in all probability the teacher meets with the students one day a week for 45 minutes to 1 hour or sometimes less. Art specialists cannot begin to give the children the in-depth experience they deserve. Art teachers can become more valuable if they are also used as a resource persons for the classroom teacher, so that additional activities can take place in the classroom. Ask them questions, talk to them about ideas you might have, tell them what you're working on in the classroom, see if you can collaborate with them on a lesson or two, and borrow visual aids from them and use these aids however you can. Because of financial concerns, the school may not have an art specialist on staff, therefore making the total art instruction of each student the responsibility of the classroom teacher.

The key to art instruction is to connect it to the many activities of the classroom and its children. Art is not a separate entity, separate from the rest of life. Artists have always drawn content from the full knowledge of the world. Mathematics can be found in the Egyptian pyramids, in the order of Greek architecture, in the perspective of the Renaissance. Science is reflected in the color explorations of the impressionists and in the experiments and writings of Da Vinci. We know volumes about humankind's history through art, and we are learning more and more about other cultures because of their artwork. It is extremely valuable to take a interdisciplinary approach to teaching, not fragmenting subjects into separate parts, but rather creating a rich wholeness that draws content from all of our knowledge. The classroom teacher is in the perfect situation to make connections between subject areas.

Giving a visual shape to a concept, whether it be in science, math, or social studies, adds meaning that could not be obtained any other way. Art is still being taught and will not suffer from this integration. Instead, both the subject areas and the art concepts will be stronger because of this connection. Drawing, painting, crafts, clay, sculpture, and weaving can all be connected to other subject areas. Art history can be included. Other cultures can be shown to have also used these arts. Aesthetics can certainly be added with a discussion about what the students see and can describe and how they feel when they see the artwork. How art fits into the time frame and how it both reflects and influences the period can be a valuable piece of knowledge.

Art should not be just a recreational diversion or a time filler, although any child will tell you that art is *fun*. In the initial planning for a lesson, include art as part of the lesson, whether it be as simple as drawing to illustrate or a more complex art activity. Art and drawing is a child's natural means of expression and it should be exercised. Keep in mind that when learning is given form through art, it becomes a part of the child's life and continues to enrich his adult life.

Idea seeds

The following is a list of possible subjects to be used with students to encourage them to work with ideas as well as art media. These are only beginning points and should be elaborated upon to make them more useful. They can be used in many ways: as a short activity when students have finished a lesson, as a point of departure to other units of art activity, or to connect with previous or current art activities.

Draw yourself in a mood; sad, happy, angry, silly, etc.

Draw your greatest fear.

Finish the sentence, "If I were a frog. . . ." Illustrate.

Illustrate yourself playing a game.

Draw your dream room or playhouse.

Design your own coat-of-arms or shield.

Design an advertisement for yourself.

Create a self-portrait by looking into a mirror. Create one looking into a spoon.

Draw what you might look like in 10 years, 25 years, or 50 years.

Make a design using your name as the basis for that design.

Draw yourself at a party with many friends.

Illustrate yourself as the tallest person in the world.

Illustrate yourself growing wings.

Illustrate yourself shrinking to microscopic size.

Design your own ride at an amusement park.

Illustrate all you know about noses.

Illustrate "It was a dark and windy night."

Draw things that float, or have flavor, or that roll, or that close.

Create your own game, or comic strip, or action hero.

Draw things that come from an egg.

Illustrate buildings from the past such as Egypt, Native American, etc.

Illustrate a city built in a bubble under water, or in space.

Draw a city at night.

Draw a poster to advertise yourself.

Draw an imaginary animal, bird, or insect in an imaginary landscape.

Illustrate looking out the window, showing the inside and the outside.

Draw an Egyptian side view of arms, legs, face, and front view of eye, and body.

Paint the most beautiful day using only the primary colors of red, yellow, and blue.

Create a book of textures.

Draw a time line and place illustrations of the most important events of your life.

Design your own personal stamp.

Illustrate words such as up, down, inside, outside, together, apart, crazy, sane, etc.

Make one of your drawings larger or smaller.

Make a window with a piece of paper and slide it over one of your drawings and paintings until you find an interesting part. Then, enlarge that part.

Invent a new alphabet.

With a pencil, see how many values or shades you can create.

Study costumes of a certain culture and draw a life-sized costume.

Build a castle out of paper by folding, cutting, tearing, and pasting.

Make a puppet out of different materials so that it moves.

Write a short story about one piece of your artwork.

Choose a newspaper article and draw or paint it.

Make a weaving with different materials.

Draw a trail of an imaginary insect as it crawls over objects in the room.

Make a collage with cut-out magazine pieces using one color (monochromatic).

Try origami.

Make a design using a letter or number to begin the design.

Make optical illusions.

Illustrate things that smell sweet, sour, fresh, or rotten.

If you were an ant, draw what you would see. If you were a bird, draw what you would see.

Design a record album cover or a sticker for a CD disk.

Draw new characters for Star Wars.

Draw a common tool, slowly changing it through four steps into a animal, bird, or insect.

Create a sculpture using only paper strips.

Given a paper tissue, think of 20 things you can do with it and illustrate a few.

Design your own bumper sticker.

Make a illustration only using tints (colors mixed with white). Use only shades (colors mixed with black).

Make as many different colors as you can using only primary colors and black and white.

Create a design using complimentary colors.

Beginning with a fat dot, make an imaginary plant grow to fill the paper.

Design your own license plate (for a bike or family car).

Design a new outfit for . . . (pick a person).

Definitions of art

One could easily be tongue-tied if challenged to give a definition of art; it has worn many styles and intentions through the ages. All of the definitions listed here have been vigorously argued, but all probably have some essence of what we think of as art. Different definitions most likely apply to different types and styles.

1. The expression of human experience (Dewey).
2. The formal expression of a conceived image in terms of a given medium (Cheney).
3. Intuition (Bergson; Croce).
4. An expression controlled by a certain aspect of the mind.
   a. Emotion (Tolstoy).
   b. The will (Nietzsche; Freud).
   c. The intellect (Aquinas).
5. The making of a form produced by the cooperation of all the faculties of the mind.
   a. Significant form (Bell).
   b. Eloquence (Burke).
   c. Unexpected inevitability of formal relations (Fry).
   d. A unified manifold which is pleasure giving (Mather).
   e. A diagram (or paradigm) with a meaning that gives pleasure (Listowel).
   f. That which gives pleasure apart from desire (Aquinas).
   g. Objectified pleasure (Santayana).
6. Imitation (Note: what is imitated?).
7. Right making; skill (Note: skill at making what?).
8. Propaganda. Emphasis on communication rather than expression. Implies some conscious effort to influence conduct.

Some, if not all, of these are obviously subject to interpretation. Their introduction would most often spark a lively debate. There is no unanimous agreement on any *one* of them!

Art, aesthetics, art history

We generally think that we can recognize art when we see it but, as can be seen from the previous section, it has had many divergent definitions. What is art for one person may not qualify as art for another person. The nature of art history seems self-evident; it is a vast subject with occasional new discoveries and frequent reinterpretations. Aesthetics, according to one dictionary reference, pertains to the appreciation or criticism of the "beautiful." It is a compound of objective analysis, psychology, sociology, and philosophy of art. Aesthetics is a complicated subject on which much has been written and little totally resolved! This is particularly true with the introduction of the term *beauty.* Definitions of beauty have changed with the times and are changing radically in our lifetimes. In some circles, beauty is regarded as obsolete.

The average teacher does not need total immersion in the study of art history and aesthetics. Some study, however, will yield benefits in the classroom. It will help discrimination in the selection of artworks to be displayed and studied in the classroom and will provide the teacher with information to be dispensed on the origins and possible purposes of those artworks. Additionally, the accumulated knowledge will give some foundation for the discussions of art (as recommended earlier in the book).

Art history is objective, but aesthetics is subject to a variety of opinions. In some instances, the discussions might alter opinions as to the value of a work, but one must be careful not to *impose* values. Younger children will probably decide on favorites independent of any explanation, whereas older students may be inclined to change their opinions, particularly as regard recent art, as the artist's intentions are made clear. Examination of ethnic and geographically exotic art is interesting and should be encouraged. We think such studies will be fascinating and instructive to both the teachers and their pupils!

Most of us associate art with beauty and *expect* art to be beautiful even if unable to define what that beauty is. In the previous section of this book, a definition of art is not easily found—beauty is equally elusive. It has meant different things to different people throughout history. The field of aesthetics evolved in an effort to find an answer to that critical and confounding question: What is beauty?

Historical cultures have had their own concepts of beauty and our contemporary responses to them vary. For the ancient Greeks, beauty was in the idealized human form and, in most cases, we can accept this as beauty. We can also accept the somewhat revised Roman version of Greek art, although it is sometimes too realistic for us. Medieval art is still indigestible for many of us, but Renaissance art is almost a seminal type of beauty for a great number of our contemporaries. Raphael, for instance, is the epitome of this kind of beauty, though some find it overly saccharine. A good deal of the art following the Renaissance is reasonably acceptable until stumbling blocks were erected during the nineteenth century.

During that century preceding our own, there were many momentous changes in art that confounded the public (and many artists who clung to the old ways). Impressionism, generally looked on with favor today, found a hostile audience. The Postimpressionism that followed experienced only slightly mitigated hostility. With the advent of Cubism, Expressionism, Abstraction, Futurism, and the other "isms" of the twentieth century, the separation between innovative artists and the layperson became an ever-widening abyss. The accelerating changes in every phase of our lives were paralleled by unavoidable corresponding changes in art and most people were not able to adapt to them. The practical results of change (automobiles, washers, television) could be appreciated but nonutilitarian art changes were not easily accepted. There is a ray of light, however; our technology has made all forms of art (artistic beauty?) accessible and it seems that some of the barriers to expanded taste have gradually eroded.

Let us see what aspects of art history have been of some repugnance: Greek—generally liked, but nudity displayed; Roman—less idealized, the *un*-pleasant coexisting with the pleasant; Medieval—a rather alien language of art to many, but considered "beautiful" by some; Romanticism—the occasional violence and unfamiliar settings are thought by some to be distasteful; Postimpressionism—radical change of styles from those preceding, frequently depressing instead of exalted subjects; Cubism and other "isms" (many quite different from each other)—no visible subject matter, seemingly inept and irrational, satirical and impenetrably personal.

But what is liked? Judging from the above we like, first of all, the familiar—an inheritance of taste from family, friends, and associates. We like the understandable, even though there is frequently little effort to understand the nonunderstandable. Perhaps, above all, we like certain subjects that can be recognized. They must also be reasonably familiar and understandable, acceptable to our peers, somewhat idealized or sentimental and "pleasant" as opposed to moody or threatening in their themes.

If *subject* is so important to us, it merits further investigation. Regrettably, as with art and beauty, subject is another term that is almost undefinable. Superficially subject designates objects, themes, and persons. There is also subject in abstract art, though less visible. In such art, the subject may be simply an idea or a particular use of an element or elements. For most laypersons the subject needs to have the instant recognizability of those objects, themes, or persons because beauty is often judged by this re-presenting.

There are qualifying factors, however. As stated before, the subject should be moral, pleasant, or uplifting. But a complication enters. What if we have a work that meets these criteria but is badly executed? Would it be beautiful? On the other hand, imagine a work that has none of those criteria but is expertly executed; could it be beautiful? Many great artists have created (beautiful?) works based on gross subjects. And, surely, not all persons, even of similar backgrounds, would agree on the beauty of a given subject.

There are conclusions to be drawn from this: Beauty, to the beholder, must be based on the artist's vision, skill, and interpretation of a subject irrespective of the nature of the subject. Additionally, the observer must be endowed with similar gifts, in some degree, to detect and appreciate the beauty; it is a two-way street. The emergence of a new style, or a new way of looking at things, in art can produce some consternation and a period of evaluation. Thus, we must often have the consensus of sensitive experts through the years to finally affirm the merits of artworks, and, ultimately, the public may be willing to accept this assessment. The average person does not have the background of an expert, but he or she can view visual art, study it, and learn from it, and, in the process, advance his or her understanding and taste. Yes, beauty is in the eye of the beholder, but we must ask what lies behind that eye. It was once said of an artist that "he only has an eye, but what an eye!" An interesting comment with an equally interesting implication; obviously there must be more than the eye involved in the creation and appreciation of beauty.

Beauty, whatever it is, does not seem to be universally sought in much of today's art. Many artists are in revolt against idealistic or comfortable subjects and refined technique. There are styles of intense realism in which such considerations might be inappropriate. The artists who produce such work might conceivably consider it beautiful (although they would be unlikely to use the term), but it would be an alien type of beauty for many of us. Perhaps beauty is ripe for redefinition.

Safety in the art classroom

In recent years, people have become increasingly aware of the dangers of pollutants in the environment. Concerns have rightly so extended into the classroom. Although we have always been dimly conscious of the need for safety, the scope of such dangers was little known, and a systematic study of the effects of the use (more often misuse) of materials employed in the educational system. This situation has been remedied over the last several years. Various agencies are imposing regulations and limitations on the use of supplies and equipment considered to be hazardous. Previously, artists and art students were using, without restraint or protective devices, threatening materials such as resins, lacquers, acids, asbestos, and various solvents. Serious injury and even death sometimes resulted. Secondary to this is the threat to teachers and administrators of liability suits.

Although the more dangerous items are not ordinarily found in the elementary and junior high schools, there are still enough dangers to indicate the need for caution and careful supervision. Some states have passed legislation that bans the use of dangerous art materials.

Dangers can arise from unexpected sources, and there is a need to disseminate information on these sources to those involved in art. A great deal of this information is available in a book written by Charles Qualley listed in the Art Resources Appendix of this book. Additionally, the Center for Occupational Hazards collected reports on hazardous substances and practices. The information was circulated by means of books, lectures, and articles in several publications.

One article so clearly illustrated the incipient dangers, that it is reproduced here in its entirety. It is entitled, "The Young at Art" and was written by Monona Rossol, M.S., M.F.A. It is, of course, one of many such articles that were written on the subject.*

> Some of the most important and interesting calls received at the Center for Occupational Hazards are those from Poison Control Centers asking for our help in determining the ingredients in art materials. The frequency of these calls has increased greatly since November 1979, when our service was added to the list of resources on POISONDEX—the computer-generated poison control identification and management system available to nearly 900 Poison Control Centers in the U.S. and Canada. An examination of some of the calls received by the Center for Occupational Hazards demonstrates the need for continuing and increasing efforts in disseminating art hazard information.
>
> The most common calls from Poison Centers involve ingestion of an art material by a child. Among them are calls about children who have eaten artists' paints. One toddler chewed through a tube of flake (lead) white oil paint; another child ate dyed crystal paper (for transfer dyeing); still another ate the colored knobs from the ends of the center spikes of artificial flowers; and a number of children have eaten a variety of materials related to ceramics, such as glazes and stains.
>
> Almost a third of the calls we receive from Poison Control Centers involve ceramic materials. Besides those about children, others have been about adults. One woman accidentally inhaled a powdered ceramic stain which spilled into her

---

* From Monona Rossol, "The Young at Art" in *Art Hazard News.* Copyright © Center for Occupational Hazards, New York, NY. Reprinted by permission.

face when she tried to retrieve its container from a high shelf. Another call concerned a 58-year-old woman with an irregular electroencephalogram which her doctor attributed to her use of manganese dioxide as a clay colorant.

Then there are miscellaneous calls: A boy, with lead-poisoning symptoms, who had the habit of chewing the ends of his oil paint brushes while he worked; a girl with suspected cyanide poisoning from a silverplating accident; two complaints about fumes from heat-pressing decals on polyester T-shirts; a series related to an outbreak of dermatitis among young adults who attended a face-painting party; a question about inhalation of smoke from burning ironwood and newsprint; an inquiry about fumes from using dye strippers (to remove dye from fabric); a boy who accidentally injured his eye with a colored copy pencil; and a 17-year-old boy who, for some reason, chewed a considerable quantity of "Dippity-Do" dyed paper.

Poison Control Centers usually call us when they lack information about ingredients in a particular art material which may be affecting someone's health. Although we often can provide this information, in many cases it is not readily available. In a number of instances, Poison Control Centers have called us after they have been unable to reach the manufacturer at the address on the product label because the company has moved or changed its name. In these cases, calls to large art suppliers or to trade magazines which advertise similar products have been useful. Often tracking down a manufacturer can take a day or longer. In one case, we never have been able to find the company, and we believe it is likely that the firm was very small and has gone out of business. We have had equally bad luck in reaching foreign manufacturers.

A day or longer in answering Poison Control calls is sometimes far too long. When a call involves accidental ingestion and when emergency room personnel are standing by for ingredient information, we do not have time to track down elusive manufacturers. In these cases it is sometimes possible to use other label information to narrow down the number of likely ingredients. For instance, if a product is known to contain organic solvents and the label also states that the product is inflammable, we can eliminate many solvents because only a limited number are inflammable. Sometimes the label's directions for use will contain clues about ingredients. For example, some ceramic products are called glazes, but the directions show that they are not to be fired but are to be applied to the finished ware and left to dry. This information means that the product is not actually a glaze, but a varnish or paint material. But the directions on a container of true ceramic glaze, too, can be useful. By combining information about the firing temperature, the type of kiln in which the glaze is to be fired, and the glaze color, we can narrow possibilities of actual compounds in the glaze.

Using label information to guess about ingredients is not ideal. And we resort to this step only when better information is not available.

There is no substitute for accurate knowledge of a product's ingredients. Some simple rules can help artists and others avoid situations in which ingredient information is unobtainable.

1. Don't buy unlabeled products or products whose labels are damaged or covered by price stickers.
2. Keep label information with the product at all times. Do not transfer products to unlabeled containers, remove labels, or allow spills to obliterate labels.
3. Write to manufacturers for Material Safety Data Sheets and other toxicological data. At the time of purchase ask the supplier for any additional product information he might have.
4. Keep a file of package inserts, directions, Material Safety Data Sheets, and other collected information. Make sure that the file is kept in good order and is handy in case of accident.

Although these rules apply especially to situations where young children might come in contact with art materials, our file of Poison Control calls suggests that accidents involving art materials can happen to anyone, no matter what age. Every studio, whether used by the young or old, warrants such vigilance.

One cannot, in every case, anticipate and forestall accidents. With some simple precautions one can make the classroom a safer place to work. The teacher must always be vigilant while overseeing a class in which dangerous situations can develop; even a pen point can cause a puncture wound. Scissors should always have blunted tips. Small children should use draw tools for linoleum cutting. Even simple tools can cause damage. It would be wise to take inventory to determine whether tools should be altered or replaced. When possible, materials should carry the label CP or AP indicating certification by The Art and Craft Materials Institute, Inc. The label certifies the nontoxicity of the item. In California, Tennessee, Oregon, Illinois, and Florida (where the use of toxic art materials in the classroom is banned), labels listing acute and chronic health hazards are mandatory on all art and craft products that contain toxic ingredients. Other labels may warn of danger, and if material is seen to be or suspected to be dangerous, it should be stored in an inaccessible, locked storage area.

In the ideal situation, a school nurse should always be available during school hours. The teacher should establish a close working relationship with the nurse, making him or her aware of the perils that can accompany an art program. Therefore, the nurse can see that appropriate medical supplies are stocked. Parents should be queried as to any known allergies the children may have. This information should be on file for emergency treatment.

In most cases, troubles arise as the result of the following:

1. *Inhalation* This trouble suggests the need for adequate ventilation, particularly where fumes and gases are involved.
2. *Ingestion* Materials used should be nontoxic and carefully monitored while in use. Children love to put things in their mouths.
3. *Absorption* Some materials can be absorbed through the skin and affect internal organs. Aprons, gloves, and sometimes even goggles must be worn.
4. *Electrocution* Cords and plugs should be inspected. All electrical equipment must be grounded properly.
5. *Burns* These can result from the careless use of irons, stoves, and molten materials, as well as acids and alkalis.

The Department of Health Services—State of California has developed a list of acceptable art products to be used in the elementary classrooms. This 40-page list entitled "Art and Craft Materials Acceptable for Kindergarten and Grades 1–6" and the California guidelines for the safe use of art and craft materials in schools are available from the Center for Safety in the Arts as a public service. The cost is minimal and includes any updates done by the California Department of Health Services during the year following your purchase.

Center for Occupational Hazards offers a wealth of information on hazardous materials and practices. Obviously, space forbids the inclusion of all of this information; we can, however, reproduce a partial list of art materials too toxic for use in public schools:

Lead-containing materials

- Lead-pigmented paints and print-making inks.
- Enamels fired onto metals (except Vitrearc brand).
- Lead glazes, ceramic glaze chemicals, and lead fruits.

Asbestos

- Sculpture stones, soapstones, steatite, serpentine, greenstone.
- Asbestos gloves and other products.
- Some talcs used in some glazes, white clays, and slips.

- Instant papier-mâchés.
- Vermiculite.

Aerosol spray cans

- All aerosol sprays are too hazardous except for outdoor use or in ventilated spray booths.

Materials, too toxic for children under 12

- All solvents, such as mineral spirits, turpentine, and solvent-containing rubber cements, glues, shellacs, paints, inks, and permanent felt-tip markers.
- Some oil paints.
- Ceramic glazes and enamels.
- Paints or pigments in powdered form and pastels.
- Photographic chemicals.
- Wallpaper Paste.

Known or suspected carcinogens—shop equipment

- Some solvents like benzene, carbon tetrachloride, and chloroform.
- Some ceramic glaze chemicals including chrome oxide, chromates, and uranium oxide.
- Some paint and print-making pigments including barium yellow, chrome yellow, diarylide yellow, lithol red, molybdate orange, pthalocyanine blue and green, strontium yellow, and zinc yellow.
- Tools that require cutting, piercing, pounding, squeezing, pinching, and heating must be watched carefully. In addition power tools, when available, constitute a great threat; quite often it is recommended that the instructor control these tools. There is also a recommended safety reading list for schools; all are published by the Center for Occupational Hazards:

Articles (a partial listing)

- "Electric Kiln Emissions and Ventilation"
- "Health and Safety in Schools"
- "Teaching Art to High-Risk Groups"

Data sheets (a partial listing)

- "Are Public School Art Materials Safe?"
- "Art Painting"
- "Asbestos Substitutes"
- "Ceramics"
- "Children and Art Materials"
- "Children's Art Supplies Can Be Toxic" (lists products authorized to bear the CP Certified Products Seal and the AP Approved Products Seal of the Certified Products and Certified Labeling Bureau of the Arts and Crafts Institute, Inc.)
- "Craft Dyeing"
- "Labeling Problems of Arts and Crafts Materials"
- "Lead Glazes and Food"
- "Safety Rules for Power Tool Operation"
- "Silk Screen Printing Hazards"
- "Silver Soldering"
- "Stained Glass"

- *Health Hazards in the Arts and Crafts* (a 16½ × 20 inch multicolored wall chart, with hazards and precautions)

Computers in art

Computers have arrived! They have made their presence felt thoughout our lives in one way or another. The field of art is no exception; in fact, it is a natural use of the computer since it is a visual media.

Computers are now being used in many ways, from creating art to viewing the arts of masters. It is easy to study and compare, with split-screen subject matter, the style and technique of artists from different time periods. A virtual tour of famous museums is at our fingertips. Slide shows are created, and animation is just a matter of clicking the mouse. The Internet has allowed us to connect and share opinions and thoughts with other artists and educators half a world away.

Computers are also a wonderful way to help the exceptional student. If need be, the computer can be specially adapted to help with the mainstreamed students who would otherwise have difficulty with a pencil or a brush.

Machinery and software is constantly and quickly changing and becoming more powerful and faster. Don't wait until the ultimate one arrives—it never will. So start with what you have. How the computer will be used in a classroom depends on a number of factors:

1. Are you willing to expend the effort and do the work necessary to integrate the computer into the curriculum? What is your attitude?
2. Do you have any computers in the room? If so, how many? Should they be upgraded? Are you on the Internet?
3. What programs does the computer have? Does it have a word processing program? Does it have a desktop publishing program? Are there any CD-ROMs available?
4. Do you have a printer? Is it black or color? Do you have a scanner? Do you have a presentation TV? Do you have a VCR?
5. Is there a computer lab available? How many computers are contained there? What other equipment is available, such as printers, presentation TV, scanner, VCR, and software?

It is important to inventory and learn what is available before deciding if more needs to be obtained. Once that is determined, make a modest "wish list" in order of priority, and begin to explore the possible ways of obtaining it. Be creative.

If there is only one computer, decide how to use it. Will it be for a special project? Will names be drawn to decide who will use it? Will it be used to reinforce another lesson? Could a TV be hooked up to it? If there are more computers, it becomes easier to decide how to use them. If there is a computer lab, find out when it is free.

Decide what the objectives are

What do you want students to learn? Can the strands of DBAE be addressed with the use of this media?

Here are some hints:

With whatever is available, explore and learn all that you can about it. Some students know a great deal about computers and are totally unafraid. Let them teach you and other students.

The computer is a great link between cultures and subjects, and students love to use them.

Start slowly and use one or two basic programs. Add more if you really need them.

Classes or workshops are offered by districts. Colleges or universities may have a workshop or class that would be helpful.

Constantly evaluate. Are you meeting your objectives? How could you meet them more effectively? Encourage the student to evaluate and make suggestions.

The following are some of the programs available at this time. Keep in mind that this list enlarges and changes very quickly. Be sure to check what system is necessary for each program and also if it is formatted for Windows or Mac or is a hybrid which will work with either format.

The Art Lesson CD-ROM, Primary

This program is based on the early art experiences of renowned children's book author, Tomie dePaola. Students can watch the story and investigate the art activities, video interview clips, sound, and animation. Fourteen activities allow children to experiment with art tools, the use of color, collages, funny faces, and more. Children can create and print their own pictures, and all parts of the program are accessible from a separate menu. The artist explains his illustration process as he takes the students on a CD-ROM tour.

You Can Draw! CD-ROM, Intermediate and Jr. High

An art teacher takes the students through six different sections—Gesture, Line, Shape, Value, Volume, and Perspective—and helps students develop their design and drawing skills. Each section includes three more subsections, including Techniques, Exercises, and Artists. In Techniques, students take art lessons, and in Exercises, students practice the many methods they learned in earlier presentations. The Artists section reveals how master artists employed techniques to express moods and feelings in their works. The final section, Media, lets students explore different types of drawing utensils and surfaces available.

Kid Pix Studio® Deluxe CD-ROM, Primary and Intermediate

Students can draw use drawing, coloring, and creating tools, including the "Wacky Brushes," eight different color palettes, and hundreds of rubber stamps. This multimedia tool allows students to prepare a slide show with special effects, including sound and screen transitions. Text, sound, and graphics allow students to expand their narrative from static images to storytelling sequences.

HyperStudio, Primary to Adult

This program is used for creating multimedia projects. Virtually any multimedia element (graphic, movie, animation, etc.) can be added to a project in under 60 seconds. Projects can be easily linked to Internet locations, and an entire project can be exported as one or more Internet Web pages with just a few mouse clicks. There are direct digital camera support, cross-platform compatibility, and the abundance of third-party support materials.

Fun with Architecture CD-ROM, Primary to Adult
Program from the Metropolitan Museum of Art allows students to design houses, factories, pyramids and entire city scapes in ultra-realistic to imaginary creations, adding landscape components to enhance the structure. Second half of the program teaches the shapes, elements, and language of architecture.

Kai Super GOO CD-ROM, Primary to Adult
GOO takes images and turns them into liquid goo image effects. Pinch, twirl, smear & smudge, move & nudge, or grow & shrink any element. Blend the nose of one face with the eyes of another or with facial features from the program's library—which includes images of boys, girls, animals, world leaders, and so on. Import your own images from digital cameras, scanners, and CD-ROMs. Animated movie can be made by clicking the mouse for each frame. Print the finished work or export as a PICT, TIFF, GIF, or JPEG file or as Photoshop documents.

Dabbler™ 2 CD-ROM, Intermediate to Adult
Hundreds of tools and textures respond just like traditional art materials. Finished work looks more like "real" art, not just computer art. Create frame-by-frame animations or use the photo-cloning tools to trace photos and turn them into paintings using Natural-Media brushes. Includes step-by-step art lessons with built-in multimedia tutors. *Drawing Cartoons* by Bill Blitz and *Cartoon Animation* by Preston Blair.

Painter Classic, Grades 6 to Adult
More sophisticated than the Art Dabbler. Omits the animation tools, but has a streamlined set of Painter 5 tools. Includes six extra-large brush libraries and more—seamless tiling for graphic Web projects. Script actions, then play them back as a custom curriculum presentation.

Painter 5.5, Web Editions, Grades 6 to Adult
Painter combines a comprehensive set of image-editing features with new Natural-Media technologies. Dynamic, new plug-in floaters create layers of special effects. Updated features include Web authoring enhancements. Web Edition features Client-Side image mapping "hotspots" with click-to-link capabilities. Includes scores of new calligraphic brushes and thousands of Web friendly buttons, background titles, and images. Supplements programs such as Photoshop, Illustrator, Freehand, and others with paint and sculptural effects.

Painter 3-D, Grades 5 to Adult
Painter 3-D joins the technology of Detailer with the richness of Painter 5 to make an application for teaching skills in 3-D art and design. Contains hundreds of Natural-Media tools and effects which let students create surface maps that control the appearance of a 3-D object. Textures, bumps, reflections, highlights, glow, and environmental effects can be created with control and flexibility.

Poser 3, Grades 5 to Adult
Create lifelike human and animal models with hands and faces that can be posed. Animate fingers and hands for realistic gestures and synchronized speech. Animals can be posed and have animated body parts, including tail, ears, and mouth positions. The extensive library of 3-D props, hair, facial expressions, animations, sounds, camera, and lights gives you a complete animation studio.

Bryce 3-D, Grades 6 to Adult

Create photo-realistic and surrealistic movies and images for video, Web pages, multimedia, and electronic visual art. Set every part of the 3-D world in motion, including clouds, heavenly bodies, random star fields, fog, and haze. Create landscapes, sculpt valleys, peaks, and so on. Surfaces can be controlled inside and out. Can be used effectively with MetaCreations Poser, Detailer, and Ray Dream.

Wacom® Intuos Graphics Tablet Systems, Grades 6 to Adult

Includes an ergonomic tablet and Intuos Pen with 1024 levels of pressure sensitivity and 2540 lpi resolution for the smoothest curves and gradual transitions. Includes a built in eraser and allows for precise control for rendering and editing in programs such as Photo Shop or Painter. New programmable menu strip allows teachers to program keyboard shortcuts specific to classroom instruction. Software included is Painter Classic. Plus PenTools enables students to create distortions with Super Putty. Virtual Airbrush included.

Adobe® PhotoDeluxe™ 3.0, Grades 4 to Adult

Teaches image-editing and manipulation foundation skills as preparation for teaching Adobe Photoshop. Improved, easy-to-use color management system and a simplified way to import photos into the computer. Save and print photo creations in standard sizes, post photos on a Web page, attach photos to an e-mail message as a multimedia slide show or export photos to another file format. Includes 50 step-by-step guided activities and dozens of templates.

Adobe® PageMill™ 3.0, Grades 5 to Adult

Making colorful, dynamic Web pages is as simple as using the word processor. This program uses familiar drag-and-drop operations rather than HTML, the language of the Web. The intuitive WYSIWYG interface, animations, and over 10,000 Web-ready images, animations, and sounds provide excellent support.

Art appreciation and art history

Look What I See CD-ROM, Primary and Intermediate

Art masterpieces from the Metropolitan Museum of Art combined with wildlife photography. Wide range of activities using skills of finding, changing, looking, and comparing. Encourages experimentation. Audio instructions and simple icons facilitate independent use of program.

With Open Eyes CD-ROM, Primary and Intermediate

Explore the Chicago Art Institute with no reading required. Features over 200 works of art. Multimedia museum tour with point-and-click graphic interface to access a variety of background material for the individual pieces of art. Child-oriented icons guide students through historical and geographical information. Audio tracks, timelines, scrapbook, and more.

A Is for Art, C Is for Cezanne CD-ROM, Primary to Adult

From the Philadelphia Museum of Art, Introduction features Cezanne, his friends, and other famous artists. Images are organized into three categories: People, Places, and Things. Students can shuttle between images in each category and compare how Cezanne and different artists painted the same subject. Includes animated clips, games, puzzles, and more.

The Louvre: Museums of the World for Kids CD-ROM

Full-screen images and close-ups can be accessed from the interactive map and timeline. Includes 150 treasures. Includes audio clips, a slide show, challenging games, and a virtual gallery.

ArtRageous 2.0 CD-ROM, Grades 4 to Adult

The students make their own "artrageous" masterpieces with this interactive trip through the wondrous world of art. They do more than look at paintings; they can manipulate the colors, positions, shapes, and perspective, and see how it affects each piece. See why the masters made the decisions they did as the students face the same creative choices. The program's fully searchable database furnishes background information on some of history's greatest artists and their work.

Impressionism in the Twentieth Century-The Masters-from Monet to Matisse CD-ROM, All Levels

Introduction to the works of impressionist and postimpressionist masters—Cezanne, Gauguin, Seurat, and van Gogh; the early masters Monet and Degas; and the early works of Picasso and Matisse. Overview considers many significant nineteenth century European artists.

Early American History Through Art CD-ROM, Grades 4 to Adult

Comprehensive history of colonial America and Native Americans through the art they created. A tool to compare and contrast works created at the same time, in the same country, but from two very different cultures.

National Museum of American Art CD-ROM, Grades 5 to Adult

Includes 750 objects from the Smithsonian's collection dating from the colonial period to the twentieth century. Students can investigate a specific piece through searches by artist, title, date, subject matter, theme, style, or medium; access the "Library" section which contains the full text and visuals of six collection catalogs; and even listen to some of the artists themselves in the "Artwork" section, which consists of several artists' biographies. A media-enhanced guided tour features nearly two hours of supplementary video, audio, slide presentations, and animated segments illustrating numerous genres from American portrait painting to bottle cap folk art.

Masterstrokes CD-ROM, Grades 5 to Adult

Created by artist Saul Bernstein, this program shows how these great masters—including Michelangelo, Rembrandt, and van Gogh—constructed some of the most revered artwork in history. Six tutorials: Color, Composition, Animation, Light & Art, Special Techniques, and Hidden Images & Storytelling reveal the "underdrawings" of some of these artists' works and explain step-by-step how they were executed.

Masterpiece Mansion CD-ROM, Grades 5 to Adult

Featuring 40 games and puzzles that encompass 150 works of art, this interactive program traps students in a haunted mansion where they have to solve various problems in order to escape. Students may have to reconstruct a scrambled picture, identify a vanishing point, answer questions about an artist's life or work, or place a group of paintings in chronological order. The program also contains two reference sections students can access for more in-depth information. The "Art

Period Explorer" outlines five eras in the development of Western art, including Greek and Roman, the Renaissance, Dutch realism, Impressionism, and the twentieth century. The "Biography Explorer" profiles the lives and works of 46 artists.

Exploring Modern Art CD-ROM, Grades 5 to Adult

Features 150 works from Britain's Tate Gallery. Program has 10 different options to let students explore twentieth century art, encompassing painting and sculpture made in Britain, Europe, and America. Students can investigate the galleries of the artists Pablo Picasso and Barbara Hepworth, or view the works in the "Pop Art Gallery," the "Modern British Sculpture Gallery," the "Dynamism Gallery," and the "Men and Women Gallery." The "Archive" sections contains material on each gallery, including information on the lives of artists, descriptions of their work, and explanations of historical and technical terms.

Bulletin boards and display areas

The basic purpose of a bulletin board, tack strips, or any display area is communication. There should be a place to display work in each classroom. It is a great advantage to have display areas in the hallways that surround the school community and visitors with examples of all the school activities and the students' involvement.

The displays may be children's finished work, work in progress, or announcements of coming events and in general may be a record of the happenings in the class or school. The displays should be changed frequently and out-of-date material removed to maintain student interest.

Displaying student artwork allows children to view their own work and the works of others in a nonthreatening manner. To see their work from a greater distance than their own desk or table gives students a different perspective, allowing

Display areas may feature an artist, a style, a subject, or a design element and become a key to teaching concepts.

them to see their work in a new way. This provides a good way for the students to assess their own works without a formal critique. Displaying the work of artists of the past or artwork from other cultures with a bit of information can be a excellent way to introduce to the students the connections between art and art history and between the arts of our culture and other cultures. It takes very little time, it's interesting, and it encourages the student to really look and observe.

A showcase is very much like a bulletin board display, but it needs to have some three-dimensional qualities to be effective. It also is a good place to display clay objects and fragile items because the artwork is protected. Whether the bulletin board or display area is effective as a tool of art education depends upon its composition or arrangement. The elements that need to be considered are size, shape, color, texture, value (light and dark), variety, balance, and repetition.

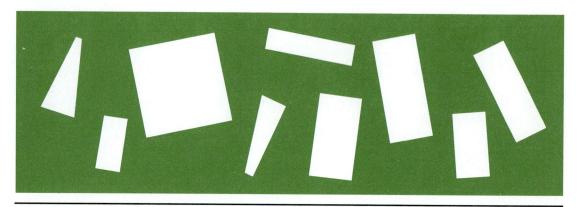

Avoid an arrangement that is too busy or confused.

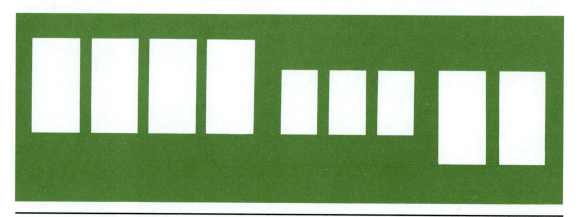

It is better to arrange the elements in an orderly manner.

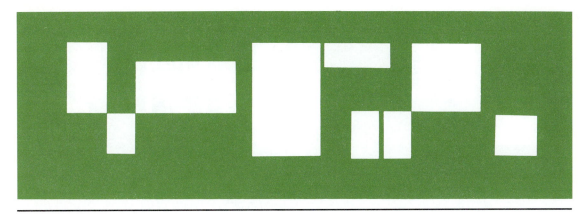

The background areas should be as interesting as the shapes themselves.

3-D objects may be attached to a board and will attract attention to the display.

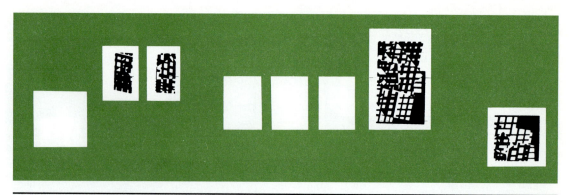

One element such as value, color, or texture can be used in different parts of the display to unify the display.

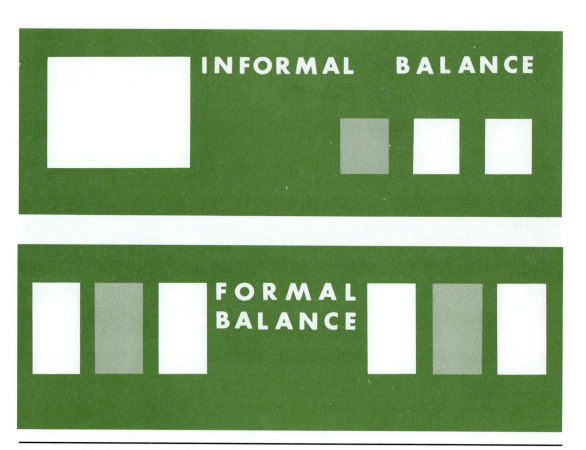

INFORMAL BALANCE

FORMAL BALANCE

Be aware of the balance of the display. Informal or formal balance may be used.

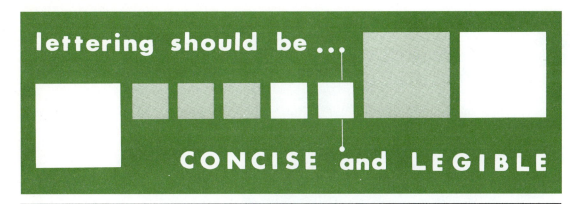

Lettering may be included in the display, but it should be legible, concise, and considered part of the composition. The style of lettering should be kept simple.

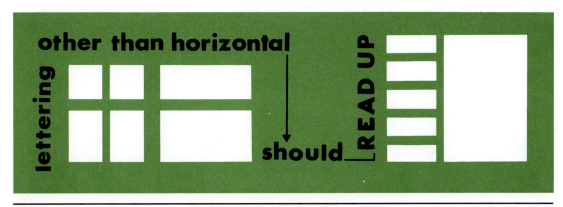

Avoid lettering to be read diagonally or from top to bottom.
Lettering should be horizontal or read from bottom to top.

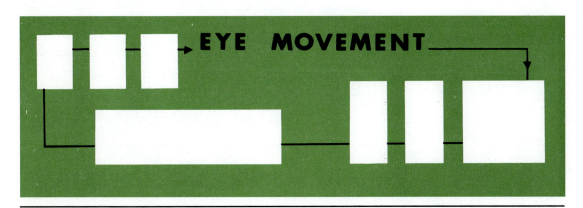

Colored string, yarn, ribbon, or narrow pieces of paper can also be tacked in place to direct the eye movement through the arrangement.

Display areas may be interactive with the use of questions or things placed on the display that are meant to be touched.

design

2

The elements of art

The elements of art are line, shape, value, texture, and color. Line does not exist in nature, but the artist uses it to define the edges or boundaries of objects. This is often referred to as *outline*. Lines may be long or short, thick or thin, and dark or light (value). They may also possess color and may be straight, angular, or curved. The character of a line is determined by the drawing instrument such as pencil, pen, or brush. All of the factors cited have certain compositional functions. They also have expressive properties, particularly when augmented by color. Lines can be used to suggest texture and value through squiggles, hatching, and cross-hatching. The comparative values, thicknesses, and directions can also promote the appearance of space.

Shapes are outlined or filled-in areas. They may be rectilinear (straight lines), curvilinear (curved lines), or a combination of the two. When an artist uses shape, whether or not he or she is attempting to reproduce something, there is normally a search for balance, related directions, and controlled importance (through size, value, shape, contrast, location, and color). Shapes may indicate space through those same means or by using traditional perspective. Different shapes have traits that can produce emotional reactions.

Line

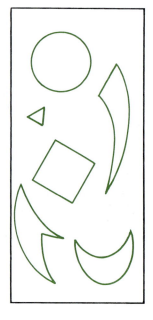

Shape

The Elements of Art Structure

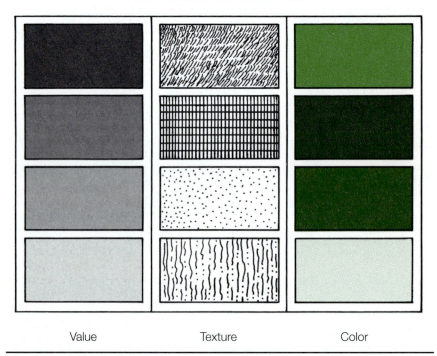

Value   Texture   Color

These are extremely simplified examples of each of the art elements; they may further consist of the following. Line: Angular, zig-zag lines; curved spiral, circular, serpentine, or any combinations of these types; Shape: Square, triangle, octagon, oblong, circle, oval, free-form; limitless possibilities and combinations; Value: Numerous variations from snow-white to pure black; Texture: Simulated (copied from rugs, wood, towels, grass, etc.), invented (entirely the product of the artist's imagination), or abstract (freely interpreted from existing textured surfaces); and Color: An infinite number of hues with their numberless variations of value and intensity.

Value refers to degrees of darkness or lightness. All of the other art elements exhibit value. Value can describe objects, create shapes, and suggest space. The value of an object (local value) most likely could be affected by highlights and shadows that are values in themselves. Dark values in an artwork can project a mood of gloom, mystery, and menace, while light values are more cheerful and less threatening.

Texture has four categories—actual texture is the way the surface of a real object looks and feels, simulated texture is the artist's attempt to re-create that effect, abstract textures are simulated textures modified for artistic reasons, and invented textures are created (rather than re-created) by the artist. Selections from this group can lend reality, warmth, decoration, and psychological qualities to an artwork.

Color is produced by the light waves reflected by an object (in art, pigments). They are warm or cool, light or dark, and they have varying degrees of brightness (intensity). We all react emotionally to different colors; in various situations they can appeal to us or repel us. Contrasting colors are exciting, but harmonious colors are calming. The artist can use color to reproduce natural effects, to attract attention in varying degrees, and to produce spatial suggestions (bright colors advance and dull colors recede).

The elements of art are mixed and controlled by the artist so that they work in concert to transmit his or her responses to persons, places, and things.

Visual composition

Visual composition is probably an area that restricts itself to the upper grade. Each artwork is unique, with its own set of unique design problems, and good design is, in large part, a thing instinctive in the artist. Nevertheless, there are some guiding principles of which we need to be reminded periodically, and which, if repeated often enough, can become a part of the artist's instincts.

Design is perhaps more accurately called *composition.* The artist works with elements (lines, shapes, values, textures, and colors)—sometimes representing recognizable subjects, sometimes not—just as the music composer works with notes, harmonics, tempi, rhythms, and dynamics. The function of *visual* composition is to make the material legible, interesting, and expressive of the artist's feelings about the subject. The artist's *form* (total composition) may be directed by logic or instinct. Some artists are more cerebral than others; their work is dissected and analyzed as it develops. Other artists seem to work more out of their subconscious motivations, but there is still logic to their artwork. Every artist realizes that there are limits to his or her format (the area on which the artist works) and that this surface becomes an arena of visual forces that must work to his or her advantage. Things must be tied together so that they lead comfortably from one to the other, and there must be assurance that an appropriate amount of emphasis is given them—all of this while working for pictorial equilibrium, or balance. Obviously, these goals are not easily reached; a well-designed work is the result of considerable alteration.

To achieve *balance* the artist must have some feeling for the visual weight of the elements and images being drawn. The weight is, of course, an illusion, but it is real to the artist. Visual weight derives from size, lightness or darkness, placement, general configuration, and complexity. A large shape is usually (not always, depending on what else the artist does to it) heavier than a small one, a dark shape heavier than a light one, a shape at the lower part of the drawing heavier than one at the top, and some shapes, simply because of their character, are seemingly heavier than others. These factors may be intermingled in an image, increasing or reducing the apparent weight. One cannot put such factors into the scales, so the artist must develop some sensitivity to the weight represented. Once this sensitivity is achieved, it is possible to scan a work and respond to its balance or imbalance. Balance is generally sought and can take two forms: symmetrical balance or asymmetrical balance. In symmetrical balance, similar or identical images are given similar or identical placement on either side of a work. This is a rather simple and often monotonous form of balance. In asymmetrical balance, unlike images are given dissimilar placement in such a way that a total feeling of balance is produced.

When placing the images, other design criteria must be observed. It is possible that although balance has been achieved, placement has caused some images to lose some of the importance they deserve; in other words, the relative dominance has been disturbed. *Relative dominance* refers to the degree of significance the artist attaches to each image. Obviously if everything is of equal importance, the work is difficult to read and the artist's message is lost. Dominance is manipulated by the same factors that create weight: a larger image is interpreted as being more important, and so forth. When balance is achieved but relative dominance is lost, the artist must go back to the drawing board. He or she must juggle the factors until the needs for balance and relative dominance are both satisfied. By now it can be seen that composition is not unlike a game; not an easy one, but one that is very rewarding if the answers are found. In this game the artist creates his or her own problems, each of which is unique, and experiments until the problems are solved. This problem-solving function necessitates some sacrifices for the benefit of the total image.

Balance Diagram

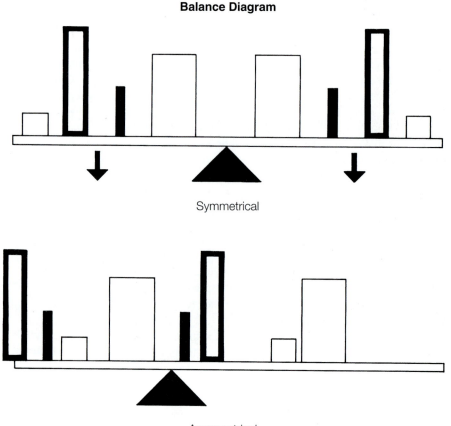

Symmetrical

Asymmetrical

Assuming that problems of balance and relative dominance have been solved, there remains the task of relating the imagery in terms of the observer's perusal of the work. Although the observer may not be aware of it, the artist *directs* this perusal. Transitions are created between areas of interest. The directions implicit in these areas may be, or can be made to be, participants in this directional sweep, augmented by newly introduced passages. When this final matter is settled to the artist's satisfaction, presumably we have a work that attracts the observer's attention, which is then comfortably directed from point to point, each point occupying its own importance scale in the work.

This discussion has isolated compositional problems in such a way that it seems that there is a predictable sequence to them. On occasion, the artist may direct his or her attention to each individual problem, but usually the problems are considered en masse. So we find that the development of a work is not usually intellectual or methodical, but instinctive, with the artist's feeling for rightness directing the proceedings.

Harmony and variety

The two most important factors in composition are harmony and variety. Harmony refers to sameness and variety to difference. The composition may be unbalanced in favor of one or the other, but both must be present to some degree. Harmony leads to close relationships and, when overused, dullness. Variety creates excitement and, in the extreme, chaos. Any of the elements illustrated thus far may be modified in various ways to produce either harmony or variety. An example in color might be a scheme that is largely made up of reddish hues (harmony) or one that uses clashing colors or all the colors in the rainbow (variety). In dealing with shapes, one could devise some that are entirely made up of straight lines (harmony) or straight and curved lines (variety). The characteristics of the elements just cited are among their physical properties; there are many that can be manipulated. If harmony and variety are appropriately blended to suit the expressive needs of the artist, it can be said that the work is *unified*.

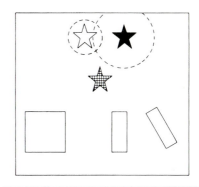

The circles represent the areas of attraction of the stars. The black star circle is larger because that star, because of its contrast, is more dominant. The rectangle on the right has more dominance than its size justifies because it is tilted. All elements or images have degrees of attraction because of factors such as these.

Venus and Adonis. Titian. National Gallery of Art, Washington Widener Collection, 1942.

This diagram demonstrates the basic movements of the preceding work. The eyes of the observer are directed along these paths. Secondary movements or relationships could also have been indicated.

chapter two: design   **41**

It would probably be foolish to show concern for the design abilities of the very young, for the verbalization of such a concept would be unintelligible to them. Most young people already have a good instinctive sense of design that is frequently lost with the advancing years. It has already been noted that maturity is a variable and that the realistic stage, when reached, can present many problems. One of the problems is that, in their preoccupation with realistic imagery, young people may lose contact with their compositional needs. If this occurs, it may be advisable to point out (without neglecting the importance of good drawing) that "likeness" is not the only answer in creating good art. Competent artists realize that visual reality (likeness) often has to be adjusted or reevaluated for effective composition. Those who are gaining competence in realistic drawing do not usually welcome or see the need for such sacrifices. It requires a great deal of diplomacy to convince such persons that the real aim of art is the expression of something that cannot be communicated by faithful copying, no matter how skillfully it is done.

The development of an artwork

Every artwork has the illusion of a certain amount of space, whether planned or unplanned. This spatial illusion is the product of the elements listed previously and the images they create; dark lines move ahead of light lines, large shapes move ahead of small shapes and bright colors move ahead of dull colors. Artists use these physical properties of the art elements to control the space in their works. When art elements are close together in space, that space is called *decorative space*. When art elements are separated, the space is either shallow or deep space. Other devices used for space control are size, position, overlapping, transparency, interpenetration, sharp or diminishing detail, converging parallels, and linear perspective.

Any attempt to impose compositional concerns on young children would be fruitless. Children produce exciting and expressive images but the images lack the coherence of a mature work. Only as children mature does the importance of composition become reasonable—and that very slowly. People involved in personal creativity can evoke this realization most successfully.

For the sake of interest, here is the way an artwork *may* develop; works do not always develop in the same order. An artist must begin with an idea, or germ, that will eventually develop into the concept of the finished artwork. The idea may be the result of aimless doodling, a thought that has suddenly struck the artist, or a notion that has been growing in his or her mind for a long time. If this idea is to become tangible, it must be developed in a medium selected by the artist (clay, oil, paint, watercolor). The artist not only controls, but is controlled by, the medium.

Through the medium the elements of form emerge, with their intrinsic meanings. These meanings may be allied with a representational or nonrepresentational image; in either case, the bulk of the meaning will be in the form created by the elements.

While working on the artwork, the artist will be concerned with composition, or formal structure, as the most interesting and communicative presentation of the idea is explored. During this process abstraction will inevitably occur, even if the work is broadly realistic; elements will be added, eliminated, or generally edited. The abstraction happens with an awareness, and within the parameters, of the principles of composition.

As the creative procedure unfolds (not always directly, neatly, or without stress and anguish), the artist fervently hopes that the result will be unified. This refers to the culmination of everything being sought in the work. Put simply, it means that every part not only fits, but that each one contributes to the overall content or meaning. At this point, however arduous or circuitous the artist's route, the work is finished—or is it? Having given the best of themselves artists are never sure of this! Perhaps the perspective of a few days, months, or years will give the answer. How fortunate are the grade-schoolers that they can just pitch in and avoid such worrisome matters!

To learn about the many considerations involved in striving for compositional unity in art, it is recommended that the reader study some of the many books on the subject. Prejudice dictates that a reading list be headed by *Art Fundamentals,* produced by the publisher of this book, and written, in part, by one of the authors of this text. Details on this and other recommended books can be found in the Art Resources Appendix.

Through the exploration of 2-D and 3-D media, older or more talented students may discover, select, and transform ideas from personal experience into subject matter in their artworks. They thus learn art concepts and art vocabulary from practical experience. When these students study their own artwork or historical artwork, they learn how art critics, historians, and society have perceived artworks, and thus they improve their ability to express themselves.

The elements of line, shape, color, value, and texture have been discussed in some detail; the compositional concepts include balance, pattern and repetition, rhythm and movement, unity, emphasis, and contrast and variety. Some of these are germane to certain activities and, in some cases, these are pointed out. The objectives of the activities may be expanded because of the choice of subject and the emphasis placed on different aspects of the lesson.

color

3

The spectrum

Color can be an immensely complicated field of study. There are many color theories, some of them devised for specific conditions or applications of color. Fortunately, the readers of this book need only a basic understanding of the color principles that artists and physicists have given us.

In dealing with the color of light, we can see that its rays are divided into constituent colors as they pass through a glass prism. This array, known as the *spectrum,* demonstrates violet, dark blue, blue, green, yellow, orange, and red as well as other colors invisible to the naked eye.

The colors we detect in objects are visible because these are the only colors reflected back to our eyes; the rest are absorbed by the surface of the object. This is, of course, also true of the media used by the artist, whether it be chalk, watercolor, oil paint, pastel, or tempera. When a ribbon of red oil paint is squeezed from the tube, the paint reflects only the color red back to our eyes.

Color inherently fascinates all of us and particularly children, who are as fearless in its use as they are with any medium within reach. Most of us are aware that colors affect us psychologically, and this means that color selection is of primary consideration in creating the mood of an artwork. Young children seem to know this instinctively, and in any case, it is foolish to burden them with such considerations; however, when one deals with children on the threshold of the realistic stage, it might be appropriate to point out the symbolic and expressive properties of color.

Color relationships

Many colors come prepackaged, and many people use the colors just as they find them, direct from the tube. On occasion this may be appropriate, but in doing so consistently one misses the opportunity to learn something about color relationships and the fun that comes from mixing colors. It is always a delight to see what happens when colors are added to each other. Experimentation should not be discouraged, but there should be some *planning* of the color mixtures; only through methodical mixing can one get some idea of the infinite color possibilities.

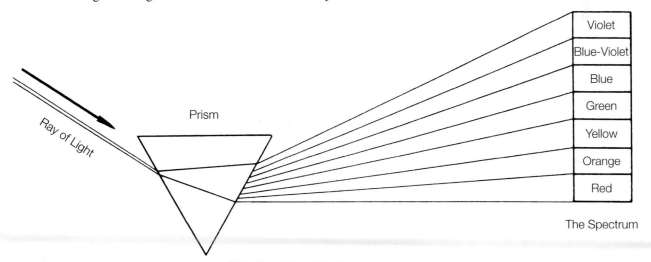

Ray of Light

Prism

| Violet |
| Blue-Violet |
| Blue |
| Green |
| Yellow |
| Orange |
| Red |

The Spectrum

The rays of red have the longest wavelengths and those of violet the shortest. The angle at which the rays are bent, or refracted, is greatest at the violet end and least at the red.

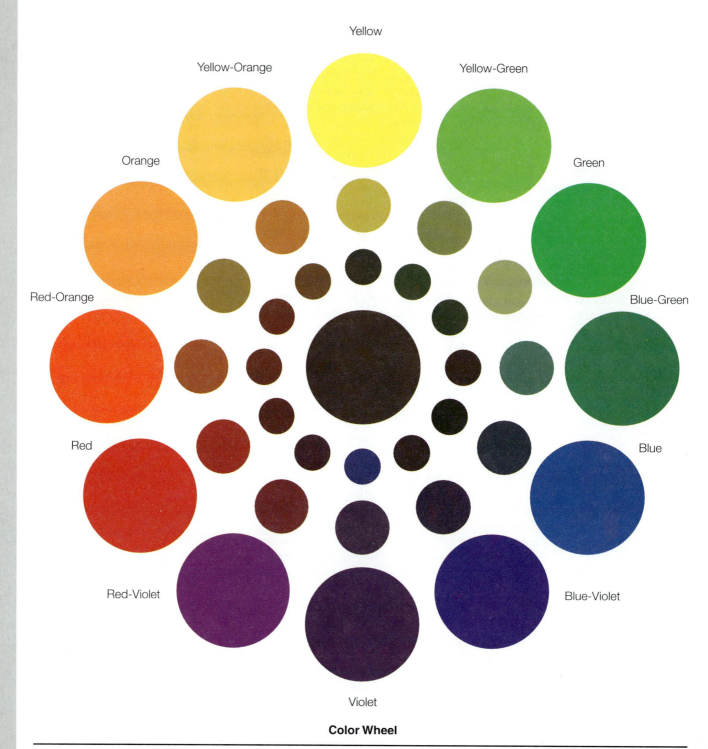

Color Wheel

The outer ring of hues includes the primaries (red, yellow, and blue) and secondaries (green, violet, and orange). Were we to insert new colors appropriately between each of these, they would be called tertiaries. One could continue doing this ad infinitum, as there is no limit to the modifications of hues.

As the hue moves inward it is being neutralized by its complement (the hue directly opposite on the wheel) until it reaches a neutral, or gray. As in the case of the hues, intensities can be infinitely modified. This is also true of values; each of its hues or intensities could receive increasing amounts of white and/or black (not shown).

Hue

Colors are also known as hues. The basic hues from which all others evolve are the *primaries*—red, yellow, and blue. The first step in this evolution occurs when the primaries are mixed equally to produce the *secondary* hues. The equality of color mixing should be optical, not by measurement. Some hues are stronger than others and tend to dominate. For example, if we mix blue and yellow for a green and let the blue dominate, the result would not be green but blue-green. This would mean that we had moved a bit beyond the green into an *intermediate* hue. The color wheel illustrates the hues that can result from mixing.

Intensity

Hue can be modified in its *intensity* or brilliance. A pure hue could be said to be at maximum intensity. Anything added to this hue would affect its brightness, but most artists use a complement when dulling a hue. Complementary hues are those directly opposite each other on the color wheel, with violet and yellow being examples. If the violet used to neutralize the yellow is not a true violet (red and blue balanced), the intensity will be reduced, but the hue will change, being inclined to lean toward either orange (too much red) or green (too much blue). It is theoretically possible to achieve a true gray by balancing out any two complements, but the nature of pigment used in art media is such that different complements will produce somewhat different grays.

Value

The third property of color is *value*—the darkness of a given hue. Color value is a consideration too often neglected in art. In looking at the color wheel, it should be apparent that yellow is much lighter than violet, and if the wheel were photographed in black and white, each hue would display its own characteristic value. The diagram illustrates this quite clearly.

The pattern created by the use of value contrasts in a composition is an important factor in the effectiveness of the work. The darkening and lightening of hues is usually accomplished by adding black or white. It is theoretically possible to do so without changing the intensity; but in fact, the addition of any color to hues will change both value and intensity to some degree. In some cases hue is changed as well; some black additives result in a greenish hue. The characteristics of media vary, even according to manufacturer, and are not entirely predictable.

To confirm what has been said here and, in the process, learn something of color relationships, it is recommended that a color wheel be attempted along with experiments in both intensity and value. There are limitless possibilities, so great in fact that even in hue, the colors produced are so many that there can be no standard identifying names for them—although they can be seen to be reddish, bluish, or whatever. By neutralizing and darkening and lightening these hues, the possibilities expand almost geometrically.

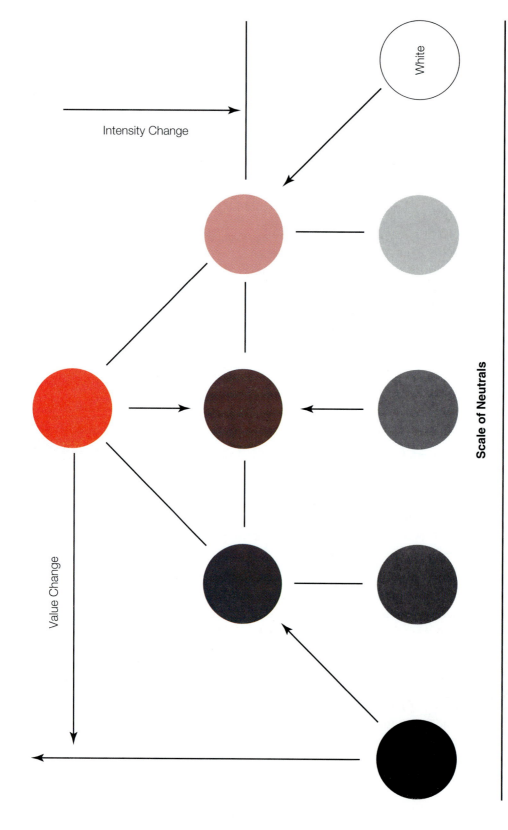

Scale of Neutrals

The red at the top of the illustration is presumably at spectrum intensity (pure red). As we move down one step we can see that the red has been slightly neutralized in its intensity. If we move right we can see this neutralized red has had its value changed by the addition of white; moving to its left it becomes darker (black added). The bottom circle (two steps below red) represents the ultimate neutralization of the red; this, in turn, moves toward white (right) and black (left).

part one: foundations

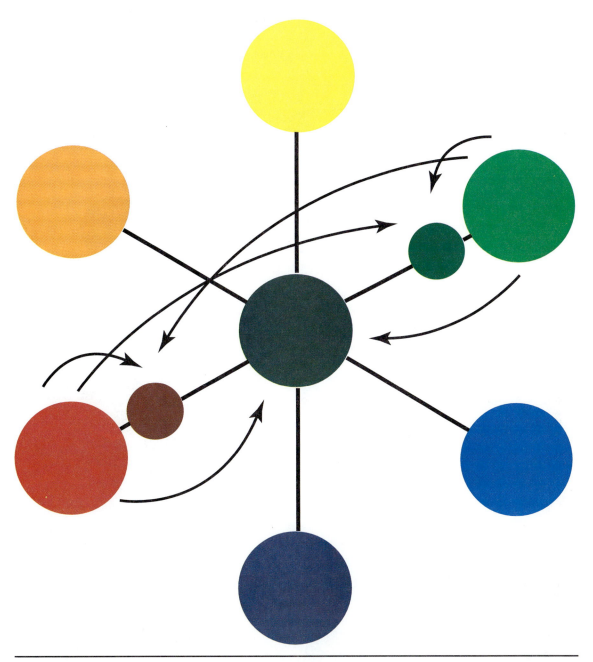

These two diagrams (above and on p. 48) illustrate the four means of changing the intensity of color. (1) In the diagram on p. 48, as white (a neutral) is added to bright red, the value is changed, but the resulting color is lowered in intensity. (2) In the same way, the addition of black to bright red creates a dark red closer to the neutral scale because the intensity is changed. (3) When a neutral gray is added to the spectrum color, the intensity is lowered, but the value is neither raised nor lowered. (4) The diagram on this page indicates change of intensity by adding to a color a little of its complement. For instance, by adding a small amount of green to red, a gray red is produced. In the same way, a small amount of red added to green results in a gray green. When the two colors are balanced (not necessarily equal amounts), the resulting mixture is a neutral gray.

White

High light — Yellow

Yellow-Orange — Light — Yellow-Green

Orange — Low light — Green

Red-Orange — Medium — Blue-Green

Red — High dark — Blue

Red-Violet — Dark — Blue-Violet

Violet — Low dark

Black

This chart shows the value of each of the hues illustrated at maximum intensity (not neutralized). It can be seen that pure yellow is the lightest of the hues, corresponding to "high light"; red-orange is somewhat darker, matching up with "medium" value. Violet is the darkest of the hues shown (low dark). Any changes in any of the hues would move them up (lighter) or down (darker) on the value scale.

A "hands-on" study of color should begin with painting a color wheel consisting of at least 12 hues (yellow, yellow-orange, orange, red-orange, red, red-violet, violet, blue-violet, blue, blue-green, green, and yellow-green). Following this procedure, each hue should be taken through a number of modifications of its value and intensity.

Color schemes

Once the many possibilities are appreciated, selection of color schemes can begin. Artists use color according to their own feelings. Excitement can be the product of a complementary plan, while relative calm is the result of analogous hues (those hues near each other on the color wheel). Colors can be warm (red, orange, yellow) or cool (blue, green, some violets). The color temperature is another ingredient in the mood evoked. Sometimes artists use triadic schemes; the primary triad is red, yellow, and blue; the secondary triad is orange, green, and violet. Other triadic systems with similar hue separation are, of course, possible.

Split complements are often used, this entails the use of a hue plus those colors to either side of its complement on the color wheel.

Some artists stay fairly close to *local* hues (the hues normally associated with objects), but they are rarely entirely literal in their transcription of color;

nature is entirely too complex to treat with complete fidelity. Those artists closest to nature are termed *naturalists,* and those who distance themselves somewhat are called *realists.* Other artists find that natural colors are inadequate for their needs. Such artists use nonlocal hues (green faces, purple cows, etc.); the hues are employed to achieve decorative, symbolic, or expressive effects. Despite the differences in their artistic goals, these artists are collectively known as *expressionists.*

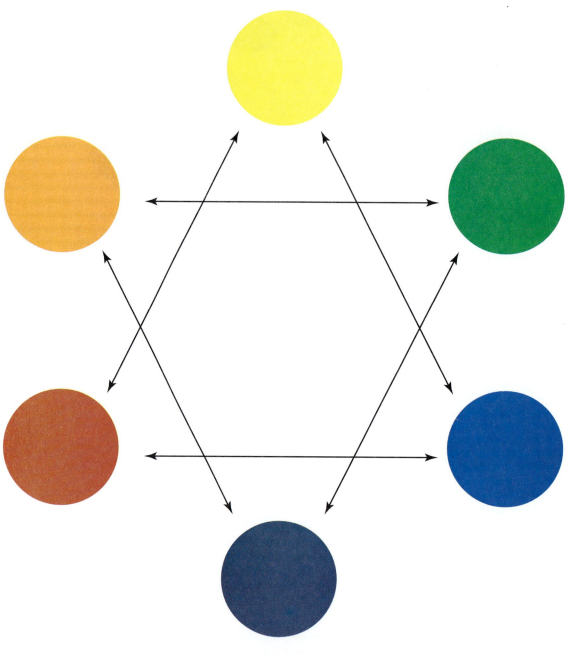

Triadic Color Interval
(Medium contrast)

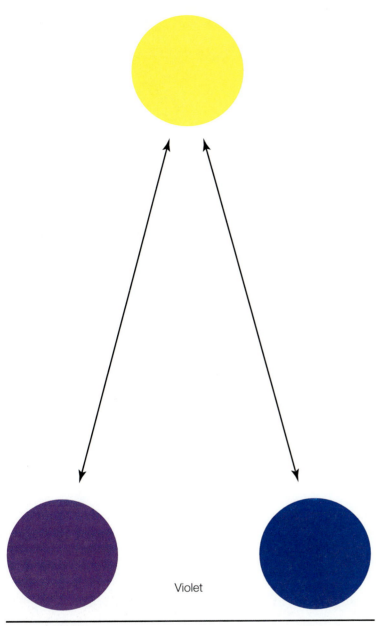

Violet

This example shows yellow and its split complementary colors, red-violet and blue-violet, on either side of yellow's complement, violet.

activities
part two

an introduction to the art activities

The activities in this volume are so named because they produce action and as an alternative to the term *problems,* a term often associated with art assignments. Problems are usually assigned as a specific segment of art for which a solution is sought, and the solution is often found through an intellectual process. Fine art is produced by using varying degrees of the intellect and the intuition, the proportions depending on the artist, the work, and the difficulties encountered. Although there is some amount of problem-solving involved in these activities, more for some children than others, the balance in this book would favor intuition. Younger children do not ordinarily intellectualize their works. In supervising very young artists, it is wise to provide motivation and enthusiasm, allowing their instincts to guide them; as the students grow older or show evidence or precocity, reason will come into play.

All children are different; they cannot always be accurately classified by age, grade, or any other standards. They also respond differently to art and with different degrees of creative maturity (see "Art and Teaching," pp. 6–10). Students within the same class may be at different stages of development, the manipulative, symbolic, or realistic stages. Some may be exceptional in art, some in other fields. Certain activities will be more challenging or more interesting to some students than to others, but most of the activities will be received by all with some degree of enthusiasm and will have some benefits for all. With creativity having such elastic boundaries for such a wide range of individuals, teaching art requires a flexible and sensitive teacher.

We have listed the general benefits which could be associated with art activities. We hope that you will recognize them in your situation:

Appreciation Showing a deserved degree of regard for a product or performance based on an adequate understanding of the difficulties involved.

Concentration Stretching the interest span. Focusing on a particular task without being unduly influenced by distractions.

Conceptualization Foreseeing the results of certain actions. Planning in one's mind's eye the thought and its subsequent portrayal.

Cooperation Relating to and contributing to social growth. Constructive teamwork. Productive participation.

Correlation The ability to see, understand, and exploit relationships between things. May include relationships between certain areas of art and other subject areas.

Dexterity Neuromuscular coordination; eye-hand control. The ability to handle physical tasks.

Family relationships Children usually like to represent their family and direct their work toward it. They expect a positive response from relatives.

Individual growth Improvements in behavior, attitude, and performance in matters both personal and social.

Interest in nature Children usually show an automatic interest in natural items or occurrences. This can be enhanced and exploited by the teacher.

Perception Not just looking at, but *seeing* things with a degree of accuracy. Noting certain things beyond the obvious.

Resourcefulness The motivation and energy required to develop ways of problem-solving.

Self-esteem An outcome of individual growth. Recognition of one's ability to perform things with confidence. Self-awareness of skills and abilities. The teacher's positive remarks are especially helpful here. Pride, but not to excess.

Social growth Adapting one's responses to those of other people. Thinking of one's efforts as part of a *total* effort. Cooperating unselfishly in group activities.

Stability Acceptance of constructive criticism without rancor, such criticism made only as adequate maturity is reached; rarely applies to younger children.

lettering and calligraphy

4

Lettering

The art of using lettering is called *typography*. Lettering and calligraphy is an art form that benefits from the knowledge of certain rules in order to be attractive and legible. Ellison machines, press type letters, and now the computer have given us access to hundreds of styles of lettering called *typeface*. Each of the letters, numbers, punctuation marks, and symbols that make up a particular typeface is called a *character*. The arrangement of the characters is called *typesetting*, and the size of the characters is measured in *points*.

The typeface can also have variations. *Roman* has characters that stand straight, and *Italic* has characters that slant to the right. Characters that are thin are called *light*, and those that are strong and heavy are called *bold*.

The strokes at the ends of some characters are called *serifs* and those typefaces without serifs are called *sans serif*. Capital letters are called *uppercase* and the smaller letters are called *lowercase*.

Each typeface has a different look and a different feeling. A written word can produce a different response by using different typefaces.

A rough layout of the letters done in pencil is recommended before inking. The form of the letters, size, placement of words on a page, and the spacing between the letters and words should all be given consideration.

Only the fundamental rules of the Gothic letter structure are illustrated here. A variety of lettering can be created from this basic type, as is shown in the illustration.

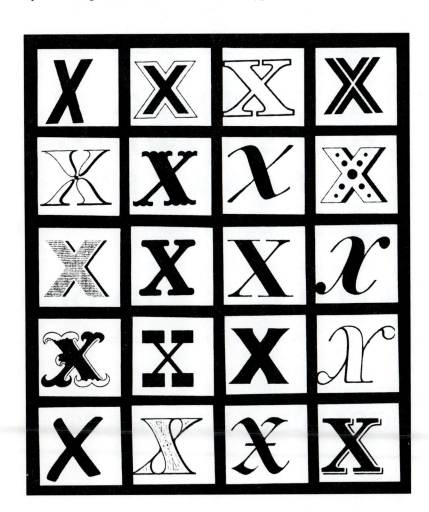

CAUTION: Some of the activities in this chapter call for the use of X-acto knives. Extreme care and supervision must be taken whenever X-acto knives are used. Safety instructions should be given before **EVERY** use of the knives. X-acto knives are now sold with safety caps, but separate caps may be purchased for older knives. Heavy corrugated cardboard should always be placed under the paper or material being cut. The X-acto knife is held like a pencil, with the fingers holding the knife on the textured ring. The slanted, sharpened edge should be directly over the line to be cut and the position of the knife or the paper should be changed if the line changes direction. Keep the fingers of the holding hand out of the way of the blade, usually above the cutting area. Remind students often to check themselves and the position of the knife and their hands.

supplies

supplies

1. Ink
2. Lettering pen and pen holder, or felt pen
3. Paper
4. Ruler
5. Pencil

Ink or felt pen lettering

procedure

1. The axes of all Gothic letters are perpendicular to the line upon which they rest and are of uniform thickness.

   PERPENDICULAR | **perpendicular**

2. Capitals, or uppercase letters, are all the same height—usually two spaces high for children.

   A B C D E F G H I J K L M N
   O P Q R S T U V W X Y Z ·
   1 2 3 4 5 6 7 8 9 0

3. Capital letters are of three different width groups—wide, average, and narrow.

   Narrow letters   Wide letters

   E F I J L T   **G M O Q W**

   There are no serifs or dots on the basic Gothic letters I or J, as indicated above, unless used on all letters.

4. A serif is a cross stroke on the end of the individual lines of a letter. (When serifs are used, they must be used on *every* letter.)

   COLOR   ART   CRAFT

5. Horizontal line intersections generally should be above or below the middle of the letter for greater legibility.

Letters with horizontal line intersection above the middle:

BEFHX

Letters with horizontal line intersection below the middle:

AGKPRY

6. Correct spacing is absolutely necessary to make lettering or manuscript writing legible and attractive. Measured spacing produces a lack of unity in lettered words. Spacing should be done with feeling for the *area between* the letters. When lettering, leave the width of an average letter between words.

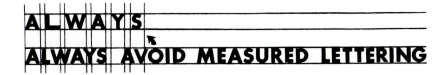

7. Lowercase, or small letters, are usually divided into thirds for the convenience of young children.

abcdefghijklmnop

qrstuvwxyz

8. The lowercase Gothic alphabet can be divided into three families of letters:

Short letters

aceimnorsuvwxz

Letters with ascenders

bdfhklt

(Note that the letter t extends only halfway into the top space.)

Letters with descenders

gjpqy

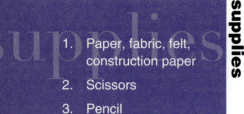

Cut letters

This style of lettering is especially useful for bulletin boards, display areas, posters, and reports. It is a good fold and cut lesson. The letters are easy to cut, and, when the technique is perfected, the letters may be cut any size, with any foldable material, and can even be distorted if desired.

procedure

1. Cut a number of strips of the material to be used the height of the proposed letters.
2. If the letters are to be used for a particular project, such as a bulletin board or poster, write out the words and count the number needed for each letter. Several letters may be folded and cut at the same time depending on the thickness of the material used.
3. Letters fall into three categories, wide, average, and narrow, and these refer to the width of the letters. The wide letter is a square and the average has some paper removed from one side with additional paper cut away for the narrow letters.

Wide letters: C G M O Q W

Average letters: A B D H K N P R S U V X Y Z

Narrow letters: E F I J L T

Average letters

A—The top of the letter A must be cut half as wide as the final thickness of the letter.

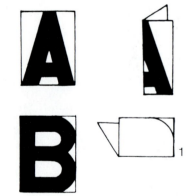

B—Fold in half and cut around the corner to form the curved edge of the letter (Ill. 1).

Fold top edge to middle crease and cut opening (Ill. 2).

Fold bottom edge up to the bottom of opening and cut larger opening (Ill. 3).

Unfold and cut out triangle. The bottom of the B will be larger than the top (Ill. 4).

D—Fold the bottom edge up and cut the opening and corners.

H—The crossbar of the letter H must be cut half as wide as the final thickness of the letter.

K—The first two letters K (Ills. 1 and 2) are cut by folding; the third is not folded (Ill. 3).

N—The N cannot be folded to cut.

P—Fold top edge down below the middle and cut out shape.

R—The opening in the letter R is cut like the P; the remainder of the letter is cut without folding.

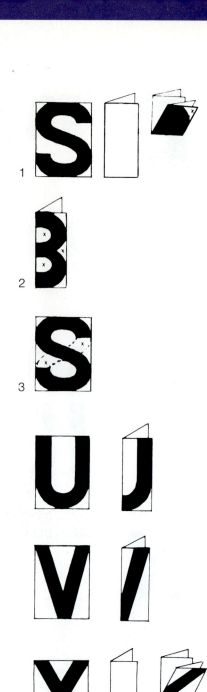

S—Fold paper in half, then in half again. Cut a rounded corner (Ill. 1).

Open and cut away the areas marked with X (Ill. 2).

Open and cut away the excess paper from the figure 8 to form the letter S (Ill. 3).

U—Fold in half and cut opening and corners.

V—The bottom of the letter V must be cut half as wide as the final thickness of the letter.

X—The center of the letter X must be cut half as wide as the final thickness of the letter.

Y—The stem of the Y must be cut half as wide as the final thickness of the letter.

Z—The Z cannot be folded to cut.

Wide letters

C—Fold paper in half, then in half again. Cut quarter circle for both outside and inside of letter.

Open and cut away section as indicated.

G—Fold paper in half, then in half again. Cut quarter circle for outside of letter only.

Unfold and cut out openings in areas indicated. Open and cut away parts indicated.

M—The middle of the letter M must be cut as wide as the final thickness of the letter. The sides of the M are vertical. The middle of the M should go to the bottom.

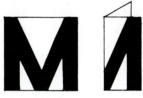

O—Fold paper in half, then in half again. Cut quarter circle for both inside and outside of letter.

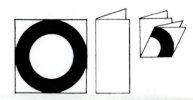

Q—Fold paper in half, then in half again. Cut as shown.

Open and cut away the extra tails; or cut like the letter O and add for the tail.

W—The middle of the W must be cut half as wide as the final thickness of the letter. The sides of the W slant: The middle of the W should go to the top.

Narrow letters

E—Shorten the middle arm of the E. The middle arm of the E must be cut half as wide as the final thickness of the letter.

F—Shorten the middle arm and remove bottom leg. The middle arm of the F must be cut half as wide as the final thickness of the letter.

I—Cut to match the thickness of the other letters.

J—The letter J is a narrow letter but is cut like a U.

L—The L cannot be folded to cut.

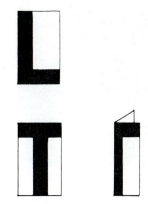

T—The stem of the letter T must be cut half as wide as the final thickness of the letter.

The top or bottom of the following letters can either be pointed or flat, but all must be of the same style when used together in forming a word. Pointed letters should extend either above or below the line.

AA VV NN ZZ
WW MM

Folded three-dimensional letters

Simple three-dimensional lettering is interesting to use and easy to make.

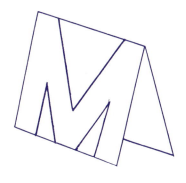
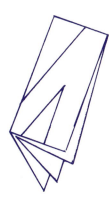

Fold a sheet of paper so that it is twice the height of the intended letter. Fold the paper in half again if the letter can be folded to cut. Make sure when cutting that each letter is held together by some part of the fold.

Mount the bottom of the letters on a poster or bulletin board—the spring in the paper will give the top half a three-dimensional effect.

connections

Alphabatics by Suse MacDonald, Aladdin Paper Backs, New York, 1992

The Jungle ABC by Michael Roberts, Callaway Edition, Inc., New York, 1998

Alphabet City by Stephen T. Johnson, Viking, Penguin Books, New York, 1995

Old Black Fly by Jim Aylesworth, Illustrated by Stephen Gammell, Henry Holt & Co., New York, 1992

ABC book

This could be a cooperative project with each student contributing one letter with illustration for the finished book. It is important to choose a particular theme for the book before beginning. The book could be connected with many different subjects such as the rain forest, children's games or activities, animals, birds and so on. It is important that each student have an idea to go with their letter before they begin the lesson.

procedure

1. Each student will make one of the letters of the alphabet, using colored paper or material. Cut letters work well for this lesson.
2. Place the letter on a sheet of 9″ × 12″ paper, but do not glue.
3. Make the object that begins with the cut-out letter and background. This could be done with cut paper or paint or any other color media.
4. Decide on the arrangement or composition and paint or glue all shapes in place.
5. The pages may be laminated or not. They may be put in order in a scrapbook format.

Poster art

With the use of lithography in the 1800s, it became possible to make formats that would convey ideas and events to a wide audience. The first posters were created usually to advertise art exhibitions.

Posters are a serious art form that ties art to commerce. This art is used for the promotion and marketing of ideas, events, and products. The poster needs to attract attention, should have an economy of information, and the letters should be part of a pattern unit. A person should be able to read it quickly and from a distance.

procedure

1. The older student should do several small possible arrangements or layouts so that he or she can select the best on the basis of readability, color, pattern, movement, composition, and appeal. Keep in mind that the lettering should be a part of the design.
2. On the selected poster material, draw a neat frame around the edge. Draw the selected layout on the poster in pencil. Use chalk and Craypas to fill in color carefully.

connections

Oskar Kokoschka
Egon Schiele
Henri de Toulouse-Lautrec
Pierre Bonnard
Other possibilities:
    Program covers
    Package design
    Disk covers

Primary poster art

procedure

1. Prepare a poster layout with rub-on letters, stencil letters, cut letters, or hand lettering. Include all the information of when, where, what. Leave a framed space for the illustration.
2. Run the layout off on a copier machine. Have each of the students create an illustration that will fit in the space left on the layout.
3. If the student works with a black fine line marker or a soft drawing pencil, the poster could be run off again with the illustration in place.

Lettering as part of a composition

Lettering has been used as a composition or part of a composition on artwork, particularly by the pop artists. The painting by Robert Indiana is an example of the letters of the word *love* forming the composition. The colors are simple and strongly contrasting and reminiscent of billboards. Other artists that have used words and letters in their work include Stuart Davis, Andy Warhol, and Maxfield Parrish.

supplies

supplies

1. Pencils and erasers
2. Rulers
3. Color media could include markers, tempera, or acrylics
4. Brushes for paint
5. Water containers for paint

procedure

1. Think of the letters as shapes.
2. The letters may make up the entire composition or be a part of the composition.
3. The letters may spell words.
4. Draw the letters and the shapes of the composition in pencil.
5. When satisfied with the composition, paint or fill with color very carefully. Keep the edges of the letters as neat as possible or when complete, go over the edges with black marker.

Different typeface used as texture and value

The artist now has access to hundreds of typefaces and can use them in many different ways. Not only can the type be used as a means of communication, but also as a means of creating both value (lights and darks) and texture (how something might feel). Each typeface, when it is repeated, has a definite character. It may be thick and dark or very thin and airy in character. Each letter, because of its shape, can create a different texture when it is repeated many times.

supplies

1. Computer and printer
2. Scissors
3. Pencils
4. Glue or glue stick
5. Mounting paper, 9″ × 12″ or larger

procedure

1. The student will need to experiment with different fonts, different sizes of fonts, and different styles to check their character. Different letters, uppercase or lowercase, punctuation, or numbers can be used.
2. The subject of the compositions may even be the letters used for the different parts of the composition. For instance, if the subject is the cockatoo, the letters of the word *cockatoo* could be used.
3. Print out sheets of the letters to have a large enough piece to cut the necessary shapes for the subject.
4. Cut out the shapes and lay the shapes on the mounting paper. Glue in place.

Calligraphy

Calligraphy is simply the art of beautiful writing. It is a manual art in contrast with printing, which is a mechanical process. The term *printing* is often mistakenly used for writing; the term *lettering* is more appropriate. The words *calligraphy* and *lettering* are often used interchangeably, although, in most cases, people think of calligraphy as being more florid and elegant. Calligraphy is cursive, the letters being connected as in standard handwriting; in lettering there is usually no connection. Earlier generations may remember their handwriting instruction in which particular emphasis was placed on this skill; more recently this has been somewhat neglected. We are probably most familiar with calligraphy through manuscripts of the Middle Ages, Islamic script, and the brushwork of Asia (principally China and Japan). In the case of China, calligraphy is considered a pure art.

The invention of printing and the use of movable type made inroads on calligraphy, but a revival occurred in the nineteenth century as a form of protest against industrialization. Most contemporary calligraphy is mistakenly called *lettering;* it may be done with brush or pen. Even lettering has been considerably aborted by the introduction of *press-type,* in which printed letters can be adhered to a sheet through rubbing.

Such Western calligraphy as exists today is generally less flamboyant than that of earlier years. The initial letters in the Book of Kells (Irish, A. D. 800) for example, while beautiful, are virtually illegible. Much modern lettering is associated with commercial applications and requires great legibility as well as impact. The florid style is largely passé.

Most calligraphy, whether with pen or brush, depends on carefully controlled pressures to produce swelling and tapering lines. Asian artists hold the brush upright in contrast to Westerners who hold the instrument at an angle. Earlier masters used black carbon, iron-gall, bistre, and sepia inks. The writing was done with quill, reed, and metal pens as well as brushes. There are specific metal points designed for calligraphy. Many of the pens in use today do not contain a permanent ink; it will fade badly if left exposed to the light. Furthermore, most household pens do not have points with the needed flexibility.

Lettering and calligraphic surfaces are very important, and not all of the paper available today is suitable. Generally the work is done on a smooth surface such as illustration board, although some artists prefer a slight "tooth" (texture). The ink will not penetrate some papers; in others it has an unfortunate tendency to spread. Historical surfaces included parchment, vellum, and wood paneling. Occasionally a ground was painted over the surface to prepare it for the work. If permanence is a factor, the work should be done on paper that has a pure rag content and that is of neutral pH (acidity). Most papers are made of wood pulp, which tends to discolor and deteriorate with the passage of time.

Ordinary handwriting, or *chirography,* is first taught in the elementary grades. Instruction usually begins with script, or manuscript, writing. By the time the student is in third or fourth grade, the writing becomes cursive with slanted and connected letters. Either kind can be done with distinction; if particularly skillful and beautiful, the latter could be called *calligraphic.*

supplies

1. Tilt drawing table. (Very helpful, but not essential)

2. Drawing board. (May substitute for above; about 16″ × 20″)

3. "T" square. (Adjustable crosspiece and raised plastic edges are helpful)

4. Paper. (There are many types; experiment. Illustration board usually works well)

5. Pencils. ("F" type)

6. Erasers. (For both ink and pencil; also a kneaded type)

7. Pen holders. (Whatever is comfortable)

8. Pen points. (Fine-pointed, hard and rigid, soft and flexible)

9. Brushes. (Sables are best; they should have fine points)

10. Tempera paint. (Black and white for retouching)

11. Compasses. (One for pencil and one for ink if possible)

12. Ink. (Permanent and waterproof)

The tools of calligraphy

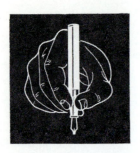

Pens specially designed to reproduce the italic style of handwriting:

Speedball lettering pens

Speedball steel brush

Mitchell round-hand no. 0

Mitchell italic

Osmiroid broad oblique

Pelikan graphos pen

Platignum broad italic

The Pens   These, of course, are the basic tools. There are many kinds and styles of flat pens available today, and each comes in a variety of sizes, or width of nib.

They fall into two categories. Each has its own characteristics as to weight, length, and degree of flexibility. It is essential that you find the style of pen which permits you the greatest ease in handling.

The first kind are the nonautomatic feed pens, the most popular of which are the Speedball C series, in seven sizes. They are expensive, easy to use, with much flexibility. They do, however, require frequent filling and, unless the automatic feed is used, can be troublesome since the ink flow is not controlled. Included here, too, are the steel brushes, which are flexible layers of metal, up to 3/4″ wide, allowing letters up to 6″ high. Other nonautomatic pens are shown, each with qualities of their own. It is advised that you obtain one of each make and find which suits you.

The automatic-feed fountain pens have the big advantage of controlling the ink flow, so important in any work requiring uniform strokes.

The Osmiroid pen is an automatic feeder and is useful to those preferring a short nib and an edge that is not as sharp as the Speedball nib.

The Pelikan Graphos has a longer and more flexible nib than either of the above, with a very thin and sharpened edge. It is easy to clean due to a swivel-edge top layer.

The Platignum is the most popular of the fountain pens for lettering calligraphy. It lies midway in length and weight, with a well-sharpened edge, in a variety of widths up to 1/8″, which allows for a letter 1″ high.

It will be necesssary for the serious student to experiment with all or most of these pens before finally settling on the pen and holder which are most comfortable in the hand.

There are water-base and permanent felt tip calligraphy pens available in both black and other colors.

Higgins
pen cleaner

From "Construction of the Basic Alphabet" (pp. 4–12), "The Tools of Calligraphy" (p. 112) in Hand Lettering Today *by Abraham Switkin. Copyright © 1976 by Abraham Switkin. Reprinted by permission of HarperCollins Publishers, Inc.*

It should not be necessary for relatively inexperienced artists to delve too deeply into letter styles. The basic styles are five in number: Roman, Italic, Gothic, Script, and Block. There are many possible variations on each of these and, as progress is made in the mastery of the basic styles, the artist can move on to more complicated styles. There has always been, and is today, a ready market for skilled lettering and calligraphy, but it is a skill not easily acquired. There are many books on the subjects, some of which can be found in the Art Resources appendix of this book.

The tools of informal script

Red sable rigger

Red sable pointed tip

Smaller red sable pointed tip

Fountain pen (for a smooth, firm line)

Calligraphy pen (with different-sized flat nibs)

Grease pencil (for texture)

Under the big top

thrilling adventures

children of all ages

Lions, tigers, and bears

The Circus

From Lettering Art in Modern Use *by Raymond A. Ballinger. Copyright © 1952 by Van Nostrand Reinhold Company. Reprinted by permission of the publisher.*

From The Art of Hand-Lettering *by Helm Wotzkow. © 1952 by Watson-Guptill Publications. Reproduced by arrangement with Watson-Guptill Publications, a division of BPI Communications, Inc.*

This is an example of Islamic calligraphy. It is the opening of the surat Maryam (Mary), from al-Qandusi's 12-volume Quran, which was completed in 1849. The poem in chikeste script (1893) was transcribed by Mahmud Khan (Iran). (From Khibati, A., Sivelmassi, M. The Splendour of Islamic Calligraphy. *New York: Rizzoli International Publications, 1976.)*

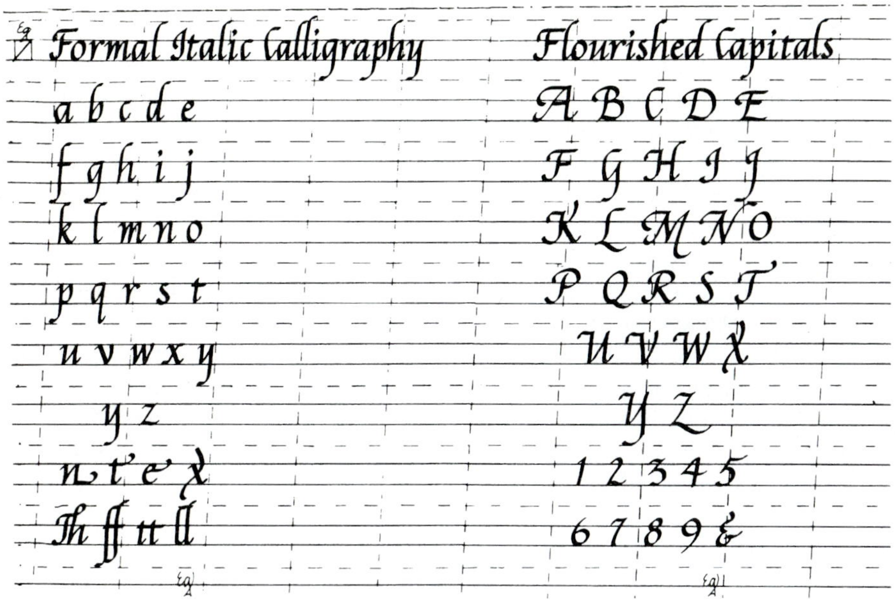

Formal Italic Calligraphy

a b c d e
f g h i j
k l m n o
p q r s t
u v w x y
y z
n t e x
Th ff tt ll

Flourished Capitals

A B C D E
F G H I J
K L M N O
P Q R S T
U V W X
Y Z
1 2 3 4 5
6 7 8 9 &

Calligraphy samples. Courtesy of Elmer Girten.

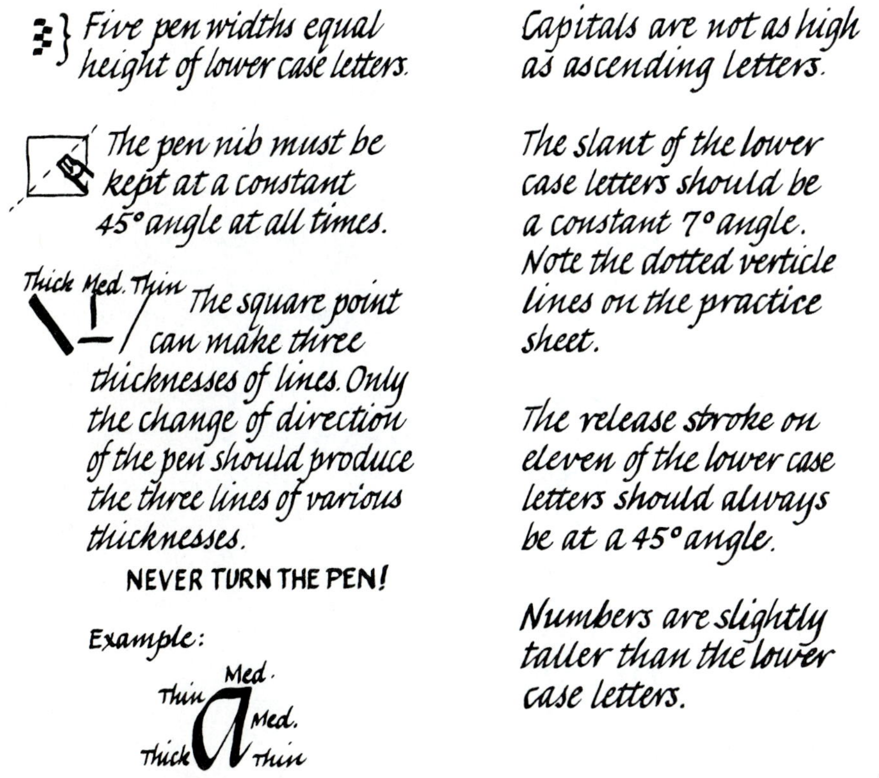

Five pen widths equal height of lower case letters.

The pen nib must be kept at a constant 45° angle at all times.

Thick Med. Thin The square point can make three thicknesses of lines. Only the change of direction of the pen should produce the three lines of various thicknesses.

NEVER TURN THE PEN!

Example:

Thin Med.
Thin Med.
Thick Thin

Capitals are not as high as ascending letters.

The slant of the lower case letters should be a constant 7° angle. Note the dotted verticle lines on the practice sheet.

The release stroke on eleven of the lower case letters should always be at a 45° angle.

Numbers are slightly taller than the lower case letters.

Courtesy of Elmer Girten.

1. Pencil and eraser
2. Tempera paint, acrylic paint watercolors, markers, or colored pencils. Metallic markers are great to use
3. Heavy paper or illustration board

Illumination

Illumination refers to drawing and painting independent illustrations in the margins and the embellishments of initial letters.

During the Middle Ages, monks produced most of the books by hand. Illuminated manuscripts are handwritten books produced on vellum and embellished with a combination of miniature pictures, ornamented letters, or designs often used with gold or silver leaf.

Different styles developed in different parts of Europe, including Anglo-Irish, Byzantine, English, French, and Irish styles.

Decorations included animals, branches with leaves or berries, geometric designs, ornamental letters, braids, and scroll work.

Illumination was one of the major art forms, especially in the early Middle Ages, and through this medium, important traditions of art from classical antiquity were transmitted.

procedure

1. Draw a frame around the edge of the paper.
2. Select one Gothic, Celtic, or Classical Roman letter and draw it carefully on the paper so that it touches as least two of the frame lines.
3. In the space around the letter, arrange plant life, animals, birds, people, and patterns.
4. Add color to the design.
5. Metallic acrylics, tempera, markers and colored pencils may be used to add color to the design.

clay

5

1. Local or commercial water-base clay

2. Two containers for mixing clay (galvanized or plastic buckets, crocks, earthenware crocks, etc. A tightly fitting lid is desirable)

3. Hammer or mallet

4. Cloth bag

5. Sieve or piece of window screen

6. Plastic bags or aluminum foil for storing clay

7. A plaster slab is ideal for absorbing excess moisture from the clay

Nature of the clay medium

Clay (simple dirt, to many!) is a material of organic and mineral composition. It exists in several forms and grades, some of practical application. Clay is malleable when wet, retains water, and holds together when dry. The earliest humans made clay pottery. Ancient hieroglyphics inscribed in clay still exist. Many brick and adobe building structures have been made of clay. White clay is used commercially as a coating for paper.

Making clay

Any local clay can be easily transformed into pliable clay for classroom use by the following method. This same method is used in reconditioning any unfired clay.

procedure

1. Break the moist clay into small pieces, and allow them to dry thoroughly.
2. Place the pieces of dry clay into the cloth bag and pound them with the hammer or mallet until they are almost a powder.
3. Fill the container half-full of water and pour the broken or powdered clay into it until the clay rises above the surface of the water. Moist clay will not disintegrate when placed in water, so be sure it is bone dry and broken into pieces. The smaller the pieces, the more quickly the dissolving process will take place. This process is called *slaking*.
4. Allow the clay to soak for at least an hour. This period will vary according to the size of the pieces.
5. Stir the clay thoroughly with a stick or the hands until all the lumps are dissolved. This clay mixture is called *slip*.
6. Pour the slip into the second container through the sieve to remove any foreign matter, and allow it to stand overnight. If there is any excess clear water, pour it off.
7. Remove any excess moisture by placing the clay on the plaster slab. Allow the water to be absorbed until the clay can be kneaded without sticking to the hands.
8. Store the clay in a container with a lid, or cover the container with a damp cloth. Small amounts of clay can be kept moist by using plastic bags or aluminum foil.

Suggestions on handling water clay

1. Pliable clay should be kneaded (wedged) to remove all air bubbles before working.
2. Clay objects should dry slowly to prevent cracking. Thinner forms will dry more quickly than thicker forms. The thin form may be wrapped with a damp cloth to equalize the drying.
3. Cover the clay objects with a damp cloth or paper towels and wrap in a plastic bag or place in a zip-lock plastic bag to slow the drying process or to keep the clay moist from day to day.
4. If a project needs to be kept for a later work period, it would be handy to have some kind of small plate to put under the clay while working with it. Such a plate can be made by covering corrugated cardboard with vinyl wallpaper and taping it securely on the bottom with a plastic tape. The plate along with the covered clay work can be placed into a zip lock bag and will keep very well until the next session.
5. Cut the clay with a wire; an opened paper clip works well.
6. Moist clay will not adhere to dry clay due to shrinkage.
7. Clay appendages, or details that are to be added to pots or figures, must be of the same consistency as the piece to which they are to be attached. The two areas that are to be joined should be scratched or scored with a sharp tool, and covered with a slip (liquid clay) or wet slightly before being placed together. Then, the joints should be fused into one piece with a smooth tool or the fingers.
8. Slip can be made by crushing dried clay and mixing it with water to a pudding consistency. When joing pieces of clay together, slip is applied with the fingertip after the surfaces of the pieces are scored or scratched. After the pieces are joined, it is also a good idea to smooth the two edges with the finger or tool to assure that the seam will hold.
9. Holes maybe made in flat pieces by pushing soda straws through the moist clay. Holes can be carved or pierced while the clay is leather-hard.
10. Dry clay objects (unfired clay is called *greenware*) must be fired to a temperature of at least 1500°F, or 830° C, to be hardened. An electric kiln is the best method for firing. However, the primitive open campfire method can be used.
11. Glaze can be applied to bisque (a piece of clay that has been fired once is called *bisque*) by dipping, spraying, or with a brush. The piece is then retired. All glaze must be wiped from the bottom or the foot of the piece with a sponge or cloth before firing.
12. A simple, low-fire glaze can be purchased commercially.
13. If no kiln is available, the greenware can be finished by waxing, painting with enamel, shellac, or varnish, or with tempera or acrylic paint. Varnish, shellac, or clear plastic spray, either matte or glossy, can be applied over tempera or acrylic paint for permanency.
14. Overhandling of the clay will cause it to dry rapidly, which in turn causes cracks or crumbling.

Clay decoration

Clay can be decorated by pulling or pushing it into a new shape. This can be done by using fingers or hands or by paddling with a piece of wood. Designs can also be carved into leather-hard clay with a sharp tool. Wire loops on a stick are also used to carve patterns.

Fingers were probably the first things used to make designs into the surface of a still wet vessel. Natural objects such as stones, pieces of bone, shells, and sticks were used to make interesting patterns. These things are still used and many more objects have been added to the list: utensils such as craft sticks, tongue depressors, pencils, forks, knives, nuts, and bolts and any other thing that can be pressed into or dragged across the clay to make a design. Stamps can be designed and made by filing, sawing, or drilling into small pieces of wood or the ends of dowels. A piece of moist clay can be made into a stamp by pulling and elongating one end to make a handle, flattening the opposite end and pressing simple tools into the flat end. After the stamp has dried and been fired, it can be used over and over to make patterns on a moist clay form.

A technique traditionally used by many Native Americans is called *slip decoration*. Liquid clay or slip (see the section, Making Clay) of a contrasting color is brushed on the moist clay form. It is allowed to dry and is fired. Sgraffito (meaning "scratching through") is another method that uses slip and was used with great success by the Greeks. The slip is painted on the leather-hard clay and when the slip and clay are almost dry, a sharp tool is used to scratch a pattern or design through the slip. The underlying color of the clay is allowed to show through the scratches. When the piece is completely dry, it is fired and usually it is sealed with a clear glaze. Engobes are slips with more color and with additives to help them adhere to the clay body.

connections

Indians of Central America

Native Americans

Greek Vases

Polychrome Vase, eighth-century Maya. The Mayan Indians of Central America created beautiful and sophisticated ceramics. Indiana University Art Museum, Raymond and Laura Wielgus Collection. Photograph by Michael Cavanagh and Kevin Montague.

An example of decorative ceramics. Lucy M. Lewis "Jar," 1956, earthenware, slipped and painted, 6" ×7 ¾". Photo courtesy of the U.S. Department of the Interior, Indian Arts and Crafts Board.

Clay modeling

procedure

Method a

1. Beginning with a basic shape of the object to be modeled, squeeze or push the clay to form the features (arms, legs, head, for example). Think of the object as a whole, rather than separate parts.
2. Between working sessions, wrap the clay piece with a moist cloth or paper towels and place in a plastic wrap or zip-lock bag to retain plasticity.
3. Allow the piece to dry slowly at room temperature.
4. Check for firing details.

Method b

Beginning with a basic shape of the object to be modeled, use a modeling tool to carve away all unnecessary parts until the piece is formed.

Method c

Beginning with a basic shape as in method a, additional parts may be added if correct methods are used. Both parts should be scored at the place of attachment, wet with one finger dipped in water and after they are pressed together, the edges are smoothed together with the the finger or a tool. (Scoring means to scratch the clay in two directions with a sharp tool such as a wire to make the surface of the clay look like a window screen. This technique must be used if separate pieces are to stay together.)

supplies

Local or commercial water-base or self-hardening clay. For small projects, Crayola Model Magic or Fimo could be used.

NOTE: Clay is especially good to use with special-needs students since it is nonthreatening.

Clay may be formed with fingers, hands, and tools (tongue depressors, wood blocks, modeling tools, etc.).

Clay modeling—clay castles

(Uses clay modeling Method C.) Show many pictures of castles, and discuss the different types of castles and the reasons for those differences.

Begin with a portion of clay for the base or ground under the castle. The base may be domed or hollowed out later when it is leather hard. The castle should be built from the center out. Every piece that is added must be scored and wet or slipped where the pieces meet each other and the base. Walls can be made by flattening pieces of clay with the heel of the hand. Towers can be made by rolling coils for round towers and taking short coils and flattening them by taping them on each of the four sides on the work surface. Stairs can be made with small coils and steps pushed in with a tool such as a small stick. Windows can be added by pushing the large end of craft stick into tower. Doors may be added. A moat needs to be shallow so that it will not make the base too thin. Add textures to walls, or towers, roofs, grass, or rocks. Add trees and bushes.

When dry, fire and if desired paint or treat with color.

Clay modeling — mythological creatures (dragons and gargoyles)

Holy Terrors: Gargoyles on Medieval Buildings by Janetta Rebold Benton, Abbeville Press, 1997 New York.

Book of Dragons by Michael Hague, William Morrow & Co., New York, 1995

Dragons: A Natural History by Karl Shuker, Simon & Shuster, New York, 1995

A Book of Dragons & Monsters Victoria and Albert Museum, Abbeville Press, Inc., New York, 1992

Zoo animals

Rain forest creatures

Lizards and frogs

Fish in the plants

Pre-Columbian figures

(Uses combined clay modeling Methods A and C.) Begin with a basic shape to form into a body and pinch out the main appendages of the creature. Add other parts such as horns, mouths, tongues, eyes, etc. Remember to score and wet or slip each piece and the main shape where it is added.

Dry slowly and fire. May be colored with paint.

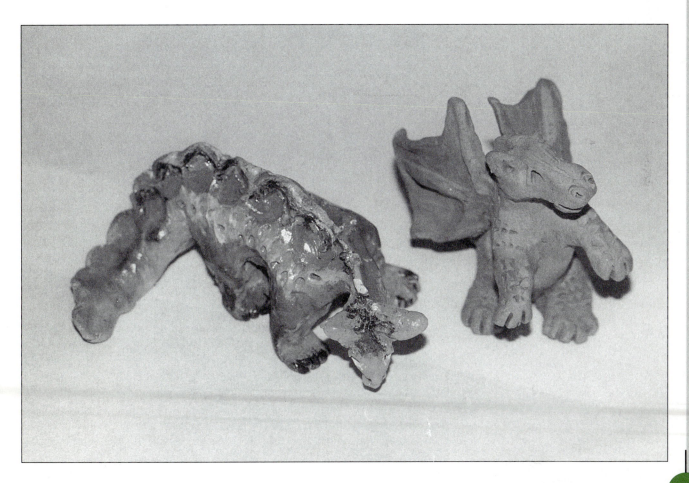

Local or commercial
water-base clay or
self-hardening clay

Pinch pot

procedure

1. Knead (wedge) the clay until it is of a workable consistency and the air bubbles have been removed.
2. Roll a ball of pliable clay between the palms of the hands to form a sphere approximately the size of a small orange.
3. Hold the sphere in the fingers of both hands. The thumb should be free to press the clay to form the pot. Keep the thumbs pointed up and form the pot upside down. (See Ill. 1, p. 86.)
4. Press the thumbs gently into the center of the sphere and at the same time press with the fingers on the outside while rotating the ball of clay.
5. Continue pressing with both the fingers and thumbs while rotating the clay until the ball is hollowed and the walls are of uniform thickness (approximately ½ inch). Cracks may appear if the clay is too dry or if it is pressed into shape too quickly or forcefully. Repair any such cracks immediately by gently rubbing the fingers over the clay until they disappear.
6. The finished pot, if built correctly, will not have any flat areas. To flatten the bottom of the pot, hold it gently between the fingers with both hands and tap it lightly on a tabletop.
7. Press the end of a key, hairpin, paper clip, etc., into the top edge of the pot, creating a single and interesting decoration.
8. Allow the pinch pot to dry slowly at room temperature.
9. See pages 96 and 97 for firing details.

VARIATION: Clay Animal Bells

Small clay bells with handles that are animals or animal heads, similar to those crafted by the Mexicans, can be made as a basic pinch pot with some additions. The pot needs to be higher rather than wider and with walls that are of even thickness. The top edge of the pot must be smooth and even. Another piece of clay is used to make the animal, bird, or fish shape for the handle. The bottoms of the handle and the pot should be scored, water or slip applied, and the two blended together. Two holes made with a straw should be put in the bottom of the pot on each side of the handle. Roll a small piece of clay and pierce a hole to make a bead for the clapper. Fire the bell and clapper. Tie an overhand knot in one end of a short piece of jute or string, put it through one of the holes of the bell, and string the bead. Pull the string through the other hole in the bell and tie another knot.

 Mexican clay animals
Mexican handbells

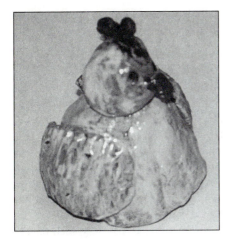 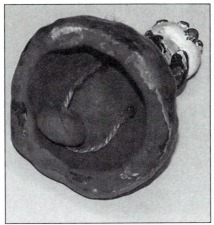

VARIATION: Connected Pinch Pots

Several pinch pots can be put together by simply scoring or scratching the pots where they are to be joined, applying slip or water to the joints, and smoothing the pots together. If a little space is needed between the pots, buttons of clay can be placed between the pots as long as all surfaces that touch are scored and wet to be blended together.

VARIATION: Bottle

Two pinch pots can be joined by scoring and putting slip or water on the top edges of both pots. They are then pressed firmly together and smoothed and sealed with a tool or a finger. It is sometimes helpful to put a coil of fresh clay at the seam to help blend the two pots into a hollow clay ball. With a wire (open paper clip), carefully cut a hole in the top of the ball. This edge should be textured or smoothed as desired if no neck is to be added. It is a good idea to smooth with a tool or finger the inside of the seam where the two parts are joined. A neck for the bottle can be made by rolling a slab of clay and cutting a narrow rectangle with the wire to make a cylinder that will fit the hole in the top of the pot. Remember to score and wet with water or slip the two ends of the rectangle and the edge of the cylinder and the hole. Seal the cylinder to the hole. A small coil of fresh clay at the point where the neck joins the pot is helpful in sealing the two parts.

 Miniature Cameroon
grain container

1. Local or commercial water-base clay
2. Modeling tool
3. Small container for mixing slip

Coil pot

procedure

Method a

A coil pot consists of coils built on a pinch pot base as done by the Native Americans.

1. Knead (wedge) the clay to a workable consistency.
2. Roll a ball of pliable clay between the palms of the hands to form a sphere approximately the size of a small orange.
3. Hold the sphere in the fingers of both hands. The thumb should be free to press the clay to form the pot. Keep thumbs pointed up and form the pot upside down.
4. Press the thumbs gently into the center of the sphere and at the same time press with the fingers on the outside while rotating the ball of clay (Ill. 1).
5. Continue pressing with both the fingers and the thumbs while rotating the clay until the ball is hollowed and the walls are of uniform thickness (approximately ½″). Cracks may appear if the clay is too dry or if pressed into shape too quickly or forcefully. Repair any such cracks immediately by gently rubbing the fingers over the clay until they disappear.
6. The pot, if built correctly, will not have any flat areas. To flatten the bottom of the pot, hold it gently between the fingers with both hands and tap it lightly on a tabletop.
7. Roll another piece of clay into round strips or coils of approximately ½ inch in diameter, making sure the strip makes a complete turn to ensure its roundness (Ill. 2).
8. Scratch the top edge of the pinch pot base (Ill. 3) and apply a thin coat of slip (liquid clay) over the scratches (Ill. 4). The slip helps the coil adhere to the pinch pot base.
9. Place the coil on the slip-covered edge of the base (Ill. 5). Cut both ends at the same angle so that they fit snugly (Ill. 6). Gently press the coil to the base and fuse the joint both on the outside and inside (Ill. 7).
10. Scratch the top edge of the first coil, apply slip (Ill. 8), and add the second coil (Ill. 9). Remember to fit the ends together tightly. Gently press the second coil to the first coil, and fuse them together.
11. Repeat procedure 10 until the coils create a completed form.
12. Allow the pot to dry slowly at room temperature.
13. Check pages 96 and 97 for firing details.

connections

Native American pots
African pots
Mexican pots

1

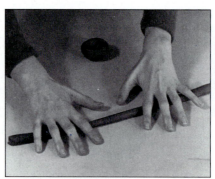

2

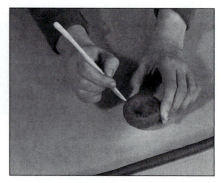

3

4

7

5

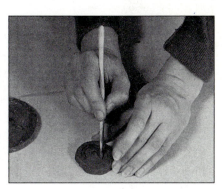

6

8

9

Method b

1. Knead (wedge) the clay to a workable consistency.
2. Roll the clay into round strips or coils of approximately ½ inch in diameter, making sure the strip makes a complete turn to ensure its roundness (Ill. 2).
3. Wind the strip into a tight coil to the desired size for the base. Fuse the coil together with a small tool or the fingers until all traces of the round strip disappear (Ill. 9). A ball of clay flattened on a damp cloth to approximately ½ inch thickness also makes a good base for a pot when cut to the desired diameter.
4. Scratch the outside top edge of the base, and apply a thin coat of slip (liquid clay) over the scratches. The slip helps the base adhere to the first coil.
5. Place another coil on the slip-covered edge of the base. Cut both ends at the same angle so they fit snugly. Gently press the coil to the base, and fuse the joint both on the outside and inside.
6. Scratch the top edge of the first coil, apply slip, and add the second coil. Remember to fit the ends together tightly. Gently press the second coil to the first coil, and fuse them together.
7. Repeat procedure six until the coils create a complete form.
8. Allow the pot to dry slowly at room temperature.
9. Check pages 96 and 97 for firing details.

connections

Native American pots
African pots
Mexican pots

Whether by the use of coils, pinching, or other manipulations, clay ceramic ware has been created for thousands of years. © James L. Shaffer.

VARIATION: Container Coil Pot

A coil pot can be made inside of a plastic bowl so that there is a stable form to hold the coils in place. Make a flat, round slab of clay to put in the bottom of the plastic container. The slab should be large enough to come a little way up the side walls of the container. Gently push the clay slab into the bottom of the bowl with the fingertips. Score and wet or apply slip to the top edge of the slab. Roll coils, score, and apply slip or wet and place them on top of the edge of the slab and each other. Patterned flat buttons can be made by pressing a small piece of clay with the palm of the hand and making designs on one side with any tool. Place the button with the pattern toward the plastic bowl and surround with coils and other buttons. Seal the inside of the coils and buttons together by blending them together with the finger or a tool. The clay pot will come out of the plastic bowl when it is partially dry because of the shrinkage of the clay.

VARIATION: Trivet

Coils can be woven together to make hot pads or trivets from the clay. Wherever the coil touches itself or another coil, it should be scored, slip should be applied on each surface, and then it should be blended together with a tool or finger. Spirals of clay can also be joined in the same manner.

Clay tiles

procedure

1. Knead (wedge) the clay to a workable consistency.
2. Spread the damp cloth on a smooth tabletop.
3. Place the two sticks on the damp cloth parallel to each other. The space between the sticks will be the width of the finished tile.
4. Roll a ball of clay and place it between the sticks (Ill. 1 on page 90).
5. Flatten the clay by running the rolling pin along the parallel sticks. The clay will be flattened to the thickness of the sticks (Ill. 2 on page 90).
6. Cut the slab of clay into tiles, and allow it to become almost dry, or leather-hard (Ill. 3 on page 90).
7. Plan a design on thin paper, the size of the clay tile.
8. When the clay is almost dry, place the paper design over the tile and transfer the design by retracing the lines with a sharp pencil or instrument.
9. The following three methods of decoration are possible:
   a. Incised—scratch the design into the leather-hard clay with a sharp tool.
   b. Relief—carve away the background areas and allow the design to stand out.
   c. Inlaid—carve out areas of the design and replace with clay of a different color, making sure both clays are of the same consistency.
10. See pages 96 and 97 for firing details.

VARIATION: Mirror Frames

Make a slab as described under the section, Clay Tiles. Cut a rectangle or a square from the middle of the slab. Decorate, dry, and fire the frame.

VARIATION: Coasters

Make a round pattern as large as the top of a glass. Using the pattern, draw and carefully cut out the shapes with a wire. Decorate the disk and gently bend up the edges of the circle. Dry and fire the coaster.

VARIATION: Cylinder Seal

The cylinder seal was invented by the Sumerian people around 5,000 years ago in the southern Mesopotamian region. With the growth of commerce and trade in this advancing civilization, Sumerians developed the cylinder seal as a way for business people to sign their names to validate business agreements. Individuals created their own unique seals by carving pictures or designs into the surface of a clay or stone cylinder. When the cylinder was rolled across a wet clay surface, these carvings left behind a personalized imprint which served to seal business deals.

To make a cylinder seal, a cardboard can, such as that used for frozen juice, makes a good form to cast plaster. Follow the directions on mixing plaster (p. 125). After the plaster has been cast in the cylinder form, peel the cardboard can away from the plaster and allow it to dry. Make a design the same size as the cylinder by rolling it on a piece of newsprint to get the necessary dimensions. Follow the directions for carving under Carved Plaster Bas-Relief in Chapter 14, Sculpture. When the carving of the design is completed, roll the cylinder using firm and even pressure over a slab of moist clay. The cylinder seal can also be used in activities involving clay slabs.

supplies

1. Local or commercial water-base clay
2. Rolling pin
3. Two sticks ½" thick
4. Damp cloth
5. Knife, scissors, or wood stick (recommended)
6. Thin paper
7. Sharp pencil

connections

Spanish tile
Persian ceramic glazed tile

connections

Cylinder seal

Slab pot

A slab pot is built with flat pieces of clay that are joined together to form a container.

procedure

1. Knead (wedge) the clay to a workable consistency.
2. Spread the damp cloth on a smooth tabletop.
3. Place the two sticks on the damp cloth, parallel to each other. The space between the sticks will be the width of the finished tile.
4. Roll a ball of clay, and place it between the sticks (Ill. 1).
5. Flatten the clay by running the rolling pin along the parallel sticks (Ill. 2). The clay will be flattened to the thickness of the sticks.
6. Place the cardboard pattern over the flattened clay. Using it as a guide, cut around the pattern with a knife (Ill. 3).
7. Using the same cardboard pattern, cut three more slabs and allow them to stiffen to a leather-hard condition.
8. To assemble a pot, score the edge of each slab with a knife (Ill. 4).
9. Put slip on scored edge (Ill. 5), and place two pieces together.
10. Prepare a small roll of clay, and press into the joint of each corner (Ill. 6). Continue this procedure until all four sides are together and smoothed inside and out.
11. Score the edges of a fifth piece, which will be the bottom.
12. Press the four sides on the bottom and complete (Ill. 7).

1. Local or commercial water-base clay
2. Rolling pin
3. Two sticks, approximately ½" thick and 12–20" long
4. Damp cloth
5. Knife, scissors, or wood stick (recommended)
6. Water container for mixing slip
7. Cardboard pattern

NOTE: A cylindrical slab pot is made from one slab (Ill. 8) placed on a round base (Ill. 9). Decorations can be done with a syringe filled with slip of a different color. Squeeze syringe, and trail design. Stamp any design in leather-hard clay.

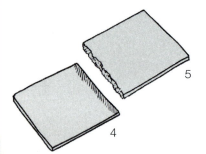

1

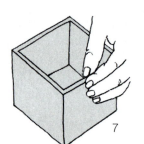

2

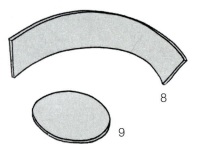

3

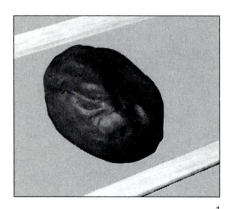

4

5

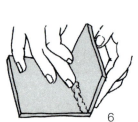

6

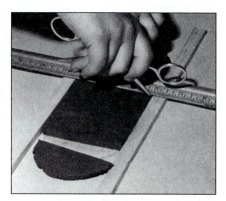

7

8

9

Pocket pot

procedure

1. Knead or wedge clay.
2. Roll out the clay to form a slab, using the rolling pin.
3. Cut one large piece from the slab, using an open paper clip. This is the back of the pot.
4. Cut a second piece from the slab, one-half the size of the first piece. Paper patterns may be used to facilitate this step.
5. Using a soda straw, make a hole close to the top center on the larger slabbed piece. Press and carve designs into the top half of this same piece of clay.
6. Press or carve patterns in the smaller slabbed piece.
7. Wad a tight piece of newspaper or toweling and place it on top of the bottom portion of the larger slab. Score or scratch the bottom face edge of this larger piece of clay.
8. Score or scratch the inside (or underside) edge of the smaller piece of clay.
9. Moisten the fingertips with water or slip and apply to the scratched edges. Now put them together. Seal by pressing both slabs together at the edges.
10. The newspaper wad keeps the shape open while the pot air dries. When the pot is completely dry, remove the paper and fire in a kiln.

1. Local or commercial water-base clay
2. Rolling pin
3. Cloth
4. Paper clip
5. Soda straw
6. Two flat sticks, ½″ thick
7. Pressing tools—spools, forks, nails, screws, etc.
8. Water container
9. Newspaper or paper toweling

Wind chimes

supplies

1. Location of commercial water-base clay or self-hardening clay

2. Rolling pin

3. Cloth

4. Paper clip

5. Two flat sticks ½" thick

6. Pressing tools—spools, forks, nails, screws, etc.

7. Soda straw

8. Fishing line

connections

Japanese wind chimes
Mobile—Alexander Calder

procedure

1. Knead or wedge clay.
2. Slab clay. (See Clay Tiles, p. 89.)
3. Cut largest piece, the top of the wind chimes, from the clay slab by using an open paper clip. Any shape may be cut, but be careful of thin projections—they tend to break while drying.
4. The top shape will need one hole for each chime near the lower edge. It will need at least one hole near the upper edge. These holes are made by pushing and turning a large soda straw into the clay. Make sure the holes are far enough away from the edge of the shape so that they will not break. Press and carve designs on both sides of the hanger by using pressing tools.
5. Cut the chimes from the rest of the slab. Put a hole at the top of each. Put patterns on both sides of each chime. Remember different shapes are more interesting.
6. Allow the pieces to dry at room temperature—fire when completely dry.
7. String chimes to hanger by using cords and tying overhand knots.

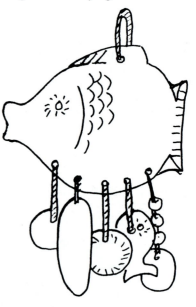

Slab clay mask

procedure

1. Make an armature or support for the mask by using newspaper and masking tape. Push it tight and mold it with the hands. An empty soft drink bottle could also be used as a support for the clay mask.
2. Roll out the wedged clay by placing the flat sticks on each side of the clay and rolling over the clay and the sticks with the rolling pin.
3. Place the clay slab on the armature and trim excess from the edge of the mask shape.
4. The base piece may be pierced to make designs, depressions can be pressed into the surface and the scrap clay may also be used to form the features on the face of the mask. Experiment with the shaped scraps before joining them to the base. When ready, join the pieces to the main part of mask by scoring and wetting or applying slip to both surfaces.
5. Many different types of patterns and textures may be added, depending on the type of mask being studied.
6. With plastic partially covering the mask, allow it to dry slowly.
7. Fire. If desired, add color and attach any other materials.

supplies

1. Local or commercial water-base clay (self-hardening clay may be used)
2. Cloth
3. Rolling pin
4. Two flat sticks, ½″ thick
5. Tools for pressing or carving into the clay
6. Paper clip
7. Newspaper and masking tape, or a large empty plastic soft drink bottle

connections

African mask
Native American mask
Japanese theater mask
Mexican mask

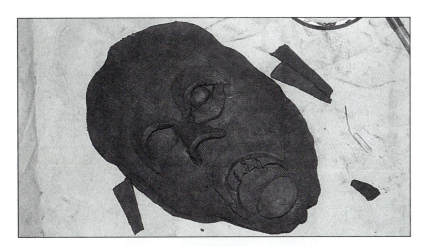

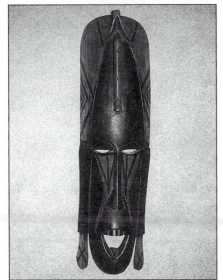

Bells and beads

1. Local or commercial water-base clay (self-hardening clay may be used)

2. Cloth

3. Rolling pin

4. Two flat sticks, ½″ thick

5. Soda straw

6. Tools for pressing or carving into the clay

7. Empty cardboard cone from inside yarn

8. Paper clip

9. Cord or jute to string bells

Japanese bells

connections

procedure

1. Knead or wedge clay.
2. Roll out the clay to form a slab, using the rolling pin.
3. Wrap the slab around a cone by laying the cone on the center of the clay, bringing the sides around the cone. Trim away the excess clay with an open paper clip so that the edges overlap. Seal the edges together by pressing with fingers.
4. While the clay is wrapped around the cone, trim the bottom and the top, remembering to keep a small hole in the top of the clay cone. Apply designs and patterns by pressing and carving with any tools (nails, scissors, spools, spoons, forks) available.
5. When finished with patterns, gently remove clay cone from cardboard cone with a twisting motion. Allow to air dry.
6. With the scraps of the slab left, or a new slab, make the clapper for the bell by cutting out a shape with an open paper clip. Make sure the shape will fit inside of the cone. Apply designs or patterns to both sides of clapper and put a hole near the top by using a soda straw.
7. Make at least two beads (more are nice) by rolling clay into bead-size balls or other shapes and inserting a soda straw through the shape. Make patterns on the beads and gently remove the straw.
8. Allow all pieces to dry slowly. Fire in a kiln.
9. String bells by putting one end of cord or jute (about 36 to 40″) through the hole in the clapper. Bring the ends of the cord together with clapper in the center. Make an overhand knot approximately 2″ above clapper.
10. Push both cords through the hole in first bead with a twisting motion. Make an overhand knot just above the bead. String cord ends through the top of the cone from the inside.
11. Make an overhand knot in cords, and string a second bead. Make an overhand knot (if additional beads are to be added, always put an overhand knot between the beads). Finish with a final overhand knot at the loose ends of cords.

VARIATION: Make a pattern from newsprint for the long rectangle for the bell. Bring the two small ends together to make a cylinder. If the rectangle is too long cut to the desired size. Place the pattern on the clay slab and cut with a wire. While the slab is still flat, put patterns and designs on the clay slab. When completed with design, use the inside cardboard roll from paper or roll newspaper to use as an armature. Roll the clay around the armature and seal the two ends of the rectangle together after scoring and wetting or slipping. It may be necessary to put a thin coil of clay on the inside behind the seal and smooth it in place to make sure the seam is sealed. Push the four sides of the top of the cylinder together, but do not seal until there has been scoring on the surfaces that will touch and water or slip applied. Pinch the excess clay together leaving a small hole in the center of the top. Finish with beads, clapper, and cord.

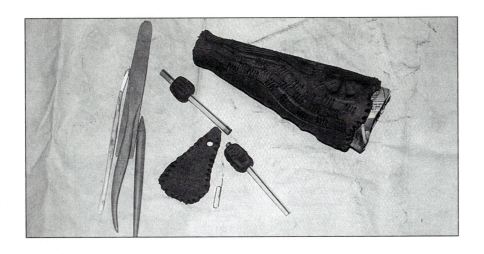

Special Effects

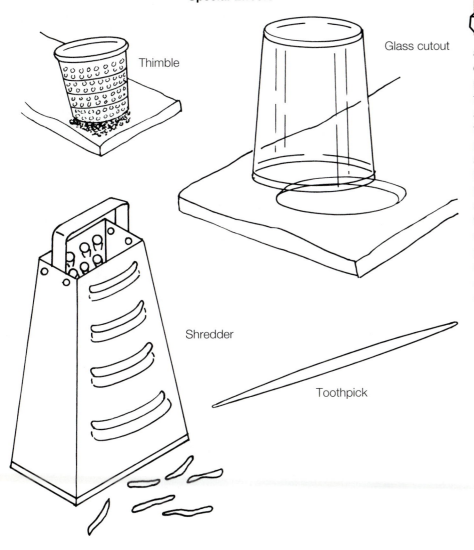

Thimble

Glass cutout

Shredder

Toothpick

NOTE: The clay can be manipulated in various ways with common objects or instruments to achieve special effects. Textured objects such as a thimble can be pressed into the clay to produce a textured surface. Glasses, bowls, and the like can be forced through the clay for cut-out shapes. Large pieces of clay can be drawn across a shredder to produce clay slivers to be used in building up or decorating pieces. Toothpicks, nut picks, sticks, and other similar items can be used to manipulate or texture the clay. Glazes can be applied to the clay to provide a watertight glossy or matte coating. They are available in many colors. See the section, Kilns, in this chapter.

supplies

1. Vented kiln

2. Kiln shelves

3. Shelf supports

4. Kiln furniture (stilts, triangles)

5. Pyrometric cones

6. Kiln wash (Glaze drippings are easily removed from shelves coated with kiln wash)

7. Kiln cement (for repairing cracks and chips in kiln wall)

NOTE: Children should not be near any active kiln.

Kilns

Clay pieces that have just been completed are called *greenware* and should dry naturally before being fired in a kiln. Artificial heat is likely to cause the piece to crack. All decorations must be completed on the product before the piece is completely dry.

When the clay is completely dry (bone dry), it is ready to be placed in the kiln for firing. Firing will not only vitrify, or fuse, the clay but will burn out any impurities.

There are numerous kilns of all sizes, shapes, and prices, which are fueled with gas, oil, coal, or electricity. Most electric kilns use 220-volt current.

The inside firing chambers of table model kilns have a large range and usually a maximum of 2300° F, which is more than adequate. Several inside firing chamber sizes of electric table model kilns are: (Ill. 1) 14⅜ inch opening, 13½ inches deep, 1.37 cubic feet; (Ill. 2) 17.5 inch opening, 18 inches deep, 2.63 cubic feet; and (Ill. 3) 23⅜ inch opening, 27 inches deep, 7 cubic feet.

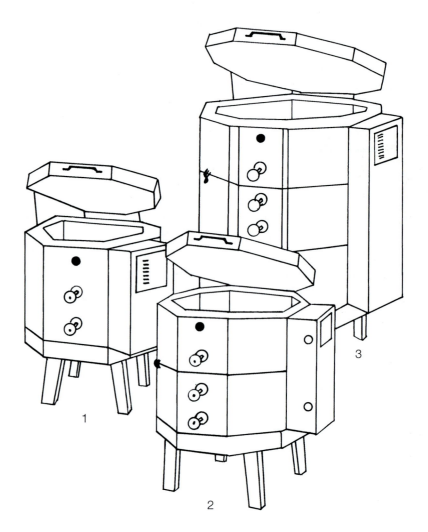

Most kilns will have a switch control for low, medium, and high temperatures. Some will come equipped with a pyrometer, an indicator for reading the kiln temperature. These are ideal, but much cheaper and equally accurate are pyrometric cones (Ill. 4), which are used to indicate fusion.

Three or four of these cones with different fusing points are placed at a slight angle to one of their faces (not on their edge) in a piece of pliable clay (Ill. 4). The clay is allowed to dry, then placed in the kiln so the cones can be seen through the spy hole in the kiln door. A piece of fire brick may be necessary to lift the cones high enough to be seen.

The kiln will heat slowly and a periodic check of the cones through the spy hole will let you know the approximate temperature of the heat as the cones begin to melt. When the last cone (Ill. 5) is beginning to melt, the kiln can be turned off, as the desired temperature has been attained.

Many kilns now come with timers so that the number of hours the kiln is to fire can be programmed at the beginning. A kiln sitter can be attached, which employs small junior cones to serve the same function as the larger cone, melting at the proper temperature and shutting off the kiln at that point. Newer kilns can be electronically controlled with digital firing. This eliminates the need for any cones and allows for more precise control and less time spent monitoring firing. Kilns are now better insulated often with 3″ of firebrick.

A piece fired only once is called *bisque,* or biscuitware, and it can be glazed and fired again. A glaze will give the pieces a glasslike finish. Glazes can be purchased from a commercial company that will give instructions for use and the temperature cone at which the glaze matures. (Avoid any glazes not certified by the manufacturer as being free of lead and nontoxic.) The glaze is applied by spraying, brushing, or dipping. Dipping a piece in and out of a bowl of glaze may be the most practical method. Fingermarks are removed by daubing glaze on the spots with a brush.

4

5

CAUTION: It is extremely important that there is good ventilation for a kiln. Several good systems are on the market.

Cone temperature chart

Pyrometric cones

	Fahrenheit	Centigrade		Fahrenheit	Centigrade
Cone 018	1328	720	Cone 05	1904	1040
Cone 016	1463	795	Cone 04	1940	1060
Cone 015	1481	805	Cone 03	2039	1115
Cone 014	1526	830	Cone 02	2057	1125
Cone 013	1580	860	Cone 01	2093	1145
Cone 012	1607	875	Cone 1	2120	1160
Cone 011	1643	894	Cone 2	2129	1165
Cone 010	1661	905	Cone 3	2138	1170
Cone 09	1706	930	Cone 4	2174	1190
Cone 08	1742	949	Cone 5	2201	1205
Cone 07	1814	990	Cone 6	2246	1230
Cone 06	1859	1015			

Temperature equivalents figured at firing rate of 300° F or 149° C per hour.

Nonfiring clay

There are a number of other clay mediums on the market that do not require firing in a kiln. Some of these products will set if they are air dried. Others need to be placed in a low temperature oven or toaster oven for a specific length of time. Read and follow directions carefully. All of these products are nontoxic, but proper safety precautions should always be followed. Don't eat the clay; don't use tools for clay and then food; don't eat while working, and don't overbake clay.

Mexican Pottery Clay, nontoxic and self-hardening, will dry hard and durable without kiln or oven firing. Resembles Indian pottery when dry. Can be decorated with tempera, enamels, lacquers, or Rub 'n Buff®. Finish with shellac or varnish.

Marblex, self-hardening gray clay, comes in ready-to-use moist form. Objects dry hard and permanent without firing, but will not hold water. May be painted with showcard paint, enamels, lacquers, and so on. Finish with shellac or varnish.

Crayola® WetSet Clay is a soft, pliable clay which is indefinitely workable with no special care or covering. It is recommended for grades 4 and above. An assortment of armatures may be used. Won't shrink or crumble. When you decide to set it, immerse the piece in cool water for three or more hours. Once hardened, piece may be painted with a variety of paints or decorated with assorted materials.

Crayola® Model Magic Modeling Compound is recommended for primary through intermediate grades. The compound is soft, clean, pliable, and light-weight and dries to a firm consistency. Dried pieces can be carved, sanded, or painted with acrylic, tempera, watercolor, glossy enamels, or markers. Decorative materials can be inserted into the pieces before drying or can be glued on after the piece is dry. Permanently dries in 24 hours without firing or baking. Doesn't flake or crumble, with little clean-up. Available in 4 oz. packages or 2 lb. tubs.

Polymer clays need to be baked in an oven or toaster oven. Work on a piece of paper or cardboard to keep the work surface clean. Wash hands before and after working with the clay. Use the heat of the hands to soften the clay. Save all the little scraps in resealable bags, but be sure the different colors are wrapped separately. Never try to harden the pieces in a microwave and never heat above the recommended temperature or overbake. Heating polymer clays above 375° F will cause decomposition and the release of toxic fumes. *Do not inhale fumes.*

Friendly Clay™ is good for miniatures and wearable art ornaments. Soften in the hand, shape it, add color, or blend with other colors. The finished piece is placed in a preheated oven or a toaster oven for at least *30 minutes at 265° F.* After cooling, add accessories.

Fimo® is another polymer clay which hardens in the oven. It has brilliant color, is fade-proof, and is odorless. Fimo or soft-kneaded Fimo (a softer version) can be used again and again if it is well-packed in plastic and stored at room temperature. Any desired shade can be achieved by kneading together basic colors. White Fimo will lighten the tone of other colors, and transparent Fimo can be added to give the tone a translucent quality. Larger pieces or pieces with projecting pieces should be supported with an armature. Fimo Soft takes a shorter time to condition and is easier for children to model. Fimo may be added to and baked again. It can be carved, sawed, filed, cut, and painted. It is watertight and washable.

Sculpey bakes permanently hard in a home oven and is nontoxic, nondrying, and always pliable. Can be painted, carved, and sanded. Sets at 275° F in an oven.

The polymer clays seem to work best with smaller things such as jewelry, scarabs, beads, and miniatures.

Cat by Juliet Clutton-Brock, Alfred A. Knopf, New York, 1990 (Eyewitness Series).

Dog by Juliet Clutton-Brock, Alfred A. Knopf, New York, 1991 (Eyewitness Series).

Reptile by Colin McCarthy, Alfred A. Knopf, New York, 1991 (Eyewitness Series).

Amphibian by Dr. Barry Clarke, Alfred A. Knopf, New York, 1993 (Eyewitness Series).

Insects by Laurence Mound, Alfred A. Knopf, New York, 1990 (Eyewitness Series).

Japanese netsukes

Mexican clay animals

Beads

Egyptian scarab

chalk

6

Nature of the medium

Chalk and pastel

Chalk was a common graphic medium at the end of the fifteenth century. The original chalks for drawing, some still used today, were pure earth, cut and shaped into tools. Chalks used by the early masters were limited to reds (sanguine), black, and white. The addition of a binder, such as gum solution, created a fabricated chalk that we know as pastel. The colors have greatly increased in number. One of the first artists to work totally in pastel was Rosalba Carriera. Extremely successful, she was in great demand for her portraits. She also influenced many of the artists of her day and those that followed. Maurice Quentin de La Tour pushed pastels to its technical limits in the eighteenth century. It was one of the ideal mediums of the impressionists with its luminosity of color and spontaneity of application.

Some artists apply pastels in separate strokes, letting the color blending take place in the viewer's eye. Others are not reluctant to blend colors, and do so successfully, although there is a danger of the colors being muddied.

Chalk or pastel drawing is best done on a paper with *tooth,* or a slightly coarse, abrasive surface. This texture helps the paper trap and hold the chalk particles. Many papers have this character, including watercolor paper, manila, and construction paper.

Chalk or pastel can be drawn on a surface with light, delicate lines or with bold blocks of color, depending on how the pastel or chalk is held and how much pressure is used.

Pastels now come in a number of forms; the softer pastel, usually round, the medium pastel, square in shape, and the harder pastel, also square. Pastel pencils are also available.

Chalks and pastels are brittle and easily broken. They are impermanent and smear easily. They can become dirty, and it is helpful to wipe them with tissue and store them in rice. They can also be cleaned by putting them in a jar of rice and shaking them.

Blending tools include the tortillon, a tight twist of paper that comes in various sizes. As they get dirty on the end, the end can be peeled away to create a clean point. Cotton swabs or cotton balls can also be used to blend. Many artists prefer to use fingers as a blending tool since none of the color is lost. Kneaded erasers are handy since they can be shaped to a point to remove tiny areas of color. Fresh bread that is kneaded into a ball is ideal for erasing soft pastel. Soft, short watercolor brushes are good to help retrieve the tooth of the paper surface when it becomes filled with pastel. Wet Wipes are very good to keep hands clean between colors and to wipe down pastels to keep down dust.

The chalks used on paper are **not** designed for use on chalk boards—they are nearly indelible.

At some point in time, it will be necessary to protect the pastel or chalk with a fixative. When the work is finished, it will need to be fixed; sometimes during the building up of colors, it is also necessary to fix the work so that each layer will not become muddied by the next layer. There are many plastic fixatives on the market, although inexpensive hair spray may also be used.

CAUTION: It is imperative that proper safety precautions be taken. Pin the work to a vertical surface. Spray outdoors in a well-ventilated but wind-free area. With a sweeping motion, spray from the top to the bottom of the work. It may be necessary for the instructor to do the fixative.

connections

Artists:

Eugene Delacroix, early nineteenth century

Claude Monet

Camille Pisarro

Berthe Marisot

Edgar Degas

Mary Cassatt

Pierre-Auguste Renoir

Henri de Toulouse-Lautrec

James Whistler

Odilon Redon

Drawing with chalk or pastel

1. Chalk and pastels
2. Dark-colored paper
3. Fixative or hair spray
4. Tissues to keep chalk or pastels clean
5. Wet Wipes are handy for cleaning hands

procedure

1. *White chalk on darker paper* Add color chalk or pastel. Keep the colors light so that the student can see the good contrast between the media and the background.

2. *Chalk or pastel on gray paper* Begin the composition with white chalk. A middle-tone paper allows for good contrasts in both light and dark chalk or pastels. The contrast is developed more effectively if some of the paper is allowed to show through.

3. *Chalk or pastel on colored paper* Begin the drawing with white chalk. Subtle and bold contrasts may be achieved, depending on the colors chosen.

Charcoal with pastel

procedure

1. Draw main shapes of composition with the charcoal. Add simple lines just to indicate background of composition.
2. Begin to block in some color by using the flat of the pastel.
3. Add colors in loose broad strokes. Add whites for highlights. Blend with finger.
4. Use charcoal to add more form. Spray with fixative to hold media in place.
5. Add more charcoal into darker parts of the composition.
6. Continue to build up colors.
7. Use fixative.

CAUTION: It is imperative that proper safety precautions be taken. Pin the work to a vertical surface. Spray outdoors in a well-ventilated but wind-free area. With a sweeping motions, spray from the top to the bottom of the work. It may be necessary for the instructor to do the fixative.

supplies

supplies

1. Charcoal, can be in pencil form. Willow charcoal. Compressed charcoal is harder to alter once it's on the page

2. Soft pastels

3. Fixative

4. Blending tools

5. Wet Wipes

Chalk or pastel textures

supplies

1. Chalk or pastel
2. Thin drawing paper
3. Pencil or crayon
4. Textured surfaces
5. Mounting paper
6. Glue stick
7. Scissors

procedure

1. Hold a thin paper against a surface that has a definite texture and rub the chalk over the paper. The texture will be transferred to the paper by the chalk.
2. Place the paper against another texture and transfer it to another portion of the paper.
3. Textures may be overlapped.
4. The textures may be fixed and cut in shapes to be used as a collé by mounting them on another sheet of paper.

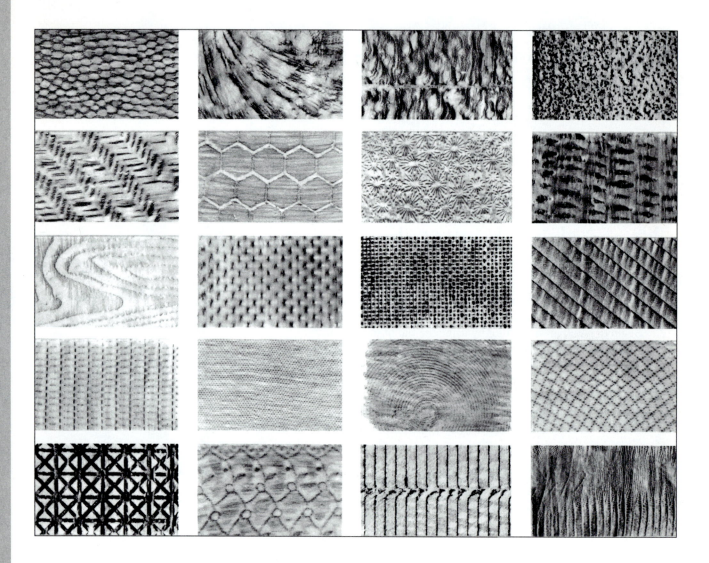

Wet paper chalk or pastel drawing

procedure

Draw over damp paper with the chalk or pastel. This will make the colors brighter and more exciting than those applied to dry paper. It is possible to use wet and dry techniques on one drawing by painting plain water over some areas prior to drawing. The paper should be of fairly heavy stock so that it will not wrinkle and curl.

Water can also be sprayed on top of chalk or pastel paintings that have been done on watercolor paper, and can be worked with a watercolor brush to move color around on the paper.

 NOTE: Soaking the chalk sticks for 10 minutes in a strong solution of sugar water before use reduces the tendency to smear.

 CAUTION: It is imperative that proper safety precautions be taken. Pin the work to a vertical surface. Spray outdoors in a well-ventilated but wind-free area. With a sweeping motion, spray from the top to the bottom of the work. It may be necessary for the instructor to do the fixative.

supplies

supplies

supplies

1. Paper
2. Chalk or pastel
3. Sugar
4. Water container
5. Water

Chalk or pastel painting

procedure

1. Mix 6 or 8 tablespoons of sugar into a small amount of water until dissolved into a thin solution.
2. Soak the chalk sticks in the sugar water solution for 10 to 15 minutes.
3. Use soaked chalk stick as a paint brush.
4. When chalk strokes become hard and dry, the chalk will not rub off.

 CAUTION: It is imperative that proper safety precautions be taken. Pin the work to a vertical surface. Spray outdoors in a well-ventilated but wind-free area. With a sweeping motion, spray from the top to the bottom of the work. It may be necessary for the instructor to do the fixative.

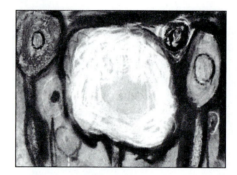 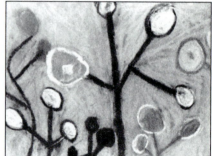

Chalk/Pastel and tempera print

procedure

1. Make a light pencil outline drawing on paper.
2. Mix tempera or latex paint to the consistency of cream.
3. Dip end of desired colored chalk into chosen color of paint.
4. Apply paint with chalk stick in brushlike strokes.
5. Continue until picture is completed.
6. Detail can be added with plain chalk.

supplies

1. Chalk or pastel
2. Tempera or latex paint
3. Paper
4. Clear spray

 CAUTION: It is imperative that proper safety precautions be taken. Pin the work to a vertical surface. Spray outdoors in a well-ventilated but wind-free area. With a sweeping motion, spray from the top to the bottom of the work. It may be necessary for the instructor to do the fixative.

Chalk/Pastel and tempera paint

supplies

1. Chalk or pastel
2. Tempera paint
3. Paper
4. Large brush

procedure

1. Complete a design or drawing with colored chalk on a piece of good quality paper. Be sure to use the chalk heavily.
2. Coat another piece of paper of the same size with white tempera paint. Use a large brush and paint in both directions to smooth the paint over one entire side.
3. While the tempera is still wet, place the chalk drawing face down in the tempera paint.
4. Rub firmly over the paper with fingers and/or the hand.
5. Separate the two papers before they are dry.
6. Two prints will result—the chalk will have merged with the print on both prints (Ills. 1, 2).
7. Experiments with different colors will produce numerous effects.

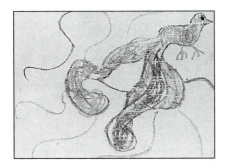

1

2

supplies

1. Liquid starch
2. Powder tempera
3. Brush
4. A scratching instrument, such as a stick or a spoon
5. Chalk or pastel
6. Two sheets of paper

Chalk/Pastel, tempera, and starch print

procedure

1. Mix the liquid starch and tempera paint to produce a dripless paint (Ill. 1).
2. Brush the mixture on a sheet of paper (Ill. 2).
3. Scratch a design in the wet paint (Ill. 3).
4. Coat another sheet of paper with colored chalk (Ill. 4).
5. Place the second sheet, chalk side down, over the wet paint surface (Ill. 5).
6. Lightly rub the back of the top sheet (Ill. 5).
7. Pull off the top sheet (Ill. 6).

crafts

7

supplies

1. Cardboard
2. Construction paper
3. White glue
4. Assortment of seeds or natural objects
5. Food coloring
6. Pencil
7. String or yarn
8. Clear spray or a brush-on finish

 NOTE: Additional details may be added to the picture with heavy yarn, string, or other decorative materials (for whiskers, stems, and so forth).

Relief mosaic from seeds or beads

procedure

1. Sketch the design on construction paper, carefully defining the areas where seeds are to be placed.
2. Using glue, mount the construction paper on cardboard, the same size as the construction paper.
3. Spread the glue on one area of the design at a time, and press the seeds, beads, or natural objects into place, filling the area. (For a neater appearance in the design, it is best to outline each area, then proceed to fill the rest of the area.)
4. When placing small pieces, it is helpful to put a dab of glue on the end of a toothpick to pick up and place each seed.
5. When the glue is completely dry and excess pieces have been shaken off, spray the design with three thin coats of clear spray. Clear brush-on finish may be a better choice.

CAUTION: It is imperative that proper safety precautions be taken. Pin the work to a vertical surface. Spray outdoors in a well-ventilated but wind-free area. With a sweeping motion, spray from the top to the bottom of the work. It may be necessary for the instructor to spray the structure.

Stick construction

procedure

Method a

1. First, cut the wooden pieces for the back and front of the structure. (The hole for a wren house should be 1 inch in diameter.)
2. Sticks are then glued to the edges of the front and back pieces to enclose the shape.

Method b

1. Various bowls or other constructions can be created by laying sticks on top of one another, much like laying bricks. Place a drop of glue where sticks cross one another.
2. Continue the process until bowl is built to desired height.

 CAUTION: It is imperative that proper safety precautions be taken. Pin the work to a vertical structure. Spray outdoors in a well-ventilated but wind-free area. With a sweeping motion, spray from top to bottom of the work. It may be necessary for the instructor to spray the structure.

supplies

1. Popsicle sticks or tongue depressors
2. Fine sandpaper
3. Glue
4. Enamel spray paint or fast-drying clear finish
5. Wooden pieces for back and front of structure

 NOTE: Various combinations of sticks may be used to create figures, creatures, or objects. **A brush-on finish may be a better option.**

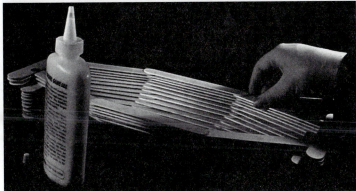

String picture

procedure

1. Make a light pencil drawing on a sheet of paper. Use colored paper if white string is to be used.
2. Trail the glue over the pencil lines and place the string or yarn on the glue. A popsicle stick is helpful to press the string or yarn down.

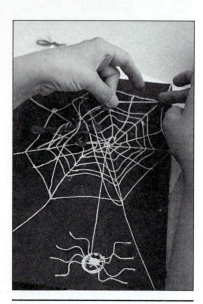

Study of line

Sealed nature pattern

procedure

1. Cut two sheets of waxed paper that are of equal size.
2. Lay one sheet flat and arrange the plant life on it to create the desired pattern.
3. Place the other waxed sheet over the first, covering the plant life.
4. Iron over the second sheet with a *warm* iron. This will seal the waxed sheets together, preserving the plant life.
5. If used with very young students, teacher should handle the iron.

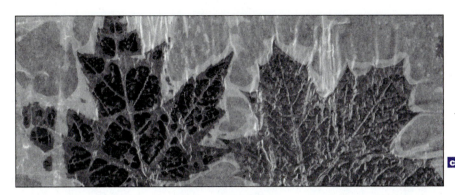

supplies

1. Interesting forms of *flat* plant life such as leaves, weeds, or grasses
2. Waxed paper
3. Iron

NOTE: Interesting effects using yarn, string, colored paper, and other assorted flat materials may also be used. Suggested uses include table runner, blackboard frieze, and window transparencies.

connections

Leaf identification composition

Sewn seed jewelry

procedure

1. After determining the sequence in which the seeds will appear, string the seeds on a predetermined length of thread, making allowance for knots at the ends.
2. Thread the seeds on the thread until there is just room for a triple knot at the end.
3. Tie the knot and, if desired, spray with an acrylic to preserve the seeds.
4. For young students, holes could be put in the seeds before stringing. If the students are using needles, *stress safety!*

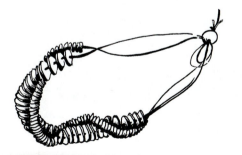

supplies

1. Variety of dried seeds, such as corn, beans, cantaloupe, watermelon, grapefruit, apple, pumpkin, or tree pods
2. Needle
3. Heavy buttonhole cotton thread

NOTE: Ornamental objects such as beads can be spaced between the seeds. Cold water will soften the seeds. Shell macaroni can also be used. Dip the macaroni in hot water to soften.

connections

Seed necklaces and bracelets are made by local people of the area of the Pacific and Caribbean Islands

chapter seven: crafts 113

Stained glass windows

procedure

Method a

1. Draw a design on paper with pencil. Add lines on the picture surface to divide it to simulate the look of a stained glass window.
2. Draw over all the pencil lines with the black glue.
3. Allow the glue to dry and fill in the areas between the glue with any of the color agents.

supplies

1. Black glue
2. Heavy paper or tag board
3. Markers, oil pastels, crayons

 NOTE: Black glue can be made by mixing Elmer's Glue and black acrylic paint or black tempera. Mix thoroughly before using.

 connections Stained glass of Gothic period

Notre Dame of Paris

Marc Chagall

Method b

1. Fold black construction paper or papers in half, either vertical or horizontal.
2. Cut the outside shape of the window on the open edges of the black paper.
3. Draw shapes on the folded edge, allowing about ¼ inch between each shape and the top and bottom of the paper. Remember it is a folded paper so draw one-half of a symmetrical shape.
4. Open the black paper and carefully fold the right edge of the window to the middle crease. Cut additional shapes on this fold leaving spaces between them. Keep the shapes if they are to be used as patterns for the left side of the window.
5. Open the black paper and repeat step 4 on the left side of the window.
6. Tape or glue pieces of colored cellophane or tissue on the one side of the black paper, usually on the side where the pencil lines appear.

supplies

1. Black construction paper
2. Scissors
3. Colored cellophane or tissue paper
4. Tape
5. Glue

NOTE: Two sheets of black paper may be cut at the same time. The cellophane or tissue is sandwiched between the two sheets so that both sides have a clean finish.

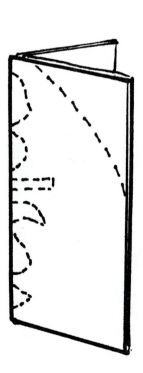
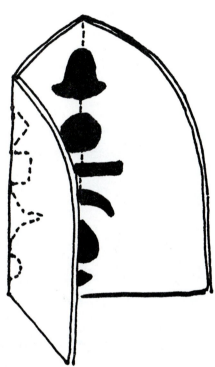

supplies

1. X-acto knives No. 11 blade

2. Corrugated cardboard

3. Black construction paper

4. Scissors

5. Colored cellophane or colored tissue

Method c

1. Draw the outside shape of the window and cut with scissors.
2. Within this shape, draw a thick line to make the main shape of the window. Draw connecting lines in the background and within the main design shape to simulate the lead of a stained glass window.
3. Cut carefully with an X-acto knife. **Remember the safety rules.**
4. Carefully cut and fit colored cellophane or colored tissue over the openings.
5. Tape or glue the colored pieces neatly in place.

CAUTION: Extreme care and supervision must be taken whenever X-acto knives are used. Safety instructions should be given before **Every** use of the knives. X-acto knives are now sold with safety caps, but separate caps may be purchased for older knives. Heavy corrugated cardboard should always be placed under the paper or material being cut. The X-acto knife is held like a pencil, with the fingers holding the knife on the textured ring. The slanted, sharpened edge should be directly over the line to be cut and the position of the knife or the paper should be changed if the line changes direction. Keep the fingers of the holding hand out of the way of the blade, usually above the cutting area. Remind students to check themselves and the position of the knife and their hands often. The safety cap should be on the knife at all times except when in use.

Transfer picture

procedure

1. Tape the photographic print face up on the waxed paper (Ill. 1).
2. Paint the print with six or seven coats of clear polymer. Alternate the direction of each coat, allowing 10 to 15 minutes of drying time between each coat (Ill. 2).
3. Allow one hour for all of the coats to dry.
4. Soak the coated print in warm, sudsy water until all of the paper can be peeled from the back of the picture (Ill. 3). In some cases the paper may have to be rubbed from the back. The soaking time may take an hour, depending on the thickness of the paper. Be careful not to tear or stretch the remaining film of ink and polymer.
5. Allow the print to dry.
6. Apply the print to any surface by first brushing a coat of clear polymer on the surface. Adhere the print while this coating is wet (Ill. 4).
7. Remove any bubbles by pressing out from the center. If any bubbles persist, puncture them with a pin.

supplies

1. Color photograph printed on high-quality glossy paper
2. Clear polymer medium (painting medium for acrylic paint)
3. Paint brush
4. Tape
5. Waxed paper
6. Material or object to which the print is to be transferred
7. Small roller

NOTE: With proper mounting on clear acetate or plastic, the transfer photographs can serve as slides for projectors (Ill. 5). They are ideal for mapmaking.

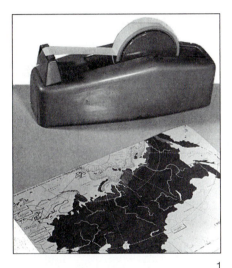

1

2

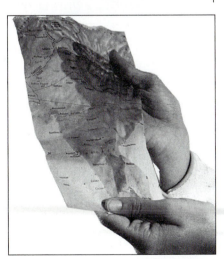

3

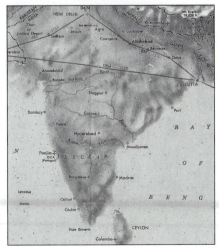

4

5

Embossed metal

1. Colored aluminum foil, 38 gauge. Color on one side with bright aluminum on the other

2. Modeling tool (anything that will not cut or scratch the metal, such as a dull pencil, a sharpened wooden dowel, or a craft stick)

3. Pad of newspaper or towel

4. Pencil and newsprint

5. Acrylic paint, latex paint, India ink permanent markers

6. Paper towel or piece of cloth

procedure

1. Cut the foil to the size of the finished work.
2. Develop a design on paper the same size as the piece of foil.
3. With a pad of newspaper or a cloth under the foil, fasten the design on top of the foil with a piece of tape and draw over the design with a dull pencil.
4. Decide which areas of the design are to be raised (traditionally, the main shapes are raised). Begin tooling with the foil facing down on the pad. Using a suitable tool, make short coloring strokes side by side. Emboss the foil from both sides to avoid wrinkles. Remove the pad, place the foil on a smooth hard surface, and work around the raised portions to flatten the background.
5. India ink, or black acrylic or latex paint, can be wiped over the surface of the foil and quickly wiped off to give the look of oxidation.
6. Colored permanent markers with bullet points can be used to color the foil, particularly if the aluminum side is used as the front.

VARIATION: Design Coins
Cut 2 circles of the foil. Cut a slightly smaller circle from mat board or cardboard to be the core for the two sides of the tooled coin. Antique the coin surface with the India ink, or black acrylic or latex paint. Glue the sides of the coin to the cardboard core and crimp the edges.

VARIATION: Egyptian Mask
Using some of the Egyptian masks (such as the gold mask of Tutankhamen) as examples, draw the shape of the mask on the foil. With the gold side as the front, tool lightly on both sides of the foil. Using permanent markers, add color to the headpiece, at the eyes, eyebrows, and the collar piece.

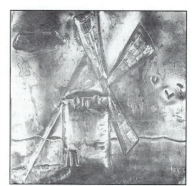

Repoussé

Repoussé is the technique of making patterns in relief on metal usually by hammering. Patterns can also be made by stretching the metal with a simple wooden or plastic tool. Deepest relief can be obtained by tooling all the areas to be recessed from the one side and then tooling all the remaining areas from the other side.

procedure

1. Cut the foil to the size of the finished work. Be careful of the sharp edges.
2. Develop a design on newsprint the same size as the piece of foil. Do not make small details.
3. With a pad of newspaper or a cloth under the foil, fasten the design on top of the foil with a piece of tape and draw over the design pressing hard with a pencil.
4. Decide which areas of the design are to be raised (traditionally, the main shapes are raised). Begin tooling with the foil facing down on the pad. Using a suitable tool, make short coloring strokes side by side.
5. When the raised areas are finished, turn the foil over and begin tooling the recessed areas from the front side of the foil.
6. If wrinkles develop, press a flat tool in the direction of the wrinkle with the foil on a flat, hard surface.
7. Copper foil can be oxidized (blackened) by brushing or wiping Liver of Sulphur over the front surface of the foil. When the surface is darkened, wash the foil under running water and allow the foil to dry. Make sure there is adequate ventilation, because Liver of Sulphur smells like rotten eggs.
8. Clean and polish the foil with steel wool. The fine steel wool is good for the final polish. The oxidizing will remain in the low areas.

supplies

1. Copper, aluminum, or brass foil, 36 gauge
2. Modeling tool (anything that will not cut or scratch the metal, such as a sharpened dowel, popsicle stick, tongue depressor, dull pencil, and commercial tools for this technique)
3. No. 000 steel wool, No. 0000 for final polish
4. Pencil and newsprint paper
5. Pad of newspaper or cloth (a Turkish towel is excellent)
6. Oxidizing liquid, Liver of Sulphur (adequate ventilation is a must)

NOTE: Numerous textures can be embossed to give richness to the modeling. Polish the foil with fine steel wool before applying the Liver of Sulphur. Oxidation will work even better if the metal can be warmed first. Holding the metal under running warm water will work.

connections

Tibet

India

Linear string

1. Heavy string or cord
2. Waxed paper
3. Glue
4. Pencil
5. Paper
6. Tape
7. Small flat tray for glue

NOTE: If color is wanted, the string can be dyed before or painted after the design is completed and dry. Paint the design before removing it from the waxed paper. These objects can be incorporated into mobiles.

connections

Study of line

procedure

1. Make a pencil drawing of the desired subject.
2. Cover the pencil drawing with waxed paper, and fasten it in place with tape.
3. Puddle glue in a flat tray to soak string.
4. Place glue-covered string on waxed paper over the line drawing.
5. When the glue is dry, remove the string from the waxed paper.

Mailing tube containers

This project can be used to make banks, napkin rings, pencil and brush holders, planters, or bracelets.

procedure

1. If a base is needed, place a piece of cardboard under the end of the tube, trace around it, cut it, and affix the base to the mailing tube with the polymer or glue.
2. Paint the surface of the tube with polymer or diluted glue.
3. Tear pieces of the tissue paper and press them on the surface of the tube, or use a printed photo.
4. Continue with layers of glue and paper until the desired degree of richness is achieved.
5. Spray surface for protection.

 CAUTION: Use adequate ventilation when spraying.

 NOTE: If a bank is desired, cut the top as the base, cut in half, cut out the coin slit, then glue together on the top (Ill. 1).

If a pencil and brush holder is desired, cut the top and drill holes in the top before gluing to the tube (Ill. 2).

The object can be further decorated with wrapping string, transfer pictures, or decorative paper strips (Ill. 3). The interior may be lined with felt.

Small rings can be used for napkin rings with decoration added (Ill. 4). If designed as a planter, line the inside with plastic before use (Ill. 5).

1

2

3

4

5

String and pin plaques

supplies

1. Upsom board, ½" thick
2. Straight pins or finishing nails
3. Assorted colors of thread or string
4. Piece of felt or cloth
5. Tape or glue

NOTE: Individual creative designs may be produced by experimenting with pin placement.

procedure

1. Decide on the size and shape of the plaque, and cut it from a piece of Upsom board.
2. Cover the Upsom board with a piece of felt or cloth. Pull the cloth over the edges, and fasten in back with glue or tape. Be sure the cloth is stretched tightly.
3. Push enough straight pins into the cloth-covered Upsom board to form a design. Measure the distance between the pins if the design is to be geometric (Ill. 1).
4. Tie a string or thread to one pin, then wind around other pins to form the design (Ill. 2).
5. Tie the string when one color of the design is completed. Tie another color of string to a pin, and begin to form another part of the design.
6. Place a hook in back so plaque may be hung.

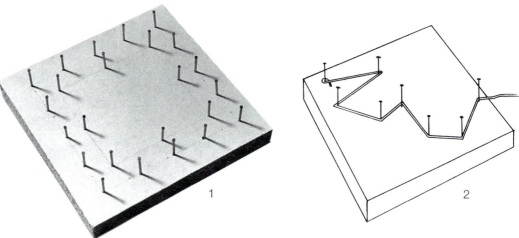

1

2

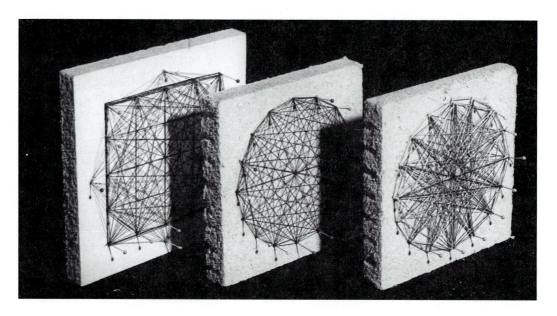

Strata carving

This project is so named because its nature reminds one of stratified rock. It could easily be correlated with a study of geology.

procedure

1. Mix one part of glue with five parts of whiting and add enough water to produce a consistency that can be painted rather thickly.
2. Divide the mixture into several jars, and add contrasting tempera colors to each jar. Mix well.
3. Brush the surface of the base object with a moderate thickness of the first of the color mixtures (this will be at the bottom). Allow to dry.
4. Continue superimposing color mixture layers until all are used. Allow each layer to dry between each application.
5. Make a drawing on thin paper the size of the item just completed.
6. Transfer the drawing to the top layer. Carbon paper may be used, or the back of the paper can be covered with graphite from a pencil; then the paper is placed on the surface and the drawing is redrawn.
7. Carve through the mixtures to the depth required to expose the desired color. Experiment with carving tools.
8. If desired, the surface may be preserved with the application of a clear spray.

 CAUTION: It is imperative that proper safety precautions be taken. Pin the work to a vertical surface. Spray outdoors in a well-ventilated but wind-free area. With a sweeping motion, spray from the top to the bottom of the work. It may be necessary for the instructor to spray the work.

supplies supplies

1. Liquid glue
2. Whiting
3. Container for mixing the paste and several small containers for the separate colors
4. Tempera paint in a number of colors
5. Painting base (block of wood, box, or heavy cardboard)
6. Brush
7. Pencil and paper
8. Carbon paper (optional)
9. Carving and scratching tools, such as nails, knives (with caution), chisels, or hair pins
10. Clear spray (optional). There are clear brush-on finishes on the market. These may be a better option

Pressed nature notepaper

1. Notepaper or place cards
2. Leaves, delicate flowers, lacy ferns, grasses, and other natural objects
3. Newspapers
4. Glue
5. Clear Contact paper
6. Ruler
7. Scissors

procedure

1. Collect flowers, ferns, leaves, grasses, and other natural objects, and dry them by pressing between sheets of newspaper weighted with books or other heavy objects. Let them dry about one week, changing newspapers occasionally.
2. Arrange these natural objects where they appear to be most pleasing on the notepaper or place cards.
3. When satisfied with the arrangement, place dots of glue on the backs of the natural objects, just enough to hold them in place until the Contact paper can be applied.
4. Cut a square or rectangle of clear Contact paper large enough to cover and extend a little beyond the design.
5. Peel the backing from the Contact paper and carefully apply it, pressing it firmly to the place card or notepaper. If a bubble forms in the Contact paper, prick it with a pin and press it out.
6. **Use safety scissors if possible.**

Plaster mixing

procedure

Mix the plaster as follows:

1. Pour the desired amount of water into the mixing container (Ill. 1).
2. Add the plaster to the water by sifting it through the fingers or gently shaking it from a can or small cup (Ill. 2).
3. Continue adding the sifted plaster to the water until the plaster builds up above the surface. Allow to soak 20 or 30 seconds to thoroughly blend the mixture (Ill. 3).
4. Stir the plaster thoroughly with the hands until it is smooth and creamy, making sure that any lumps of plaster are broken, and stir gently to avoid bubbles (Ill. 4).
5. Once the plaster is mixed, do not add more water to thin, or more plaster to thicken, because the same consistency cannot be regained.
6. Pour the plaster into a container, which can be used for the mold. Gently agitate the mold to bring any bubbles to the surface (Ill.5).

supplies

1. Molding plaster
2. Container for mixing plaster
3. Water
4. Newspaper and paper towels for cleaning
5. Container to be used as mold

NOTE: Begin to clean up immediately after pouring the plaster in the mold, as it will harden rapidly once the chemical reaction takes place. Any remaining plaster should be wiped from the pan immediately with paper towels and rolled in newspaper so that it can be disposed of more easily. Do not wash plaster down any drain. When cleaning the hands, tools, and mixing pan, be sure the water runs continuously. Instructor should do most of the clean-up.

1

2

3

4

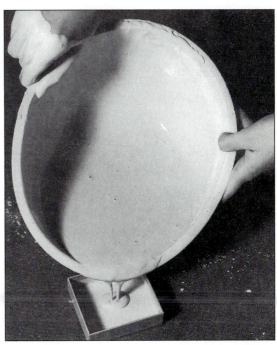

5

Plaster tile mosaic

1. Piece of wood or masonite the size of the mosaic to be made

2. Scraps of thin, colored, plastic floor tile (all must be the same thickness)

3. Molding plaster

4. Bowl in which to mix plaster

5. Pliers

6. Glue

7. Straightedge wider and longer than the tile to be made

8. Tweezers

procedure

1. Place the wood or masonite to be used as the tile on a sheet of paper and trace around it with a pencil. This will provide a pictorial area the same dimensions as the completed tile.
2. Create a drawing within this area.
3. Transfer the drawing to the wood or masonite.
4. Break the plastic into small pieces with the pliers, and glue in place on the tile. Allow a small space between each piece as it is placed. If pieces are too small they can be picked up with tweezers.
   a. Avoid light-colored tiles, as they will not contrast with the white plaster surrounding each piece.
   b. If the entire tile is not to be covered with mosaic, be sure a border is included.
5. Mix the plaster (see illustrations, p. 125).
6. Pour the plaster over the tile, which has been placed on newspaper, and work it between the mosaic pieces.
7. Level the plaster by pulling the straightedge over the surface. (Thin pieces of mosaic should be used, as thick pieces will be pulled out of place.)
8. Fill in all bubbles and repair any flaws before the plaster becomes too hard.
9. Only a thin film of plaster should appear on the mosaic tiles after scraping with the straightedge.
10. When almost dry, clean film from the tile pieces with fingers, tissue, or rag.

 NOTE: Begin to clean up immediately after pouring the plaster in the mold, as it will harden rapidly once the chemical reaction takes place. Any excess plaster remaining should be wiped from the pan immediately and rolled in newspaper so that it might be disposed of easily. Do not wash plaster down the drain. When cleaning the hands, tools, and mixing pan, be sure the water runs continuously.

 Mosaics of Pompeii

Ravenna (fifth century)

St. Marks of Venice (thirteenth century)

Miniature mosaics of Italy

Mosaic jewelry

Mosaics were widely used in the classical cultures. Floor Mosaic from Antioch. (Roman) 2nd century, A.D. *Courtesy of Bowling Green University.*

Mosaic plaster plaque

procedure

1. Place the container to be used as a mold on a sheet of paper and trace around it with a pencil. This will provide a pictorial area of the same dimensions as the completed work, on which the preliminary drawing may be done. Divide the subject matter in the drawing into interesting sections that can be easily cut from the linoleum or plastic tile.

2. Transfer the various parts of the design to the linoleum or floor tile of the desired color and cut out with scissors. Break into pieces with the pliers if brittle plastic is used.

3. Place a small spot of paste on the face of each piece and fasten face down in the cardboard mold to form the original design (Ill. 1). Approximately ⅛ inch space should remain between the various sections and the edge of the mold.

4. Mix the plaster (see illustrations, p. 125).

5. Pour the plaster into the mold to the desired thickness (Ill. 2). Gently agitate the box to make sure the plaster completely surrounds the individual pieces of the design and to also bring any bubbles to the surface. If a wall plaque is desired, a wire hook can be placed in the plaster before it hardens completely.

6. Allow the plaster to dry thoroughly before removing the cardboard box mold. If the cardboard adheres to the plaster, wash it off under running water.

7. Smooth any of the sharp edges by scraping with any available tool. Repair any flaws that might appear at this time.

8. The finished plaque can be soaked in a solution of white soap flakes and then wiped dry with a cloth. This will produce a glossy, high-polish finish.

 NOTE: A plaster relief can be created by carefully lifting out the pieces of plastic tile or linoleum. Instructor may need to do the cutting for younger students.

supplies

1. Cardboard container to be used as a mold
2. Scraps of thin-colored or textured linoleum or thin plastic floor tile
3. Molding plaster
4. Bowl in which to mix plaster
5. Heavy-duty scissors
6. Paste
7. Pliers

 NOTE: Warming the linoleum will make it easier to cut.

 NOTE: Begin to clean up immediately after pouring the plaster in the mold, as it will harden rapidly once the chemical reaction takes place. Any excess plaster remaining should be wiped from the pan immediately and rolled in newspaper so that it might be disposed of easily. Do not wash plaster down the drain. When cleaning the hands, tools, and mixing pan, be sure the water runs continuously.

1

2

Salt and flour relief

1. Combine three parts salt with one part flour and enough water to bring solution to the consistency of dough. This will create a mass suitable for sculptural modeling; the thickness may be modified for individual needs or desired methods of application by varying the quantity of water

2. Heavy cardboard or piece of wood

3. Watercolor paints

4. Brush

5. Water container

NOTE: Topographical maps or aerial views are especially suitable for treatment in this manner.

procedure

1. Cover the cardboard or wood with a thin film of salt and flour mixture.
2. Keeping a design in mind, create a semiround relief, building up masses of the salt and flour mixture to various heights. Additional salt and flour may be added when the first application has dried enough to support another layer.
3. When the modeling is completed, it may be embellished by the addition of color while still moist.
4. Additional interest may be created by pressing objects, textures, and patterns into the wet salt and flour.

Sand candles

procedure

1. Pack damp sand into a box or bucket (Ill. 1).
2. Hollow the shape of the candle in the damp sand. These shapes can be created with your hands, a bottle, pencils, sticks, or any type of tool that can be pressed into the sand to make a hollow.
3. Place a wick into the mold by tying one end to a stick suspended across the top of the mold (Ill. 2). On the other end, tie a weight and drop it into the hollow. Make sure the wick is centered and stretched tight. A candle itself may be inserted to form the wick.
4. Melt the wax in a double boiler to a temperature of 190° F to 230° F, or 88° C to 110° C (standard pouring temperature). Use a thermometer to make sure, for wax reaches a flash point at approximately 400° F, or 204° C.
5. Add colored crayons to the melted wax to reach desired color.
6. Grip the container of melted wax with gloves or hot pad, and pour melted wax into moist sand mold (Ill. 3). Different colored wax poured in layers makes interesting effects.
7. Leave wax in sand until completely hard. Wash off excess sand.
8. If bottom of candle is uneven, it can be leveled on a hot surface.

CAUTION: In case of fire, cover the flame with a lid or baking soda. Never use water to extinguish the flame. Children are merely observers in this activity.

supplies

1. Wax (old candles work best, but clean and cut off burned wick). Paraffin could be mixed with the old wax, as could beeswax
2. Wicks, cotton twine (old candle wicks)
3. Can or old pan (for melting wax)
4. Colored crayons (for coloring wax)
5. Double boiler
6. Thermometer (candy thermometer)
7. Box or bucket
8. Damp, fine sand
9. Gloves, hot pad, or cloth

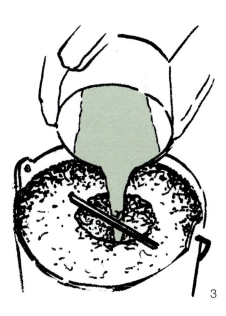

Beads from soda and cornstarch mixture

1. 1 cup cornstarch
2. 2 cups baking soda (1 lb. box)
3. 1¼ cups water
4. Saucepan
5. Stove or hot plate
6. Aluminum foil
7. Food coloring
8. Plastic bag
9. Watercolors, tempera, or acrylic paint
10. Clear commercial spray or a brush-on finish
11. Scrap Styrofoam or ball of clay to use to stick toothpicks in for the beads to dry
12. Toothpicks
13. Rolling pin or glass jar

procedure

1. Combine cornstarch, baking soda, and water in a saucepan. Cook over medium heat, stirring constantly.
2. When the mixture is thickened to doughlike consistency, turn out on a piece of aluminum foil or breadboard.
3. Food coloring may be worked into the clay when it has cooled slightly.
4. Cover the clay with aluminum foil or plastic to keep it pliable when not in use, and store it in the refrigerator.
5. Pinch off a lump of the mixture, and shape into a bead. Spheres and cylinders can be formed easily by rolling the mixture between the palms of the hands.
6. Roll out the mixture flat with a rolling pin or glass jar, and cut flat beads from it.
7. Punch a hole through each bead with a toothpick. Leave the toothpicks in the beads, and stick them into the ball of clay for drying. Turn the toothpicks in the beads occasionally to keep them from sticking.
8. Use a commercial spray or a brush-on finish on the beads, and when they are dry, string them.

 CAUTION: Any cooking should be done by the supervisor. If a commercial spray is used, it is best to do the spraying outdoors where there is very little wind. Spraying should also be done by the supervisor.

 connections

African beads
Native American beads
Egyptian beads
Ethnic beads of any culture

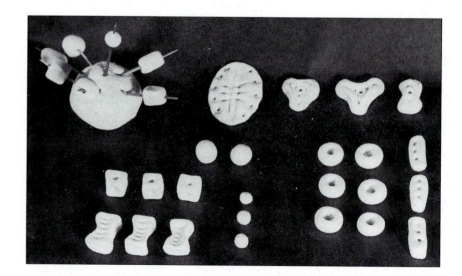

Collage

Collage is a word that comes from the French word *coller,* meaning "to glue." The word is often used to include both the techniques of collé and assemblage. Pasted paper even though it can include some other materials is usually referred to as *collé. Assemblage* refers to a combination of three-dimensional objects glued to a surface.

Some of the earliest examples of paper collage are the work of twelfth-century Japanese calligraphers who prepared the surfaces for their poems with bits of paper and fabric clued to a background. Collage was used in the fifteenth and sixteenth centuries in the art of bookbinding in the East. Artists in medieval times used gemstones, fibers, relics, and metals to decorate religious images. Renaissance artists of the fifteenth and sixteenth centuries in Europe pasted fabric and paper to decorate the backgrounds of coats of arms in genealogical records.

Pablo Picasso used patterned oilcloth in a cubist still life, and George Braque incorporated wallpaper in his artwork. The two artists experimented with paper collé as an extension of cubist principles.

Collage was also employed by the dadaists, such as Marcel Duchamp, Kurt Schwitters, and Max Ernst. Surrealists also used collage techniques.

procedure

1. Arrange the items into a design or picture. Take time and think about the composition.
2. Glue on the cardboard only when satisfied with the arrangement.
3. Other details can be added with paint, crayons, ink, or any other tool.

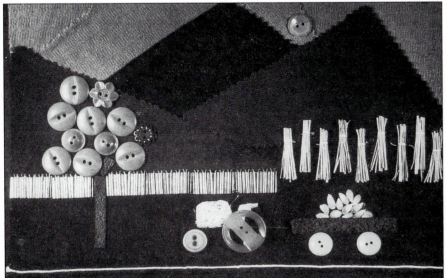

supplies

supplies

1. Piece of cardboard, matt board, illustration board

2. A collection of items, such as pieces of cloth, various kinds of paper, wallpaper, magazine pages, newspapers, grocery bags, gift wrap, confetti, receipts, paper towels, labels, train schedules, programs, wax paper, posters, construction paper, crossword puzzles, old cards, and so on

3. Scissors (safety scissors)

4. Glue stick, Elmer's Glue-All, Sobo Craft and Fabric Glue

connections

Artists:
Robert Motherwell
Robert Rauschenberg
Jasper Johns
Claus Oldenberg
Miriam Schapiro
Romare Bearden

connections

Children's Book Illustrators:

The Paper Crane by Molly Bang, William Morrow & Company, New York, 1987

The Snowy Day by Ezra Jack Keats, Viking Children's Press, New York, 1996

Alexander and the Wind-up Mouse by Leo Lionni, Alfred A. Knopf, New York, 1987

Water for One, Water for Everyone by Stephen Swinburne, Millbrook Press, Brookfield, Conn., 1998

Letter collé

procedure

1. Select a number of magazine letters of various sizes and colors.
2. Cut out selected letters. **Use safety scissors if available.**
3. Combine two or more letters to create figures, scenes, or a design.
4. Arrange this group of letters on a piece of background paper.
5. Paste the letters in place when satisfied.

supplies

1. Colored magazine letters to be used as texture
2. Scissors
3. Paste or glue stick
4. Sheet of white or colored paper for background

Magazine collé

supplies

1. Colored magazine pictures to be used as texture
2. Scissors
3. Paste or glue stick
4. Sheet of white or colored paper for background

NOTE: Do not use the texture to create the subject matter from which it came—instead adapt it to other uses (that is, an illustration of corn flakes could be cut to represent a plowed field, haystack, rumpled hair, and so on).

procedure

1. Select a number of magazine pictures containing areas that may be used for textural effects.
2. Cut these areas into shapes that, when combined, will create a scene or design. **Use safety scissors if available.**
3. Arrange these paper shapes on background paper.
4. Paste the paper shapes in place when satisfied.

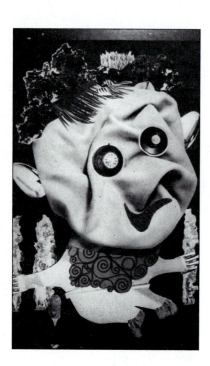

Kites

The first kites may have originated in China and later spread to neighboring countries, such as Korea, India, Malaysia, Indonesia, Burma, and Japan. At first, it was thought that they were built for practical purposes, such as measuring distance, and they seem to have had some religious significance. Kites later became more decorative and more beautiful.

In Japan, until recently a Boys' Festival was celebrated on May 5, the fifth day of the fifth month. If a boy had been born to a family during the past year, a kite was flown in celebration. Usually, this kite was in the form of a brightly colored paper wind sock with a carp adorning its sides. The *carp* is the symbol of courage and strength. Today the festival includes girls, and it is called Children's Day. In China, on the ninth day of the ninth month of each year, it is traditional to hold a kite-flying festival, and the day is called *Kites Day*. On the fifteenth day of the year in Korea, tailed kites are flown for good luck.

Kites may have come to Europe via trade contact with the East. It is known that wind socks appear in drawings as far back as A.D. 105, when the Romans used wind socks shaped like dragons as military banners. The wind sock had a set of wings added by the fifteenth century so that it could fly at an angle like a kite. The pennon kite came into use during the medieval period with the outside of the dragon remaining but with the head as a flat plane supported over two cross spars or supports. Da Vinci also experimented with kites, which may have led him to his interest in flying machines.

In the United States, Ben Franklin used a kite to prove electricity in the atmosphere. Marconi raised the aerial for his intercontinental radio hookup by kite, and the Wright brothers began their experiments into flight with kites.

Kites can be very complex, but the simple ones are not difficult to make and fly. In designing the kite, the decoration should always relate to the kite's basic form. Since the design on the kite will be seen from a distance, it should be simple and bold in general layout. Colors should be strong and clear. Movement with fluttering edges and tails also add another element to the design of a kite.

Words to know

Covers The material used to cover the frame of a kite, including nylon, cloth, PVC sheeting, tissue, or butcher's paper.

Spars Supports of the kite, sometimes of bamboo, lightweight wood, or even folded paper or poster board.

Bridles Short strings from the kite to the main flying line. The bridle is to hold the kite at the correct angle to the wind while flying.

Tails The length not the weight is what is important to balance the kite. The tail is generally five times the height of the kite frame.

Simple kite

1. 8½″ × 11″ white or colored paper

2. Markers or any other color agent

3. 18″ wooden dowel or lightweight wooden stick

4. 3′ long pieces of ripstop nylon, ribbons, thin plastic strips, or other thin lightweight material for tail

5. Clear tape

procedure

1. Fold on center fold and continue by folding down the two wings on each side at the slanted lines.
2. Open up so that the student can decorate both sides of the kite. The center of the kite will be folded into itself, so it will not be necessary to decorate this portion. Just line up the decoration when drawing so that the two wings will line up. The bottom should be decorated.
3. When the kite is decorated, top and bottom, continue by putting the folds back in and putting a hole in the two circles for the string.
4. Tape the stick across the line close to the top edge.
5. Tape tail strips at the small marks at the bottom of the kite.

 Almost any subject, including fantasy, could be connected with this kite

This drawing has been reduced 50%. It may be enlarged and used as a pattern.

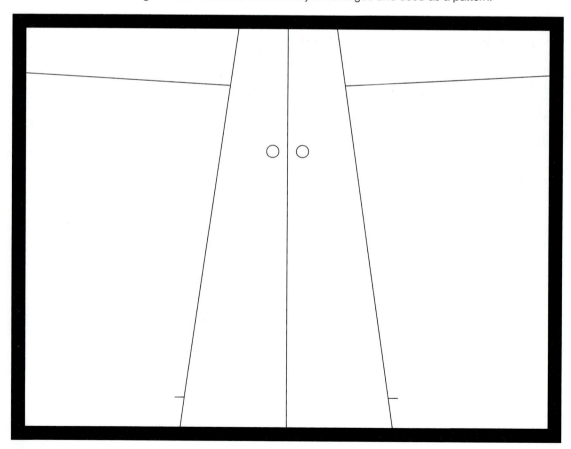

Wind sock

The wind sock is basically a long tube with the top end kept open with the use of reed, wire, or a circle of poster board. The bottom of the tube can be decorated with strips of material, ribbons, or tissue strips.

procedure

1. Cut material to be used for the kite into two long halves. Remember there will need to be a right and a left side. One piece can be used and made into a cylinder later, depending on the material selected.
2. Decorate with other tissue paper, markers, or glitter glue. In the case of fabric, use fabric paint or fabric crayons, following directions for their use.
3. If you have decorated two separate sides, put them together with glue, with the decorated sides to the outside of the kite.
4. Fold over the top edge and glue or sew to form a sleeve to accept the top support to hold the top open.
5. Attach the bottom ribbons or strips to the kite.

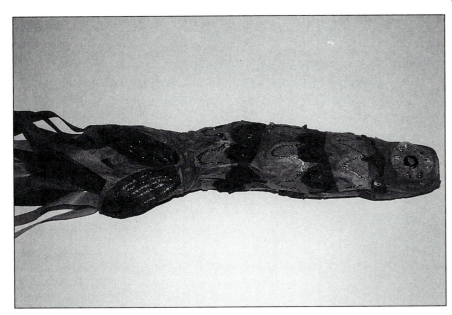

supplies

1. Tissue, lightweight paper nylon material, polyester material
2. Markers, fabric crayons, glitter glue
3. Glue or glue stick
4. Ribbons, thin strips of material, ripstop nylon
5. Lightweight floral wire, thin bamboo, pipe cleaner

connections

The Dragon Kite by Nancy Luenn, Harcourt Brace, San Diego, Calif., 1993

Dragon Kite of the Autumn Moon by Valerie Reddex, Lothrop Lee & Shephard, New York, 1992

Rome

Japan

Fish

Wind

Almost any subject, including fantasy, could be connected with this kite

Tetrahedron frame kite

supplies

supplies

1. Six plastic straws that will not bend
2. 3 ft. piece of yarn
3. Colored tissue paper
4. White glue or glue stick
5. Scissors
6. Pencil
7. Kite string, can be embroidery floss
8. Ribbons
9. Colored felttip pens
10. Glitter, sequins, feathers, and other lightweight trim

procedure

1. Begin to make the frame by stringing three straws together with yarn to form a triangle. Tie the one end of the yarn to the other part of the yarn, leaving enough of an end to tie later.
2. String two more straws onto the long piece of the yarn to form a diamond shape. Run the string through one of the first triangles' straws in order to string the last straw on and to be able to tie at the short end of the yarn that had been left earlier.
3. Tie a tight knot.
4. Place one triangle of the tetrahedron frame on a piece of tissue paper, and mark around it with a pencil, allowing 1″ extra on each side so that the tissue can be folded over the straw. Being careful to allow enough tissue for the center of the kite, tip the frame over to draw around the other triangle forming the diamond shape. Again allow the 1″ allowance for a fold over.
5. Carefully fold the allowance over the straws and glue in place. Do one end of the diamond first before proceeding to the other end.
6. Trim any excess tissue off the points.
7. Cut a head and stomach for your bird out of colored tissue paper. Glue them in place on the frame.
8. Glue decorations onto the kite. Make scales, feathers, and designs using tissue. Sequins, glitter, or glitter glue may also be used.
9. Cut a piece of thread or line about 24″ long. Poke a small hole in the paper cover at the head and tail for the line to pass through and tie the line to the center straw.
10. Tie a 1″ loop in the bridle so that the kite will hang at a 45-degree angle.
11. The kite line, about 25 to 50 feet long, should be attached to the loop on the bridle and the other end wrapped around a strip of cardboard.

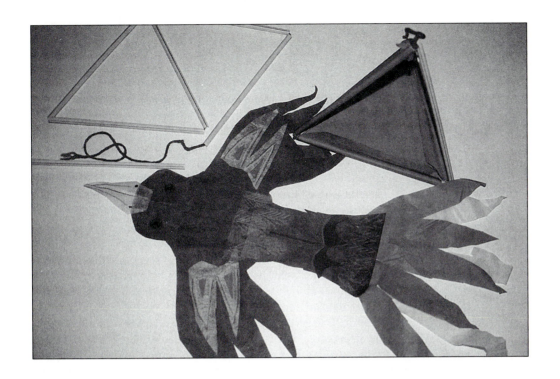

supplies

1. Stiff lightweight paper, twice as long as wide. Can range from 5½" × 11" to 18" × 36". Butcher paper works well for the larger sizes

2. Tape

3. Bridle string

4. Tail streamers, can be crepe paper

5. Stapler, scissors, ruler, pencil, and paper punch

 NOTE: A 1" strip of poster board could be stapled into the accordian folding to help strengthen them. Decorate after the spars have been formed and the holes have been punched for the bridle.

Sled kite

procedure

1. Fold the paper into thirds with the outer section turned toward the middle.

2. Fold the outer sections in half with the outside flaps away from the middle.

3. Draw a dot on the outside edge, one-third of the way down on the outer flaps. Draw a line from each corner of the fold to the dot on the outside edge and cut away excess.

4. Lightly fold in the center of the middle section to mark the center of the vent. The top end of the vent should be ⅓ of the way from the bottom of the kite. The size and shape of the vent may vary.

5. Fold the half left from the outer sections in half toward the center. Fold again. The bigger kites may have this strip doubled over several times. Staple several times along the fold length to form a paper spar.

6. Reinforce the outside corners with tape. Punch holes through the tape where the bridle is to be attached on each side of the kite.

7. The bridle string should be as long as the kite is wide, with additional length for the loops at the bridle points and a loop at the center of the bridle where the flying line will be attached.

8. Tape on narrow crepe paper or ripstop nylon streamers about 3 ft. long for smaller kites and up to 6 ft. long for large kites.

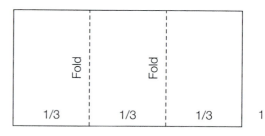

Paper is twice as long as it is wide

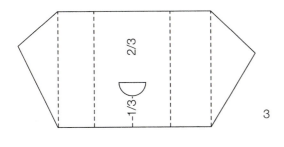

3

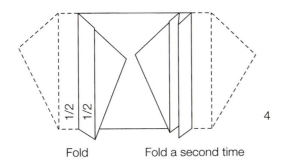

Fold   Fold a second time

4

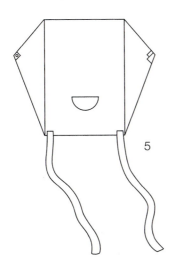

5

crayons and oil pastels

8

Nature of the medium

Crayons

Wax crayons are one of the most familiar art materials. Most of us were introduced to them at a tender age, which may explain why we tend to think that crayons are beneath the dignity of more mature artists. Such is not the case; examples abound of distinguished drawings executed in this humble medium, although few can be dated before the nineteenth century.

Crayons consist of an oily or waxy binder impregnated with pigments. Records exist of a variety of prescriptions for binders, involving soap, salad oil, linseed oil, spermaceti, and beeswax. Crayons are of various types, some soft, some semihard; some are specifically designed for lithographic work, others for general classroom use.

Crayons work well on most papers. They do not blend well; when attempts are made to do this, the wax often "tears." Thus, most drawings are linear in character. Crayons can be scraped thin to produce semitransparent layers of subtle color, and they can be coated with black and scratched through for crayon etchings.

This is an ideal medium for children; it is bold, colorful, clean, and inexpensive.

There are many types of crayons available. They include:

1. *Neon or fluorescent* Bright extra-vivid color.
2. *Multicultural* Includes many flesh tones.
3. *Glitter crayons* Glitter sticks to the paper as the colors are used.
4. *Pearl Brite crayons* Pearly accents show up in the light.
5. *Metallic crayons* Gold, silver, and copper crayons for special effects.
6. *Construction paper crayons* Completely opaque when used on colored construction paper.
7. *Watercolor crayons* This crayon becomes liquid with the addition of water. The crayon can be dipped in water and applied to the paper or the crayon can be colored on the paper and the water brushed on top.

Oil pastels

Oil pastels use oil as a binder and produce a rich depth of tone and a degree of transparency. Oil pastels feel sticky at first, but work over the surface of the paper more easily as they get warmer. They can be modified by using turpentine.

Ordinary construction paper makes a reasonable base for the simple use of the oil pastel. Textured oil paper or oil board works well as a base for many of the techniques available. Oil pastels can be thinned to create washes of color that can be blended or they can be applied very heavily and in layers of color to create **impasto. Sgraffito** or "scratching lines" can be used through the top layer of oil pastel to show the underlying color.

Some oil pastels are water soluble. A number of different techniques may be used with this type of oil pastels (with the exception of resist techniques) with the addition of water. The oil pastel can be dipped in water, water can be brushed on after the pastels have been applied, or a water mist can be sprayed on top of the oil pastels.

Oil pastel on colored paper

procedure

1. Discuss the subject to be used for the work. Show pictures.
2. Encourage drawing large. It is much easier to mix colors on larger shapes.
3. Point out that the mixed colors will look different depending on which color is used first. Experiment.
4. Save black until last. Use a piece of newsprint to help shield the side of of the hand so that it will not smear the work. White is useful to use as an addition where the color needs to be brightened.
5. It is most effective when very little of the original color of the paper can be seen.

supplies

1. Oil pastels
2. Pencils or white chalk
3. Colored construction paper

The Little Wood Duck. by Brian Wildsmith, Oxford University Press, Oxford, England, 1983

James McNeil Whistler

Wassily Kandinsky

Joan Miró

Paul Klee

Marc Chagall

Marsden Hartley

Oil pastel on black paper

1. Oil pastels, except for black unless it is mixed with another color
2. Pencils
3. Black paper

connections

Georges Rouault
Max Beckman
Karl Schmidt-Rottluff
Ernst Ludwig Kirchner

procedure

1. Discuss the paintings of Georges Rouault, particularly the color, subject matter, shapes, and use of dark lines used around the shapes.
2. Illustrate with a simple subject how to leave space around the shapes to keep a black outline. After producing the original drawing, it is helpful to draw a second line about a ⅛″ to ¼″ away from the original line. The space between the two lines would be kept free of any color.
3. Encourage mixing of color and liberal use of white to brighten the colors. Colors need to be applied heavily to simulate oil paints. Black should be avoided unless it is mixed in small amounts with another color.

Crayon or oil pastel etching

procedure

1. Cover the entire surface of the paper with a heavy coat of brightly colored crayons or oil pastels in either a free or a planned design. Avoid using dark colors. The heavier the colors are applied, the better the final result. No definite drawing or design is necessary at this point.
2. Color over the brightly colored crayon or oil pastel with black, violet, or any dark color, until none of the original color shows. Rub the crayon surface with a piece of tissue, cloth, patting powder, or chalk dust over the first layer of crayon to help the second layer of dark color adhere.
3. Dark-colored tempera paint mixed with detergent can be used in place of the dark-colored crayon or oil pastel. It should be brushed on the colored surface with smooth, even strokes and allowed to dry.
4. Having a definite design or drawing in mind, scratch or scrape through the dark surface to reveal the colors beneath.

supplies

1. Wax crayons or oil pastels
2. Dark-colored tempera paint with a few drops of detergent
3. Drawing paper (white or manila)
4. Scraping tool, such as scissors, stick, hairpin, comb, nail, or nail file

connections

The Boy and the Ghost by Robert D. San Souci, Aladdin Paperbacks, 1992

Paul Klee

Ben Nicholson

Mark Tobey

Crayon or oil pastel over tempera paint

supplies

1. Tempera paints and brush
2. Wax crayons or oil pastels
3. Paper
4. Sponge

procedure

1. Create the desired painting with tempera paints.
2. Work a contrasting color over each area with crayon or oil pastel, using moderate pressure.
3. Immerse the sponge in water: then "wash" the painting until the underlying tempera paint begins flaking off. The result will be a mottled, textured quality in which the residual crayon or oil pastel will supplement and accent the varied tempera tones that remain. The degree of flaking may be accelerated by brushing or, if it has gone too far, retouching may be done with the crayon or oil pastel.

NOTE: This procedure may be modified by applying the crayons more heavily, then holding the drawing under water that is just hot enough to melt the crayon. The use of the hot water necessitates a degree of caution. The instructor may decide to do this procedure for the student.

connections

Max Ernst
Jean Dubuffet
Paul Klee
Oskar Kokoschka

Crayon or oil pastel resist

procedure

1. Color the drawing or design heavily with crayons or oil pastels, allowing areas of paper to show.
2. Cover the entire surface of the paper with watercolor paint. The paint will be absorbed by the uncolored paper and resisted by the wax crayons or oil pastels.

supplies

supplies

1. Wax crayon or oil pastels
2. Paper
3. Brush
4. Watercolor paints
5. Water container

NOTE: If light-colored or white crayons are used, a dark watercolor wash will be the most satisfactory.
Using only black and white crayon or oil pastel over the pencil lines of a design is an excellent way of doing color mixing with watercolors. The wax or oil forms a barrier so that the colors stay within the boundary lines.

 Paul Klee
Oskar Kokoschka
Henri Matisse
Pierre Bonnard

1. Crayons
2. Manila paper
3. Pencil
4. Watercolors
5. Brush

connections

Indonesia
China

Crayon resist batik

procedure

1. Make a light drawing in pencil on manila or heavy wrapping paper.
2. Using the pencil lines as a guide, draw lines and shapes with the crayon, allowing areas of the paper to show through.
3. Soak paper in water and crumple into a ball.
4. Uncrumple the paper, flatten, and blot off excess water.
5. Paint the entire surface with watercolor paint or diluted tempera paint. The paint will be absorbed by the uncolored paper and resisted by the wax crayon, creating a weblike or batik pattern.

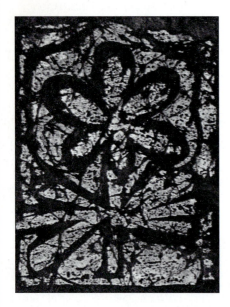

Crayon or oil pastel textures made by rubbing

procedure

1. Make an outline drawing or design with pencil on thin drawing paper.
2. Hold the drawing against a surface that has a definite texture, and rub the crayon or oil pastel over all areas of the drawing in which the texture will create a pleasing pattern. The texture will be transferred to the paper by the crayon or oil pastel.
3. Place the paper against another texture, and transfer this texture to another portion of the drawing.
4. Textures may be repeated or overlapped.
5. Unusual effects can be obtained by using several colors.

supplies

1. Wax crayon or oil pastel
2. Thin drawing paper
3. Pencil
4. Textured surface

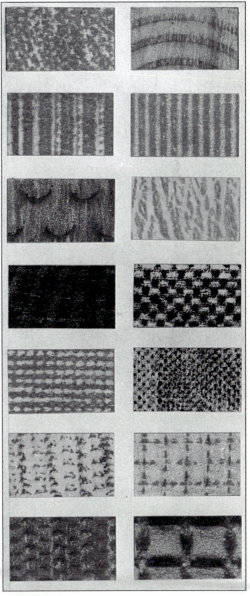

Encaustic painting

Encaustic is a method of painting in which colored waxes are applied to a surface and the color is fixed by heat. Encaustic paintings were found in some of the portraits at Pompeii and the Roman portraits found in Fayoum, Egypt.

1. Wax crayons, or see formula for encaustic paint.
2. Old muffin tin
3. A 100 or 150 watt light bulb and extension cord, or an electric skillet
4. Stiff bristle painting brushes (the use of melted crayon will render the brushes unusable for any other media)
5. Any durable painting surface, such as wood, canvas, board, plaster, masonite, or heavy cardboard
6. Turpentine and soap for cleaning brushes

procedure

1. Sort out the pieces of crayon in a muffin tin according to color.
2. To melt the crayons, float the muffin tin in water in an electric skillet and slowly heat the water. A light bulb placed close to the muffin tin can also be used to melt the crayons. **This step must be closely supervised.**
3. Paint directly on the chosen surface with the hot melted crayons. Many varied effects of luminosity, texture, and tone are unique to encaustic painting.
4. When the painting is finished and cooled, it may be polished with a soft cloth.

 NOTE: Encaustic painting is also possible by soaking fine crayon shavings in a small amount of turpentine for twelve to fifteen days. The finer the shavings, the quicker they dissolve. The dissolved crayons should be a smooth, creamy medium for painting. **With the use of wax or crayons and heat, extreme caution must always be taken.** Never melt wax or crayons in direct head. Use a double boiler, or float the pan holding the wax in another container with water in it. Baking soda should always be at hand in case of fire.

 Fayoum Portraits

connections

Melted crayon

procedure

1. Hold the crayon briefly over the flame of the candle until it softens, then press, drip, or drag the softened crayon onto the paper. A definite design or drawing can be sketched on the paper beforehand to serve as a guide, or the idea can be created with melted crayon directly.
2. Should the crayon become too short to hold over the flame, a long pin stuck into the crayon will solve this problem.
3. A number of different colors melted on top of one another will not only create an unusual textural effect but will greatly enrich the color.

 CAUTION: Because this procedure uses an open flame, it is suggested that every precaution be observed. White and yellow crayons can be heated but should not be held in the flame for long, as they will carbon.

supplies

1. Paper
2. Crayons with paper wrapping removed
3. Candle

connections
Vincent Van Gogh
Berthe Marisot
Roderic O'Conor

supplies

1. Paper
2. Pencil
3. Crayons, oil pastels, or paint

NOTE: The top doodle was the beginning of each drawing below it. Colored circles indicate the starting points of the doodles.

Original doodle

Horizontal design from doodle

Vertical design from same doodle

Crayon or oil pastel doodle designs

procedure

1. Cover the entire area of the paper with a continuous line drawn with complete spontaneity in light pencil. Make sure this line contains numerous directions made by a variety of straight and curved lines.
2. Look for shapes that are created by the lines and draw them in with a heavy pencil line. Many interesting abstract designs, as well as subject matter, can be found.
3. Color with crayons, oil pastels, or paint.

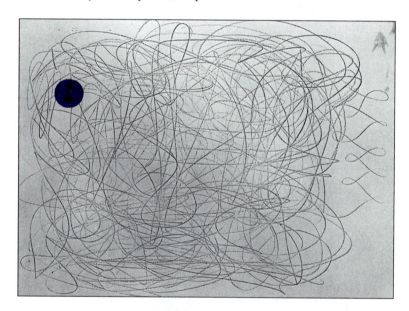

Original doodle

Design from doodle

Crayon on cloth

procedure

1. Draw directly on the cloth with the crayons, using considerable pressure.
2. Melt the crayon into the cloth by placing it under a heat lamp or ironing over it between sheets of paper.

NOTE: The color will be semipermanent only if the fabric is washed in **cool** water with a **nondetergent** soap. **Caution should be observed in handing an iron.**

Finger painting over crayon

procedure

1. Cover the paper with brightly colored crayon.
2. Lay the crayoned paper on a smooth flat surface.
3. Spread finger paint of a contrasting color over the crayon.

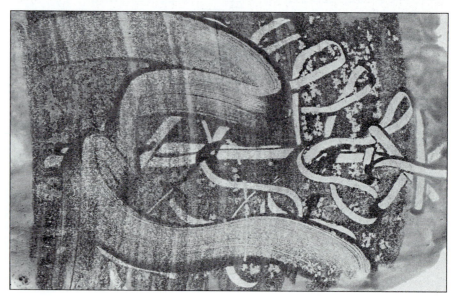

Fabric crayons

procedure

1. Draw a design on newsprint with a pencil.
2. Color the design with fabric crayons, using considerable pressure.
3. Remove any loose crayon specks and turn the paper design face down on the synthetic cloth, which is on an ironing pad of several layers of paper.
4. Set the iron on the cotton setting and allow it to heat up. Apply the iron to the design, holding it in place for thirty seconds. Lift the iron and move it to the untransferred areas of the design. If the iron is moved excessively, the design may blur.
5. "Sneak a peek" by holding the design and lifting one corner to check the strength of the color and design. Apply the heat until the design is completely transferred.

supplies

1. Fabric crayons
2. White paper
3. Synthetic cloth
4. Newspaper
5. Iron (with no steam vents)

NOTE: As this procedure involves the use of a hot iron, precautions should be observed. Instructor should probably handle the iron. Pillows, wall hangings, table cloths, soft sculptures, banners, clothing, and wind socks are all possibilities with fabric crayons. Articles can be machine washed using warm water and gentle action. Do not use bleach or put in dryer. The color can be reapplied to the newsprint and the design used again.

supplies

1. Crayons
2. Wax paper
3. Iron
4. Dull knife, opened scissors, crayon sharpener
5. Newsprint or newspaper

Pressed crayon laminations

procedure

1. Shave the crayons on a piece of wax paper placed on newspaper, creating the image by pushing the shavings around with a small piece of cardboard.
2. Cover the crayon-covered wax paper with another piece of wax paper.
3. Cover both pieces of wax paper with a piece of newspaper and iron with a warm iron.

NOTE: Variations are possible by cutting the wax laminations into various shapes and putting them into a design pressed again between two new sheets of wax paper. For younger students, the instructor should handle the iron. By punching a hole the wax lamination can be used in a mobile.

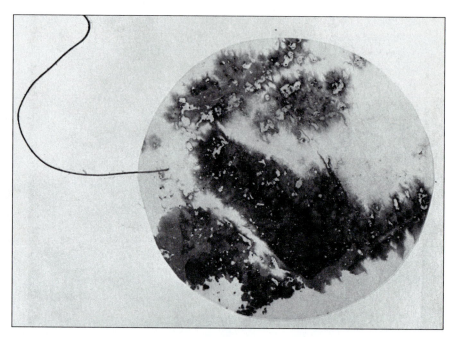

murals

9

Murals

A mural is a large work of art usually designed for a specific location and intended to be viewed by large numbers of people.

A small mural may be produced by the individual student, whereas a larger work is readily adaptable to classroom work as a group enterprise. As such, and because of its mass audience, it can be developed from a theme of general interest selected from any subject area. Properly handled it can be an effective educational aid.

The quality of artwork in a class-produced mural can be easily diluted by its commitment to subject and audience. (A review of the section, Basic Concepts of Art Instruction on pages 3–9, will refresh the reader on the perils inherent in the subjugation of art to other disciplines.) From an art standpoint, little is to be gained from the mural if it is to be confined to a strictly factual presentation. On the other hand, much may be gained if the subject under consideration is studied and researched (on a collective and personal basis) and then submitted to the interpretive abilities of the students. Under such a system of instruction the students could freely debate and vote on the general presentation of the theme and volunteer for selected passages of this theme. The overall plan or layout of the composition could be left in the hands of one student, or it could be produced by the instructor, providing the sketch is not too specific or rigid.

As a public work of art, some consideration should be given to effective placement of the mural in terms of traffic, lighting, and other factors. When the location has been determined, the space available will help to decide the total shape of the mural. Architecture may be a friend or foe; in any case, it must be considered.

Students participating in the design of a mural should be of a narrow age range. When older students are mixed with younger children, there is often an unfortunate tendency to compare. Actually, when ages vary, the products are non-comparable, but this is not always understood, and the general reaction could be frustrating and embarrassing to some students.

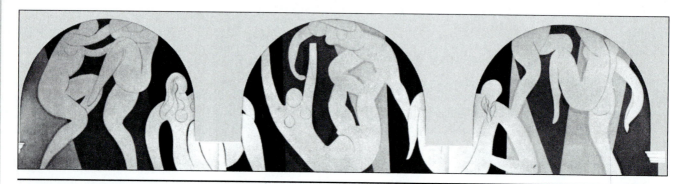

Matisse has designed these figures to work within a specific architectural area. Photograph © 1996 by The Barnes Foundation. All rights reserved.

When the main composition has been sketched, the surface (wrapping paper is cheap, strong, and quite adequate) may be divided up into a working area for each student. Because of spatial restrictions, it is not always possible to have all artists working simultaneously. Work could proceed on a shift basis, integrating this project with other scheduled activities.

It is usually advisable to restrict the work on a mural to one or two media. Materials are variable in strength, and the design could be chaotic if all media were used, unless they were subject to some type of coordination. Some media, such as chalk, are perfectly satisfactory but quite impermanent and could be easily smudged during the process of the work. To avoid this, a fixative or plastic spray could be used to protect the drawing, but this would ruin the surface for further drawing. Crayon is cheap and permanent; poster paint is effective but may flake off if the mural is rolled up. Cut or torn paper is a simple and effective medium and easily combined with other media. Collage techniques may be employed by pasting up fabrics and other textured materials, and papier collé may be used according to the instructions under the activity Collage. A cartoon grid and overhead projector could be useful. If written material is to be included, refer to the section on lettering.

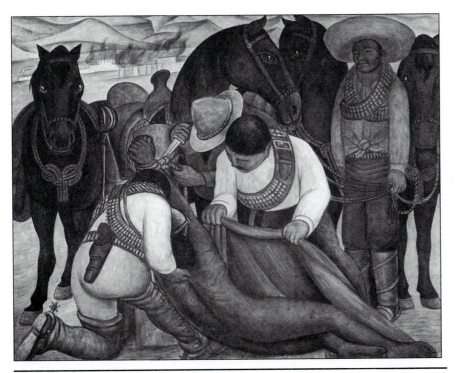

Rivera, a well-known muralist, shows his concern for the underprivileged. Diego Rivera, The Liberation of the Peon, *1931 Fresco, 6 ft. 2 in. × 7 ft. 11 in. (1.88 × 2.41 M). Philadelphia Museum of Art: Gift of Mr. & Mrs. Herbert Cameron Morris.*

supplies

1. Paper
2. Crayons
3. Wrapping paper
4. Scissors
5. Masking tape
6. Pencils
7. Latex paint (semigloss) acrylic paint
8. Brushes, large and small
9. Rollers
10. Sponges
11. Old shirts (for smocks)
12. Cans with lids, to hold various colors of paint

NOTES: Have a group of clean brushes and wipe up any spills. **Use safety scissors if available.**

In order to scale up a drawing, lay a tracing paper over the original sketch. Draw regular squares across it. Draw the same number of squares on a new piece of paper, but make the squares bigger. Copy each square of the original sketch onto the new square so that the part in that square matches the smaller original square.

Mural techniques

procedure

1. Discuss and show examples of murals. Discuss and show pictures of the selected theme.
2. Make idea sketches.
3. Enlarge or scale up the selected sketches on larger paper.
4. Cut out the larger drawings like paper dolls.
5. Stretch wrapping paper below the wall where the mural will be rendered.
6. Arrange the cutouts on the wrapping paper. Use small rolled pieces of masking tape to hold the cutout in place. Shift the objects until satisfied with the composition or arrangement.
7. Place the cutouts in the same position on the wall and draw around them. Tape them back on the wrapping paper when finished so that they can be referred to for details.
8. Paint the wall design with latex or acrylic paint, giving all the students an opportunity to paint.
9. Complete background and details with brush or sponge (see sponge painting).
10. Black and/or white paint may be used to outline or add detail.

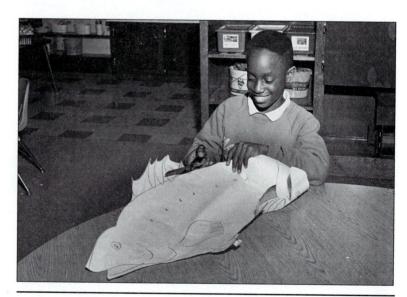

© James L. Shaffer

© James L. Shaffer

NOTE: In order to scale up a drawing, lay tracing paper over the original sketch. Draw regular squares across it. Draw the same number of squares on a new piece of paper, but make the squares bigger. Copy each square of the original sketch onto the new square so that the part in that square matches the smaller original square.

Murals and different media

The procedure for any mural, whatever the media, should first include a discussion of murals with pictures and a discussion of the subject for the proposed mural with available pictures.

This discussion should be followed by idea sketches enlarged on wrapping paper.

Chalk mural

If the mural is to be in **chalk,** it can be rendered on wrapping paper to be mounted on the wall or bulletin board, or it may be rendered directly on the chalkboard if the proper chalk is used.

Crayon/Oil pastel mural

Crayon or **oil pastel** murals should be created on paper and then mounted.

Cut/Torn paper murals

Cut or torn paper murals can have the cut or torn paper pieces pinned, glued, or double faced and taped to a paper background or pinned to a bulletin board.

Tempera mural

Tempera murals are usually painted directly on the paper background. They could also be painted, allowed to dry, and then cut out and fastened to a background.

Clay and copper mural

Clay can be used for permanent murals. Clay by itself lends itself beautifully to murals because all ages can work with it and because clay comes in a variety of colors or can be colored by stain or glaze.

procedure

1. Murals and pictures of murals along with the pictures of the proposed subject should be discussed.
2. Drawings are done by each student with the subject (in this example, the subject is the ancient world, its people, its buildings, its animals, its myths and beliefs).
3. The technique of Repoussé is used with the copper foil.
4. After the copper has been tooled and oxidized, it is put aside for a time.
5. Clay is slabbed and made into tiles. Extra clay is made into buttons. (In some cases, shapes have been drawn on the clay; in other cases the emphasis is on pattern).

After the clay has been fired, the backing for the mural is prepared. The copper pieces are glued on the luan plywood with a dab of silicone glue, and the edges are crimped around the wood. The copper pieces are arranged along with the clay pieces on the backing. When the arrangement or composition is acceptable, the wood and copper are nailed with copper nails to the backing and the clay pieces are glued with the clear silicone.

supplies

supplies

Repoussé

1. Copper foil, 36 gauge, cut to size

2. Modeling tool—anything that will not cut or scratch the metal, such as a sharpened dowel, popsicle stick, tongue depressor, dull pencil, or commercial tools used for this technique

3. No. 000 steel wool, no. 0000 for final polish

4. Pencil and newsprint paper

5. Pad of newspaper or cloth

6. Liver of sulphur

Clay Tiles and Buttons

1. Clay

2. Canvas or desk covering

3. Modeling tools and stamps

To Assemble Mural

1. Clear Silicone glue

2. Luan plywood, ⅛", cut slightly smaller than copper pieces

3. Copper nails

4. Wooden backing, plywood is fine

pencil, paint, and ink

10

Nature of the medium

Pencil

Pencil is the most important of the drawing media. The lead pencil is actually made of graphite, which is a mixture of clay and the mineral *graphite*. This mixture is in the form of a rod that is encased in cedar wood. The graphite pencil ranges from a hard 8H to a soft 8B. A pencil with a larger diameter of lead is a good choice for younger students since it tends to be stronger and makes a intense line on most paper surfaces.

Charcoal is often used as a drawing medium and comes in various hardnesses, ranging from very soft to a harder form. Charcoal produces a velvety surface that is easy to blend.

Charcoal pencils are also available with the charcoal encased in cedar wood. The white charcoal pencil is a chalklike medium which is used on colored paper.

From black to gray water-soluble pencils are good for light to dark value drawings, or the pencil application can be diluted with water to make a wash of varying tones of gray.

Colored pencils are not like pastels in that they cannot be blended. Building up layers of cross-hatching can make an optical mix of color. An optical mix of color is a visual effect whereby overlaid colors appear to blend together.

Water-soluble colored pencils produce colored lines that dissolve on contact with water to give a colored wash that can be manipulated with a brush.

Erasers come in many forms. Gum and soap erasers are relatively inexpensive. Plastic erasers are more expensive, but are far superior and can be used on almost all papers. Kneaded erasers are pliable and nonabrasive, are excellent for highlighting, and can be molded into a point to lift out marks.

Watercolor

Watercolor is a brilliant, transparent, water-soluble painting medium. The pigment is available as color blocks in pans or in the more expensive and professional tubes.

The distinguishing property of watercolor is the sparkling quality resulting from its transparency. Most painters strive for a spontaneous effect by using whiteness of the paper and the fluid blending of the colors. Watercolor requires planning, as does any art form, but there can be a good deal of improvisation. Unlike oil paintings, watercolors are worked up quickly and rarely reworked.

The prerequisite to the successful use of watercolor is familiarity with its effects, achieved only through experimentation. Prior to painting, the paper should be dampened; then use bold, wet washes, with intermingled colors. Bold and fine strokes should be attempted, both wet and dry. In addition, try wet-on-dry techniques, blotting, tilting the paper to control the flow of color, various resists, and combinations of watercolor with other media. For serious efforts, the paper should be fastened to a board with paper tape after soaking, to allow the painting to dry without distorting the paper.

Three types of professional paper are available for watercolor painting:

Hot-pressed A smooth paper, for detailed work
Cold-pressed Moderate texture, and the most common
Rough Highly textured surface, producing clear, sharp effects

These professional papers are, however, beyond the needs and means of most children. A paper of fairly heavy weight, such as manila (or its equivalent) is a satisfactory, inexpensive paper for general classroom use.

Brushes used for watercolor painting should be washed frequently, and the cleaning water should be replaced often. Smocks or aprons are useful, as are newspapers and paper towels. Expect a mess; it's the only way to learn.

Tempera paint

Tempera is a water-soluble paint that is available as a liquid or a dry powder. It is an extremely versatile medium for classroom experiences in art and works well on a variety of surfaces. (When painted on nonporous materials, a small amount of liquid detergent should be added.)

Tempera may be spread by brush, roller, sponge, stick, or, if slightly reduced with water, it can be sprayed. Lights and darks are controlled by additions of white or black.

Unlike watercolor, tempera is an opaque medium; the appearance of the paper is not such a factor, nor does it have to be stretched. The paint may be mixed semidry and built up to create a textured surface. The other possibilities are too numerous to list here, but include screen printing, block printing, finger painting, and lettering.

Young children using a potentially messy medium, such as tempera, should wear smocks if possible. Clear water should be kept handy for keeping brushes clean. Small plastic or paper cups can be provided for the various colors.

Inks

A liquid vehicle and a soluble pigment are required for making ink, and this is satisfactory only if it can flow evenly and has good tinting strength. The earliest ink known, black carbon, was prepared by the early Egyptians and Chinese. This was followed by iron-gall (from growths on trees), bistre (burnt wood), and sepia (a secretion from cuttlefish). Today, there is a wide variety of inks, transparent and opaque, water-soluble and waterproof. Perhaps the type best known to the art student is India ink, which is really a waterproof carbon black. All of these inks serve effectively for *line* drawings; drawing *washes* are usually produced with ink sticks or watercolors. A tremendous number of inks can be made with fruit and vegetable juices, aniline, or coal dyes.

Pen and ink drawings are generally characterized by their clarity and precision. This, of course, can be modified by choice of instrument or method of control. It takes a great many strokes to produce an area of tone, which is the principal reason why pen and ink drawings are best created on a fairly small scale.

Pens

Those of us who take the familiar metal pen point for granted may not realize that it is a fairly new invention, which had not been successfully developed until the last century. The reed pen had been the pen of the ancients, and the quill pen the principal writing instrument from the medieval period to modern times. Most of us probably remember the use of quill pens in the drawings of Rembrandt and in the historical documents drawn up by the founders of our republic.

Today, the advent of ball, felt, and plastic tip pens have revolutionized the writing industry, as well as providing artists with yet another drawing tool. Artists, however, still make use of the earlier pen types on occasion, and even resort, at times, to matchsticks and other unlikely things for making ink marks on paper. Each drawing instrument leaves its own distinctive mark and helps to develop special interests and disciplines for the artist. In the hands of children, the mechanical metal points and felt and plastic tips are generally more suitable, but other kinds of pens might provide some exciting moments for the older child.

Brushes*

Brush making as a craft originated in France, later spreading into Germany. It became identified, quite naturally, with the carpenter, who turned brush maker by tying bristle to his finished handle and was known as *carpenter-brush maker.*

The art student learned from his master how to make brushes in the most elementary way—hair or bristle would be primitively washed and straightened, then tied onto a wooden handle or stick with string or cord. Modern brush making had its beginning as an industry in the early part of the nineteenth century.

Bristle is obtained from the body of hogs and boars found in Russia, Japan, Formosa, Korea, France, and Central and Eastern Europe. While all animal hair has *points,* bristle has *flags* (the individual bristle splits into two or three tiny forks on the end). Only pure natural white and black bristle with their original flags preserved are used in Liquitex® brushes.

Brown squirrel hair, known as Kazan, is generally found in the Kazan region of Russia. It has finer points and is more elastic than other squirrel hair, making it ideal for camel hair watercolor brushes.

Camel Hair is the trade name for squirrel hair and pony hair. Squirrel hair is obtained from the tails of various types of Russian squirrels (Scuirus Vulgaris Calotus).

Ox hair The best grades are selected and prepared from ox ear hair found in Central Europe and certain parts of North and South America. Ox ear hair with its strong body and fine tapered points is especially suited for brushes used in oil or heavier colors, since it will hold plenty of color, retain its elasticity, and perform smoothly. It will also perform well for show card and watercolor brushes, though here again the special qualities of red sable hair cannot be equaled.

Pony hair is obtained from pony hides. It ranges in color from light or dark brown and is straight and soft but does not have the fine points that distinguish squirrel hair.

Red sable hair The most valuable hair used in artist brushes is obtained from the tail of the kolinsky (Mustela Sibirica) found in the Amur region of Siberia, and in the Republic of Korea. Red sable hair, pale red in color with darker tips, has special qualities unmatched by any other hair—strength along with slim

Water color	Wash	Easel	Tempera and poster lettering	Oil red sable
	Round　Oval	Flat　　　Round	Round　Flat	Flat
Water color Wash, rendering ceramics, textile, leather-craft etc.	Water color Wash, sky rendering and tempera painting.	Flat Easel painting and oil painting. Flat Chiseled Easel painting in powdered tempera and other mediums. Round Camel hair for easel painting bristle for oil and easel painting.	Round Lettering and poster. Flat Lettering, posters, water color, ceramic glazing, varnishing, etc.	Round Fine detail in oil, ceramics, textile, etc. Flat Smooth textural effects on oil, ceramics, textiles, etc.

*Courtesy Consumer Products Division of Binney and Smith Inc.

body, extremely fine points, and great resiliency. Not only does it come to a needle-fine point or knifelike edge, but it retains its full elasticity, making it virtually irreplaceable for the best brushes used in any watercolor medium.

Sabeline hair is specially treated silken ox hair, light in color with exceptional points and lots of snap.

The care and use of brushes

1. Use watercolor brushes for watercolor and oil brushes for oil. Do not mix.
2. Clean brushes after each use. Neglect will cause the brush to lose its shape.
3. Never rest a brush vertically on its hairs. Suspend it, if possible; if not, rest it on its side.

Cleaning procedures

1. Water-based brush media:
   a. Repeatedly wash in cold water.
   b. Straighten the hairs to their natural shape before drying.
   c. Rinse repeatedly in clean water while in use.
2. Oil-based brush media:
   a. Squeeze paint from the brush with waste paper or rags.
   b. Lather on the palm of the hand with soap and water.
   c. Rinse repeatedly until all paint is removed.
   d. Restore the original shape of the bristles.
3. Acrylic and polymer brush media:
   a. Clean in cold water immediately after use.
   b. Clean in warm water if the paint has hardened.

NOTES: Clean house paint, oil stain, enamel, or varnish with turpentine, proprietary brush cleaner, or paint thinner.

Clean shellac or alcohol stain with alcohol.

For lacquer, use lacquer thinner.

Detergent soaps are effective for cleaning oil, acrylic, and watercolor brushes.

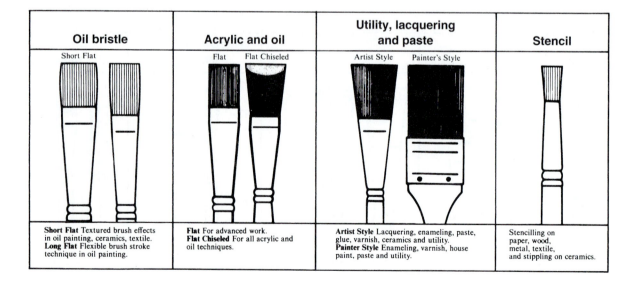

Oil bristle	Acrylic and oil	Utility, lacquering and paste	Stencil
Short Flat	Flat Flat Chiseled	Artist Style Painter's Style	
Short Flat Textured brush effects in oil painting, ceramics, textile. **Long Flat** Flexible brush stroke technique in oil painting.	**Flat** For advanced work. **Flat Chiseled** For all acrylic and oil techniques.	**Artist Style** Lacquering, enameling, paste, glue, varnish, ceramics and utility. **Painter Style** Enameling, varnish, house paint, paste and utility.	Stencilling on paper, wood, metal, textile, and stippling on ceramics.

Contour drawing

There are two contour drawing methods that are very useful in training the eye to see subtle variations in the object or objects being drawn. **Blind contour** drawing refers to the method of drawing without looking at the paper, and focusing all attention on the object. The trick is to try to get hand and eye to move at the same speed. As the eye slowly travels along the edge of the subject seeing every bump and curve, the hand and pencil or pen records this progress. It is important that this be considered an exercise and not a finished drawing. It must be stressed that this is an exercise and that there should be no peeking, which will help to improve the student's power of observation.

Semiblind contour drawing and the blind contour drawing are similar since the focus is still primarily on the subject. The difference is that the students can stop periodically to check their position with the drawing tool and the position of their eyes on the subject. It allows them to find their place. It also allows for more detail within the shapes of the subjects.

The blind and semiblind contour drawings should be done with a continuous line. Pencil and pen or marker work very well. With a pencil, it is tempting to stop and erase to make corrections, but with the use of the pen or marker, there is definite commitment because the line cannot be erased.

procedure

1. Set up several simple but similar objects to allow students to choose the objects they wish to draw. Talk about the shape of the objects; have the students handle the objects, if possible, to feel the shapes.
2. Talk about blind contour drawing as an exercise to help their powers of observation. Have them use one continuous line to draw the object without looking at their paper. If necessary, have one student hold another paper in a position to hide their drawing paper, but not the object being drawn. Keep it fun.
3. Introduce semiblind contour drawing. This is also an exercise using one continuous line to draw an object. Have students keep the attention focused primarily on the object, but glance down on the drawing paper to find their place from time to time. Have them add details on the inside of the shape, still using a continuous line.
4. Try drawing groups of objects or a person.

supplies

1. Newsprint or white drawing paper
2. Pencil, pen, or marker

connections

Aubrey Beardsley
Henri Matisse
Pablo Picasso
Ellsworth Kelly
Susan Rothenberg

supplies

1. Pencil
2. Newsprint or white drawing paper
3. Objects to draw

connections

Pablo Picasso
Henri Matisse
Aubrey Beardsley

Variation in line

Contour line is much more interesting when it has variations. Different line weights (dark and light) give the drawing more depth and make it more three-dimensional. The variation of the width of the line makes it more exciting and also adds to the depth. Light thin lines look distant with darker, thicker lines seeming close. Certain parts of the drawing are emphasized by variation of the line.

procedure

1. Students should do a simple semiblind contour continuous line drawing of several objects. Draw lightly with a pencil.
2. The students should decide which things are close and which are farther away, or which parts of the composition should be emphasized.
3. Go over the lines that are to be emphasized with more pressure on the pencil to make the lines darker and thicker.
4. Try doing a semiblind contour continuous line drawing and incorporate the heavy pressure where desired as it is being drawn. Lighten the pressure on the pencil where a thin light line is needed.

Tonal drawing

Tonal drawing refers to the use of the side of a short crayon piece or a thick felt pen to shade in the shape of the object being drawn. Objects that lend themselves to this method of drawing could include mechanical objects, plants, and other objects with more interesting shapes. Really simple shapes like balls and books are not as interesting. The drawing should be done quickly.

procedure

1. Discuss the use of tone. Liken it to drawing the shadow of the object without using line. Try one object. After the students feel comfortable, encourage them to try an object with a more complex contour or shape.
2. Try doing a tonal drawing with the crayon and no outlining. Do a contour drawing of the same object that overlaps the tonal drawing, but not necessarily matches it.
3. Try posing a student with other objects and use the drawing tool to scribble in the figure. Begin with the head and include the body, legs, arms, and feet. Don't bother with the neck. Work fast. Unusual poses are more fun. Change models often.

supplies

1. Short dark crayon piece
2. Newsprint or white drawing paper

connections

The Garden of Abdul Gasazi by Chris Van Allsburg, Houghton Mifflin, Boston, Mass., 1979

The Polar Express by Chris Van Allsburg, Houghton Mifflin, Boston, Mass., 1985

Henry Moore

Bleach drawing

procedure

1. Place colored paper on several thicknesses of newspaper.
2. Draw a picture with cotton swab dipped in liquid bleach. Give careful supervision to the use of the bleach.
3. The bleach will lighten the paper in seconds.
4. Allow the colored papers to dry separately from the newspaper.
5. Other media, such as markers, oil pastels, crayons, or ink, may be added to the picture when the bleach is dry.

CAUTION: Be very careful with the bleach. Make sure there is only a small amount of bleach in the plastic containers and that there is good ventilation.

Why Mozquitos Buzz in People's Ears by Vera Sarclemna, Dial Books, New York, 1975

connections

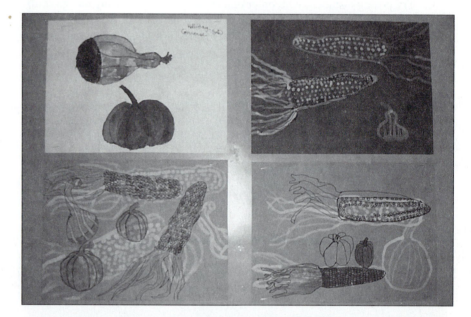

Playing with line

Line has different qualities, such as direction and thickness, and may be organized in many different ways. The lines of a given form, such as a curved line, if placed side by side, will make a pattern of line. The emphasis is on the relationship of the lines and the space between the lines.

procedure

1. Using any drawing subject, the shape is outlined lightly in pencil.
2. Each part of the drawn subject is filled with marker lines drawn parallel, repeated in variation. Explore many possibilities.
3. The pencil lines should be erased so that the form is visible because of the change in line patterns.

Linear perspective

Perspective refers to the method of creating the illusion of space by changing sizes, shapes, placement, and so on, into a unified spatial order. Linear perspective came into great use during the Renaissance. The artist focuses on one view seen from one position at a certain time. The use of eye level, guide lines, and vanishing points gave art using this method a view of mathematical exactness. A knowledge of perspective, for the older student, can be very helpful in placing objects and their shapes and sizes in a picture plane. It must be understood that drawing in perspective should be viewed as an exercise. Some students will see it as a solution to problems they may have drawing, while other students will have difficulty understanding or "seeing" perspective. Consequently, the introduction of perspective is fine, but care must be taken not to view it as a total solution to spatial relationships in a drawing or painting.

One-point linear perspective

One-point perspective refers to the view when one is **face on** a flat plane, such as the end of a room, a hallway, or a long frontal view of buildings, streets, and lines of trees or light posts down a street.

procedure

1. Draw a straight line lightly across the paper. This is the **horizon line** or **eye level line.** This line refers to the artist's height and usually is a little above the center of the paper. With the end of the ruler at the top of the paper and the edge along the side edge, measure down 4″ to 5″ and put a dot. Do the same on the other side edge of the paper. Join the dots so that this line is straight.
2. Put in the **vanishing point.** This point can be close to the center of the horizon line, but can be interesting if it is off center.
3. Establish the flat plane in the picture. Draw from the corners closest to the vanishing point to the vanishing point. This will be the angled shape of the sides. Draw straight lines to connect the angled lines. The lines should follow the edges of the original plane.

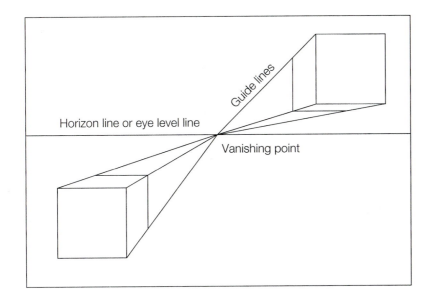

NOTE: Some possible subjects to draw in one-point perspective:

A room
A hallway
Looking down a street with buildings on each side
Looking down railroad tracks
Rectangles and squares in space
Block letters in space

connections

Felippo Brunelleschi
Leon Battista Alberti
Sandro Botticelli
Antonio Canaletto
Edward Hopper
Vincent Van Gogh

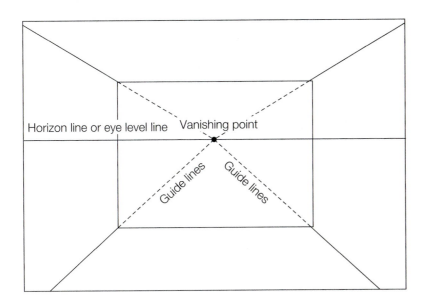

Two-point linear perspective

Two-point perspective is used when the artist views a corner or leading edge instead of a flat plane, such as a wall. This will make the shapes seem to be at angular positions.

procedure

1. Begin by drawing in the horizon or eye level line. This line is relative to the height of the artist. To make a straight line, measure from the top of the paper and make a guide dot on one edge or end of the paper. Do the same on the other end and draw a light line joining the two guide dots. The vanishing points should be placed one on each end of the horizon line.

2. Begin drawing the subject by drawing a vertical line for the corner closest to the artist. From the top and bottom corners of the vertical, guide lines are drawn to each of the vanishing points. This establishes the sides and tops and bottoms of the shape. The width of the shape is determined by other vertical lines. The lines in a two-point perspective are drawn to the vanishing point, or they are vertical lines.

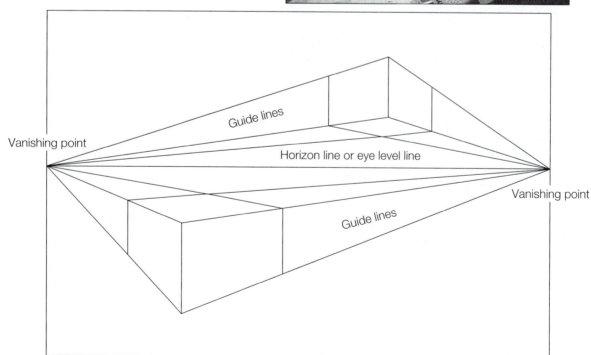

Drawing with ink

procedure

1. Pen and ink drawing is capable of arousing great interest if approached in an experimental manner. For instance, pen points of different types create varied lines, and these lines in turn may be combined with each other to create stippled, crosshatched, scumbled, and other textural effects.

2. Brush and ink drawing is a highly expressive medium due to the flexibility of the brush line. The quality of line may be controlled by the type of brush (bristle or sable), wide or narrow, fully or sparsely haired; the hand pressure applied; the quantity of ink carried by the brush; and the calculating or spontaneous attitude of the artist.

   As in most drawing, greater freedom is obtained from the brush by avoiding the grip used in writing. Instead, hold the brush between the thumb and forefingers while supporting the hand on the other three fingers. The movement of the brush should be initiated with the body ("body English") and directed through the arm. Drawing done with the fingers or wrists is more suited to the development of surface details.

3. Stick and ink is a lesser-known drawing procedure, but one that has enough individuality to justify its frequent use. In technique it is very simple—merely dip an absorbent piece of wood into the ink, allow it to become semisaturated, and draw as you would with a pen. Interesting effects may be obtained by using sticks with frayed, sharp, broad, and smooth ends.

connections

Henry Moore
Rembrandt Harmenozuon van Rijn
Honoré Daumier
Giovanni Batista Tiepolo

NOTE: Ink is very effective when used with other media. It may be added to watercolor, tempera, and crayon to enhance the brilliance of colors or provide accents and outline. The above may, in turn, be used over ink. When ink is used on wet paper, the results are unexpected and interesting.

Rembrandt used both pen and brush in this drawing. The Metropolitan Museum of Art, New York, The H. O. Havemeyer Collection. Bequest of Mrs. H. O. Havemeyer, 1929. (29.100.934)

chapter ten: pencil, paint, and ink

Stippling or ink dots

supplies

1. Marker; Sharpie black works well. Dark or soft pencil may be used

2. White drawing paper

procedure

1. Draw the design lightly on a piece of white paper.
2. Begin to place dots of ink by touching the marker point to the paper, lifting it and putting it down again. Begin with the darkest values.
3. By placing the dots very close together with little space between them, the area will be shaded and dark. By allowing more space between the dots the value will be lighter.

Plastic or felt tip pen or marker drawing

Many different kinds of markers are available, and all can be useful for different projects. Permanent markers are markers that will not smear or dissolve if water or anything moist is put on top or near the marker line or area. Permanent markers come in many different colors, and the points or tips may be extra fine, fine, chisel point, wedge point, or broad point. Permanent markers sometimes have an unpleasant odor, and clean up is a little more difficult.

There are even more types of watercolor markers or pens on the market. The watercolor marker or pen will smear or diffuse if water or a moist material is placed near it. These pens have different types of tips and many different colors.

Classic colors usually refer to the primary and secondary colors with the addition of black and brown.

Tropical colors are pastels and include gray.

Bold colors are intermediate colors.

Fluorescent colors are very bright.

Multicultural colors include all different flesh tones.

Crazy tips are markers with split nibs.

Changeables use a color changer that looks white, but when it is drawn over the other colors in the package it will turn that color into a new one. Yellow turns to fuchsia and so on. This type of marker is wonderful to use to make patterns.

Overwriters come with two different kinds of markers in the package. Under colors are used on the paper first and over colors are used on top of the first color.

procedure

1. Use a preliminary light outline drawing in pencil on the paper.
2. Draw over the pencil lines with marker or pen and fill in with color.

supplies

1. Paper, paper-covered object, or cloth
2. Multicolored plastic or felt tip pens or markers
3. Pencil

NOTE: Experimenting with different kinds of markers is very exciting. They can be used with any subject, the results are immediate, and the colors are wonderful.

Water-based pen marker and watercolors

procedure

1. Discuss the subject chosen. Discussion should include pictures of the subject and pictures of the subject as illustrated by artists of the past.
2. Draw main parts of the design lightly on the white paper.
3. When satisfied with the composition, add lines with the water-based pen or marker on some of the main lines.
4. With the tip of the brush, stroke water and color next to the line on the inside of the shape. It's important to use single strokes going in the same direction to apply the paint and water. the ink will "fuzz" into the paint stroke. A back and forth stroke will make the color very muddy.

connections

Follow the Dream by Peter Sis, Alfred Knopf, New York, N.Y. 1991.

Komodo by Peter Sis, Greenwillow, New York, N.Y. 1993.

Owen by Kevin Henkes, Greenwillow, New York, N.Y. 1993.

William Blake

George Groz

Eugene Delacroix

Ernest H. Shepard (Winnie the Pooh)

Raoul Dufy

Alternative watercolor techniques

Add other techniques, such as printing the watercolor brush. Dip the brush into paint, fan the bristles with one finger and touch them down to the paper and up, and down again. This creates modeled color. It dries quickly and other colors can be printed on top. The fanned brush can also be dragged across the paper to create thin parallel lines on the paper.

Dry brush refers to having a little water mixed with color on the brush and dragging it across a textured surface. The color picks up on the high points of the texture, leaving the lower points free of the color applied. In the case of painting on paper, very often a wash or light coat of color is applied first and that color shows through the dry brush.

The brush handle can also be used. Over a damp painting, details can be put on the painting by dipping the end of the brush handle in paint and drawing with it. This results in an interesting irregular line.

John Marin, Phippsburg, Maine. 1932, watercolor, h. 15¼ w. 19⅞ in. Marin let the white paper show through, as does the rubber cement. The Metropolitan Museum of Art, Alfred Stieglitz Collection, 1949. (49.70.145)

Watercolor painting on damp paper

supplies

1. Transparent watercolors
2. Brush
3. Drawing paper
4. Water container
5. Blotting material such as a rag, sponge, or paper towel

 connections

The Missing Tarts by B.G. Hennessy, Viking, New York, 1988

Morris's Disappearing Bag by Rosemary Wells, Dial Books, New York, 1993

Why Mosquitos Buzz in People's Ears. by Vera Aardemna Dial Books, New York, 1975

Chicken Sunday by Patricia Polacco, Philomel Books, New York, 1992

Aunt Chip and the Great Triple Creek Dam Affair, Philomel Books, New York, 1996

Wassily Kandinsky

Emile Nolde

Berthe Morisot

William Morris

William Blake

Albrecht Durer

J.M.W. Turner

John Constable

Winslow Homer

Paul Klee

John Marin

Auguste Rodin

Paul Cézanne

Edouard Manet

Paul Gauguin

Sir Edward Burne-Jones

procedure

1. Soak the paper thoroughly in water.
2. Lay the wet paper on a desk top or drawing board and smooth out all the wrinkles.
3. Blot up any pools of water with the blotting material.
4. Paint directly on the damp paper. Make sure to use more pigment than water, for the colors tend to lose their brilliance when dry. Paint the light colors first, and add second and third colors before the paper dries, so colors will mingle and blend into spontaneous and soft shapes. After the paint is applied, avoid reworking.
5. Leave some areas unpainted to add sparkle.
6. Details, if necessary, can be painted in when the painting is dry.

 NOTE: Damp paper watercolors painting must be done hurriedly to be lively. Don't expect complete success on the first try, for only experience will tell just how wet the paper must be and how much paint should be used. Clean the brush and the water in the container often.

Watercolor wax resist

procedure

1. Place wax paper over the drawing paper.
2. Draw heavily on the wax paper with a pencil or the wooden end of a brush. The pressure will transfer the wax to the drawing paper.
3. Remove the wax paper and paint over the drawing with transparent watercolor. The lines drawn with the pencil will remain white.

supplies

1. Wax paper, wax stencil paper. Paraffin or a wax candle can also be used for drawing and will achieve the same result

2. Pencil

3. Paper

4. Transparent watercolors

5. Brush

6. Water container

connections

Marc Tobey
Henry Moore

supplies

1. Watercolor
2. Cotton Swabs
3. White paper

connections

Paul Signac
Camille Pissarro
Georges Seurat

Pointillism

The impressionists' theories on light and color led to a more scientific approach to painting. Georges Seurat and Paul Signac divided all colors into their primary parts and then applied small dots or dabs of pure colors to the canvas to build up variations of shade without losing the brightness of the colors. This technique, called *divisionism* at first but now called *pointillism,* relied upon the viewer's eye to mix the color. For instance, if yellow dots are placed next to blue dots, the color area will look like green from a distance and the value and intensity of that green will vary depending upon the number and color of dots used.

procedure

1. Draw a design lightly on white paper.
2. Fill in the main objects with color by touching the cotton swab first into color and then touching it down on the paper within the pencil lines. Continue to print the dots close together but with a bit of white paper between them.
3. The dots will dry quickly, particularly with watercolor, and dots of another color can be put in between and overlapping the original color.
4. More than two colors can be used but the original form should still be visible.
5. The background space around the main objects should also be filled in with dots of color to finish the painting.

Small colored dots were excitingly juxtaposed, with our vision sometimes blending them together. Georges Seurat, Study for Le Chahut, *1889—oil on canvas 21–7/8 × 18–3/8". Albright-Knox Art Gallery, Buffalo, New York, General Purchase Fund. 1943.*

Soda straw painting

procedure

1. Place several little pools of variously colored paint on the paper with a brush.
2. Point the end of the straw at the pools of paint and blow air in the other end of the straw, pointing the straw in the direction the paint is meant to move.
3. Remind the students to take breaths.
4. Overlapping the colors creates numerous blending effects.
5. Add details with paint, paper, or other media when the blown paint has dried.

supplies

1. Paper
2. Watercolor paint or thin tempera
3. Soda straws
4. Brush

connections   Chinese painting

Sponge painting

1. Sponge or cellulose sponge cut into a variety of sizes and shapes

2. Scissors

3. Watercolor or liquid tempera paint

4. Paper

5. Brush

procedure

1. Soak the paper thoroughly in water.
2. Lay the wet paper on a smooth surface and remove all the wrinkles and excess water.
3. Use small pieces of moist sponge as a brush by dipping them into the tempera paint.
4. Apply the paint to moist paper that may have general areas of a design marked with a pencil.
5. Details and accents can be added with a brush when the painting is dry.

VARIATION: Try sponge painting with the paint on dry paper rather than wet paper. The paint will dry fairly quickly and additional sponge painting in different colors may be done on top of the original sponge painting.

Tempera resist

procedure

1. Paint some areas of the paper with tempera as necessary to suggest the design. Leave much of the paper unpainted to allow the ink to be absorbed by these areas. The paint should be a fairly heavy body. The paint must be painted on the paper and not over another color.
2. When the paint is completely dry, paint over everything—tempera and paper—with India ink.
3. When the ink is dry, hold the drawing under running water, allowing the force of the water to dislodge the ink. Should this ink prove stubborn, its removal may be accelerated by light strokes of the finger. A certain amount of caution should be exercised in removing the ink. Excessive washing could remove too much of the paint and ink. However, many seeming disasters have turned out beautifully at second glance. Furthermore, any lost color can be replaced with watercolor, ink, crayon, or tempera.

connections

Oskar Kokoschka

Tempera painting on damp paper

1. Dry or liquid tempera paint
2. Brush
3. paper
4. Water container
5. Blotting material, such as a rag, sponge, or paper towel

NOTE: Damp paper tempera painting must be done hurriedly to be lively. Don't expect complete success on the first try, for only experience will tell just how wet the paper must be and how much paint should be used. Clean the brush and the water in the container often.

connections

Jacob Lawrence
Thomas Hart Benton
Andrew Wyeth
Ben Shann
Paul Klee
Peter Hurd
Charles Demuth

procedure

1. Soak the paper thoroughly in water.
2. Lay the wet paper on a desk top or drawing board and smooth out all the wrinkles.
3. Blot up any pools of water with the blotting material.
4. Paint directly on the damp paper. Make sure to use more pigment than water, for the colors tend to lose their brilliance when dry. Paint the light colors first, and add second and third colors before the paper dries, so colors will mingle and blend into spontaneous and soft shapes. After the paint is applied, avoid reworking.
5. Leave some areas unpainted to add sparkle.
6. Details, if necessary, can be painted in when the painting is dry.

Fold and dye

procedure

1. Fold the paper in different patterns.
2. Dip the corner of the folded shape into the dye and lift immediately.
3. When the corners have been dipped, allow the paper to dry before unfolding. Unfold very carefully.

These are a few of the folds possible. Experiment to find others.

Fold in half, fold in half again.

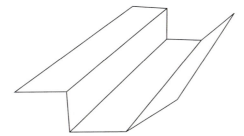

NOTE: This is a great way to introduce tie and dye. It is also a good way to investigate color mixing.

Fold the fold-over into triangles as illustrated.

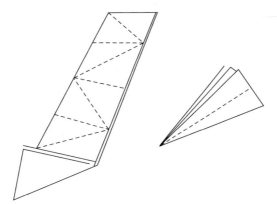

Fold the paper into accordion pleats. Fold the fold-over into small squares as illustrated.

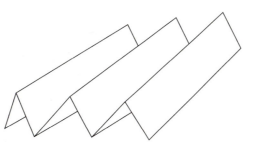

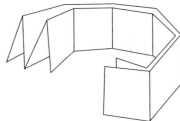

Try possible folds below.

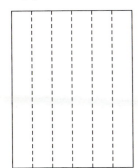
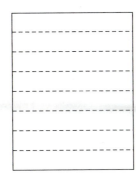
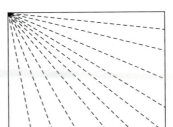
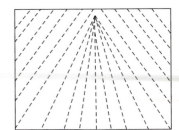

Finger painting

supplies

1. Finger paint (recipe on p. 393)
2. Glossy or glazed paper
3. Sponge
4. Iron
5. Acrylic media
6. Water must be available in a sink or large container, to soak the paper

connections

Very Hungry Caterpillar by Eric Carle, Putnam Publishing Group, New York, 1984

Animals, Animals by Eric Carle, Philomel Books, New York, 1989

NOTE: It is suggested that only a few children work at one time unless a large room with adequate table space is available. Finger painting can be used to decorate items of many kinds including wastebaskets, book jackets, or portfolio covers.

Colored paper cut to particular shapes and pasted in place on finger paintings adds further detail.

A comb or piece of notched paper will give good results if it is drawn through the wet paint.

A stencil cut from paper and pasted over a finger painting is another variation. If finger painting is used as a decorative covering, it should be painted with acrylic medium for permanence.

procedure

1. Soak the paper in water in any of the following ways, making sure both sides are thoroughly wet.
   a. Put the paper under the faucet in a sink, or
   b. Roll the paper into a tube and submerge it in a container of water, or
   c. Spread the paper on a table and soak it with sponge and water. The paper adheres more firmly to a surface if wet on both sides.
2. Place the wet paper on a smooth and flat surface. Do not place it too close to the edge of the tabletop, as the paint may drip over. Make sure the glossy side of the paper is up and all wrinkles and air bubbles are smoothed out. Satisfactory finger paintings cannot be made on an uneven or unsteady surface.
3. Place approximately 1 tablespoonful of finger paint on the wet paper. If powdered finger paint is used, sift it lightly over the entire paper; more can be applied later if necessary. Paint applied too heavily will crack or chip off when dry.
4. Spread the paint evenly over the entire surface of paper with the palm of the hand or the forearm to create the background of the finger painting.
5. Varied movements of the hands and forearms in various positions will create interesting effects. The side of the hand, when held rigid and pulled over paper, makes long and delicate leaves. This same hand position moved in a zig-zag motion creates an altogether different effect. Experiment with a variety of hand and arm movements and positions. An infinite number of effects are possible by using the closed fist, bent fingers, open palm, heel of the hand, wrist, etc. Other various effects can be obtained by using a comb, a small notched piece of cardboard, etc. Areas of color can also be cleaned away with a sponge.
6. New beginnings can be made until the paper loses its gloss. If the finger paint becomes too sticky, sprinkle a few drops of water on the paper to allow the hand or arm to slide easily over the paper.
7. Spread the paper or newspaper on the floor in a seldom-used area. Lift the finger painting by two corners and lay it on some newspapers.
8. Allow the painting to dry. Press it on the unpainted side with a hot iron. **The iron should be left in the hands of the teacher.**

Gouache

Gouache, pronounced gwăsh, is a technique that mixes watercolor with another material, usually gum arabic, to make it opaque. In this case, white powdered tempera is mixed with the color to make it opaque and make a tint of that color.

procedure

1. Draw lightly on the colored construction paper.
2. Dip the brush in water and in paint and finally touch the brush into the powdered white tempera.
3. Paint.
4. Paint will dry quickly, and additional details can be added to enrich the painting.

supplies

1. Watercolors
2. Brush
3. White powdered tempera
4. Dark-colored construction paper

Max in Hollywood, Baby by Maira Kalman, Viking Penguin, New York, 1992

Hippopot by J. Patrick Lewis, Dial Books, New York, 1990

Camille Pissarro

Pablo Picasso

Fernard Leger

Mark Tobey

Jacob Lawrence

Marc Chagall

Morris Graves

Jacob Lawrence, Cabinet Makers, *1946. Gouache with pencil underdrawing on paper. 21 3/4 × 30 in. (55.2 × 76.2 cm). Hirshhorn Museum and Sculpture Garden, Smithsonian Institution, Washington, D.C. Gift of Joseph H. Hirshhorn, 1966. Photograph by Lee Stalsworth.*

Dot painting

1. Many of the paintings are done in ochre colors that are adjusted to produce other desert colors. It might be well to limit the colors. Thickened watercolor or acrylic paints should be put in small containers. Pan watercolors would work well

2. Small dowels, swabs

3. White drawing paper, or earth tone paper. Smaller-size paper might be advisable

The Aboriginal people of central Australia produce paintings on bark, paper, canvas, and other materials by painting or printing dots in patterns of color. These dots of color are very unlike the dots or dashes of color applied by the impressionists. The emphasis with this indigenous art is on the pattern and the stories they tell rather than the optical mixing of color. The art is a means for the Aboriginal people to pass on the history, customs, and beliefs of their people. These "dreaming stories" using land, plants, animals, and spirits as subjects keep their culture alive. The art is part of their culture and is part of their lives, not separated from it. Depending upon the particular group or people doing the painting or craft, the designs may be abstract or geometric. The designs used in ceremonial body painting and sand painting are reflected in the painting done today. Aboriginal art has become connected with other cultures.

procedure

1. Discuss the Aboriginal culture and the dreaming stories. Show books and pictures of the Aboriginal dot painting. What symbols are used by the Aboriginal people to convey the story? Discuss symbols to be used.
2. Draw the design lightly with a pencil on the drawing paper.
3. Put colors in small containers or have the students use pan watercolors.
4. Using swabs or small dowel sticks, apply paint to the surface of the paper. There should be a little space between the dots of color. Fill in the areas of the design with dots of the chosen colors.

Aboriginal work—Australia

Line painting

Line drawing in ochres is another traditional painting technique used by the Aboriginal people of Australia. The line paintings can still be found in the undercuts of some of the rock formations that have been sacred for generations. Monochrome figures and images are also common at these art sites. Ochres, naturally occurring pigments, are still the media of choice for some of the artists. Ochres are similar to the Western acrylics of yellow ochres, light reds, and white. Charcoal from campfires was used for black. To prepare the pigment, the artist would crush or grind the ochre or charcoal into a fine powder. Water and a binding agent were mixed with this powder. Traditionally, animal blood, egg white, beeswax or resin from plants were used as a binding agent. PVA glues are now used as a substitute. Brushes were made from natural fiber such as grasses or reeds or human hair. Bark or rock was the traditional painting surface, but now heavy thick cotton rag paper is used.

Before the lines are painted, a background is applied to the surface. This background was traditionally painted in red ochre although other colors are now used. A textured background is sometimes produced by blowing pigment from the mouth or spraying it from a spray gun. All figures or objects are kept in the picture surface. The artist uses a thin brush to create "rarrk" (or hatching and cross hatching) using smooth strokes away from the artist with the point of the brush directed toward the artist. Layer upon layer of lines are applied. Often, internal structures or organs are depicted, and the name *X-ray art* is sometimes used for this style of painting.

Subjects usually include animals, fish or birds, snakes, plants and spirits. The rainbow serpent is one of the most important of the subjects used with this technique.

procedure

1. Discuss the Aboriginal people and the use of art to convey the beliefs and values of their culture to their children. Show pictures of the art.
2. Unless working on a colored surface, paint the surface of the heavy paper to prepare it.
3. Draw the plan for the painting on the surface.
4. Paint the outlines of the design with a thin brush. Some areas may be painted with solid pigment, but others are painted using parallel lines, usually at a slant, often with other parallel lines going across the first lines to form cross-hatching.

VARIATION: Make a line painting combined with a print technique as a variation to use with younger students. Cut different sizes of cardboard or mat board. Place ochre yellow, red brown, black, and white paint in shallow pans, dip the edge of the piece of cardboard in the paint, and print lines close together within the drawing. When that dries, print lines close together to simulate the cross-hatching. Brushes could be used to paint in some of the parts of the drawing.

supplies

1. Paint, acrylic works well
2. Thin brush
3. Heavy white drawing paper or illustration board. Heavy-colored paper could be used
4. Pencil

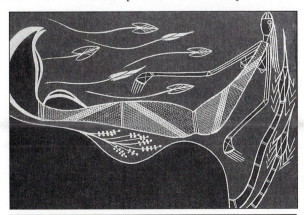

Aboriginal drawing — Australia

chapter ten: pencil, paint, and ink   195

paper and cardboard

11

Paper textures

The flat surface of a piece of paper can be changed into a textured surface by many methods, five of which are suggested below. Also see Paper Sculpture.

procedure

Method a

Cut or slit a paper with a cutting instrument, and push the shapes out from the back. Be sure to have a piece of cardboard under the work when cutting with the X-acto knife.

 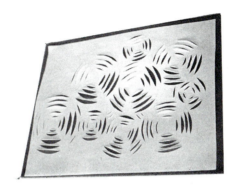

CAUTION: Extreme care and supervision must be given whenever X-acto knives are used. Safety instructions should be given before **every** use of the knives. X-acto knives are now sold with safety caps, but separate caps may be purchased for older knives. Heavy corrugated cardboard should always be placed under the paper or material being cut. The X-acto knife is held like a pencil, with the fingers holding the knife on the textured ring. The slanted, sharpened edge should be directly over the line to be cut, and the position of the knife or the paper should be changed if the line changes direction. Keep the fingers of the holding hand out of the way of the blade, usually above the cutting area. Remind students often to check themselves and the position of the knife and their hands. The safety cap should be on the knife at all times except when actually in use.

Method b

Form numerous small three-dimensional paper shapes of various colors, and fasten to a piece of paper in a contrasting color to form a texture picture.

A   Enlargement of A

supplies

1. Paper
2. Scissors or X-acto knife
3. Paste, glue stick, or thick white glue
4. Piece of cardboard (to be placed under work when cutting)

Method c

Curled paper strips, fastened close together on a piece of paper, will also create an interesting texture.

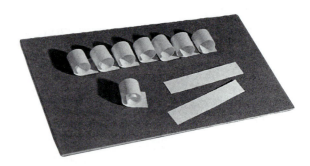

Method d

Strips of paper with one edge cut in a decorative manner and the other edge folded to a right angle, and then fastened close together on a base paper, create interesting textures.

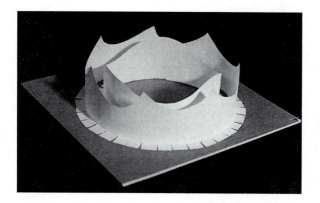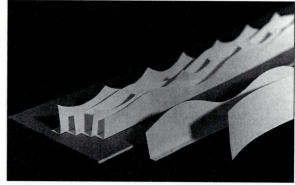

Method e

Scoring and folding a flat sheet of paper will create numerous three-dimensional textures. Scoring is achieved by pressure with a comparatively dull, smooth instrument, such as closed scissors or a metal file, drawn across the paper in order to dent the paper so it can be folded more easily. After folding and creasing the paper on the scored lines, it can be opened and forced into lowered and raised creases.

Mat board—Cut and peel

supplies

1. X-acto knife
2. Colored mat board

procedure

1. Cut lightly into the surface and around each shape that has been previously drawn on colored mat board. **X-acto knives must be used with safety precautions and supervision.**
2. Peel out each area after it has been cut.
3. Contrasting color areas can be added with colored paper, paint, crayons, or colored pencils.

⚠ CAUTION: Extreme care and supervision must be given whenever X-acto knives are used. Safety instructions should be given before **every** use of the knives. X-acto knives are now sold with safety caps, but separate caps may be purchased for older knives. Heavy corrugated cardboard should always be placed under the paper or material being cut. The X-acto knife is held like a pencil, with the fingers holding the knife on the textured ring. The slanted, sharpened edge should be directly over the line to be cut, and the position of the knife or the paper should be changed if the line changes direction. Keep the fingers of the holding hand out of the way of the blade, using the space above the cutting area. Remind students often to check themselves and the position of the knife and their hands. The safety cap should be on the knife at all times except when actually in use.

supplies

supplies

Cardboard relief

procedure

1. Cut a cardboard base on which to build a design.
2. Cut a second piece of cardboard into shapes of different sizes and glue to the cardboard base.
3. Cut a third piece of cardboard into shapes smaller in size than the previous pieces and glue in place.
4. Continue to cut and glue smaller and smaller pieces until a design of different levels results.
5. Cut and add details, if necessary.
6. **Use safety scissors if available.**

supplies

1. Soft cardboard such as tablet backing or shirt boards
2. Glue
3. Scissors
4. Paint
5. Brush

Three-dimensional picture or poster

supplies

1. Colored construction paper
2. Pencil
3. Scissors
4. Paste, glue, or tape

procedure

1. Cut the subjects from a drawing or painting. **Use safety scissors if available.**
2. Make a number of small cardboard stilts of various sizes, and paste them on the back of each cutout. A narrow strip of cardboard folded into a square shape and fastened with a piece of tape makes an ideal stilt. Jacob's ladders may also be used. (See Paper Sculpture chapter.)
3. Paste each cutout on background paper, making sure that any subject that is meant to appear close to the viewer projects higher from the paper than those meant to be in the distance.

   Try other methods of creating a three-dimensional effect in the paper.

supplies

1. White drawing paper
2. Markers, crayons, or oil pastels
3. X-acto knives or scissors
4. Corrugated cardboard

 connections

Alexander Calder

Stabile

procedure

1. Draw a frame around the edge of the paper to ensure a solid base.
2. Draw the picture lightly, keeping the shapes from overlapping except when it is necessary to support the weight of the shape. Don't allow the shapes to be too tall.
3. Add color to the shapes. Color around the shapes on the base is optional.
4. Cut the sides and tops of the shapes, leaving the bottom edge as a hinge to fold up and support the shape. **Scissors or X-acto knives may be used, but remember to use caution.**

CAUTION: Extreme care and supervision must be given whenever X-acto knives are used. Safety instructions should be given before *every* use of the knives. X-acto knives are now sold with safety caps, but separate caps may be purchased for older knives. Heavy corrugated cardboard should always be placed under the paper or material being cut. The X-acto knife is held like a pencil, with the fingers holding the knife on the textured ring. The slanted, sharpened edge should be directly over the line to be cut, and the position of the knife or the paper should be changed if the line changes direction. Keep the fingers of the holding hand out of the way of the blade, using the space above the cutting area. Remind students often to check themselves and the position of the knife and their hands. The safety cap should be on the knife at all times except when actually in use.

Pierced paper

procedure

1. Discuss the subject chosen. Talk about the subject. Showing pictures of stained glass windows may be helpful because the look is similar.
2. Plan the design on newsprint. It is important to remember to have connections between parts of the paper, so there will need to be "bridges" of paper left between the cutout shapes. Therefore, the main piece of construction paper will not fall apart and the image will be clear.
3. Draw a frame around the edge of the construction paper. This will serve as a reminder for the student not to draw or cut past the frame line.
4. Draw the design on the construction paper. Begin cutting with the X-acto knife. It is important to observe all safety rules.
5. When all of the shapes are cut out of the construction paper, begin fitting pieces of colored material over the openings. Use the side with the pencil lines. Glue in place.

CAUTION: Extreme care and supervision must be given whenever X-acto knives are used. Safety instructions should be given before *every* use of the knives. X-acto knives are now sold with safety caps, but separate caps may be purchased for older knives. Heavy corrugated cardboard should always be placed under the paper or material being cut. The X-acto knife is held like a pencil, with the fingers holding the knife on the textured ring. The slanted, sharpened edge should be directly over the line to be cut, and the position of the knife or the paper should be changed if the line changes direction. Keep the fingers of the holding hand out of the way of the blade, using the space above the cutting area. Remind students often to check themselves for the position of the knife and their hands. The safety cap should be on the knife at all times except when directly in use.

supplies

1. Newsprint
2. Colored construction paper—black paper gives the most contrast
3. Pencil
4. Glue stick, or thick white glue
5. X-acto knife, and corrugated cardboard
6. Scissors

NOTE: The colored materials to place under the openings can include oil pastel on paper, watercolor, other pieces of colored construction paper.

connections

The Emperor and the Kite by Jane Yolen, World Publishing Co., Cleveland, Ohio, 1967

Color Zoo, by Lois Ehlert, J. B. Lippincott, New York, 1989.

Color Farm by Lois Ehlert, J. B. Lippincott, New York, 1990

Colored tissue paper

supplies

supplies

1. Colored tissue in desired colors
2. Mounting board, canvas board, or heavy cardboard
3. White glue
4. Clear spray
5. Scissors

 NOTE: Colored tissue paper may be used to decorate a wide variety of items in the home, such as mirrors, wastebaskets, planters, or recipe boxes. Tissue blends with glue; work light to dark.

 connections *The Very Lonely Firefly,* by Eric Carle, Philomel Books, New York, 1995

Animals, Animals by Eric Carle, Philomel Books, New York, 1989

procedure

1. Cover the board with a thin solution of the glue and water.
2. Cut or tear pieces of colored tissue: press these in place on the glue-covered board while glue is wet. **Use safety scissors if available.**
3. Add additional layers of the paper with glue solution between each layer, until the desired richness of color is achieved.
4. Apply clear spray to protect the design. **Adequate ventilation is necessary when spray is used.**

VARIATION: Use black crayon or permanent marker to draw on the mounting board before applying the tissue and glue. Drawing can also be done after the tissue dries and before it is sprayed.

Colored tissue transparent discs

procedure

1. Soak the larger reed in water until it can be bent into circles without breaking. (A fine reed may bend without being soaked.)
2. Cut to make the size circle desired, using the fine reed for the small circles and the medium reed for the larger ones. **Use safety scissors if available.**
3. Overlap the ends of the reed at least ½ inch on the small circles and more on the larger ones, then fasten with small strips of masking tape. Allow the reed to dry thoroughly. (It may be easier to allow the reed to dry partially before fastening with masking tape, as the tape will hold better.)
4. Cut a circle out of tissue paper a little larger than the reed frame.
5. Apply thick white glue to the reed and press onto the tissue circle.
6. Cut tissue designs in various colors.
7. Cover the design with thick white glue and place on tissue circle. Two, three, or more tissue designs may be placed one on top of another to achieve a really beautiful effect. These may be the same color or different colors.
8. Trim away the tissue extending beyond the frame.

supplies

1. Tissue paper in many bright colors
2. Fine and medium basket reed
3. Masking tape
4. Thick white glue
5. Sharp scissors

 NOTE: Above all, for the best results, work neatly. Draw circles with a compass and handle the tissue gently when applying the glue. The decorative discs may be used as units in a mobile, to decorate windows, plastic bottles, glass panels, or put on straight reed stems and arranged in a container as a bouquet.

Geometric design

procedure

1. Cut geometric shapes that are varied in size and color. **Use safety scissors if available.** Cutting some of these shapes into halves or quarters not only offers more variety of shapes but also correlates well with teaching fractions.
2. Group a number of geometric shapes together until they form a picture.
3. When satisfied with the arrangement, paste the shapes in place on background paper.

Fernand Leger, Three Women *(Le Grand dejeuner). 1921. Oil on canvas, 6′ ¼″ × 8′3″ (183.5 × 251.5 cm). The Museum of Modern Art, New York. Mrs. Simon Guggenheim Fund. Photograph © 1996 The Museum of Modern Art, New York.*

Corrugated cardboard

procedure

Method a

1. Cut out pieces of colored construction paper, corrugated cardboard, or both. **Use safety scissors if available.**
2. Paste these pieces on a piece of corrugated cardboard to form the desired pattern.
3. Accents can be added with ink, tempera paint, or crayon.

supplies

1. Corrugated cardboard
2. Scissors
3. Colored paper
4. Paste or thick white glue
5. Ink, paint, or crayon

Method b

1. Cut through the paper surface of a corrugated cardboard box with a *sharp knife* and peel out areas to expose the corrugations. **Use X-acto knife with caution.**
2. Color can be added with paints or crayons when the picture is complete.

supplies

1. Corrugated cardboard box
2. X-acto knife
3. Paint, ink, or crayons

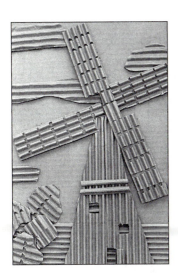

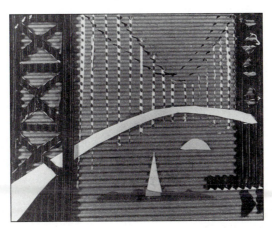

1. Corrugated
   cardboard

2. Tempera paint

3. Brush

4. Water container

Method c

Interesting effects are created by painting directly on the corrugated cardboard. Try painting in the ridges, on top of the ridges, or across the ridges. Further interest may be obtained by using one color inside the ridges and another one on top of the ridges.

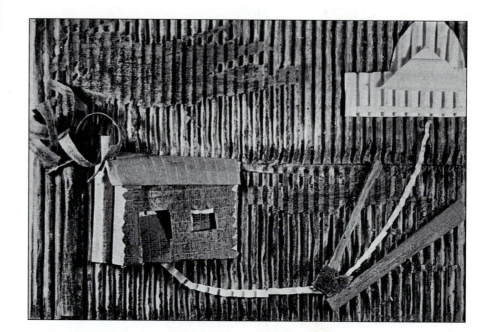

Cut paper design

procedure

1. Fold the paper into eighths as in illustration 1.
2. Cut numerous small shapes out of the paper until there is more paper cut away than there is remaining (Ill. 2). **Use safety scissors if available.**
3. Carefully unfold the paper so as not to tear it when opening.
4. The design can be mounted on a contrasting colored paper. Numerous designs can be created through an inventive approach using variously colored, shaped pieces under the cut design (Ill. 3).

1

2

3

Paper quilling

supplies

supplies

1. Corsage pin or round toothpick
2. Paper, cut into ¼"-wide strips, or commercial quilling strips may be used
3. White craft glue
4. Acrylic media
5. Wax paper

procedure

Method a
Two-Dimensional

1. Draw design on paper.
2. Tape design to hard surface with wax paper taped over design.
3. Roll piece of strip (approximately 3 inches long) around corsage pin or toothpick. Glue end to coil or quill to keep it from unrolling.
4. Make additional quills, shaping them as desired.
5. Place quills on wax paper over design and begin gluing quills together, using a toothpick or pin to apply glue. Do not glue to wax paper.
6. Glue from the center of the design out to the edges of the design (Ill. 1).
7. When complete, seal the finished quilling shape with clear acrylic media.

Method b
Three-Dimensional

1. Follow steps 1 through 4 in method a.
2. Glue quills to a solid three-dimensional armature or shape, such as a blown egg, box, or Paris craft object (Ill. 2).
3. Seal with acrylic media.

Basic Rolls

 Loose Roll

 Tight Roll

 Eye Roll

 Rain Drop

Square

Triangle

Heart

Scrolls

Scroll

 "S" Shape

 Heart

 "V" Shape

 Decorative Scroll

1

2

Method c
1. Follow the same steps in method a, but use strips of construction paper 1" thick and wrap the strip around a pencil point or a thin dowel. This will create a large version of the quilled shape.

Paper mosaic

A mosaic is a design made by the close placement of small pieces of colored material. Historically, mosaics can be traced back to classical antiquity. They were composed of small pieces of colored glass or stones imbedded in a binding agent.

procedure

1. Make a light pencil drawing on the background paper.
2. Cut the colored paper into small fairly uniform sizes. **Use safety scissors if available.** (Try to keep the pieces sorted by color to save time later when pasting.)
3. Apply the paste or glue to the individual pieces and place them on the drawing. Leave a narrow space of background color between the pieces of paper. A corsage pin will help in picking up the bits of paper.
4. Continue pasting until the design is completed.

supplies

1. Scissors
2. Colored-paper scraps or colored magazine pictures
3. Paste, glue stick or thick white glue
4. Corsage or hat pin (for lifting pieces of paper)
5. Pencil
6. Background paper

NOTE: Other interesting mosaics can be made with confetti, seeds, grain, punched paper bits, and so on.

connections

Cleopatra by Diane Stanley and Peter Vennema, Morrow Junior Books, New York, 1994

Roman Mosaics

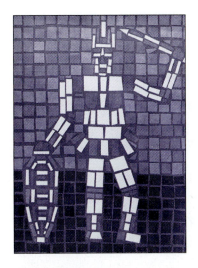

supplies

1. Colored paper
2. Scissors
3. Translucent paper, such as tracing paper, onion skin paper, or tissue paper
4. Thick white glue

Distance silhouette

procedure

1. Make an outline drawing on paper with pencil.
2. Cut out the shapes to appear in the background, and glue them to a sheet of white paper (Ill. 1). Use safety scissors if available.
3. Place a piece of the translucent paper over the cutout shapes, and hold in place by folding and the gluing to the back (Ill. 2).
4. Cut out shapes, and rubber cement these for the middle ground of the original drawing on the above translucent paper (Ill. 3).
5. Cover this with another translucent paper, and hold it in place by folding over and gluing to the back (Ill. 4).
6. Complete the picture by rubber cementing objects on the top of the translucent paper (Ill. 5).

Doug Maguire,
Peter Bruegel the Elder
J.M.W. Turner

NOTES: As long as the first silhouette is visible through the translucent paper, the procedure can be continued. Translucent paper that is too heavy reduces the number of silhouettes. Designs cut from colored cellophane and placed between translucent paper make interesting window decorations.

This is a good way to introduce aerial perspective.

Atmospheric (aerial) perspective is the illusion of space produced by lightening values, making details indistinct, lessening the contrasts in value, and making the colors of objects appear more neutral as they recede.

1

2

3

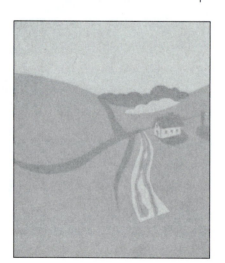

4

5

Cut paper rubbings

procedure

1. Cut related shapes from pieces of construction paper (Ill. 1). **Use safety scissors if available.**
2. Arrange the shapes on another piece of paper; if desired, the pieces may overlap (Ill. 2).
3. Fix the pieces in place with glue.
4. Place another piece of paper over the affixed shapes (Ill. 3).
5. Rub crayons over the paper, using overlapping strokes. The images of the cut shapes will appear (Ill. 4).

 NOTE: Textures may be rubbed onto a piece of paper from any rough surface by laying the paper over the object and rubbing the paper with graphite pencil, crayon, oil pastel, or colored pencils.

supplies

1. Scissors
2. Crayons, oil pastels, or colored pencils
3. Drawing paper
4. Construction paper or tag board
5. Thick white glue

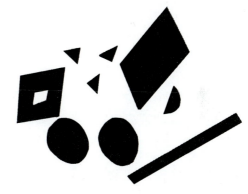

1

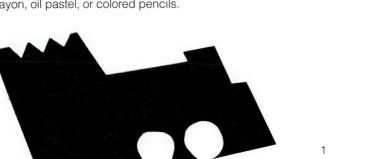

2

3

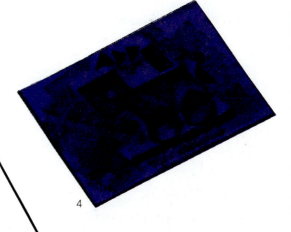

4

Torn paper picture

procedure

1. Determine the subject to be treated, and tear the paper into shapes adaptable to the subject.
2. Arrange these torn shapes on a piece of paper that will serve as a background.
3. Paste each piece in place to complete the picture.

VARIATION: Begin with the main shape of the object to be made from the torn paper. Overlap and glue other shapes of torn paper to the main shape. Add details in torn paper on top of the shapes to add interest to the form.

Paper script design

procedure

1. Fold the paper in half.
2. Write a word or name in script with a crayon along the creased edge. The crayon is used to ensure enough thickness of line to permit you to cut letters on both sides.
3. Cut on both sides of the crayoned line, making sure each letter is held together by the fold. **Use safety scissors if available.**
4. Paste the cutout letters on contrasting colored paper. Additional cut paper may be added to develop a suggested image.

VARIATION: A three-dimensional form can be created by gluing the design so that parts are lifted above the mounting surface.

supplies

1. Scissors
2. Paper
3. Paste, glue sticks or thick white glue
4. Crayon

NOTE: A word containing a letter that extends below the line (such as f, g, j, p, q, y) must be written above the fold so that only the extension of that letter reaches the fold. View the accompanying illustrations from the side in order to see the original name from which the design is created.

supplies

1. Colored paper
2. Paste, glue sticks or white glue
3. Scissors

NOTE: Many variations and allover patterns can be created by changing designs and color. In a pure positive-negative design, no scraps will be left over.

Positive and negative design

procedure

Method a

This is the simpler procedure of the two and the one most appropriate for young children.

1. Select one sheet of colored paper (Ill. 1) and one-half sheet of a contrasting color (Ill. 2).
2. Fold the small sheet in half (Ill. 3).

1   2

3. Cut a design directly out of the folded side (Ill. 4). **Use safety scissors if available.** (A pencil drawing may be helpful in cutting out the design.) The cutout section is the positive part (Ill. 6) and the section containing the opening is the negative part (Ill. 5) of the design.

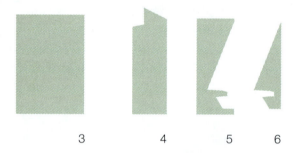

3   4   5   6

4. Unfold both parts, laying the negative section (Ill. 7) on the uncut sheet of contrasting color paper, squaring it up on one end. Paste in place.
5. Place the positive section (Ill. 8) on the other half of the uncut sheet and paste it in place.

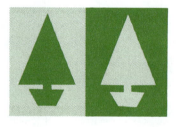

7   8

6. To carry a design farther, cut both the positive (Ill. 9) and negative (Ill. 10) pieces on the fold.
7. Alternate the positive and negative pieces, and paste on contrasting colored paper (Ill. 11).

9   10   11

Method b
An Allover Pattern

1. Select one sheet of colored paper (Ill. 1) and one-half sheet of a contrasting color (Ill. 2).

1   2

2. Cut the smaller sheet into four or eight equal parts (Ill. 3). **Use safety scissors if available.**

3   4   5

3. Fold one part in half, and cut a design directly from the folded edge (Ill. 4) (a pencil drawing may be helpful in cutting out the design). The cutout section is the positive part of the design; the section containing the opening is the negative part of the design.

    If the allover pattern is to be repeated in every respect (color and design), fold the remaining parts in half and lay the negative piece over each part in turn. Trace the design with a pencil, then cut out each part along the pencil line.
4. Unfold all of the positive and negative sections and cut along each fold so that each section is divided into two parts.
5. Paste one-half of the negative part in the upper left-hand corner of the full sheet (Ill. 5).
6. Paste one-half of the positive part so the original design is completed.
7. The allover pattern can be completed by alternating the positive and negative sections until all the sections are used and the paper is filled.

Paper mola

supplies

1. Variety of colored construction paper
2. Scissors
3. Pencil
4. Paste, glue stick, or thick white glue

Cuna Indians of San Blas Islands

procedure

1. With light pencil lines, draw a simple silhouette of a bird, simple animal, lizard, reptile, or insect.
2. Cut out the shape and erase the pencil lines. **Use safety scissors if available.**
3. Draw the second silhouette, on a contrasting color, ¼″ away from the edge of the smaller shape being used as a pattern.
4. Cut out the second shape and use it as a pattern on a third piece of contrasting color. Draw around it and cut it out. (There should be three pieces of different colors and sizes.)
5. With the scraps left from the colored sheets, cut out designs to be used with the creature. Make the shapes in the same color order as the creatures, so that the smallest shape is cut from the first color used.
6. Cut three sets of color and size for each design.
7. Carefully arrange the design around the creature in the same order of size and color.
8. Mount the largest color creature on a fourth sheet of paper after trying out different arrangements. Glue the largest shapes first, medium shapes next, and finally the smallest shapes.
9. Fill in the spaces around the larger shapes with smaller pieces of construction paper. Often these shapes are cigar-shaped. They may also have several colors of graduated sizes glued one on top of the other. These shapes form a pattern.

papier-mâché

12

Nature of the medium

Papier-mâché

Papier-mâché is paper mixed with glue or paste. It was first used by the Chinese, the Persian, and the Japanese. Papier-mâché was used extensively in Europe during the eighteenth century. During the nineteenth century, people in Victorian England used papier-mâché for boxes, trays, and sometimes furniture. In early America, papier-mâché was used to make utilitarian items before those items were manufactured in wood, metal, or plastic.

Papier-mâché is used today by stage designers and carnival float makers. It is still used in the Orient to make jewelry, boxes, and other items. Mexico still uses papier-mâché a great deal in the production of piñatas and other festival items, along with dolls and jewelry.

Papier-mâché is a very low-cost medium and the technique is simple. It can be used for very simple works and very complicated constructions. It is light weight, relatively durable, and almost any material, including beads, fur, fabric, feathers, and other forms of paper, can be glued, stapled, or sewn onto it. It should be noted that it is not fireproof, not very flexible, and can only support limited weight.

Plaster wrap

Plaster wrap is often used to make sculptural items. It is sold commercially as a fabric in a roll impregnated with plaster. It is immersed in warm water and then applied to some supporting structure or armature and modeled to create the desired forms. It usually takes fewer layers than papier-mâché to cover a form and it dries faster. It is not as light in weight as papier-mâché and is more expensive. Plaster wrap is sometimes used in place of papier-mâché.

Papier-mâché bowl

procedure

1. Cover the outside surface of the bowl with a film of liquid soap, Vaseline, or thin plastic wrap. This will keep the papier-mâché from sticking to the bowl.
2. Place the bowl upside down on newspaper or cardboard.
3. Tear or cut newspaper or paper toweling into strips, approximately ½″ wide. If cutting, instructor could use paper cutter or students could use safety scissors.
4. Mix the paste in a bowl or pan to the consistency of cream.
5. Place a strip of paper into the paste until it is saturated. Remove the strip from the bowl, and wipe off the excess paste by pulling it between the fingers.
6. Apply the paste-saturated strips directly on the soap or plastic wrap–covered surface of the bowl. One or two layers of strips of wet paper applied directly to the bowl before applying the paste-saturated strips will serve the same purpose as greasing the bowl.
7. Continue to apply strips until the entire bowl is covered. Repeat until at least six layers of paper strips are applied. The number of layers can be readily counted if a different kind or color of paper is used for each layer. The strength of the finished bowl will be much greater if each layer of trips is applied in a different direction. Also, make sure all wrinkles and bubbles are removed before a new strip is added.
8. Allow the papier-mâché to dry thoroughly before removing the bowl.

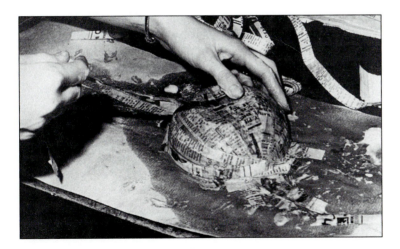

NOTE: The paper used may be cut or torn. Cut paper can be cut into specific shapes to make a pattern much like fish scales. Torn paper will blend together better for a smooth surface. If the paper is torn, tear in the direction of the grain of the paper. Test first by tearing in a horizontal and then a vertical direction. The torn edge will be less irregular when torn with the grain.

 Burma

Thailand

Kashmiri boxes

9. Trim the edges of the papier-mâché bowl and apply additional strips to strengthen and smooth the edges. Other imperfections can be repaired at this time.

10. When everything is completely dry, sandpaper the surface until smooth and decorate.

11. If tempera paint is used to decorate, it will need to be sealed with clear acrylic medium, shellac, or varnish.

 CAUTION: If spray sealer is used, make sure there is adequate ventilation.

 CAUTION: If wallpaper paste is used, it may contain an insecticide; check this for safety. Some instant papier-mâché contains asbestos. Paper cutter should be employed by the teacher.

Papier-mâché jewelry

procedure

1. Shape a piece of Styrofoam to correspond identically to the desired piece of jewelry.
2. Tear or cur paper into ¼" wide strips.
3. Mix the paste in a bowl or pan to the consistency of cream.
4. Immerse a strip of paper into the paste until it is saturated. Remove the strip from the bowl, and wipe off the excess paste by pulling it between the fingers.
5. Apply the strips directly to the Styrofoam.
6. Continue to apply strips until the entire piece of jewelry is covered. Repeat until several layers of paper strips are applied. The number of layers can be readily counted if a different kind or color of paper is used for each layer. Make sure that all wrinkles and bubbles are removed after each strip is added.
7. Add any desired particular features. This can be done either with papier-mâché or by adding other materials.
8. Allow the papier-mâché to dry thoroughly.
9. Sandpaper the surface until smooth and then decorate.
10. If tempera paint is used for decoration, the surface should be sealed with acrylic medium, shellac, or varnish. **If a spray sealer is used, be sure to have adequate ventilation.**
11. Fasten earring or pin to the back of dry papier-mâché jewelry using glue mixed with a small piece of cotton.

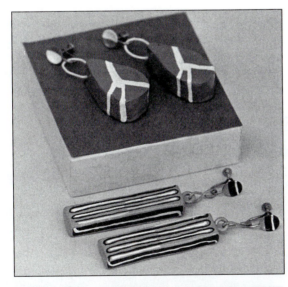

supplies

1. Small pieces of Styrofoam
2. Paper toweling, tissue, or any absorbent paper
3. Safety scissors or paper cutter (to be used by instructor)
4. Paste thinned to the consistency of cream, such as wheat paste, PVC or white glue, or Metylan (available as Ross Art Paste)
5. Container for mixing paste
6. Sandpaper
7. Paint, such as tempera, latex, oil, enamel, or acrylic
8. Brush
9. Acrylic medium, shellac, or varnish for protective finish
10. Thick white glue
11. Jewelry findings, such as pin or earring backs

connections

Egyptian collar necklace
Egyptian earrings
Kashmiri pins
Kashmiri bracelets

Papier-mâché over balloon

supplies

1. Newspapers, paper toweling, or any absorbent paper

2. Scissors or paper cutter

3. Paste thinned to the consistency of cream, such as wheat paste, PVC or white glue, or Metylan (available as Ross Art Paste)

4. Container for mixing paste

5. Balloon

6. Sandpaper

7. Paint, such as tempera, latex, enamel, oil paint or acrylic

8. Brush

9. Acrylic medium, shellac, or varnish as a protective finish if tempera is used. **If a spray finish is used, make sure there is good ventilation**

connections

Masks of Tibet, Mexico, Central America.

procedure

1. Tear or cut newspaper or paper toweling into strips approximately ½" wide.

2. Mix the paste in a bowl or pan to the consistency of cream.

3. Inflate the balloon to the desired size and tie it closed.

4. Place a strip of paper in the paste until it is saturated. Remove the strip from the bowl and wipe off the excess paste by pulling it between the fingers.

5. Apply the paste-saturated strip directly to the balloon.

6. Continue to apply strips until the entire balloon is covered. Repeat until at least six layers of paper strips are applied. The number of layers can be readily counted if a different kind or color of paper is used for each layer. The strength of the finished object will be much greater if each strip is applied in a different direction. Also, make sure that all wrinkles and bubbles are removed before another strip is added.

7. Allow the papier-mâché to dry thoroughly.

8. A number of different and interesting objects can be created at this point.

   a. A perfect sphere can be used as a foundation for two masks, two bowls, or one of each. If a mask is desired, openings can be cut for the eyes, and features added either with papier-mâché or by fasten-

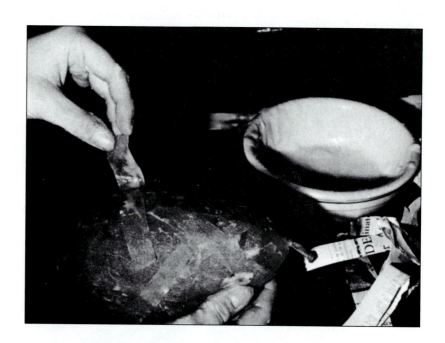

ing other materials in place, such as yarn or fun fur for hair, kernels of corn or pieces of Styrofoam for teeth, or cut paper or felt for ears.

b. A perfect sphere can be used to make a globe or planets from the solar system. The continents on the globe can be painted or built in relief with papier-mâché or with a salt and flour mixture.

c. An opening can be cut carefully into the side of the shape. Within this shape, a scene can be built.

d. The shape of the papier-mâché balloon might suggest an animal, bird, fish, or insect. Its particular features can be applied with papier-mâché or by fastening other material to the form.

Sandpaper any of the above objects if they are to be decorated by painting. If tempera paint is chosen for decoration, the surface should be sealed with acrylic medium, shellac, or varnish. **If a spray is used as a sealer, make sure that there is adequate ventilation.**

 NOTES: Torn paper will blend together better for a smooth surface. If the paper is torn, tear in the direction of the grain of the paper. Test for the grain by first tearing in a horizontal and then a vertical direction. The torn edge will be less irregular when torn with the grain.

If the paper is to be cut, the instructor should use the paper cutter or the students should use safety scissors.

1. Dry papier-mâché balloon

2. Newspapers, paper toweling, or any absorbent paper

3. Cardboard rolls, tag board, cardboard boxes

4. Tape

5. Safety scissors or paper cutter to be used by instructor

6. Paste thinned to the consistency of cream, such as wheat paste, PVC or white glue, or Metylan (available as Ross Art Paste)

7. Container for mixing paste

8. Thick white glue

9. Crepe paper or tissue paper

10. Material for details

Piñata

The piñata is an old tradition used for festivities in Spain, Mexico, Central America, and South America. Traditionally, the piñata takes the form of a animal or a bird, but almost any shape could be used. The piñata is constructed of papier-mâché covered with tissue or crepe paper, and the hollow center is filled with candies and treats. The piñata is hung from the ceiling on a cord that will allow it to be moved easily. The game has the participants, one at a time, blindfolded and given a long stick to try and hit the hanging, and moving, piñata. Usually, the blind-folded person has three chances to hit it. The object, of course, is to hit the piñata hard enough to break it and bring all of the treats to the ground to be scooped up by the guests.

procedure

1. To make the piñata, follow the directions for making the Papier-Mâché over Balloon. When the form is dry, cut a small hole in the top of the shape in order to inset the treats. Close the hole with tape and a sheet of newspaper. If the piñata is not going to be used but will only be a decoration, the hole is not necessary.

2. Add features to the original shape using tape to hold cardboard cylinders, wadded newspaper, cardboard triangles, boxes, or tag board. Papier-mâché over the new features and over the body or balloon shape. Only a couple of coats are necessary since it will be broken later. Allow the pinata to dry thoroughly.

3. When the piñata is dry, cover with crepe paper that has been cut in folded-over loops or in fringing. The folded crepe paper works better than the rolls. The loops or fringe should be put on in overlapping layers much like shingles, using thick white glue to attach them to the form. If the form is an animal, begin with the feet and work toward the head.

4. Add details to finish the form. If it is an animal, add eyes, tails, etc.

Papier-mâché over bottle

procedure

1. Cut or tear newspaper or paper toweling into strips, approximately ½″ wide.
2. Mix the paste in a bowl or pan to the consistency of cream.
3. Submerge a strip of paper in the paste until it is saturated. Remove the strip from the bowl, and wipe off the excess paste by pulling the strip between the fingers.
4. Apply the paste-saturated strips directly to the bottle or bottles.
5. Continue to apply strips until the entire bottle or bottle grouping is covered. Repeat until at least six layers of paper strips are applied. The number of layers can be readily counted if a different kind or color of paper is used for each layer.
6. Place the bottle or bottles on a crumpled piece of paper and allow it to dry thoroughly. The crumpled paper allows the air to circulate around the piece.
7. When the papier-mâché over the bottle or bottles is dry, sandpaper the surface until smooth. The surface can then be decorated with a choice of three-dimensional materials that are held in place with glue or paste-covered strips.
8. If tempera paint is used for decoration, the surface will need to be sealed with acrylic medium, shellac, or varnish. **If a spray is used, make sure there is adequate ventilation.** One bottle may be used for the armature or several containers may be grouped together. If a grouping is used, the bottles should be fastened securely together with tape and wadded newspaper should be stuffed between them to fill any spaces.

supplies

1. Newspapers, paper toweling, or any absorbent paper
2. Safety scissors or paper cutter (to be used by instructor)
3. Paste thinned to the consistency of cream, such as wheat paste, PVC or white glue, or Metylan (available as Ross Art Paste)
4. Container for mixing paste
5. Bottle or bottles on which to build the form
6. Sandpaper
7. Paint, such as tempera, latex, oil, enamel, or acrylic
8. Brush
9. Acrylic medium, shellac, or varnish for protecting the finish if tempera paint is used. **If a spray finish is applied, make sure there is adequate ventilation**

© James L. Shaffer

Papier-mâché pulp objects

1. Newspaper, tissue, or paper towels

2. Wheat paste, white glue, or Metylan which is available as Ross Art Paste

3. Table salt, or a few drops of either oil of cloves or wintergreen

4. Container

NOTES: Papier-mâché mash can be rolled out, squeezed, pinched, and smoothed much like clay. It can be used to make dishes, plaques, ornaments, puppets, maps, etc.

It can also be used to add details on another papier-mâché base.

NOTE: If PVA or white glue is used, mix 3 parts glue to 1 part water. Shreddi-Mix and Celluclay are the commercial products available.

procedure

1. Tear (do not cut with cutter or scissors) paper into small pieces no bigger than ½″ square. Be sure the edges are ragged.

2. Place the torn paper in a container, cover with hot water, stir, and allow the mixture to soak for as long as 36 hours. When soft, mash the paper until it forms a fine pulp. A blender can be used if enough water is used so that it doesn't overload the blender.

3. After the paper is mashed, squeeze out the excess water with the help of a strainer.

4. Add glue or paste in small amounts as needed.

5. Work the mixture into a clay consistency. 1 tablespoon of linseed oil helps to make it more workable. A few drops of oil of cloves or wintergreen will help the mixture from going sour. If the mixture is to be kept for a time, it should be kept refrigerated in a sealed plastic bag.

6. Model the forms with the mixture.

7. Allow the pulp to dry thoroughly.

8. Sandpaper the surface of the pulp object until smooth, then decorate.

9. If tempera paint is used for decoration, it will be necessary to cover the surface with acrylic medium, shellac, or varnish.

Papier-mâché with an armature

procedure

1. Build a frame or armature to the general shape of the chosen subject. Fasten the various parts of the skeleton together securely, using the wire, nails, tape, or appropriate material.
2. Tear or cut paper into strips, approximately ½″ wide. **Use safety scissors if available.**
3. Mix the paste in a bowl or pan to the consistency of cream.
4. Place a strip of paper in the paste until it is saturated. Remove the strip from the bowl and wipe off the excess paste by pulling the strip between the fingers.
5. Apply the strips directly over the frame.
6. Continue to apply strips until the entire frame is covered. Repeat until at least six layers of paper strips are applied. The number of layers can be readily counted if a different kind or color of paper is used for each layer. The strength of the finished frame will be much greater if each strip is applied in a different direction. Also, make sure that all wrinkles and bubbles are removed before another strip is added.
7. Add any particular features not incorporated in the original skeleton. This can be done either with papier-mâché pulp or by adding other materials.
8. Allow the papier-mâché to dry thoroughly.
9. Sandpaper the surface until smooth, and then decorate.
10. If tempera paint is used for decoration, the surface should be sealed with acrylic medium, shellac, or varnish. **If a spray is used as a sealer, make sure that there is good ventilation.**
11. Additional material such as yarn, buttons, fun fur, pipe cleaners, and so forth can be added to enrich the finished product.

connections

Fantasy Figures
of Mexico

1. Window screen, chicken wire, wire, paper, mailing tubes, sticks, rolled and taped newspaper, and so on (to be used individually or collectively to form the general shape of the object to be covered with papier-mâché)
2. Wire, nails, gummed paper, glue, and so on, for use in fastening the frame together
3. Newspaper, paper toweling, or any absorbent paper
4. Paper cutter (to be used by instructor) or safety scissors
5. Paste thinned to the consistency of cream, such as wheat paste, PVC or white glue, or Metylan (available as Ross Art Paste)
6. Container for mixing paste
7. Sandpaper
8. Paint such as tempera, latex enamel, oil paint, or acrylic
9. Brush
10. Clear acrylic medium, shellac, or varnish for protecting the finish if tempera paint is used. **If spray finish is used, make sure there is good ventilation**

printing and stencils

13

Printmaking—Basic processes

There are four fundamental techniques of printmaking used by the artist: intaglio, lithography, relief, and silk screen or serigraphy. *Intaglio printing* usually involves a metal plate that the artist has cut into or etched using acid. Ink is rubbed into the crevices of the plate and then wiped so that only those crevices contain the ink. Under the pressure of a press, the ink is then forced out of the plate onto the printing paper. *Lithography* makes use of stones or metal plates that are treated so that ink will be retained by certain areas. The printing is accomplished by using a press with a scraper bar. The pressure of the bar forces the ink to cling to the paper. *Relief printing* uses the concept of the woodcut: wood (or linoleum or a commercial block) is cut away, the remaining surface rolled with some form of ink, and the block pressed against the paper with a hand or spoon or other hard instrument. In *screen printing,* ink is forced through a screen onto the printing paper by pressure applied to a squeegee. The preparation of the screen determines the ink pattern.

The following methods, collographs, monoprints, and stamps have also been included. *Collagraphs* are printed collages that use many materials. *Monoprints* means that only one print is made, and it really is a combination of painting and printing. It is an excellent way to introduce printmaking because of the reversal of the image. *Stamps* are a small print that usually is repeated. It is a wonderful way to teach patterns and pattern networks.

These techniques which allow a number of prints to be made with the same block include glue prints, Styrofoam prints, relief prints, collagraphs, and screen prints. They may have numbered editions.

In intaglio printing, the ink is drawn out of the areas that have been bitten (with acid) or cut out of the plate. From John Ross and Clare Romano, The Complete Intaglio Print, © 1974, The Free Press.

In lithography, ink will be accepted by the sensitized areas and rejected by the others. From John Ross and Clare Romano, The Complete Screen Print and Lithograph, © 1974, The Free Press.

In relief printmaking, the nonprinting area is removed as in this case with a wood gouge. From John Ross and Clare Romano, The Complete Relief Print, © 1974, The Free Press.

Signing an edition of prints

Paper for a print should be trimmed so that there is 2 inches of clean paper to form a border. When two or more prints are made from the same block, it is called an *edition*. At the lower left-hand corner of the print and directly under the image, the name, if it has one, should be written. Directly under the center of the print should be the number of each copy. This is written as a fraction. The top number indicates the number of this print with the lower number showing the total number of prints in the edition. Directly under the lower right-hand corner of the print is the artist's signature. This information should all be written in pencil.

Printmakers sometimes strike the plate after all of the edition has been printed. *Strike* means that they mark the plate in some way so that it cannot be printed again.

It should be noted that the older printmakers, such as Rembrandt, did not mark their editions, and it is sometimes difficult to tell with certainty when the print was done and who was the artist.

Safety precautions for block printing

It is important to use safety precautions when doing wood block, linoleum block, or reduction block printing. The tools to be used are called *gouges* and are sharp. As a matter of fact, they should be kept sharp since a dull gouge is more likely to slip on the surface of the print block. Gouges have different shaped ends on the blade and are designed to be used to make different kinds of cuts on the block. Linozip cutters are good to use on the softer print material because they pull toward the artist.

A very important tool to be used with block cutting is the *bench hook*. This tool has a stop that fits over the edge of the desk or table and another stop on the top to hold the block securely. This helps keep hands from the front of the block and out of the way of the gouge. Bench hooks are available commercially in metal and wood. Wooden bench hooks can be made quite easily and economically and are worth the investment.

Blottos

Blottos are a type of monoprint (which simply means one print).

procedure

1. Cut a number of various-sized paper squares and rectangles.
2. Crease each paper square in the middle so that later it can be folded easily.
3. Sprinkle a few drops of paint on one side of the crease.
4. Fold the paper on the creased line with the paint inside and press—this causes the paint to be squeezed into various and interesting shapes.
5. When the paper is opened, the result will be surprising—it might resemble an insect, a flower, a butterfly, or any number of items.
6. After a number of blottos are made, cut them out and arrange them into a picture or pattern. When satisfied with the arrangement, paste them in place on a piece of paper of desired size.

supplies

1. Paper
2. Watercolor or thin tempera paint
3. Scissors
4. Paste

NOTE: It is possible to control the blotto by experimentation with the placement and choice of color before blotting.

connections

Blottos: Max Ernst
Conroy Maddox, English Surrealist

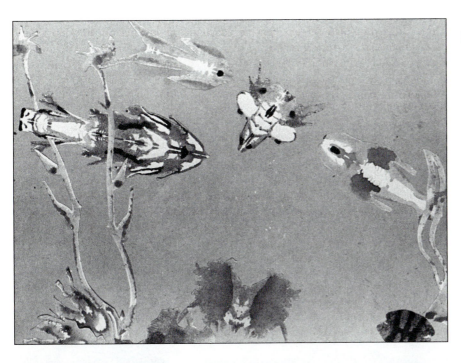

supplies

1. String
2. Paper
3. Paint or ink
4. Board, heavy cardboard, masonite, or a magazine
5. Brush or sponge

Pulled string design

procedure

1. Place a sheet of paper on a flat surface.
2. Coat the string thoroughly with paint or ink. If tempera paint is used, be sure it is thin.
3. Arrange the paint-soaked string on the paper. Twisted loops in the string will make interesting effects. Allow one or two ends to extend beyond the same edge of the paper.
4. Place another piece of paper over this string arrangement.
5. Cover this paper with a firm piece of cardboard, wood, masonite, or magazine, and hold it in place lightly with one hand. With the other hand, grasp the ends of the string and pull it gently from between the papers.
6. Carefully peel the two papers apart. The design will be duplicated on the second sheet of paper.

VARIATION: Arrange several paint soaked strings on the paper. Use different colors. Try to arrange them so that they fill the space. The strings may overlap each other. Press another paper on top of the string and bottom sheet of paper. Use the fingers or a roller to press down on the top paper. Remove the top paper and carefully remove the strings. Allow the two papers to dry. Other media may be added to the prints to enrich the string print.

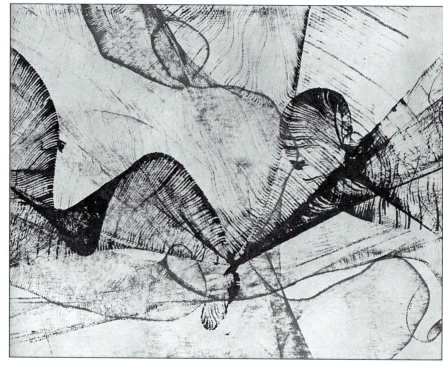

Finger paint monoprint

procedure

1. Do a finger painting directly on the tabletop or other smooth flat surface.
2. Lay a piece of paper directly on the wet painting and rub with the hand until the painting is transferred to the paper.
3. Lift the painting, and place on the newspaper to dry.
4. When the print has dried, place it face down on a flat surface and press with a warm iron. **Teacher should probably manipulate the iron.**

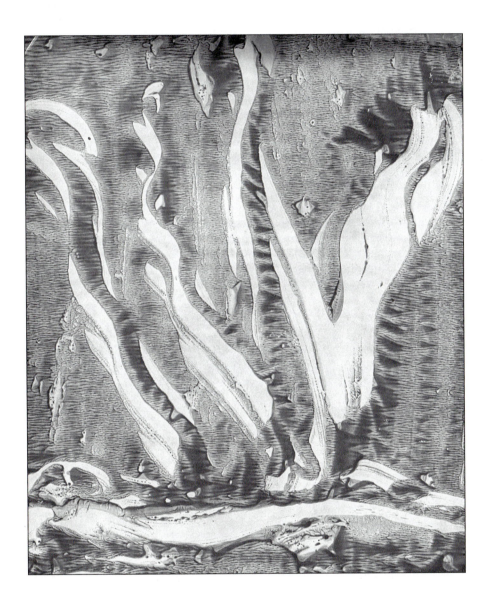

Paint monoprint

supplies

1. Smooth, nonabsorbent hard surface, such as glass, plastic, or tabletop

2. Drawing paper

3. Tempera paint

4. Brush

5. Water container

procedure

1. Discuss and show with pictures about the chosen subject.
2. Draw ideas for the painting.
3. Paint directly on a nonabsorbent surface. Keep the design simple with large colored areas. Allow to dry (Ill.1).
4. Thoroughly dampen a sheet of drawing paper. A spray bottle would work well.
5. After waiting a few moments for the water to work into the paper, press the dampened paper firmly and evenly over the painted design with the palm of the hand.
6. Carefully peel the paper from the design (Ill. 2).
7. A single impression printing will appear on the paper as a mirror image (Ill. 3).

VARIATION: Paint or ink may be rolled or painted on a smooth nonabsorbent surface. Fingers, rags, sticks, or cotton swabs may be used to draw into the ink or paint. Paper shapes can also be laid on the top of the ink or paint. The drawing paper is placed over the ink or paint and pressed down. Lift the print and allow to dry.

VARIATION: Use oil-based paint or ink on the surface of a sheet of masonite or hard surface that can be cleaned later. Lay an absorbent paper lightly on top. Draw on the back of the paper with a ball point pen, pencil, or any other tool. Lift the print and dry. Clean up with mineral spirits.

1

2

3

Sandpaper print

1. Medium to coarse grades of sandpaper of small dimensions

2. Wax crayon

3. Paper

4. Water-soluble or oil-base printers' ink (Water-soluble printers' ink is much easier to clean)

5. Brayer (roller)

6. Ink slab (9″ × 9″ floor tile, or a piece of glass with taped edges to prevent cut fingers)

7. Mineral spirits for cleaning the brayer and ink slab, if oil-base printers' ink is used

8. Newspapers

procedure

1. Draw directly on the sandpaper with the crayon. Areas or lines that are drawn with crayon will be the parts that will be reproduced—make sure they are crayoned heavily. It is not necessary to use more than one color crayon, since the prints will be reproduced in the color of the ink that is used.
2. Squeeze some printers' ink from the tube onto the inking slab.
3. Roll the ink with the brayer until it is spread smoothly. Make the roller rotate several times until it is completely covered with ink.
4. Roll the inked brayer over the crayon drawing on the sandpaper until it is evenly covered with ink.
5. Place the printing paper on top of a pad of newspapers.
6. Lift the inked sandpaper, and place the inked side down on a piece of the printing paper.
7. Hold the sandpaper in place with one hand, and with the other hand rub over the back of the inked sandpaper with a smooth instrument. (A small glass jar with a smooth bottom works well.)
8. Rub until the original drawing has been reproduced. It would be wise to peel back the corner of the sandpaper occasionally to determine whether further rubbing is necessary for a strong print.
9. Reink the sandpaper for subsequent prints.

Stick print

procedure

1. Make a light pencil drawing on paper.
2. Cut a number of sticks of different sizes and shapes, 2″ or 3″ long, making sure the ends are cut square.
3. Mix a small amount of paint on a piece of nonabsorbent scrap paper, and smooth it with a brush to an even consistency.
4. Dip the stick in the film of paint.
5. Press the stick to a scrap of paper, and print one or two images to remove any excess paint.
6. Now, press the stick to the drawing that has been placed on a pad of newspaper, and repeat until the image becomes too light.
7. Repeat steps 4–6 until design is completed.
8. A mosaic effect is obtainable by leaving a narrow space of background paper between each individual print; overlapping individual prints and colors also creates interesting effects, as does twisting the stick when printing.

NOTE: Jar lids, matchbox folders, pieces of mat board, or illustration board also may be dipped into paint and used as a printing tool.

Insulation foam print

supplies

1.. Heavy cardboard

2. Insulation foam tape (comes in rolls of various widths and thicknesses)

3. Scissors

4. Watercolor or tempera paint

5. Brush

6. Water container

7. Paper

procedure

1. Draw a design on cardboard with pencil. Remember to reverse the design, especially letters.
2. Cover pencil lines with foam insulation tape. Cut foam to fit. **Use safety scissors if available.** Do not overlap. Remove the paper back from the foam strip, and place sticky side down on top of the pencil lines.
3. Brush paint on foam.
4. Print by pressing, foam side down, on a piece of paper.

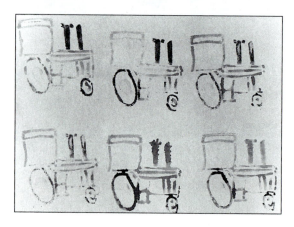

Nature print

procedure

1. Place the natural object on the scrap paper (a leaf should have the veined side up).
2. Brush or roll over the object with ink.
3. Place the printing paper over the object.
4. Hold the top paper securely with one hand, and press and brush the paper with the other hand.
5. Lift off the printed paper, turn it face up, and allow to dry.
6. Clean up oil-base ink with mineral spirits; water-soluble ink with water.

supplies

1. Natural objects that can be flattened with relative ease, such as leaves, grasses, ferns, or blossoms

2. Oil-base or water-soluble printers' ink (water-soluble printers' ink is much easier to clean)

3. Fairly stiff brush

4. Scrap paper (newspaper will be satisfactory)

5. Printing paper

NOTE: Assorted colors may be used and multiple prints may be taken on the same sheet of paper.

supplies

Potato print

supplies

1. Solid potato (see note)
2. A scratching tool, such as pencil, nail file, comb, nail, scissors, or orange stick. Small children may work satisfactorily with these tools without the dangers involved in the use of sharp-edged tools
3. A sharp-edged cutting tool, such as a paring knife or pocketknife
4. Colored construction paper, drawing paper, tissue paper, brown wrapping paper, manila paper, or newsprint
5. Paint brush
6. Water jar
7. Watercolors, tempera paint, or finger paint
8. Tray for mixing colors
9. Absorbent cloth

procedure

1. Cut the potato in half so that each surface is *flat*. If a large potato is used, it may be cut into several pieces, but each piece must be large, so that it will not break in printing.
2. Young children may incise or scratch the design into the surface of the potato with a nail file, pencil, or other tools.
3. Cut around the edge of the design to approximately ⅛″ in depth, then remove the background by cutting to the design from the outer edge of the potato.
4. Place a pad of newspapers under the paper to be printed. Have a scrap paper or paper towel available on which to try the design and to determine whether too much paint is being used.
5. Cover the surface of the design with paint and print on a scrap of paper to eliminate any excess paint. One or two prints may be tried on the scrap paper so that too much paint is not being used. The texture of the potato should be transferred for more interesting prints. Printing may now be continued. A single application of paint will serve for three or four printings, which may be combined to make an overall pattern.
6. Several different colors may be applied. If these are also applied to different areas of the potato, interesting prints will result. The water contained in the potato will make the colors blend and run, producing more colorful designs.

 NOTES: Carrots, turnips, peppers, cabbage, etc., also may be used for successful printing. This process may be used to make attractive wrapping paper, cards, program covers, decorations, place cards, and so on.

Other media, such as markers or oil pastels, may be used to fill in between the prints.

© James L. Shaffer

Paraffin or soap block print

procedure

1. After the discussion of the subject and a demonstration of the technique, the students will plan a design on paper the size of the block.
2. Smooth one side of the block with a straight-edge scraper, making sure any design is removed and the surface if flat. If paraffin is used, the surface can be smoothed by using a cloth saturated with turpentine.
3. Place the design over the block and retrace the lines with a pencil to inscribe the design on the block.
4. Carve the design in the block with any suitable tool. Cut away all areas that are not to be printed.
5. To check the design, place a thin piece of paper over the carving and rub the surface with a crayon or soft pencil.
6. Squeeze a small amount of ink from the tube onto the inking slab, and roll with the brayer until ink is spread smoothly.
7. Roll the inked roller over the carved design. Ink from side to side and top to bottom to ensure an even distribution of the ink over the entire surface.
8. Place a piece of paper over the inked surface, and rub gently and evenly with the fingers until the entire design has been covered. It would be wise to peel back a corner of the paper to determine whether further rubbing is necessary.
9. Reink the block for each subsequent print.

supplies

1. Paraffin or large bar of soap
2. Carving tool, such as nail, scissors, knife, or orange stick
3. Straight-edge scraper for smoothing surface of the soap (table knife)
4. Water-soluble or oil-base printers' ink (water-soluble printers' ink is much easier to clean)
5. Brayer (roller)
6. Ink slab (9″ × 9″ floor tile, or a piece of glass with taped edges to prevent cut fingers)
7. Paper
8. Mineral spirits for cleaning brayer, ink slab, and block design, if oil-base printers' ink is used

NOTE: To prevent distortion of the printing surface, avoid too much pressure when printing.

Collagraph

supplies

1. Piece of cardboard (if thick, edges should be beveled)

2. Polymer—acrylic medium (or gesso) for plate saturation

3. Assorted flat textures

4. Polymer modeling paste (dries slowly)

5. Polymer medium—gel form

6. Old toothbrush

7. Oil paints, colored printing inks, or tempera paint

8. Scrap piece of mat board for spreading ink

9. Mat knife or X-acto knife
   Knives must be used with caution.

The collagraph is a printed collage. After Picasso, Matisse, and Gris experimented with collage and assemblage, it opened the way for printmakers to try the possibilities of assembling many materials that could be glued onto a plate, inked, and printed.

procedure

Pieces of cardboard must be given two or three coats of polymer acrylic medium; following that, the following list indicates *some* of the things that may be done.

1. Modeling with paste on board
2. Modeling with gel
3. Embedding of textures; seal with polymer medium or gel
4. Engraving or scratching with any firm point
5. Sprinkle with grits or seal sandpaper
6. Always allow to dry completely

Printing

1. As relief—use roller or brayer to apply color
2. As intaglio—work color into depressions with toothbrush, wipe surface clean with old newspaper
3. Both—apply intaglio ink first (as in #2, above), then apply relief ink
4. Print by using printing press, clothes wringer, or rub vigorously with large spoon or some smooth hard object

VARIATION: Many flat objects may be glued securely onto a heavy surface and printed. They include rubber bands, string, textured paper, cloth, lace or trim, paper clips, buttons, coins, etc. They should be flat enough to be inked and printed.

NOTE: Excessively thick, hard, and/or sharp materials will cut the paper; check the surfaces!

Tempera dries quickly—inking and printing must be hurried!

Instructor should cut cardboard in preparation.

Materials may be applied or pressed, and gesso and other substances may be modeled to make a printing surface. From John Ross and Clare Romano, *The Complete Collagraph*, © 1980, The Free Press.

Collagraph using cardboard or rubber block print

procedure

1. Cut shapes from pieces of cardboard or inner tubes, and glue them to a cardboard background for printing. **Use safety scissors if available.**
2. Squeeze a small amount of ink from the tube onto the piece of glass or floor tile.
3. Roll the ink with a brayer until it is spread smoothly on the inking slab (Ill. 1).
4. Roll the inked brayer over the mounted design from side to side and top to bottom to ensure an even distribution over the entire surface.
5. Place a piece of paper over the inked design, and rub gently and evenly with the fingers, or with a smooth bottom of a small jar until the entire design is reproduced. It would be wise to peel back a corner of the paper to determine whether further rubbing is necessary for a strong print (Ill. 2).
6. Reink the design for subsequent prints.

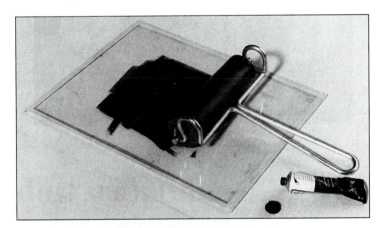

1

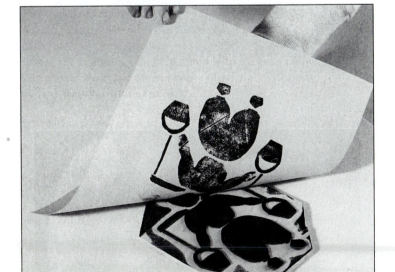

2

supplies

1. A piece of inner tube or cardboard
2. Scissors
3. Paste or glue
4. Heavy cardboard, floor tile, or a piece of wood
5. Water-soluble or oil-base printers' ink (water-soluble printers' ink is much easier to clean)
6. Brayer (roller)
7. Ink slab (9″ × 9″ floor tile, or a piece of glass with taped edges to prevent cut fingers)
8. Paper
9. Newspaper
10. Turpentine or kerosene for cleaning the brayer, inking slab, and printing block, if oil-base printers' ink is used

1. Litho-Sketch paper plate

2. Litho-Sketch solution

3. Greasy crayon or pencil, litho crayon, or India ink

4. Soft cotton pad (for spreading solution)

5. Roller

6. Litho-Sketch or woodcut ink

7. Burnisher (spoon or something similar) or press

8. Lithography tusche or Litho-Sketch tusche, if desired (for washes)

connections

Paul Gauguin

Edvard Munch

Paul Cezanne

Henri Matisse

Paul Klee

Thomas Hart Benton

Kathe Kollwitz

Fernard Leger

Francisco de Goya

Honore Daumier

Litho-Sketch printing

Lithography (explained earlier in this chapter) is fairly complex and requires equipment not normally found in the elementary or middle school. There is an alternative for this, however, in Litho-Sketch. Standard lithography is executed using stones or metal plates; Litho-Sketch uses a special paper. The printing procedure is similar.

procedure

1. It is important to have a discussion with pictures of the chosen subject. A demonstration of the technique should follow. Drawings may be made of newsprint.
2. The chosen drawing is done on the Litho-Sketch paper plate which is de-sensitized with a special solution.
3. The ink should be rolled out until it is slightly tacky.
4. Ink should be rolled over the paper, and it will adhere only to the drawing. The paper plate must always be damp while inking.
4. Place the printing paper over the plate.
5. Rub the back of the plate with a spoon or a baby food jar, or send it through a simple press.
6. The image will then appear on the paper.

Ink pad print

procedure

1. Place a pad of newspapers under the paper to be printed.
2. Press a finger, heel of hand, side of hand, or any item to be printed on the ink pad.
3. Press the inked area to the printing paper. One application of ink should serve for several impressions, which can be combined to make an overall pattern.

supplies

1. Paper
2. Ink pad
3. Newspapers

NOTE: Sticks, pencil erasers, jar lids, a cardboard shape glued to a pencil eraser, or any small flat item can be used as a printing tool.

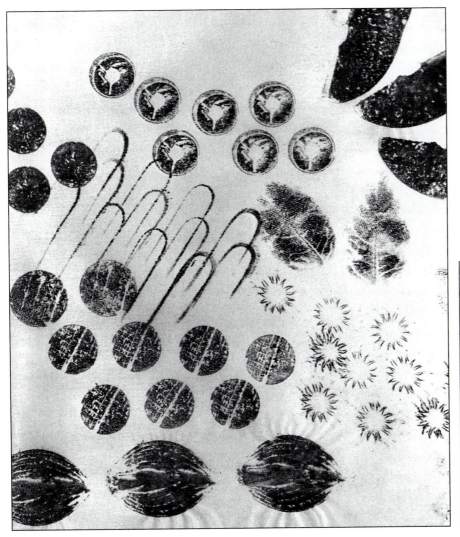

Stamps

Stamps have been used since the ancient times. The Pharaohs of Egypt used royal seals to sign documents. Stamps have been made from stone, clay, bone, wood, ivory, and metal. Clay stamps were used in ancient Mexico to make relief decoration on pottery. Stamps have been used with vegetable and mineral dyes to decorate leather, cloth, and paper. The Japanese and Chinese have used seals for centuries. Stamps have been used by African, Pre-Columbian people, and Native Americans.

Styrofoam stamp

procedure

1. Draw around the piece of Styrofoam on a piece of paper. Make a design, remembering that the design needs to be reversed.
2. Draw design on Styrofoam with pencil with enough pressure to make a good impression.
3. Using masking tape, make a handle on the back of Styrofoam stamp. Press the end of a short piece of masking tape to the Styrofoam with the other end pressed down next to the first end. The middle of the tape should stick together to make a short handle.
4. Press Styrofoam stamp on ink pad, pressing carefully with fingertips.
5. Press stamp on paper, using fingertips to make sure there is pressure on all parts of the foam. Stamp may be printed at least 2 times before reinking.

connections Adinkra prints, Ashanti people of Ghana used symbols expressing ideas such as good luck, unity, service, and forgiveness.

String stamp

procedure

1. Cover one side of the block with a thin coating of glue.
2. Deposit a small amount of glue on a piece of cardboard, and pull the string through the glue, using the fingers to give the string an even coating of glue.
3. Place the string in the glue on the block so it forms a design. Allow to dry thoroughly. Make sure the string does not overlap.
4. Paint the string on the block. (If tempera paint is used, make sure it is thin.)
5. Print:
   a. Lay the printing paper over several thicknesses of newspaper.
   b. Press the block on a scrap of paper to eliminate any excess paint.
   c. Several prints can be made from the printing block before applying more paint.

supplies

1. String
2. Glue
3. Block of wood
4. Paper
5. Tempera paint, watercolor, or water-soluble block-printing ink
6. Brush

NOTE: Instead of painting the design, a print also may be obtained by stamping on an ink pad.

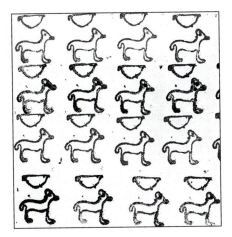

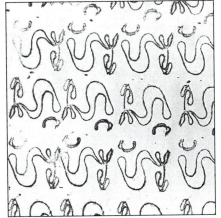

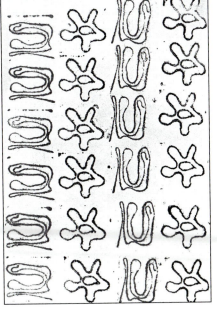

Eraser stamp

1. Art gum eraser or soap eraser
2. X-acto knife
3. Pencil
4. Paper
5. Stamp pad

connections

Adinkra prints, Ashanti people of Ghana used symbols on carved goards dipped in black dye and printed on white, yellow, or brown material.

procedure

1. Discuss the stamp and possibilities for design. If it is to be connected with African design, it is important to have some examples. Draw around the eraser on a piece of newsprint, and draw a design in that space. Remember your design will print backwards so it may need to be reversed.
2. Draw the design on the eraser.
3. Carefully cut the eraser on the lines with an X-acto knife. **Use extreme care and close supervision.** It is not necessary to cut deeply. Make sure the knife is slightly slanted toward the center of the shapes. This will prevent undercuts.
4. After the design has been outlined with the knife, carefully break out the spaces that are not going to be printed. Brush away crumbs.
5. Press the eraser firmly down on the stamp pad and then on the paper to make the print. The eraser can be printed several times before it needs to be reinked.
6. Another color ink pad can be used, but it is necessary to "stamp out" all of the previous color on a piece of scrap paper.

VARIATION: Colored watercolor markers may also be used to put color on the eraser instead of the ink pad. A very interesting variation is to use Overwriter or Changeable markers and print on top of the first layer of stamping.

CAUTION: Extreme care and supervision must be given whenever X-acto knives are used. Safety instructions should be given before *every* use of the knives. X-acto knives are now sold with safety caps, but separate caps may be purchased for older knives. Heavy corrugated cardboard should always be placed under the paper or material being cut. The X-acto knife is held like a pencil, with the fingers holding the knife on the textured ring. The slanted, sharpened edge should be directly over the line to be cut, and the position of the knife or the paper should be changed if the line changes direction. Keep the fingers of the holding hand out of the way of the blade, above the cutting area. Remind students often to check themselves and the position of the knife and their hands. The safety cap should be on the knife at all times except when actually in use.

Glue print

procedure

1. After a discussion of the chosen subject, the students should draw their design on newsprint.
2. Transfer the drawing to the cardboard. Carbon paper can be used, or the back of the paper can be covered with graphite from a pencil, the paper placed over the cardboard, and the image redrawn.
3. Squeeze the glue along the lines of the pencil design. Do not overlap the lines. Leave the cap off the squeeze container overnight if the glue is too thin.
4. Allow the glue to dry throughout (Ill. 1).
5. Coat the surface of the plate with watered down white glue or acrylic medium. This will seal the surface. Dry.
6. Roll out the ink, using a brayer as in the other print processes.
7. Use the ink-loaded brayer to roll the ink on the glue surface (Ill. 2). If only the glue areas are to print, use light pressure; if other parts of the plate are to print, greater pressure may be applied.
8. Print by placing a piece of paper over the inked image, then press, rub a hand or spoon, or roll a rolling pin or a clean brayer over the paper. Pull the print (Ill. 3).

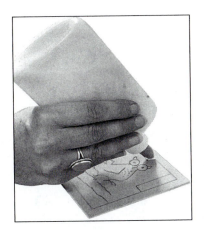

VARIATION: Do the blottos as directed but instead of laying them aside to dry, print them immediately on another sheet of paper. These prints of the blottos may be arranged as flower blossoms, fish, plants, etc. Other details may be added with paint or other media to enrich the composition.

supplies

1. White glue in a squeeze bottle
2. Piece of cardboard
3. Paper, for printing. Soft paper will probably work best
4. Pencil
5. Brayer (roller)
6. Oil- or water-base relief printing ink, or tempera paint mixed rather thick, with a few drops of liquid detergent added. (water-soluble printers' ink is much easier to clean)
7. Carbon paper (optional)
8. Spoon (or some smooth hard-surfaced object), rolling pin or clean brayer
9. Acrylic media or watered-down white glue

1

2

3

Styrofoam print

1. Cut pieces of Styrofoam. Meat trays work well

2. Heavy scissors to trim Styrofoam

3. Newsprint and printing paper

4. Tempera paint or printing ink

5. Brush or brayer

6. Water container if tempera is used

7. Ink slab if ink is used. Mixing tray if tempera is used

procedure

1. Trim Styrofoam to size. Instructor might do this.
2. Discuss and show pictures of the chosen subject. Draw designs on newsprint. When satisfied, draw designs on Styrofoam using a dull pencil or pointed stick. It should be deep enough to make a dent in the foam but not go all the way through it.
3. Place a pad of newspapers under the paper to be printed. Squeeze a small amount of ink on the ink slab and roll the ink with a brayer until there is a good even coating of ink on the brayer. If paint is used, use a tray to mix the paint to a fairly thick consistency.
4. Apply ink or paint to the Styrofoam print surface.
5. Do several test prints to check the consistency of the paint or ink and adjust if necessary.
6. Allow prints to dry.

VARIATION: Cut the Styrofoam into the shape of a object that will be repeated several times. The same procedure can be used but the printing can be done on top of a watercolor wash, a simple landscape in watercolor or water-based media, or printed with other small prints to make a composition.

© James L. Shaffer

VARIATION: The Styrofoam can be cut into a square shape and printed so that the top right corner is centered on a large square print paper. Turn the print paper and print a second time, turn and print again and finally print the Styrofoam a fourth time. This will produce a quilt line block. It is necessary to mark the piece of Styrofoam on the back in the corner that will be placed closest to the center.

 NOTE: Styrofoam may be washed with water and printed in another color. It may also be stamped out on scrap paper and reinked with another color.

1. Safety-Kut or Soft-Kut print blocks are preferred but battleship linoleum may be used with caution and supervision

2. Carving tools, such as V- or U-shaped gouges set in wooden handles or penknife. Cutting tools are available that can be drawn toward you. These reduce the risk of children cutting themselves.

3. Paper

4. Carbon paper

5. Water-soluble or oil-base printers' ink (water-soluble printers' ink is much easier to clean)

6. Brayer (roller)

7. Ink slab (9" × 9" floor tile or piece of glass with taped edges to prevent cut fingers)

8. Newspapers

9. Turpentine or kerosene for cleaning glass, brayer, and linoleum block, if oil-base printers' ink is used

Printing blocks

Linoleum has a long history in its use as a print medium. However, it tends to be hard and has a slick surface which makes it a resistant material for children to use. It also tends to get brittle as it gets older. It is always necessary to have a way to hold the linoleum in place while cutting. Even with close supervision and caution, cutting a linoleum block can be dangerous. There are new products on the market that give the student the same experience and that are much safer. These products are soft, pliable, and will grip the table while they are being cut. The same tools and the same printers' ink are used. The products are about ⅜" thick and can be cut on both sides which makes them more economical.

procedure

1. After a discussion including pictures about the chosen subject and a demonstration of the technique, plan the design on a piece of paper the same size as the block.
2. Transfer the design from the paper to the block with carbon paper and sharp pencil. If lettering is incorporated in the design, it must be drawn and carved in reverse. Do not press too firmly with the pencil.
3. Carve the design in the block by cutting all lines or areas that are not to be printed. If linoleum is used, warm it for easier cutting. **Keep the holding hand out of the path of the cutting tool.** (See supply list for safe tools.)
4. Check the design from time to time by placing a thin piece of paper over the carving and rubbing over the surface with a crayon or pencil.
5. Squeeze a small amount of ink from the tube onto the ink slab.
6. Roll the ink with the brayer until it is spread smoothly on the inking slab.
7. Roll the inked brayer over the carved block design until it is completely and evenly covered. Include the corners.
8. Print.
    a. Lay a piece of paper on which the printing is to be done over several thicknesses of newspaper. Place the inked block design face down on the paper, cover with another piece of paper to keep the block clean, and print by pressing down firmly with the hand or foot. Tapping with a mallet is also a good method.

b. Place a piece of paper over the inked block design, and rub gently and evenly with the fingers or the edge of the hand when it is in a fist position. It is wise to check the print by peeling back one corner at a time to determine whether further rubbing is necessary for a strong print.

9. Reink the block for subsequent prints.

connections

Lift Every Voice and Sing by James Weldon Johnson, Penguin, New York, 2000

Once a Mouse by Marcia Brown, Atheneum, New York, 1972

Drummer Hoff by Barbara Emberly, Simon & Schuster, New York, 1987

Linocuts—Pablo Picasso

Paul Matisse

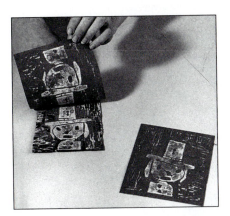

NOTE: If oil-based ink is used, the quality of the print may be improved by soaking the paper briefly in water and blotting the surface prior to printing.

A bench hook must always be used with linoleum or wood blocks for safety.

Wood-block print

1. Soft piece of pine wood

2. Carving tools, such as V- or U-shaped gouges set in wooden handles. **A bench hook must always be used with linoleum or wood blocks for safety**

3. Paper

4. Carbon paper

5. Water-soluble or oil-base printers' ink (water-soluble printers' ink is much easier to clean)

6. Brayer (roller)

7. Ink slab (9″ × 9″ floor tile, or a piece of glass with taped edges to prevent cut fingers)

8. Newspapers

9. Mineral spirits for cleaning brayer, ink slab, and wood block, if oil-base printers' ink is used

procedure

1. Plan a design on paper to fit the wood-block size, deciding which areas to cut away or leave in relief.

2. Transfer the design from the paper to the wooden block with carbon paper and a sharp pencil. If lettering is to be incorporated in the design, it must be carved in reverse.

3. Carve the design in the wood block. Cut away all the lines or areas that are not to be printed. In carving the wood, all cuts should be made in the direction of the grain. Cross-grain cuts will bind the tool and splinter the wood. **Keep the hand that holds the wooden block out of the path of the cutting tool.**

4. Check the design from time to time by placing a thin piece of paper over the carving and rubbing over the surface with a crayon or pencil.

5. Squeeze a small amount of ink from the tube onto the piece of glass or floor tile.

6. Roll the ink with the brayer until it is spread smoothly on the inking slab.

7. Roll the ink brayer over the carved wood-block design until it is completely and evenly covered.

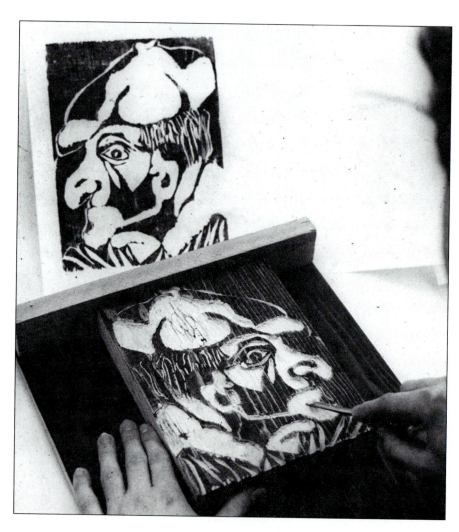

8. Print.
    a. Lay a piece of paper on which the printing is to be done over several thicknesses of newspaper. Place the inked block design face down on the paper. Cover with a piece of paper to keep the block clean, and print by pressing down firmly with the hand or foot. Tapping with a mallet is also a good method.
    b. Place a piece of paper over the inked block design, and rub gently and evenly with the fingers, a spoon, or the smooth bottom of a small jar until the entire design is reproduced. It would be wise to peel back a corner of the paper to determine whether further rubbing is necessary for a strong print.
9. Reink the block for subsequent prints.

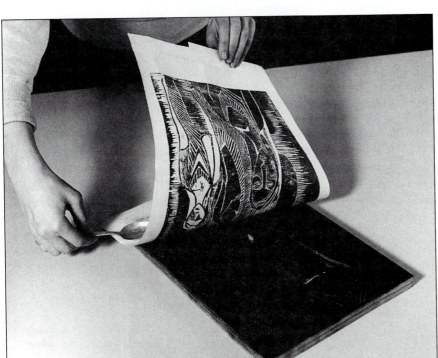

My Son John by Jim Aylesworth, Owlet Books, New York, 1997

Barn Cat: A Counting Book by Carol P. Saul, Little Brown & Co., New York, 1998

Whaling Days by Carol Carrich, Clarion Books, New York, 1996

Faraway Summers by Joanna Hurwitz, William Morrow & Co. New York, 1998

Chinese and Japanese wood block prints

Albrect Durer

Lucas Cranach

Hans Holbein

Paul Gauguin

Edvard Munch

Ernst Kirchner

Max Beckman

NOTE: To make use of the decorative advantages of the wood's grain, soak the wood in water so that the grain stands out in relief. If only certain areas of the grain are to be used, the remainder of the block may be sealed with shellac and the exposed area soaked with water. Too much soaking, however, will cause the block to warp or buckle. Brushing with a stiff wire brush will also expose the grain. The block may also be given textures by scratching the surface with various types of abrasives or tools, or by striking patterns with chisels, screwdrivers, etc. If oil-base ink is used, the quality of the print may be improved by soaking the paper briefly in water and blotting the surface prior to printing.

1. Safety-Kut or Soft-Kut print is preferred but battleship linoleum may be used. Styrofoam will work for two colors. Wood blocks may also use the reduction block technique

2. Carving tools, such as V- or U-shaped gouges set in wooden handles. If the soft material is used, the Speedball cutters or Linozips are recommended. **A bench hook must always be used with linoleum or wood blocks for safety**

3. Paper, newsprint for designing, and paper for printing

4. Carbon paper

5. Water-base or oil-base printers' ink. Water-base is easier to clean, and it should be the only ink used with Styrofoam

6. Brayer

7. Ink slab which can be a floor tile, cookie sheet, or a piece of glass that is taped on the edges for safety

8. Newspapers

9. Mineral spirits for clean-up if oil-base printing ink is used

Reduction block print

It is always best to have a discussion that includes pictures of the subject before beginning. A brief history of printmaking and a demonstration of the technique is also extremely important before students begin working on designs. Several design possibilities may be drawn and the best one chosen.

procedure

1. Cut the block to the desired size and plan the design on the sheet of paper of the same dimensions.
2. Transfer the design from the paper to the block with carbon paper and pencil. Remember that the print will be the reverse of the design. If letters or numbers are in the design, they need to be reversed to print correctly.
3. Carve the design in the block by cutting out all the areas that are not going to be printed (if printed on white paper these areas would stay white). Main outlines are usually enough for the first printing. A bench hook must be used when using linoleum. **Keep the holding hand out of the path of the cutting tool.**
4. Check the design from time to time by placing a thin piece of paper over the carving and rubbing over the surface with a crayon or pencil.
5. Squeeze a small amount of ink on the ink slab and roll the ink with the brayer until there is a smooth covering on the brayer.
6. Roll the inked brayer over the carved block design until it is completely and evenly covered. Be especially careful to ink the edges and corners so that good registration can be possible for the next printings.
7. Print.
   a. Lay a piece of paper on which the printing is to be done over several layers of newspaper. Place the ink block face down on the paper, and carefully turn both the paper and the block over. Rub the paper gently with the fingers or with the edge of the hand when it is in a fist position. It is wise to sneak a peek by peeling one corner at a time to see whether further rubbing is necessary.

8. Reink the block with the same color or different color to make other prints. Decide how many prints are to be produced. This is called an *edition*.

9. Allow the prints to dry. Decide what additional areas should be cut from the print block. These areas will remain whatever was the first color printed.

10. Cut the new areas from the block. Use the same procedure as above.

11. Choose another color of ink to roll on the block, and follow the same method except that the inked block must be lined up with corners and edges in order to print exactly on top of the original prints. This is called *registration*. Good registration means the second print color matches exactly with the first print. Off-registration means that it does not match. Sometimes, prints are done off-registration for a special effect.

12. All of the original prints should be printed a second color before cutting additional areas from the block.

13. This process can continue as desired. Often the block becomes not much more than a stamp.

Achieving registration in a multi-colored print

1. Select the sheets of paper on which the print will appear, ensuring that there will be adequate margins.

2. Lay the sheets over the linoleum or wood block, being careful of the margins.

3. Making sure that the sheets do not move (a weight may be placed on top), drive a fine nail or brad into and through the papers into the block at diagonal corners.

4. As the color is printed on each sheet, a teasing needle or the original nail or brad must be inserted through the paper and into the holes in the block; the paper is then carefully lowered straight down on the block.

5. The printing is done by rubbing over the printed area with a smooth hard object, such as the back of a wooden spoon or the bottom of a baby food jar. A printing press may also be used.

NOTE: A sharp tool is always safer than a dull tool, which tends to slip.

connections

The *reduction block* was invented by Pablo Picasso.

Serigraphy or screen print

procedure

1. Embroidery hoop, or small wooden picture frame

2. A piece of material large enough to cover the hoop or frame, such as dotted swiss or cheese cloth

3. Stapler

4. Stencil paper (the back of typewriter stencil serves as a most satisfactory and inexpensive paper)

5. Squeegee, such as a tongue depressor, small piece of linoleum with a straight edge, small plastic windshield scraper, or felt dauber

6. Paper

7. Cutting tool (scissors, knife, or single-edge razor blade)

8. Finger paint or commercial screen process ink (other paints clog the pores of the cloth). A good, inexpensive silk screen paint can be made by mixing liquid or instant powder tempera with a stiff mixture of soap flakes (not detergent) and warm water, or with a media mixer

9. Beware of commercial solvents when using oil-base silk screen products

1. Using two or three layers, stretch the material tightly between the embroidery hoops. If a wooden frame is used, tightly stretch the material, and staple it in place.
2. Cut the design from the stencil paper (Ill. 1), using paper that is a bit larger than the surface of the stretched material. The cut design must fit within the area of the stretched material. The stencil should be cut following the directions on pages 260 and 261.
3. Place a piece of paper on a flat and smooth surface.
4. Place the stencil on the paper (Ill. 2).
5. Place the screen on top of the stencil (Ill. 3). Make sure the material is in contact with the stencil to prevent the paint from running under the stencil.
6. Place some commercial screening paint, or finger paint of toothpaste consistency, in the frame or hoop (Ill. 4).
7. Hold the frame with one hand and scrape the paint across the stencil with a squeegee. In this process, the paint or ink is forced through the cloth and adheres the stencil to the screen, except where the design was cut out; these areas will be reproduced (Ill. 5).
8. Gently lift the stencil and frame, making sure the stencil remains adhered to the material (Ill. 6).
9. Place the frame and stencil on another paper and repeat steps six and seven for additional prints. Work rapidly to prevent paint from drying and clogging the material.

 NOTE: Lines and shapes may be created in this print by using crayon as a resist. The drawing should be done with the crayon directly on the material in the screen.

 connections

Victor Vasarely
Andy Warhol
Jim Dine
Ben Shahn
Robert Rauschenberg
Roy Lichtenstein
Jasper Johns
Josef Albers

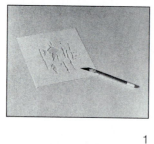

1

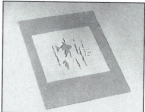

2

3

4

5

6

Crayon or oil pastel stencil

procedure

1. Tag board stencils work well.
2. The stencil may be made by folding tag board and cutting one-half of a symmetrical shape from the fold. When the tag board is unfolded, the shape will be complete. The shape piece is called the *positive* and the hole in the folded tag board is the *negative*. Putting crayon or oil pastel on the edge of any piece of scrap can work as a stencil if it is rubbed off onto another piece of paper.
3. Hold or fasten the stencil firmly in place over the drawing paper.
4. Color a heavy and thick line of crayon or oil pastel around the shape or around the edge of the negative shape. Rub the color off of the shape onto the paper and off the negative into the hole and on the paper. An eraser works as a transfer tool for crayon. Oil pastel is softer and a finger or a finger covered with tissue works well as a transfer tool.

supplies

1. Tagboard
2. Wax crayons or oil pastels
3. Paper
4. Scissors
5. Eraser or tissues

NOTE: Crayon may be stroked directly through the stencil onto the other paper, as described under chalked stencils.

supplies

1. Stencil or tag board
2. Chalks
3. Cotton or tissue (fingers may be used)
4. Paper
5. Fixative spray

Stencil with chalk

procedure

1. Cut stencil.
2. Lay the stencil over the paper. Hold or fasten it firmly in place.
3. If you are using the positive stencil, make a series of strokes with chalk, working from the outside of the opening in so as not to curl the edges of the stencil.
4. If the negative, or the cutout stencil, is being used, stroke from the inside of this stencil out to avoid the curling of stencil edges. This system will also prevent the chalk from sifting under stencil.
5. If a softening effect is desired, rub the chalk lightly with the piece of cotton or tissue, or with the fingers, being careful to rub from the stencil onto the surface of the paper.

 NOTE: The chalk may be applied directly to the paper with the cotton or tissue. Simply make strokes with the chalk on the paper, then pick up the chalk dust with the tissue or cotton and proceed as directed with step four. A separate stencil must be cut for each color.

CAUTION: It is imperative that proper safety precautions be taken. Pin the work to a vertical surface. Spray outdoors in a well-ventilated but wind-free area. With a sweeping motion, spray from the top to the bottom of the work. It may be necessary for the instructor to use the fixative.

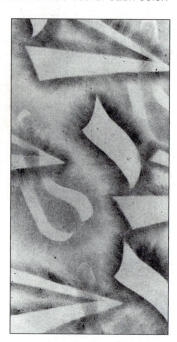

Negative stencil   *Positive stencil*

Spattered stencil design

procedure

1. Cut the stencil as directed on previous stencils.
2. Use the tape to fasten the paper in the center of the sheet of newspaper.
3. Pick up a small quantity of paint or ink with the brush (excess paint or ink will destroy the fine spatter effect).
4. Hold the screen above the paper, and rub back and forth across it with the brush or spray with pressurized can or atomizer. In the absence of window screen, similar results may be obtained by drawing a stick across the brush bristles away from the paper.

supplies

1. Tempera paint, colored inks
2. Stencil paper
3. Drawing paper
4. Small piece of window screen
5. Stiff bristle brush, such as an old toothbrush
6. Tape
7. Newspaper or wrapping paper

Sprayed stencil design

1. Thinned paint, ink, or a quick-drying commercial spray paint

2. Stencil paper

3. Insect sprayer, fixative sprayer, atomizer, or pressurized spray can

4. Drawing paper

5. Newspaper or wrapping paper

6. Tape or pins

procedure

1. Cut the stencil as directed on page 261.
2. The paper to be sprayed should be fastened to a newspaper or piece of wrapping paper. Secure the stencil over this so that it lies perfectly flat.
3. Place the newspaper on the floor, or tape it to the wall so that the stencil is at a convenient height.
4. Spray over the stencil, making sure that the open areas are fully covered with the paint.

 CAUTION: It is imperative that proper safety precautions be taken. Pin the work to a vertical surface. Spray outdoors in a well-ventilated but wind-free area. With a sweeping motion, spray from the top to the bottom of the work.

 NOTE: Variety may be added by spraying some areas more heavily than others, by using different colors on the shapes, or by overlapping the colors. In overlapping colors, it is best to permit the first coat to dry completely.

It is possible to reproduce the images of various forms of plant life by simply pinning them to the drawing paper and spraying over them.

Thinned tempera is less messy than commercial sprays.

Positive stencil

Sprayed design

Negative stencil

Sprayed design

Sponged stencil design

procedure

1. Cut the stencil as directed on previous pages.
2. Pick up the moist sponge with the clothespin or your fingers, and touch it down to the paint. Make sure that it is not saturated.
3. Put the stencil over a scrap piece of paper, hold or fasten it securely, and press the sponge lightly enough to use the sponge texture over the open portions of the stencil. Avoid scrubbing with the sponge, as this will work the paint under the stencil and create ragged edges.
4. When comfortable with the process, put the stencil design on drawing paper.

supplies

1. Stencil paper
2. Tempera paint or colored ink
3. Small piece of sponge
4. Drawing paper
5. Clip-type clothespin

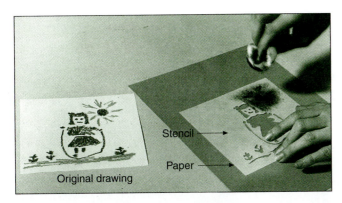

Original drawing

Stencil →

Paper →

Stencil

Finished Stencil design

Stencil with tempera

1. Tempera paints
2. Stencil paper
3. Paper
4. Stencil brush (a brush with *short, stiff* bristles)
5. Jar of water and absorbent cloth for cleaning brushes
6. Tray for mixing paints

procedure

1. Cut the stencil as directed on previous pages.
2. Hold or fasten the stencil securely in place.
3. Dip the stencil brush very lightly into the paint, and wipe the excess paint from the brush onto a paper towel or absorbent cloth. The brush should appear to be almost dry, for very little paint is needed.
4. Apply the paint with strokes, starting on the stencil and running off onto the paper, or dab, with the brush held vertically to prevent any paint from getting under the stencil.

 NOTE: Try overlapping these or new shapes with new colors for a more interesting design. A separate stencil must be cut for each color.

Textile painting with stencils

procedure

1. Cut the stencil as directed in cutting a stencil.
2. Press the cloth with a hot iron to remove any wrinkles. Tack the cloth to the drawing board or any other flat, smooth surface.
3. Place the stencil in position on the cloth, and tack it so that the stencil will not slip or slide on the material.
4. Touch the brush lightly in the paint; it is *especially* important in textile painting that a very, very small amount of paint be used. Too much paint will soak through the fabric and wash out when the material is laundered.
5. Wipe all of the excess paint from the brush with a paper towel or absorbent cloth. Running the brush back and forth across the towel or cloth will remove the excess paint and will also work the paint into the brush. The brush will appear to be nearly dry.
6. If an open stencil is being used, stroke or stipple with the brush, working from the outside of the opening in, so as not to curl the edges of the stencil. If you are using a positive stencil, stroke from inside of the shape out; this will prevent the paint from going under the edges of the stencil.
7. Experimentation will help to determine the proper quantity of paint to be used. Shading or painting one color over another in parts of the stencil will greatly enrich the design.
8. After stenciling all parts of the design (many colors may be used, but a separate stencil must be cut for each color), remove the stencil.
9. If the proper amount of paint has been used, the painted fabric will appear to be dry and the paint will not have soaked through the material. For all practical purposes, the fabric is now dry enough for handling; however, the paint should be allowed to dry thoroughly overnight before pressing with a hot iron for permanence. Be sure to read the directions on your textile paint to complete this last step.
10. Clean the brushes with a textile cleaner.

supplies

1. Stencils
2. Drawing board or flat, smooth surface to which fabric can be tacked for stenciling
3. Thumb tacks
4. Paper towels or absorbent cloths
5. Fabric that has been washed to remove sizing, such as linen, sailcloth, muslin, or gingham
6. Textile paints
7. Stencil brushes (preferably one for each color) with short, stiff bristles
8. Textile cleaner (usually included with commercial textile paint)

connections

Nigeria adire
Starch paste painted through a stencil. Stencil was made from metal and was traditionally done by men.

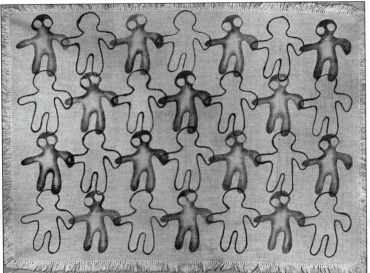

sculpture

14

Sculpture—A brief review

Sculpture is created by manipulation (clay modeling), subtraction (carving), substitution (plaster or bronze casting), and addition (welding). On occasion these may intermix (more clay added to a clay piece) or be combined. It is quite possible that this is the earliest form of art because stone pieces are the oldest artifacts extant. It might be argued that these are not art in the sense that we know it because they may have been primarily utilitarian, or for religion or magic. Perhaps it all began with stone flaking for weapons and stone forming for mortars and pestles used in grinding grain.

The historical sequence of sculpture seems to be carving, modeling (often followed by firing), and casting. These techniques persist to the present with some cultures favoring certain of them. The early Greeks, for example, specialized in carving.

New approaches have proliferated in the twentieth century. Plastics, welding, holography, fluorescent and other light forms, and synthetic metals and media have been used by contemporary artists. Some artists use computers in planning and executing their works.

Sculpture pieces may be mammoth or minuscule and massive (tectonic) or open (atectonic). Open sculpture may feature voids (passages through the work) or large open spaces between attenuated forms. A significant advance in this direction was made by Alexander Calder with his *mobiles* that not only used space but were constructed to move with air currents so that they presented constantly changing views.

A number of artists, Picasso included, have made sculpture works with objects they found, usually discarded items that could be found in junk yards. These were then assembled to form the sculpture. This concept is represented in several of these activities. Analogies from the art world can be found for all of these activities.

A great variety of materials were used to construct life-size animals. Artist: Nancy Graves (1940–1995). American. Camel VI, VII, & VIII, 1968–1969. National Gallery of Canada, Ottawa. Camels VII & VIII (camels on left and right): Gift of Allan Bronfman, Montreal, 1969. © 1996 Estate of Nancy Graves/Licensed by VAGA, New York, NY.

supplies

1. Paper (there are many kinds of paper suitable for paper sculpture—rough, smooth, thick, thin, heavy, fragile, transparent, translucent, opaque, and so on; each has its own particular quality)

2. Scissors

3. Adhesive material (transparent tape, masking tape, glue stick, thick white glue, and so on)

4. Fasteners (small staples, paper clips, and so on)

5. A ruler, compass, or paper punch would be helpful

NOTE: A number of published books deal exclusively with the three-dimensional possibilities of paper.

Paper sculpture

procedure

Experiment with the numerous possibilities of shaping the paper into three-dimensional forms. Several such forms fastened together may result in fascinating figures, animals, or birds. A textured surface can be accomplished by punching a series of holes in the paper or by cutting a series of small slits in the paper and then bending them either inward or outward to enrich the surface.

Paper generally is thought of in terms of two dimensions, such as flat cutout paper shapes fastened to a contrasting color sheet of paper. However, paper can be modeled into numerous three-dimensional forms after some experimentation. Any one or any combination of the following methods can be employed to produce fascinating paper sculpture.

Bending	Fringing	Pinking	Slitting
Curling	Illusion of a solid	Pleating	Twisting
Cutting	Joining	Rolling	Weaving
Folding	Perforating	Scoring	

The following are examples of basic techniques that can be varied in many ways to suit the needs of the artist. Also see Paper Textures, pages 197–198.

Bending—a combination of curling and fringing The fringes of any inside curves must be notched to eliminate overcrowding. The edges may then be fastened to other pieces.

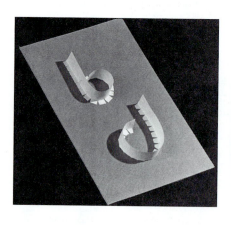

Curling A strip of paper pulled lightly across the dull edge of a scissors blade or over the edge of a table will curl the paper.

Cutting Cut a slit into a folded section, and insert another piece of paper.

Folding Cut along the solid lines of the folded paper, and push into fold on the dotted lines.

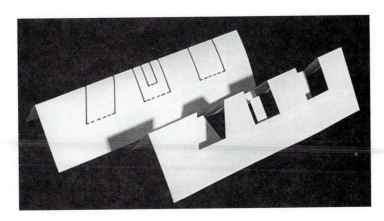

Fringing A piece of paper folded on the dotted line and cut (fringed) along the solid lines will enable the paper to be formed into numerous shapes with an edge to fasten to other pieces.

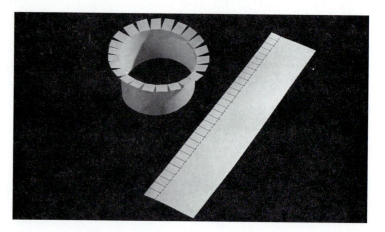

Illusion of a solid Any formal image (both sides the same) can take on the illusion of a three-dimensional form. Cut a number of desired shapes, fold them in half, and cement them together.

Joining Cut along the lines indicated, and join the two ends to produce a three-dimensional form.

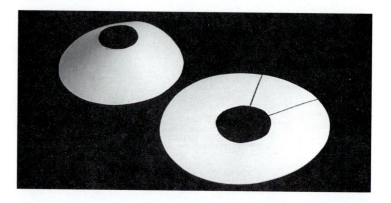

Rolling Using a thin piece of paper, begin at one corner and roll paper as tightly as possible.

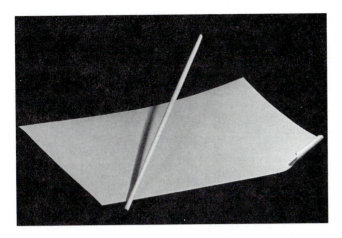

Scoring In order to fold paper along a curve, it is necessary to apply pressure with a comparatively dull instrument (closed scissors or metal nail file) along the length of the curve.

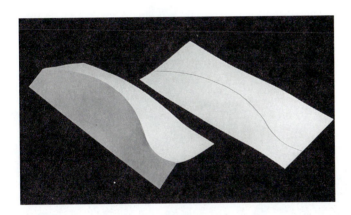

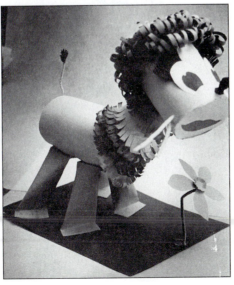

Foil sculpture

supplies

1. Foil
2. Gummed or transparent tape
3. Brush
4. Liquid detergent
5. Tempera paint

procedure

1. Crumple the foil into individual forms that, when assembled, will create a piece of sculpture.
2. Join these forms together with tape or straight pins.
3. Color can be added to the surface by painting with a drop or two of liquid detergent mixed in the tempera paint.

 NOTE: See the following page, Paper Sculpture with Foil Sculpture, for additional ideas.

Paper sculpture with foil sculpture

The combination of paper sculpture and foil sculpture lends itself to the creation of fascinating three-dimensional work. This is best discovered through experimentation with the two materials. See pages 272–275 (Paper Sculpture) and page 276 (Foil Sculpture) for suggestions.

1. Roll of gummed paper tape (the tape, when moistened, will adhere to itself)

2. Scissors (use safety scissors if available)

3. Masking or transparent tape

4. Small sponge

5. Dish for water

Paper tape sculpture

Gummed paper tape is thought of in terms of its two-dimensional applications, such as taping shut a box for mailing. However, gummed paper tape can be modeled into numerous three-dimensional forms after some experimentation. Any one of the following methods can be employed to produce a fascinating piece of tape sculpture.

Bending	Folding	Perforating
Curling	Fringing	Pinking
Cutting	Joining (several	Scoring
Fluting	pieces together)	Twisting

procedure

Experiment with the numerous possibilities of shaping the tape into three-dimensional forms. Several such forms fastened together may result in fascinating figures, animals, or birds. A textured surface can be accomplished by punching a series of holes in the tape or by cutting a series of small slits in the tape and then bending them either inward or outward to enrich the surface.

Stuffed newspaper sculpture

procedure

1. Discuss and show pictures of the chosen subject. Demonstrate the process before the students begin drawing idea sketches.
2. Draw the form chosen on newspaper and cut the intended shape from at least 4 pages of newspaper.
3. Glue or staple two of the shapes together.
4. Glue or staple the remaining two pieces together.
5. Glue or staple the edges of these two sets together, leaving approximately 4″ unglued somewhere along the edge. Allow the glue to dry thoroughly.
6. Stuff crumpled paper through the 4″ opening until the design is a three-dimensional form. Be careful not to tear the design by stuffing too tightly. Small wads of paper work best.
7. Glue and staple the opening together.
8. Paint the surface and spray with clear spray or fix with acrylic medium to keep paint from smudging. **Spray in a well-ventilated area.**
9. If desired, punch holes along the edge of the form and stitch with yarn and a large needle.

supplies

1. Newspaper, newsprint or butcher's paper
2. Thick white glue, stapler, paper punch, and yarn
3. Paint (tempera, latex, acrylic, watercolor)
4. Brush
5. Water container
6. Clear spray or acrylic medium. **(If spray is used, make sure there is good ventilation)**

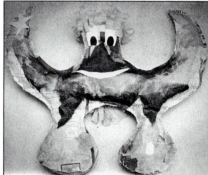

Kachina dolls

Kachina dolls come from the southwestern United States and the Hopi people. One of the Hopi beliefs is that the Kachinas are spirits of animals, plants, and people from the past. They believe that these spirits, over two hundred of them, are both powerful and helpful; and according to legend, these spirits taught the Native American arts and crafts, hunting, and other useful skills. At certain times of the year, the Hopi dancers dress as Kachinas and appear in the Hopi villages.

Kachina dolls are made by the Hopi men. The doll represents the masked dancer known as the *kachina*. The dolls are carved out of cottonwood root, coated with ground clay, and painted. Details such as fur, feathers, and so on, are fastened to the figures. These dolls are not playthings, but are given as sacred objects to the women and children who are not allowed to participate in the dances. This object is their connection to the spirit world.

method a   method b

1. Tag board or heavy paper
2. Scissors
3. Glue, glue stick
4. Scrap paper
5. Crayons, oil pastels, markers

Cylinder forms

procedure

Method a—full figure
1. Mark the center of a rectangle on the long side of the tag board or heavy paper.
2. Directly below the pencil mark, draw a figure with the top of the head at one edge of the paper and the feet at the other edge.
3. Draw all the details that would help form the basic figure into the desired character.
4. Add color.
5. Make into a cylinder by gluing and overlapping the two ends. Add other details.

Method b—full figure with arms and legs

1. Put a pencil mark at the middle of a rectangle of tag board or heavy paper. Draw the head and body of the character directly under that point.
2. Pattern and color the head and body.
3. Overlap and glue the ends of the rectangle to make a cylinder.
4. Cut two smaller rectangles to make cylinder legs. Add color and pattern. Check their size with the body cylinder before gluing.
5. Cut, color, and make two more small cylinders for the arms. Glue to the side of the body below the head. Add hands, feet, and any other details.

supplies

1. Tag board or heavy paper
2. Scissors
3. Glue, glue stick
4. Scrap paper
5. Crayons, oil pastels, markers

Totem poles

The totem poles found on the northwest coast of North America were done by the native peoples. Each pole represented a separate group of people. These separate groups all spoke different languages and each carved differently. The cedar pole was their cultural identity. It showed their family history, achievements, and rights. They believed that all living things were connected. They also believed in the supernatural and spirit world. Certain birds and animals were associated with certain behaviors, abilities, and powers. The animals and birds were often recreated in the dancer's masks.

Humans or humanlike beings were sometimes carved fully upright, but more often in a crouched position. Four-legged animals, especially the bear and beaver, are shown in the same attitude. Birds are shown perched, wings folded or outstretched, with clawed feet and beaks extended out or tucked down against the chest. Most creatures face front with some seen from above. The largest figure on the pole is the most prominent.

Cylinder forms

procedure

Method a—head

1. A single head can be constructed or multiple heads can be drawn on the tag board or paper.
2. Mark the center of a rectangle on the long side of the tab board or heavy paper with a light pencil mark.
3. Make light pencil dots on the paper where the features of the character will go when it becomes a cylinder, but do not glue it. Draw or cut out pieces of construction paper to make the features.
4. Overlap and glue the two ends to make a cylinder.
5. Add any other details that might be interesting, such as eyebrows, hair, ears, beards, glasses, and so on, for the single head. For the totem, wings, bits of fur, beaks, and so on, may be added.

supplies

1. Tag board or heavy paper
2. Scissors
3. Glue, glue stick
4. Scrap paper
5. Crayons, oil pastels, markers

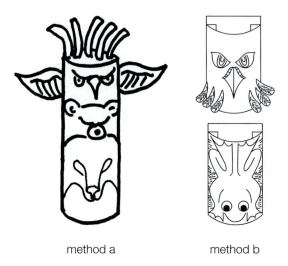

supplies

1. Brown construction paper
2. Tag board
3. Construction paper, various colors
4. White glue, glue stick
5. Marker, crayons, oil pastels

Method b—low relief form

1. Fold the long edges of the brown construction paper approximately ½″ toward the middle. This will serve as a glue tab.
2. The tag board should measure about 1″ longer and 3″ narrower than the brown paper. It will be glued onto the glue tabs so that the brown paper will bow out and form a curved relief.
3. Before fastening the tag board, glue on any of the flat features.
4. Fasten to tag board back and make other three-dimensional features to attach. Since most features will be symmetrical, it would be advisable to cut two at the same time so that they will match.
5. When the students have finished their sections of the totem, they may be mounted one on top of the other on a flat surface.

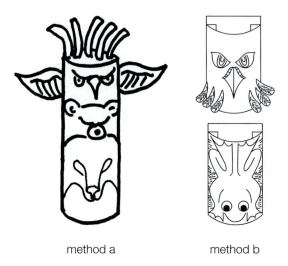

method a   method b

Shallow shadow box

A shallow shadow box may be constructed with a cardboard backing and the top, bottom, and front made from tag board. The objects in this setting may be flat or three-dimensional.

procedure

1. Glue construction paper or a painted scene on the cardboard backing.
2. Cut shapes to be used in the scene. Some of the shapes may be glued to background or they may be raised from the back through the use of Jacob's Ladders or 3D-O's®. The height of the object depends on the length of the papers used in making the Jacob's Ladders or the number of 3D-O's® placed under the object.
3. Cut out a rectangle, 4″ by 6″, 4″ from each end and 1½″ from each side. These openings may be cut several at a time using a utility knife. The knife should be used by the instructor only. The tag board could also be folded in half and the opening cut with scissors. If this is the case, the opening on the folded edge would measure 2″ by 6″.
4. Fold approximately 1″ on each of the long edges (glue tabs). Fold 1½″ from the first crease on each side. This will form a 1½″ depth for the shadow box.
5. The frame may also be decorated before gluing in place.
6. Glue the frame in place with the glue tabs on the back of the backing.

supplies

1. Cardboard such as tablet backs, lightweight corrugated cardboard (7″ by 9″ works well)

2. Tag board (9″ by 12″)

3. Various colors of construction paper

4. Assorted other media such as marker, oil pastels, colored pencils, paint. Glitter glue is fun but slow-drying

5. Thin strips to make Jacob's Ladders or 3D-O's® (Commercial foam buttons that are sticky on both sides)

6. Thick white glue

connections Subject might include undersea scene, space adventure, Native American village, medieval castle, artist at work, or zoo.

Shadow and peep boxes

The shadow and peep boxes are very similar. The shadow box is like a miniature stage set and the peep box deals more with placement of the objects inside the box and the light sources. The shadow box works well with all age levels and the peep box seems to work best with a more mature student.

Both the shadow and peep box lend themselves to scenes from stories, poems, songs, or paintings. A make-believe aquarium with suspended fish and other creatures hanging by strings and colored cellophane on the face of the shadow box or over the light sources of a peep box give the illusion of water. The shadow box may also be used as a miniature puppet theater.

It is important to discuss the chosen subject and to demonstrate the possibilities before beginning the activity.

procedures

Peep box

1. Cut a small spy hole opening in one end of a box. In some cases an opening in both ends is advisable. **Use safety scissors if available. A utility knife may be used by the instructor.**

2. Cut a number of openings or doors in the lid in order to allow light in the box. These openings can be placed strategically to allow spotlighting. Light can be controlled in the box by opening or closing the doors in the lid.

Peep box and shadow box proceed in the same manner from this point

1. Design the sides or the back of the box. Any one of a number of techniques may be used for this: potato print, crayon engraving, chalk stencil, colored paper, finger paint, acrylic, tempera, watercolor paint, etc.
2. Many methods are available for making trees, houses, barns, figures, etc. Cleansing tissue can be modeled as foliage for trees. It may be tinted with paint. Bits of sponge or foam also make good foliage when colored. Paper sculpture may be used to make objects.

Houses, barns, and other buildings can be made from tiny boxes, corrugated cardboard, or paper sculpture. These, too, may be painted with acrylic, tempera, or watercolor paints.

Figures and animals can be made from wire, pipe cleaners, clay, salt and flour mixture, papier-mâché, clothespins, etc.

 NOTES: With the peep box it would be better to put larger objects in back so that they do not obscure other forms. Small and shorter objects would be better if placed closer to the peep hole.

The possibilities of this project are unlimited. The materials and methods should be chosen to fit the age and capabilities of the students.

1. Tag board for main parts of animals
2. Colored construction paper may be used for some of the details
3. Scissors
4. Glue or glue stick
5. Crayons, markers, or oil pastels

Folded three-dimensional animals

Discuss and show pictures of four-legged animals before beginning.

procedure

1. Fold tag board in half to form a tent shape.
2. Draw and cut a rounded shape on the open edges to form the four legs. **Use safety scissors if available.**
3. Color the outside of the body and legs.
4. Cut and color additional pieces of tag board to add necks, heads, ears, tails, and anything else to make the chosen animal.
5. Glue in place. Cut and fold pieces of tag board to use as glue tabs if necessary.
6. If necessary, use glue tabs to hold legs in position so that the animal will stand.

Wooden block people

procedure

1. A discussion including pictures of sculpture, and the artist Marisol in particular, should precede the beginning of the activity. It is important to point out that the piece will be viewed from all sides.
2. The students should draw each of the sides of the figure in pencil on the newsprint. It would help to draw around the piece of wood on the paper so that the drawings will be the correct size for the wood. The front of the figure would normally go on one of the four inch sides.
3. Pay attention to details, on the face and on the body.
4. Transfer the drawing to the wood.
5. Add color.

supplies

1. Wooden 2″ by 4″ pieces of wood. The length can be determined
2. Pencil
3. Newsprint
4. Markers, or paint

connections

Marisol Escobar
Sargent Claude Johnson

Container sculpture

1. Empty milk cartons of plastic containers

2. Scissors or mat or utility knife. **When working with young students, the knife should be used by an instructor**

3. Masking tape or thick white glue

4. Tempera or acrylic paint

5. Brush

6. Small amount of liquid detergent

procedure

1. Make a decision as to the kind of sculpture desired (people, animals, machinery, buildings, cars, trucks, and so on).
2. Make the necessary cuts or cutouts with a cutting tool. (**Take care with cutting tools.**)
3. Fasten the parts together with tape or glue.
4. Paint, if necessary. A few drops of liquid detergent added to tempera paint will allow paint to adhere to waxy surfaces.

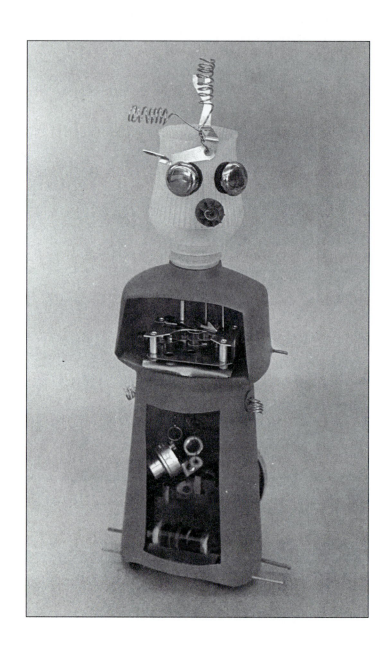

Box sculpture

procedure

The technique should be preceded by a discussion of sculpture in general and, more specifically, the materials to be used and the possibilities in the construction of different forms. Playing with the different supplies before beginning would be helpful so that the students have a chance to experiment and see the objects from different angles.

1. White glue
2. Bread
3. Lemon juice
4. Paint (watercolor, tempera, acrylic)
5. Brush
6. Plastic bag

NOTE: Various materials may be added for details.

Bread dough sculpture

procedure

1. Remove the crusts from four slices of bread.
2. Tear the bread into small pieces, mixing them thoroughly with three tablespoons of white glue and 1 or 2 drops of lemon juice.
3. Model or cut as desired, allowing 1 to 2 days for complete drying.
4. Pieces may be painted with watercolor, tempera, or acrylic paints.
5. The clay can be preserved for modeling by wrapping in plastic and placing in a refrigerator.

Plaster space forms

procedure

1. Inflate the balloon, and tie the end closed.
2. Mix the plaster (see p. 125).
3. Holding one end of the yarn, immerse it in the plaster (if the yarn is too fine, use a double or triple strand). Pull the yarn from the bowl and through the fingers of one hand, wiping off the excess plaster.
4. Place the plaster-saturated yarn on the inflated balloon in a decorative manner, making sure the yarn crosses over itself frequently.
5. Allow the plaster to harden and dry thoroughly before puncturing the balloon.
6. Hold the plaster-decorated balloon in a wastebasket or large cardboard box to catch the numerous plaster chips that fall when the balloon is punctured.
7. Gently smooth any rough edges, and paint the plaster. Spray paint will work best. **Use spray paint with optimum ventilation.** Painting before the balloon is punctured will leave the inside pure white.
8. Additional decoration of various materials can be placed inside the space form.

⚠️ **CAUTION:** Begin to clean up when the plaster begins to thicken—it will harden rapidly once the chemical reaction takes place. Any remaining plaster should be wiped from the pan immediately and rolled in newspaper so that it can be disposed of more easily. Do not wash plaster down any drain. When cleaning hands, tools, and mixing pan, be sure the water runs continuously. The instructor should handle clean-up.

supplies

1. Plaster
2. Small balloon
3. Yarn
4. Bowl for mixing plaster
5. Can of spray paint, if color is desired

1. Natural material (seeds, twigs)

2. Thick white glue

3. Acrylic medium or clear spray.

4. Paint

5. Construction paper

6. Felt

Natural object sculpture

procedure

1. Collect a number of natural objects of various sizes and colors.
2. Arrange several of these items to create a small piece of sculpture.
3. When satisfied with the creation, glue it together.
4. Paint or colored paper can be added to enhance the sculpture.
5. Paint with acrylic medium or spray to finish. **If spray is used, be sure of optimum ventilation.**
6. Glue a piece of felt to the bottom to prevent scratching.

Salt and flour sculpture

procedure

1. Discuss with the students the subject for the sculpture and show pictures if possible. Point out that the form will be viewed from all sides.
2. Mix salt, flour, and alum to the consistency of putty. Add color if desired.
3. After the pieces have dried and hardened, they may be painted with acrylic medium for permanence.

supplies

1. 1 cup salt
2. 1 cup flour
3. 1 tablespoon powdered alum
4. Mixing bowl
5. Food coloring or dry tempera (if color is desired)
6. Acrylic medium and brush
7. Alcohol for cleaning brush

NOTE: See other formulas and hints on page 390.

Sawdust sculpture

procedure

1. Mix the sawdust and thinned white glue, stirring the mixture to the consistency of plastic clay.
2. Form the desired shape with the hands. An inner support of wire or wood is needed to brace large forms.
3. When dry, the sculpture can be painted with tempera paint.
4. A clear plastic spray or several coats of shellac will preserve the finish. **Spray in a well-ventilated area.**

supplies

1. Sawdust
2. Thinned white glue
3. Brush
4. Tempera or acrylic paint
5. Acrylic medium or use clear spray

1. Molding plaster
2. Container for mixing plaster
3. Shallow box or container for mold—may be lined with plastic
4. Fine sand

Sand casting

procedure

1. Fill the shallow container with moist beach sand, and pack it tightly.
2. Form a mold by scooping out various shapes of different depths. (If a beach is handy, the pattern can be made on the spot, rather than in a box.)
3. Mix the plaster (see p. 125).
4. Pour the plaster into the mold.
5. Allow the plaster to harden before removing from the sand mold.

CAUTION: Begin to clean up immediately after pouring the plaster in the mold—it will harden rapidly once the chemical reaction takes place. Any remaining plaster should be wiped from the pan immediately and rolled in newspaper so that it can be disposed of more easily. Do not wash plaster down any drain. When cleaning hands, tools, and mixing pan, be sure the water runs continuously. The instructor should handle the clean-up.

Soda and cornstarch sculpture

procedure

1. Combine the first three ingredients in a saucepan, and cook over medium heat, stirring constantly.
2. When the mixture is thickened to a doughlike consistency, turn out on a piece of aluminum foil or on a breadboard.
3. Food coloring may be worked into the clay when it has cooled slightly.
4. When not in use, keep the clay covered with aluminum or in a plastic bag, and store it in the refrigerator to keep it pliable.
5. Clay may be rolled and cut into shapes or may be modeled into small shapes.
6. Watercolor, tempera, or acrylic may be used to paint the clay objects when they are thoroughly dry.
7. The painted objects may be sprayed with clear plastic, or acrylic medium may be brushed on. **Spray in a well-ventilated area.**

supplies

1. 1 cup cornstarch
2. 2 cups baking soda (1 lb. box)
3. 1¼ cups water
4. Saucepan
5. Stove or hot plate
6. Aluminum foil
7. Food coloring
8. Plastic bag
9. Watercolor, tempera, or acrylic paint
10. Plastic spray or acrylic medium with brush

NOTE: If the shape is to be hung, a hole may be punched in the top of the ornament while the clay is soft, or a soft wire may be inserted in the back while the clay is soft. Instructor should prepare the mixture.

Slotted cardboard structure

1. Poster board, tablet backs, any other heavy cardboard
2. Scissors
3. Pencil

connections

Naum Gabo

Berto Lardera

Nicolas Schoffer

Sidney Gordin

Isamu Noguchi used abstract images that could be taken apart and composed again. The forms fit into notches and slots. He was especially interested in space, balance, shape, and image.

A discussion of sculpture with pictures should precede the activity. A demonstration of the possibilities would be helpful.

procedure

1. Cut out squares or circles of cardboard. These shapes can be cut out or partially cut out on a paper cutter.
2. Draw a short line at the center of each of the four edges of the square shape. If using a circle, it may be easier to use a pattern to draw 4 short lines of equal distance on four edges of the circle.
3. Cut on the short line to make the cut that will hold the shapes together.
4. Begin to build.

VARIATION: Cut notches in the corners of the square.

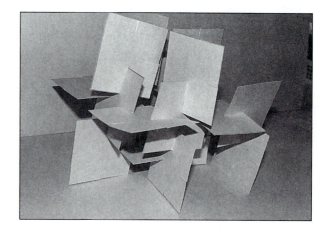

Folded cube design

This shape includes six sides and the glue tabs to make the cube. The sides may be related by subject or through the use of art elements. The subject may be varied and may range from designing letter blocks or making the cube into a human head.

procedure

1. Make a pattern from mat board or cardboard.
2. Students or instructor could draw around the pattern on white paper.
3. Cut out the shape carefully, cutting away the largest pieces of scrap first and then cutting away the small parts.
4. Fold carefully and accurately on the fold lines. This will show the sides and the glue tabs.
5. It is important for the student to identify the parts of the cube as they will relate when the cube is glued together. This will enable the student to design it as a flat shape. In this case, there will need to be a top and bottom. The top is the part of the pattern that has no glue tabs. The bottom is the center square area of the cross.
6. Design the cube on all sides in pencil first and then using the chosen media.
7. Put glue on the outside of the glue tabs on the sides that will fold up and touch the other sides. This will make a box with an open lid.
8. Put glue on the outside of the glue tabs at the top and close the lid.

supplies

1. Cardboard or mat board to make pattern for cubes
2. Paper large enough to use a pattern of the cube
3. Pencil and ruler
4. Safety scissors
5. Colored pencils, markers, pens, oil pastels, crayons, and so forth
6. Thick white glue

NOTE: Paper measuring 18″ by 24″ will make a cube with 5″ sides.

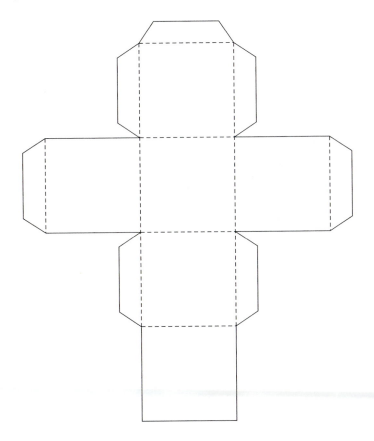

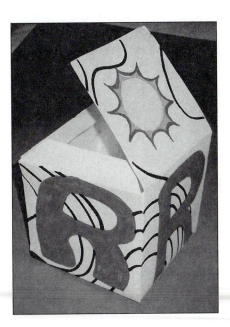

Paper cube design

The paper cube can be designed to work with almost any subject. It can depict styles of different artists or the animals of the rain forest. It can show different kinds of butterflies or display the elements of art on each side. It is also fun to try and design it in such a way that there are no obvious beginnings or ends or tops or bottoms. The design is the most important element of the cube.

procedure

1. The paper squares should be cut carefully on a paper cutter. They should be exactly square and there should be six pieces for each cube.
2. Cut strips that are 2″ wide and as long as the length of the paper square. Each frame for the cube will need 12 strips.
3. It is helpful to discuss the subject or subjects to be used on the cube, how they will connect the sides of the cube, and where they will meet on the corners. All sides should be considered, not just the four sides. It is helpful to do simple designs on newsprint before beginning work on the sides.
4. Number each of the sides in the same spot so that it will be easy to find their proper placement.
5. Draw the design in pencil lightly on all sides, and add color or value when the design is completed.
6. Make the frame for the cube. Fold each of the 12 strips in half lengthwise. Begin the fold in the middle by rolling one edge to the other edge and continue to the ends. They must be straight.
7. Make one frame by gluing four folded strips. They should meet exactly in the corner.
8. Make a second frame.
9. Glue a folded strip vertically in the corner of the first frame. Make sure it sits down in the corner.
10. Glue the second frame on top of the vertical corners.
11. Attach the sides on the outside of the frame in their proper position.

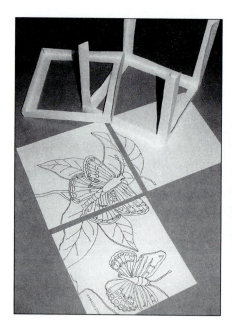
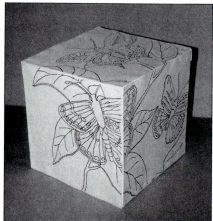

Triangular room

This simple form is a variation of the peep box. It is important to discuss different kinds of rooms and their purposes. Discuss the different kinds of things found in different rooms. For instance, a room in a museum is very different than a room in a store, and there are many different kinds of stores, such as pet, clothing, food, toy, etc.

procedure

1. Fold 9″ by 12″ tag board in half.
2. Design the inside of the room with the fold as the corner of the room. Draw with pencil.
3. Add color to the inside of the room. Color and pattern make the room more interesting.
4. When the room is finished, score the long edges of the 6″ by 9″ piece of tag board to form glue tabs about ¼″ wide.
5. Draw an opening, such as a window or a door, on the front side of the tag board. Add color and detail to the front.
6. With an X-acto knife, and a cardboard underneath, cut out the opening.
7. Put glue on the glue tabs and glue the front to the triangular room.

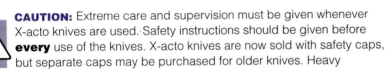

CAUTION: Extreme care and supervision must be given whenever X-acto knives are used. Safety instructions should be given before **every** use of the knives. X-acto knives are now sold with safety caps, but separate caps may be purchased for older knives. Heavy corrugated cardboard should always be placed under the paper or material being cut. The X-acto knife is held like a pencil, with the fingers holding the knife on the textured ring. The slanted, sharpened edge should be directly over the line to be cut, and the position of the knife or the paper should be changed if the line changes direction. Keep the fingers of the holding hand out of the way of the blade, above the cutting area. Remind students often to check themselves and the position of the knife and their hands. The safety cap should be on the knife at all times except when actually in use.

supplies

1. Tag board, 9″ by 12″
2. Tag board, 6″ by 9″
3. Pencil
4. Colored pencils, pens, markers, crayons, or oil pastels
5. Ruler and old scissors
6. X-acto knife, cardboard
7. Thick white glue

NOTE: Three triangular rooms can be paper clipped together and mounted on a bulletin board.

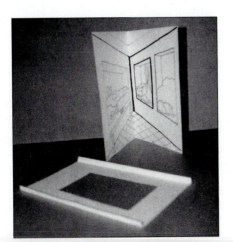

connections

Alexander Calder
Mark di Suvero
Antoine Pevsner
Alberto Giacometti
David Smith

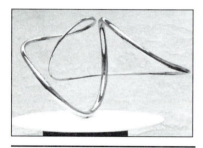

Graceful curves of the kind seen here can be produced with wire. José de Riviera, American, b. 1904, Brussels Construction, stainless steel, 1958, 118.1 × 200.6 cm. Gift of Mr. and Mrs. R. Howard Goldsmith, 1961.46. Photograph © 1996, The Art Institute of Chicago, All Rights Reserved.

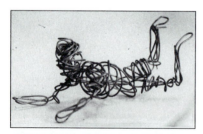

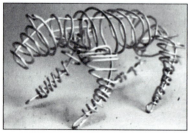

Wire sculpture

procedure

1. A discussion of sculpture with pictures would be very helpful before beginning the activity. A drawing, such as the tonal drawing (in the chapter on pencil, paint, and ink), could be a good way to begin. It must be remembered that the drawing is to be transformed into a three-dimensional work and should not be followed too literally.

2. Bend and twist the wire into the desired shapes. Coils may serve as figure elements and these may be created by wrapping the wire around such objects as sticks, pencils, or bottles. Make sure the objects can be removed.

3. Wire sculptures are generally conceived as one continuous length of wire, but they may consist of several lengths joined together. If several pieces are used, they may be hooked, wound, or soldered together.

4. Paint may be added if it is felt that color will improve the appearance of the work. Other materials, such as wood, sponge, plastics, and so on, may also be combined with the wire. The American sculptor, Alexander Calder, did a great deal of work in this medium.

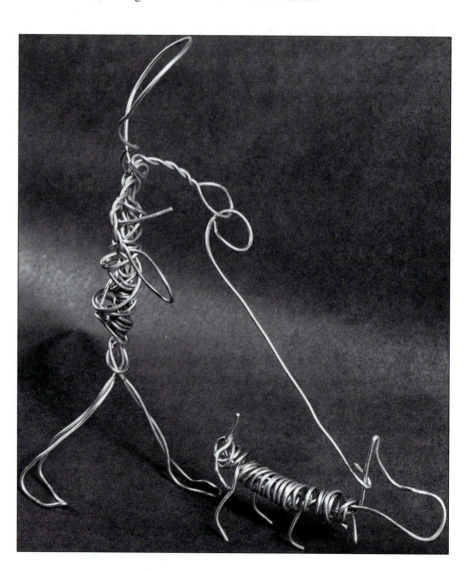

Soda straw construction

It would be advisable to have a discussion about sculpture and three-dimensional construction. A demonstration showing the triangular or a tetrahedron construction is necessary.

procedure

1. Demonstrate making a simple triangle by stringing three straws on a piece of yarn and tying the end of the yarn together.
2. Demonstrate making a tetrahedron shape by stringing three straws, adding two more straws to make a diamond shape, and one extra straw to finish the shape.
3. Colored tissue or cellophane could be added.

supplies

1. Soda straws
2. Yarn
3. A needle would be helpful

R. Buckminster Fuller

Kenneth Snelson

connections

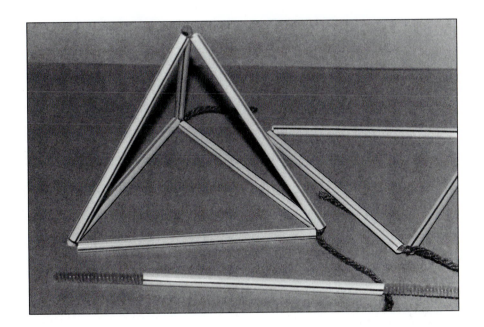

1. Thick Tacky Glue
2. Toothpicks or craft sticks

Toothpick sculpture

procedure

A discussion of sculpture, and the use of this media in particular, should precede this activity. Glue the toothpicks or craft sticks together to form various three-dimensional structures.

connections Naum Gabo

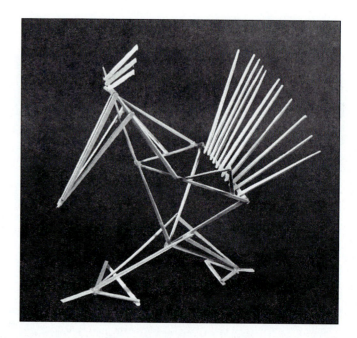

Wood scrap sculpture

A discussion of sculpture with pictures would be appropriate before beginning the activity. It should be pointed out that a piece of sculpture should present interesting views of all sides. Louise Nevelson was well known for her assemblage sculpture.

procedure

1. From a generous supply of small pieces of scrap wood of various sizes and colors, choose those piece that will work well together in creating a piece of sculpture.
2. When the arrangement is satisfactory glue all the components together.
3. Paint or crayon decorations can be added to finish the sculpture.

connections

Joseph Cornell

This is an example of "assemblage" sculpture in which pieces of wood are modified, refined, and put together. Louise Nevelson, American, 1900–1988, America Dawn, painted wood, 1962, 548.6 × 426.7 × 304.8 cm. Grant J. Pick Purchase Fund, 1967.387, photograph © 1996. The Art Institute of Chicago. All Rights Reserved.

Mobiles

Mobiles have been in existence for centuries in many countries. The Chinese glass windbells are probably the best known. A mobile is created to produce movement with changing patterns. In addition, a mobile is a problem in balance, design, sculpture, form, space, and color. Mobiles, like many other projects in this book, when simplified, are most successful in the primary grades. This form of sculpture was further developed by the American sculptor, Alexander Calder.

procedure

1. Decide the number of units to be used in the mobile and their method of construction. These objects can be made from paper, wire, papier-mâché, salt and flour, wood, and so on, or a combination of any of these materials. Remember that an effective mobile should contain objects that have some kind of relationship to each other.
2. Attach a thread to each object so that it hangs evenly. This would make a finished mobile for the child in the primary grades.
3. Cut a support (a piece of wire or small wood dowel) and suspend an object from each end, making sure that the separation is great enough to prevent the parts from touching. **Use wire cutter with caution.**
4. Place a spot of glue on the very ends of the wire or dowel to help hold the thread of each object when tied in place. The threads supporting the objects should be comparatively short but of different lengths.
5. Tie another thread to the wire or dowel supporting the mobile by the thread. Slide the thread back and forth on the wire or dowel until it finds a point of balance. Secure it with a spot of glue. This would be a complete mobile for older children. A mobile is built from the bottom up, so that this part will be the bottom if more pieces are to be added and the mobile is to become more complex.
6. The thread holding the section just completed should be tied to the end of another wire or dowel and held in place with glue. Suspend an object from the other end of the wire or dowel.
7. Balance both sections on a single thread.
8. Any number of sections can be added as long as balance is maintained.

supplies

1. Thread
2. Supports, such as heavy stovepipe wire, small welding rods, strips of wood, dowels or lightweight coat hangers
3. Wire cutters
4. Thick white glue
5. Materials for making objects to be suspended (paper, wire, plastics, cardboard, soda straws, and so on)

NOTE: A wire stretched in a seldom-used corner of the room will enable the children to hang their mobiles while working on them. There is no limit to the ways a mobile can be constructed, once the principle of movement and balance is understood.

1

Development of mobile by adding and balancing related units from numbers 1 through 7.

2

3

4

5

6

7

Plaster wrap figures

1. A piece of cardboard, to be used as a body, cut according to the desired size (a tube may be used)

2. Yarn, to be used as hair

3. Assorted fabrics

4. White glue

5. Newspaper

6. Paints (acrylic is recommended, tempera may be used)

7. Plaster wrap, (fabric, in a roll, with preapplied coating of plaster)

NOTE: This procedure describes one method for making a small figure; experimentation will lead to many other possibilities.

procedure

1. Roll up the cardboard to produce a cone. Staple or glue the ends together. Cut off the point.
2. Wad up newspaper and tape into desired head shape.
3. Tape the head on the narrow end of the cone.
4. Cut the plaster wrap into different sizes, so that small strips or pieces may be used for the head and longer strips for the body.
5. Cut fairly long strips of plaster wrap to a width suitable for the length of both arms. Cut in half and dampen so that there will be two matching arms. Attach to the cone body.
6. Cover everything with a coat of plaster wrap.
7. Allow form to dry and paint. If tempera is to be used, attach hair first with glue or the yarn may be dipped in thinned white glue and attached. If acrylic paint is used, the form can be painted and the hair attached afterward.
8. Material or all kinds of trim may be attached after painting. Discuss the character after the figure has been formed and before it is painted or dressed. It should be pointed out that the figure will be viewed from all sides. When a character has been chosen, the students should continue.

Plaster wrap with an armature

procedure

1. Discuss the subject to be used for the plaster wrap.
2. Do several sketches of the subject, remembering to think about all views of the subject.
3. Make an armature for the subject, using wire, newspaper, mailing tubes, plastic pieces, Styrofoam, etc. Tape or wire can be used to hold everything together.
4. Cut the plaster wrap into appropriate-sized strips and pieces.
5. Dip the strips into warm water and lay them in different directions over the base form. Smooth each strip before putting on the next strip. Two or three layers would be sufficient, but it is sometimes difficult to tell how many layers are on the piece because the strips are all the same color. Check for holes before allowing the piece to dry. Check edges to make sure they are smooth.
6. Allow the plaster wrap to dry. If it is still damp, the plaster wrap will feel cool to the touch.
7. Sandpaper if desired.
8. Finish. If tempera paint is used for decoration, the surface should be sealed with acrylic medium, shellac, or varnish. **If a spray is used as a sealer, make sure that there is good ventilation.**
9. Additional material such as yarn, buttons, fun fur, pipe cleaners, felt, etc., can be added to enrich the finished work.

supplies

1. Plaster wrap. Gauze impregnated with plaster
2. Water container
3. Materials for the armature or frame. This could include rolled and taped newspaper, wire, mailing tubes, plastic mask forms, Styrofoam, molded packing Styrofoam, etc.
4. Sandpaper
5. Paint such as tempera, latex, enamel, oil, or acrylic
6. Clear acrylic medium, shellac, or varnish to protect the finish if tempera is used. **If spray sealer is used, make sure there is adequate ventilation.**

connections

Max Ernst
Alberto Giacometti
Henry Moore
Pablo Picasso
Reg Butler
Kenneth Armitage
Henri Laurens
Jacques Lipchitz
Edgar Degas
Auguste Rodin
George Segal
Michelangelo
Donatello
Chinese bronze horses
Papier-mâché could also be used over an armature.

Plaster block carving

A discussion of sculpture, including pictures, would be of great value before beginning this activity. It is especially important to point out that all sides of the sculpture will be viewed.

procedure

1. Mix ½ plaster, to ¼ sand and ¼ vermiculite, or cat litter may be added before beginning to mix the plaster and water.
2. Mix the plaster as discussed in the chapter on crafts.
3. Pour mixture immediately into the wax container mold.
4. Jiggle gently and tap the sides lightly to bring any bubbles to the top.
5. When the plaster is set, remove the container mold.
6. On newsprint, draw around the shape of the hardened plaster mixture. Plan on the newsprint as if you were looking at each side of the finished work.
7. Rough in the general shapes first using a handsaw hacksaw, or a simple chisel. **Make sure the chisel is worked away from the artist's hands and body.**
8. Keep turning the piece so that there is a good view of all sides.
9. Use a wood rasp, hacksaw blade, or gouge to make smaller details.
10. Use a scraper, a table knife, or sandpaper to add other details.

Some ways to finish plaster sculptures
1. Stains are diluted color. Shoe polish can be worked in and polished to make it look shaded.
2. Paints—oil, acrylic, or tempera that has been mixed with acrylic medium works well on plaster. Details may be painted on or the entire piece can be colored and antiqued with a darker glaze.
3. Metallic finishes may also be applied.

1. Wax-coated container to use as a mold. Large milk or juice containers work well
2. Plaster of Paris or molding plaster
3. Sand, vermiculite, or cat litter adds color and texture
4. Container for mixing plaster
5. Water
6. Newspaper for cleaning
7. Handsaw, hacksaw, gouge, scraper, table knife, and sandpaper. Any sharp stick or even a nail file might be used. **Take care in handling any sharp tool.**

NOTES: Vermiculite is found in building supplies.

The block is softest when it is first taken from the mold.

connections

Constantin Brancusi

Henry Moore

Cast plaster bas-relief

procedure

1. Discuss bas-relief and show examples. Discuss the chosen subject and show pictures. Students need to draw several drawings the same size as the box to be used for the casting.
2. Fill the bottom half of the container with plastic clay.
3. Place the drawing over the clay in the container, and transfer the drawing to the clay by tracing over the lines with a sharp pencil, pressing only heavily enough to make an impression in the clay.
4. Model or carve the design in the clay, making sure that none of the edges have undercuts. **Use carving tools with caution.**
5. Brush a thin film of oil on the clay to serve as a separating agent.
6. Mix the plaster (see illustrations on page 125).
7. Pour the plaster into the mold over the clay relief to the desired thickness. Agitate the container gently to bring any bubbles to the surface. A wire hook can be placed in the plaster before it hardens completely (Ill. 1).
8. Allow the plaster to harden before removing the cardboard mold. Then, remove the clay from the plaster. Apply the final finish after repairing any flaws that may appear in the plaster. Wash off any water-base clay that adheres to the plaster (Ill. 2).
9. Any of the following type finishes can be applied to the plaster.
   a. If tempera paint decorations are applied to the plaster, clear plastic spray, shellac, or varnish can be painted over the surface for permanency. **Use spray with optimum ventilation.**
   b. A pure white glossy finish can be achieved by soaking the plaster relief for approximately 30 minutes in a solution of dissolved white soap flakes and then wiping dry with a cloth.
   c. An antique finish can be obtained by soaking the plaster cast in linseed oil. The cast should then be removed from the bath, and while still wet, dusted with dry yellow ochre or umber. Wipe off any excess coloring with a cloth until the antique finish is suitable.
   d. The plaster plaque, when decorated with enamel or oil-base paint, needs protective finish.

CAUTION: Begin to clean up immediately after pouring the plaster in the mold, as it will harden rapidly once the chemical reaction takes place. Any excess plaster remaining should be wiped from the pan immediately and rolled in newspaper so that it might be disposed of more easily. Do not wash plaster down any drain. When cleaning hands, tools, and mixing pan, be sure the water runs continuously.

connections

Jean Arp
Mary Martin
Ben Nicholson
Lorenzo Giberti
Andrea Pisano
Donatello

supplies

1. Cardboard container (lid or bottom of a box, paper plate, and so on)
2. Modeling clay (either water- or oil-base clay)
3. Modeling tool, such as an orange stick, nail file, or knife
4. Modeling plaster
5. Container for mixing plaster
6. Separating agent, such as salad oil, green soap, or Vaseline
7. Brush
8. See procedure 9 for supplies used in finishing

Clay may be formed with the hands, blocks, or modeling tools.

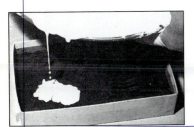
1

2

Carved plaster bas-relief

supplies

1. Cardboard container to be used as a mold (paper plate, lid or bottom of a box, and so on)

2. Molding plaster

3. Container for mixing plaster

4. Carving tool, such as scissors, knife, chisel, or nail

5. Pencil and paper

6. See procedure 7 for supplies used in finishes

connections

Jean Arp
Mary Martin
Ben Nicholson
Raoul Ubec
Lorenzo Ghiberti
Andrea Pisano
Luca Della Robbia
Donatello
Filippo Brunelleschi

procedure

1. Discuss bas-relief and show examples. Discuss the chosen subject and show pictures. Students need to draw several drawings before selecting one to use with their relief.

2. Mix the plaster (see page 125). Pour into the mold.

3. Allow the plaster to harden and dry thoroughly before removing the cardboard mold. Should some of the cardboard adhere to the plaster, wash it off under running water. A thin coating of Vaseline will prevent the plaster from sticking to the box.

4. Smooth the sharp edges by scraping with any available tool.

5. Transfer the drawing to the plaster.

6. Carve the design into the plaster, using any suitable carving tool. **Use carving tools with care.** Soaking the plaster in water will facilitate its carving. As plaster is very brittle, it is suggested that it be placed on a soft pad to avoid breakage.

7. Any of the following finishes can be applied to the carved plaster.

    a. If tempera paint decorations are applied to the plaster, clear plastic spray, shellac, or varnish can be painted over the surface for permanency. **Use spray with optimum ventilation.**

    b. A pure white glossy finish can be achieved by soaking the plaster relief for approximately 30 minutes in a solution of dissolved white soap flakes, and then wiping dry with a cloth.

    c. An antique finish can be obtained by soaking the plaster cast in linseed oil. The cast should then be removed from the bath and, while still wet, dusted with dry yellow ochre or umber. Wipe off any excess coloring with a cloth until the antique finish is suitable.

    d. The plaster plaque, when decorated with enamel or oil-base paint, needs no protective finish.

CAUTION: Begin to clean up immediately after pouring the plaster in the mold—it will harden rapidly once the chemical reaction takes place. Any remaining plaster should be wiped from the pan immediately and rolled in newspaper so that it may be disposed of more easily. Do not wash plaster down any drain. When cleaning hands, tools, and mixing pan, be sure the water runs continuously.

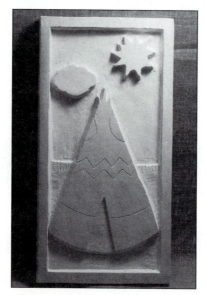

Bas-relief

It is important to have a discussion, including pictures, about sculpture in general and the bas-relief in particular. After the discussion, a demonstration would be very helpful.

Bas-relief with cardboard

Method a

procedure

1. Cut the cardboard base to size.
2. Cut out shapes to be added to the base by cutting from additional cardboard. Styrofoam is easy to cut and would work well too.
3. The relief may be finished by applying paint or paint mixed with detergent if Styrofoam is used.
4. The relief may be covered with heavy-duty aluminum foil by smoothing a coat of thick white glue on top and placing the foil on top. An attractive texture can be obtained by crushing the foil lightly and smoothing it out before beginning to glue it down. Gently press down in the low areas being careful not to tear the foil, and then smooth it over the higher relief. Extra foil can be turned to the back of the cardboard.
5. India ink can be put on top of the foil and rubbed off to create an antique effect.

supplies

1. Cardboard, one piece to be used for the back
2. Cardboard to be cut up for the relief shapes. Styrofoam cuts easily and would be suitable for younger students
3. Thick white glue
4. Paint, watercolor, acrylic, tempera
5. Detergent, if Styrofoam is used
6. Heavy-duty aluminum foil

connections

Gacomo Manzu

Auguste Rodin

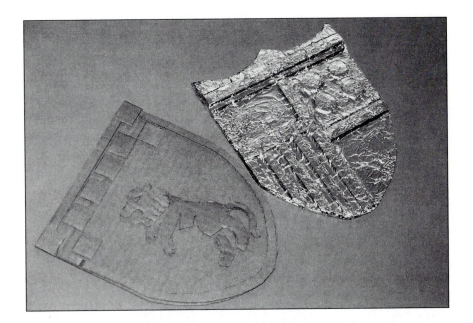

Bas-relief with plaster wrap

Method b

procedure

1. Build up the relief with the various materials as if making a collage. Experiment with using different materials.
2. Glue the materials securely to the backing using thick white glue.
3. When the collage is dry, dip the plaster wrap in water and lay the strips on top of the collage. Carefully and gently press the strips around and over the objects so that they have the desired form.
4. After the plaster wrap is dry, it may be finished with paint or sealed to remain white.

supplies

supplies

1. Heavy cardboard or Masonite for backing
2. Various materials as for a collage, for example, pieces of wood, Styrofoam, wadded newspaper, cardboard, foam core board, bottle caps
3. Thick white glue
4. Plaster wrap
5. Water container
6. Newspaper for clean-up

Bas-relief with Crayola Model Magic®

Method c

procedure

1. Using the box lid as the base for the relief, begin modeling the Crayola Model Magic®.
2. A frame may be made by making a coil of the modeling material and lining the inside of the box lid.
3. Figures, animals, birds, and so on, may be modeled first and placed into the lid. Blend the shapes together where they join.
4. When the relief is finished, it may be finished with color provided by markers, watercolor paints, acrylic paints, or tempera paint.
5. If markers, watercolors, or tempera is used it may be necessary to seal the finish by painting on acrylic medium or spraying on a clear sealer. **If a spray is used, be very careful that there is good ventilation.**

supplies

1. Box lid, a gift box works well
2. Crayola Model Magic®
3. Small tools to help with modeling: popsicle stick, pointed sticks, etc.
4. Water container
5. Watercolors, markers, acrylic
6. Acrylic medium or a clear spray finish. **Be sure there is good ventilation**

fibers

15

Nature of the medium

Weaving

Weaving has been used since ancient times because of the basic need for cloth. Weaving is the interlacing of fiber. The fiber running lengthwise is the *warp* and the fiber that crosses and is woven into the warp is called the *weft*. The first weavings were probably done with fingers and very primitive looms. Ancient people quickly learned to twine and twist fiber to produce different textures. They also used various natural dyes to produce many different colors. Now, very complicated and powerful looms produce all the fiber products needed for modern society. Computers are used to help plan the design and to render the weaving.

Still, people in many cultures cling to the old ways of producing fiber products. Hand looms are still used by many craftsmen, baskets are still woven by hand, and people still dye their own fiber. The use of color and texture, and the wide variety of available materials, have led many contemporary artists to reexamine and explore many aspects of the media. Plastics, paper, yarn, cloth strips, natural objects, reed, and cord have been used by artists. Many objects, such as bells, beads, branches, rods, and so on, are incorporated into the weavings. Almost anything that can be interwoven or wrapped is used to create both two-dimensional and three-dimensional forms.

Batik

Batik is a technique that uses molten wax to paint or draw on fabric, and then the fabric is dipped in or painted with wet dyes. The waxed areas repel or resist the dyes. Each time a new dye color is introduced on the fabric, parts of that color are waxed to preserve it until the desired color scheme is achieved.

It is difficult to pinpoint the exact origins of batik. Some fragments were found in first century Egyptian tombs, but that might have been obtained through trade. Evidence has been found that it originated in Asia and spread to the Malaysian area. Java and Bali are famous for batiks and batik garments are worn in Japan and China. Much of the paisley patterns of India and the symmetrical tribal patterns of Africa are batik.

Tie-dye

Tie-dye probably began in ancient Asia and spread down the sub-Indian continent to Malaya and across Africa. On the American continent, the earliest tie-dyed fabrics date from pre-Columbian times. Tie-dyed fabrics come from Mexico, Guatemala, Peru, Bolivia, Paraguay, and Argentina. In North America, the Pueblo people and other Native Americans used the craft at a later time.

Tie-dye is a resist technique used with fabric. The fabric is gathered or folded in various patterns and held in place by tying knots, stitching, tying cords, or placing rubber bands. Objects can also be tied into the fabric. The unusual textures are caused by the dye as it seeps around the ties. Fabrics can be tied and dyed one color, untied and then retied a slightly different way and redyed another color. This can be repeated several times. The fabric is allowed to dry and all the knots are removed.

Coiling

Coiling is a method for making baskets employed for centuries by almost every culture. Although it is still usually used for making baskets, contemporary artists have made more sculptural forms using this technique. The weft or wrapping material is the thread that wraps around the core or warp and holds the core together in a form.

Stitchery

Stitchery is the technique of using a needle like a paint brush and the yarn like paint. Yarn comes in hundreds of colors, many different weights, and different textures. There are at least 300 different stitches but it is only necessary to learn a few of the simple basic stitches. These stitches can be varied by changing the size of the thread, changing the spacing between the stitches, distorting the stitches, and combining the stitches in patterns. Stitchery can teach color relationships, balance, good spacing, proportion, and texture.

Appliqué

An appliqué is a piece of fabric fastened on another larger piece of fabric. The edges may be turned under and hemmed down or left raw and held down with stitches near the edge or over it. Stitches may become important and be decorative or the stitches may be strictly to hold appliqués in place. Quilts often use appliqué.

Appliqué may also be done in a reverse manner. Openings of any size or shape may be cut in the larger piece of fabric and another piece laid underneath to show through the opening. This may be done several times so that several colors show. The edges may or may not be turned in and stitched, and stitches may be added to the design. Molas are an example of reverse appliqué. They are unique to Panama, particularly the San Blas Islands. The oldest molas usually have three layers of black, red, and yellow, and the designs are simplified human, animal, or floral forms.

Cloth skirt (mola) made by the Chvenaque Indians of Panama. Courtesy of the National Museum of the American Indian Smithsonian Institution (Neg. #18670).

Paper weaving

procedure

1. Paper, construction paper, crepe, cellophane, metallic, tissue, butcher paper, velour, gift wrap, ribbons, cloth, tape, wall paper, and felt

2. Safety scissors. Paper edger scissors

3. Pencil

1. Fold the paper in half and cut a series of cuts that go from the fold up to approximately 1″ from the open edges. These cuts may be straight, curved, or jagged. They may be drawn before cutting. This will be the *warp* or the skeleton for the weaving.
2. Cut or tear strips of paper. These strips are called the *weft*.
3. Open the paper that was cut in step 1. Weave the strips through the slits or cuts in the paper.
4. A simple weave called a *tabby weave* is over one, under one, and so on.

VARIATION: Experimentation is fun. Try gluing a thin colored strip on a thicker strip before it is woven through the warp. Aluminum foil can be used for strips. Try using a paper punch to put holes in the weft. Try weaving on a different shape (such as a dog, cat, or other form).

VARIATION: Cut or tear strips and begin weaving using four strips in a vertical position and four strips in a horizontal position. Continue to weave to the end of the strips. A dot of glue or paste will help hold the strips in place.

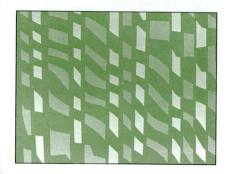

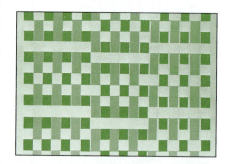

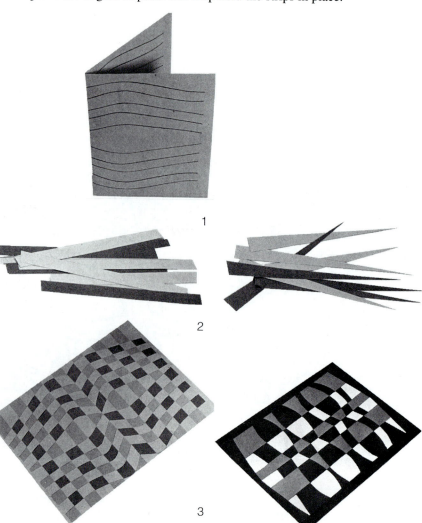

1

2

3

Straw weaving

procedure

1. Use 4 or 5 straws. Any number may be used; from 2 to as many as 10 can be held in the hand.
2. Cut as many pieces of yarn as you have straws. **Use safety scissors if available.** They should be equal and as long as you want the finished weaving to be.
3. Thread or suck each yarn through its own straw. Turn over the yarn at the end of the straw, and fasten it at the top by using a piece of tape wrapped around the yarn end and the straw (Ill. 1).
4. Keep the tape as smooth as possible.
5. Tie all the loose ends together with an overhand knot.
6. Begin weaving by tying the end of a small ball of yarn to the first straw. (Any yarn may be used, but variegated yarn will make an automatic pattern.)
7. Work the yarn over and under the straws, moving back and forth with the yarn moving up on the straws (Ill. 2).
8. To add a new color, simply tie it on and continue weaving.
9. As the weaving progresses, gently push the weaving down on the straws. If the weaving is tight, gently pull the straws up—this allows more room for weaving on the straws. Do *not* push the weaving completely off the straws; although as the weaving builds up, it will gradually go onto the yarn by itself.
10. Continue weaving until the weaving reaches the overhand knot and is tight.
11. Finish by pushing all the weaving off the straws. Cut the end of the straws where the tape holds the yarn. This allows enough yarn for another overhand knot to be tied to hold the weaving in place.

supplies

1. Common soda straws, cut in half
2. Yarn
3. Transparent tape
4. Scissors

NOTE: It is vital that a discussion of weaving and its history take place before beginning. The students also need to know the proper vocabulary for weaving. The **warp** is the string that goes through the straws and it is the skeleton for the weaving. The yarn that is woven on the straws is the **weft,** and it makes the color and pattern of the weaving. The weave produced is **tabby weave** or a simple over and under pattern.

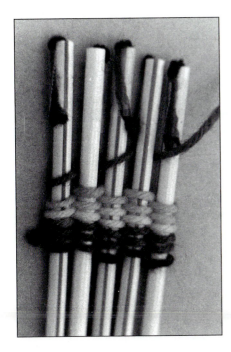

1

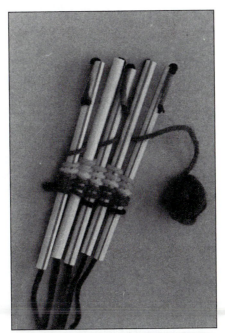

2

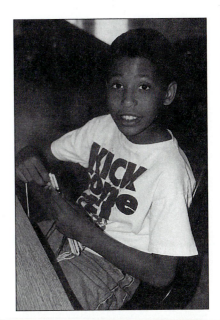

1. Popsicle or ice cream sticks (six to eight drilled sticks, 4 undrilled sticks)

2. Glue

3. Yarn

4. Pencil

5. Scissors

6. Comb

7. Fine sandpaper or an emery board

8. 9" length of ½" dowel

9. Coat hanger, 12" piece

Backstrap loom weaving

Any loom on which the warp is held taut between the weaver's body and a stationary object, such as a table or a hook, is called a *backstrap loom*. This type of weaving has been done all over the world. It is has been used in Asia and Scandinavia and is still being used in Mexico, Guatemala, and some South American countries. Native Americans of the Zuni and Navajo tribes have used this technique to make sashes and belts.

It is important to have a discussion of the technique of weaving and more specifically the use of the backstrap loom before beginning. Students should know the necessary terms before beginning.

Terms

Harness Made from popsicle sticks in this case. The warp threads go through the holes in the sticks and also in between the sticks. When the harness is raised, it divides the warp and creates a **shed** so that the yarn can pass easily over every other warp strand.

Backstrap belt Can be made of old sheets and will hold the warp beam securely to the body of the weaver.

Warp beam The rod and wire tool that will hold the warp threads next to the body.

Warp The yarns that are the skeleton for the weaving. They will be threaded through the holes in the heddle and through the slots between the sticks of the harness.

Weft The yarns that are woven through the warp.

Tabby weave A simple over and under pattern of weaving.

Shuttle A tool to help get the string through the shed from one side to another. It can be made by simply wrapping the excess weft around a piece of cardboard.

Beater A tool to comb the weft tight to the other weaving. A comb or fork works well.

procedure

1. Construct the harness for the loom. Drill a hole in the center of 6 or 8 popsicle or ice cream sticks. Place 2 undrilled sticks in a horizontal position. Place and glue 1 drilled stick at each end of the 2 undrilled sticks in a vertical position to form a square. If the sticks are placed in the corner of a sheet of paper, it is very easy to have a straight square (Ill. 1). Arrange evenly and glue the remaining drilled sticks in the space between the end sticks. Put a drop of glue at each end of the drilled sticks and place the 2 remaining undrilled sticks across each end. Place a book or weight on top until the harness dries completely.

2. String, or warp, the loom. Cut strands of yarn approximately 36 inches long. **Use safety scissors if available.** Cut one strand of yarn in one color for each hole in the harness. Cut another set of strands in another color for each space between the drilled sticks in the harness. Gather all the yarns together, and tie an overhand knot at one end. Comb the loose ends to straighten, and thread through the harness using the same color yarn for all the holes in the sticks and the other color for all the spaces between the sticks. Comb the yarn again to straighten, and tie the yarns onto the warp beam. Test the tension by bouncing the hand off the taut warp threads. If some are too loose, adjust and retie. The space between the yarn on the dowel should be the same as on the rigid heddle.

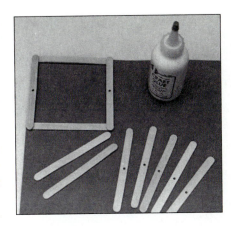

   It is also possible to tie each end of the warp by the overhand knots to two stable objects rather than use the weaver's body. If this method is used, it is necessary to weave 4 popsicle sticks into the warp next to the overhand knot and between the knot and the heddle.

3. Check the loom by raising the harness. All of the yarn going through the holes will be lifted. This forms a space, or shed, where the yarn being woven will go. Lower the harness, and all the strands going through the spaces will be in a raised position, also forming a shed. If the yarn catches in the spaces between the sticks, it may be necessary to sand lightly or use a emery board to help smooth the area.

4. Begin weaving. Make a shed again, and insert the end of a ball of yarn, allowing 2″ to hang out the left side, with the ball on the right. Change the position of the harness and push the 2″ end into the shed. Pass the ball of yarn from right to left (this weaves the end in). Continue passing the ball of yarn back and forth as the harness is changed. The yarn should be loose on the edges so that the warp is not distorted. Push the yarn together by using a comb or fork. This simple weaving is a *tabby weave.* Variety can be obtained by using different colors and different weight and texture yarns. Other materials can also be woven into the warp strands.

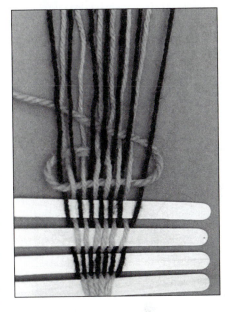

5. Loops and rya knots may also be added. (See Cardboard Loom Weaving.)

6. To finish the weaving, cut or untie the overhand knot furthest away from the weaving. Gently remove the harness. A simple overhand knot may be tied close to the weaving with the loose ends, or two warp yarns at a time may be tied together in an overhand knot close to the weaving.

1. Heavy cardboard, mat board, illustration board, or corrugated cardboard
2. Yarn
3. Scissors
4. Comb or fork
5. Ruler
6. Pencil

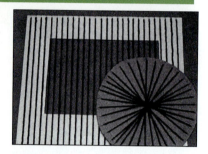

1

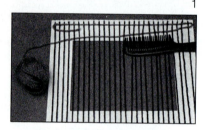

2

3

Cardboard loom weaving

It is vital that there be a discussion of the history and technique of weaving. Samples or pictures would be very helpful and a demonstration is important before beginning the weaving.

procedure

1. Construct the loom. The loom may be constructed by stapling four pieces of heavy cardboard at the corners to make a frame (Ill. 1), or by using a solid piece of cardboard. Cut small notches ½″ apart in two opposite sides of the square or rectangle. In the case of a circle loom (Ill. 1), cut notches ½″ apart all around the edge. **Use safety scissors if available.**

2. String or warp the loom by placing a knot in one end of a small ball of yarn. Place the knot in the first notch, and bring it from the back to the front of the loom. Loop the yarn around the first tooth (formed by the notches) on the opposite end of the loom. Continue looping the yarn back and forth around the teeth until the loom is finished. Knot the end of the yarn at the back of the last notch. The yarn should lie flat on the front surface of the cardboard. Do not pull the string too tight or the loom will buckle when weaving.

3. Make a small ball of yarn to weave on the loom (weft). Begin weaving by using a simple over and under pattern (tabby weave). It is not necessary to tie the yarn to the warp or to a new colored yarn. Just weave in the ends; they will stay in place. Push the rows of weaving together with a comb or fork (Ill. 2). (The comb or fork serves as a beater.)

4. Variety can be added to the weaving by adding different kinds of knots.

5. To make a loop called a *rya knot,* use a tabby weave, moving from right to left and allowing extra yarn at the right side of the loom. Take the point of a pencil or a stick and lift the weft yarn where it passes *over* the warp yarns (every other strand). While the yarn is still looped over the pencil, weave another row of tabby weave from left to right. Gently remove the pencil and comb and beat tight.

6. Ghiordes knots are a good way to use short (3″ to 4″) yarn scraps. Place the short pieces (2 or 3 work well) across two of the warp strands. Bring both ends of the short pieces down, around, and up between the two warp strands (Ill. 3). Make sure the short ends are pointing toward the existing weaving. Slide the knot up to the weaving by pulling the short ends. Continue to make knots. To make a second row of knots, skip the first warp yarn and make the first knot, using the second and third warp yarns. This will lock the first row in place. If a third row is desired, make the first knot, again using the first and second warp yarns.

7. Soumak and Egyptian are warp wrapping techniques that work well with hand weaving.

8. When the weaving is as large as desired, finish by removing the warp yarns from the teeth of the cardboard loom. Tie any loose ends.

9. Dowels or branches can be pushed through the warp loops on one end to use as a hanger.

Terms

1. *Loom* Machine or frame operated by hand or driven by power for weaving cloth.
2. *Warp* Lengthwise threads in a fabric or on a loom.
3. *Weft* The thread crossing and woven into the warp.

4. *Beater* Tool used to push weft threads together.
5. *Rya knot* Uses a continual length of cord wrapped around the warp to form a looped pile. The length is determined by the stick placed under the loops. Tabby rows hold the loops in place.
6. *Ghiordes knot* Related to the rya to create a raised pile.
7. *Soumak knot* A wrapped warp technique. The weft passes over the warp and loops behind it and then over itself in front.
8. *Egyptian knot* Also a wrapped warp technique. It is the opposite of the Soumak. The weft is passed under the warp and looped over the front, and it crosses itself behind the warp.

VARIATION: Looms can be made in many shapes. The round loom is an interesting variation.

1. To prepare a round shape, draw a line across the center of the circle. Draw another straight line at right angles to the first line so that they cross in the center of the circle. Draw two more lines, trying to space them so that the segments are equal. There will be 8 segments. On one end of one line, write a number 1. On the opposite side, write a number 2. Just above the No. 2, write No. 3. Just below No. 1, write No. 4. Cut the same number of notches in each of the segments, except the segment that contains the 1 and the 4. In that section, add one more notch.
2. The warp should be strung using a full ball of yarn so that there will be enough yarn. Begin by tying a knot in the end of the yarn and slipping it through No. 1 with the knot to the back. Stretch the yarn gently across the face of the loom and slide it into No. 2 notch. Bring the yarn through No. 3 notch and across the loom to No. 4. The yarn should cross in the center. Continue to warp the loom. When finished, bring the last line to the center and tie in a knot to gather all the strings together.
3. Weaving begins in the center, but it is better to weave a little way from the center and beat into the center with each row of weaving.

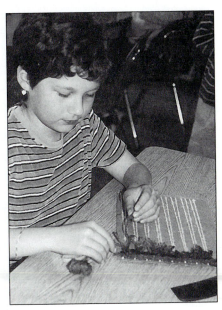

Tapestry

During the Middle Ages, tapestry was hung on the walls of castles and cathedrals and was used in parades and at tournaments.

Tapestry can be done on a simple frame or cardboard loom. It cannot be detailed, but the student will gain an understanding of tapestry technique. Tapestry is when the warp strands are divided into groups almost like small looms. Each group may be done with a different color or texture of yarn. This will create shapes on the weaving. It is necessary to do some planning before beginning.

procedure

1. Wrap the loom as instructed with the Cardboard Loom.
2. Begin weaving with a tabby weave (over and under) for a short stripe of color.
3. Count the number of warp strands.
4. Decide on the shape to weave. For instance, if there are 21 warp strands and the student wants to put a square in the center in one color with a different color on each side, the square might be 7 strands wide with 7 on each side, or it might be 15 strands wide with 3 on each side. It simply means that the weaving will be done in 3 different sections.
5. The needle is very important with tapestry because it helps when weaving on only parts of the loom at one time.
6. Where the color joins at the edge of the shape with the surrounding color may be done in 3 different ways. 1. The two colors may be linked together (Ill. 1). 2. The two colors may share the warp strand at the edge (Ill. 2). 3. The two weft may not join at all, and a split will be formed between the two colors (Ill. 3).
7. The other weaves and knots may be used with a tapestry (Cardboard Loom).

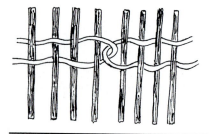

(Ill. 1) The weft strands link together.

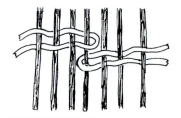

(Ill. 2) The two weft strands share one of the warp strands.

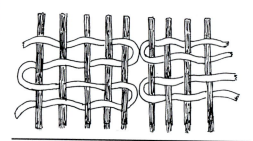

(Ill. 3) The weft strands do not link the two colors together, and a split is formed.

God's eye—Ojo de Dios

This Mexican craft involves the organized wrapping of yarn around a crosspiece of some material, usually wooden sticks. They can be wrapped in different ways to create different patterns, and they can be as small as toothpicks or as large as you care to make them.

procedure

1. Glue sticks together in a crossed position.
2. Cut a piece of yarn about 6′ long.
3. Hold one end of the yarn next to the center on one of the spokes. Bring the long end of yarn around the same spoke on top of the yarn end to hold it in place.
4. Turning the crosspiece in a counterclockwise direction, wrap the long end of yarn around the next spoke, going under and around.
5. Turn and wrap under and around the next spoke.
6. Turn and wrap under and around the next spoke.
7. At the place of beginning, lay the next wrap beside the first wrap so that the yarn will build up toward the end of the spoke.
8. Continue wrapping, always in the same direction.
9. When the spokes are filled almost to the end, put the end of the yarn through the last string and make a knot near one of the spokes.

VARIATION: A tree branch in the shape of the letter Y (like a slingshot) works very nicely as a base for the wrapping of a God's Eye.

VARIATION: With a larger God's Eye, at the midpoint of wrapping, turn the sticks over and continue to wrap the yarn from under or behind and around the sticks in a counterclockwise direction. The diamond design will appear on both the front and the back of the God's Eye.

supplies

1. Yarn. Variegated yarn will make an automatic pattern. Even short scraps of yarn can be used
2. Popsicle sticks, tongue depressors, or dowel sticks
3. White glue

NOTE: The front side should have a diamond pattern.

Coiling

1. Core material, Fiber Flex, or cotton clothesline

2. Yarn of all textures and colors or material cut into strips

3. Tapestry needle

NOTE: A discussion of the coiling technique and a demonstration is vital before beginning.

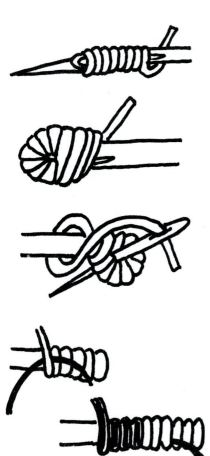

procedure

1. Taper the core end. Cut the core at an angle for 1½″.
2. Cut 3′ or 4′ of colored yarn or cloth and thread on a tapestry needle.
3. Lay the other end of the wrapping yarn along the core for about 1″ and ½″ from the tapered end. Wrap around the core and yarn end until it is long enough to bend back on itself.
4. Wrap the core and the tail end of the core together. This forms the center of the spiral. Wraps need to be tight.
5. There should be a very small opening in the center of the loop. Wrap the yarn around the cord away from the loop 5 times to hold it in place. Place two stitches through the hole in the loop.
6. The Lazy Squaw stitch goes directly across from one coil, around the previous coil and back to the outer coil to begin wrapping again. The Figure Eight stitch follows the contour of the coil being wrapped, goes between the two coils and around the previous coil, between the two coils again and begins wrapping the outer coil. From the edge, the stitch looks like a number 8 and blends with the coils.
7. Plan the number of wraps before going on, usually 5 to 7 wraps for double yarn and 8 to 10 wraps for single yarn.
8. The core should be placed in a spiral form as it is wrapped, taking stitches at regular intervals.
9. A hot pad may be made of a coiled spiral.
10. If a basket is desired, the bottom of the basket is at least 3″ wide before coiling the walls. To make the walls, as the stitch is taken, the coil is placed on top of the previous row rather than beside it. If the coil is placed directly above the previous row, a straight-sided form will result. A sloping side results when the new coil is placed slightly to the outside of the previous coil.

11. To add yarn or change color, make sure there are 6 to 8 wraps left on the old yarn. Place the end of the new yarn along the core so that both yarns are together. Wrap the new yarn around both ends and the core several times and take a stitch.

12. To finish, cut a tapered end on the core material. After wrapping to the end, take several stitches and, with the needle, pull the end of the yarn between the core and the wrap to hide and hold the end of the yarn.

The coiling technique has been used for weaving baskets for centuries by many different cultures. Native Americans have used coiling extensively. One of the natural core materials used was pine needle bunches. The bunches are held together by raffia, thread, or fine grass strands.

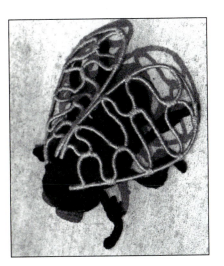

Cotton roving

1. Cotton roving (inexpensive, bulky cotton yarn)
2. Heavy white glue
3. Newspaper or a paper for covering work surface
4. Paste applicator or spreader (brush, piece of cardboard)
5. Safety scissors
6. Cardboard

procedure

1. Discuss the subject and show pictures if possible. Draw a design on heavy cardboard or matt board.
2. Cover the main shape with a heavy layer of white glue as if drawing an outline. Dampen the roving or yarn so that it is more pliable, and lay the desired color in the glue. Be careful not to stretch the roving when applying.
3. Cut the roving when the shape is completed. Use safety scissors if available.
4. Gently pat the roving into the glue.
5. Continue with a second line of roving inside the first outline.
6. Continue until desired result is obtained, changing colors if necessary.

NOTES: Roving can also be wrapped around a glue-covered shape cut from cardboard or any other three-dimensional object.

Roving takes patience. It would be better to work on a smaller piece of cardboard. Keep in mind that the background should also be considered and should be covered with roving.

connections

The Huichol people of Mexico create these yarn paintings called *Nearikas* by laying the yarn in warmed wax. The pictures tell stories about animals, birds, plants, and people, and they are somewhat abstract. They are created by the Huichol men.

Huichol Yarn Painting. 1978, Mexico. From the Girard Collection in the Museum of International Folk Art, a unit of the Museum of New Mexico. Photographer: Mark Schwartz.

Stitchery

Method a

1. Remove the selvage (the edge on either side of a woven fabric finished to prevent raveling), and pull the threads on the burlap so the sides are straight.
2. Put a dab of white glue on each corner to prevent raveling.
3. Pull interior threads and fill vacated space with colored yarn.
4. Patterns and variations can be achieved by going over two warp threads, under one, or any other combination.
5. Felt or fabrics can be appliquéd.
6. Various stitches, such as chain stitching, can be used.

Stitches

Running Stitch

Backstitch

Split Stitch

Stem Stitch

Satin Stitch

Chain Stitch

Couching Stitch

Blanket Stitch

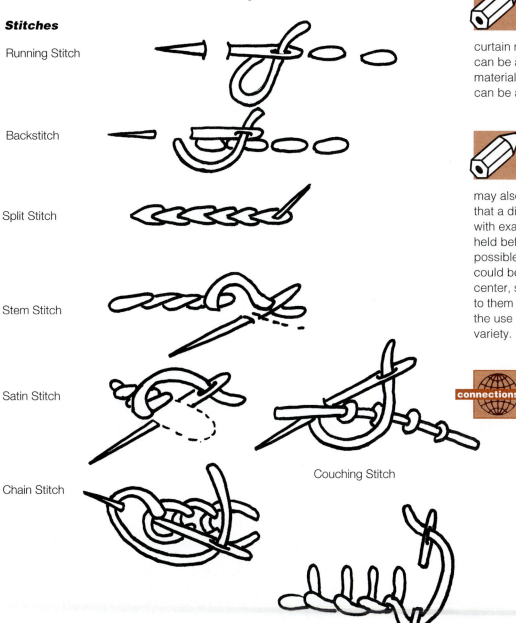

NOTE: Additional fringing can be added at the bottom for wall hangings. Small curtain rods, doweling, or sticks can be attached to the top so the material will be held straight and can be attached to the wall.

NOTE: A discussion of subjects and photos should be shown to the students. Background may also be considered. It is vital that a discussion of the technique with examples of stitchery be held before beginning work. If possible, a display of the stitches could be used as a learning center, so that students may refer to them any any time. Encourage the use of different stiches for variety.

connections

Ancient Egypt
Ancient Greece
Mesopotamia

1. Colored burlap
2. Assorted colors and sizes of yarn
3. Tapestry needle
4. Newsprint and pencil
5. Chalk or erasable fabric marker or pencil

Method b

1. Remove the selvage (the edge of the fabric finished to prevent raveling) and pull threads so that the sides are straight.
2. Put a dab of glue on each corner to prevent raveling.
3. Draw a design on newsprint the same size as the burlap.
4. If the main object is large enough, cut it out and use it as a pattern by drawing around it with chalk or an erasable fabric pencil or marker.
5. Complete the drawing of the design on the burlap.
6. Thread the needle with one end of the yarn long and one end short. The knot goes in the long end.
7. Bring the needle from the back of the burlap when beginning so that the knot will be on the back of fabric.
8. Use any of the stitches.

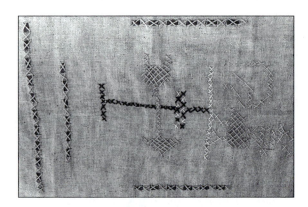

© James L. Shaffer

Appliqué

It is believed that appliqué was made in ancient times, but very little is left because fabric is so easily destroyed. Remnants of wall hangings and saddle covers have been found in Siberian tombs that date from 200 B.C. Hangings and animals wrapped in appliqué have been found in the Royal Egyptian tombs.

In the Middle Ages in Europe, appliqué was used for banners and military and ecclesiastic clothing. Appliqué developed as a way of reusing pieces of beautiful woven fabric with the other pieces of cloth. Appliqué was used instead of embroidery.

Appliqué has been used in England, America, India, Thailand, Central Europe, Tibet, Iran, Hawaii, Central and South America, and Africa.

procedure

1. The edges of the background material may be fringed before starting the picture. This will give a more finished look to the piece.
2. When the design has been decided upon, the shapes to be used in the picture may be cut and laid on the background until the arrangement is satisfactory. **Use safety scissors if available.**
3. The pieces of cloth are appliquéd to the background by using a variety of stitches chosen by the designer. A long running stitch or an overcast stitch is perhaps the easiest for young children to use.
4. The picture may be pressed with a warm iron when finished.

NOTE: The technique of appliqué can be used to make banners, wall hangings, pillows, and many other products.

supplies

1. A piece of loosely woven material cut to the size and shape of the finished picture (colored burlap is most satisfactory, as the open weave makes stitching easier)
2. Materials to be appliquéd to the background cloth (felt or any other type of material that will not ravel or fray too easily)
3. Large, blunt needles
4. Thread, colored yarn, raffia, or string for stitching
5. Safety scissors

connections

Appliqué banners used by the ruler of the Fon people of Africa include brightly colored animals, plants, and people. They tell the history and instruct the young. *Tar Beach* by Faith Ringgold, Crown Publishers, Inc., New York, N.Y., 1991

Appliqué with glue

supplies

1. Fabrics with all kinds of patterns

2. Tag board or gray cardboard

3. Fabric glue or thick white glue

4. Sharp scissors that will cut fabric

5. Permanent marker

6. Variety of trim scraps, including lace and buttons

procedure

1. Cut pieces of material into different shapes, such as squares, rectangles, triangles, egg shapes, free forms, and so on.
2. Lay the shapes on the cardboard and arrange the shapes. Try several arrangements before gluing.
3. Glue by putting glue on the cardboard and place the material pieces on top, one at a time.
4. Make sure all of the edges and corners are tight.
5. When the cardboard is completely covered with fabric, other materials such as trim can be glued in place.
6. A permanent marker can be used to simulate stitches on the edges of the material. The stitches should be different too.

connections

Mary Had a Little Lamb by Sarah Josepha Buell Hale, Orchard Books, New York, N.Y., 1995

Felt picture

procedure

1. When a design has been decided upon, the shape to be used in the picture may be cut directly from the felt, or patterns can be made of cardboard. **Use safety scissors if available.**
2. Arrange the cut pieces of felt on a felt background until satisfactory.
3. Glue or sew the pieces in place to complete the picture.

supplies

1. Colored felt
2. Scissors
3. White or textile glue
4. Needle and thread (if design is to be sewn)

Felt mola

A mola is a reverse appliqué. The material is cut through to reveal the colors of the various layers underneath.

1. Felt, 4 pieces of different colors
2. Needle and thread
3. Pins
4. Tacky Glue (to be used in place of stitching)
5. Newsprint and pencil
6. Sharp scissors

procedure

1. Using newsprint the same size as the first piece of felt, draw a design. Traditionally, the main shape is a bird, animal, reptile, insect, or human figure.
2. Cut the main shape from the newsprint to use it as a pattern to draw around on the first piece of felt.
3. Carefully cut the shape from the felt (save all of the cutout pieces).
4. Pin the cut top piece of felt to another piece of felt of a different color and mark both for additional cuts.
5. Cut and put a different color of felt under the two layers of cut felt and mark again for cuts through all layers.
6. A fourth layer of felt is put under all three layers of cut felt.
7. Pin in place and sew with small running stitches (see the section, Stitchery). It is also possible to glue the layers of felt with Tacky Glue.

NOTES: The extra pieces of felt can be used as an applied appliqué.

It is vital that there be a discussion of the Mola technique and its history, and that pictures of Molas be shown before any drawing takes place.

connections

The Mola is a reverse appliqué technique done by the women of the Cuna Indians of San Blas Island, located along the Caribbean coast of Panama. The women are the center of Cuna life. The property of the family is passed to the children by the mother. The molas as we know them are really the front and back panels of the Cuna women's blouse. They are beautifully made, using animal, lizard, bird, human, and plant motifs.

Tie and dye

Tied and dyed material is made by dipping cloth in a dye bath after having wound parts of the cloth tightly with string or cord. The tightly wound string prevents the color dye from reaching parts of the fabric, creating a resist retaining the original color of the cloth. The tied and dyed method is suitable for numerous possibilities, including scarfs, blouses, T-shirts, aprons, and so on.

procedure for tying

1. *Concentric squares* Fold materials on the two diagonals of the cloth shape, and wind string tightly at intervals from the middle.
2. *Concentric circles* Pick up the cloth from the middle, and fold as evenly as possible away from the middle point, tying string tightly around the cloth at several intervals. When dipped in dye, the areas where the string was tied will create concentric circles and remain the color of the cloth.
3. *Varied shapes* Marbles or pebbles tied in the cloth will create interesting effects. Blocks of hard wood cut in various shapes and tied in the cloth (so not so much dye is absorbed) also create different designs.
4. *Stripes* Roll the cloth into a small tube and tie it with strong knots. Cloth folded accordion-style and tied tightly with string at intervals will also create stripes.

CAUTION: Always use rubber gloves when handling dyes.

supplies

1. Enamel, glass, copper, or brass cooking utensil
2. Jars for storing dye
3. Sticks for stirring dye
4. Hot plate
5. Iron to press finished material
6. Commercial dyes
7. Cloth, such as muslin, silk, or any material that will absorb dye easily
8. String cord or rubber bands
9. Marbles, small stones, or pieces of wood
10. Rubber gloves

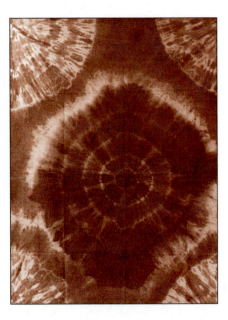

Nigeria tie-dye done by tying, folding, and stitching. Traditionally fabrics are dyed using indigo.

procedure for dyeing

1. The fabric to be dyed must be clean. Make sure all sizing is removed by washing vigorously with soap and hot water.
2. Plan your design by tying cloth in any combinations (Ill. 1). It may be wise to first experiment with a scrap piece of cloth.
3. Mix the dye as indicated on the box.
4. Dip the material in warm water before dyeing. This will tighten the tied string and also conform to the dyeing instructions on the dye box. Wring out excess water.
5. Place the cloth in dye solution, and stir constantly with a stick or hand (use rubber gloves) so materials will be dyed evenly (Ill. 2).
6. Leave the material in dye for only a few minutes or dye will penetrate the tied places.
7. Remove from the dye, and rinse in cold water (Ill. 3). Put the dye in a glass container to keep for future use.
8. If another color is to be used, untie the strings desired, retie at other spots, and put in the next color dye solution.
9. Allow the cloth to drip dry or wring out excess water.
10. Press the cloth with a hot iron while it is still damp. This will also help set the color.

VARIATION: Tie-Dye Color Cords are another way of doing tie-dye. The cords are impregnated with color dyes and the color transfers from the cords to the fabric, thus making designs. The designs are dependent upon the way the cloth is folded or tied and if cords are laid inside the folds along with being used for the tying. The color cords can be used on all cotton and rayon fabrics or cotton or rayon fabric blends. There are selected colors available in packages of 30 cords that are about 3′ long. It takes at least 4 cords per yard of material (1 T-shirt) for a simple design and more for anything complex.

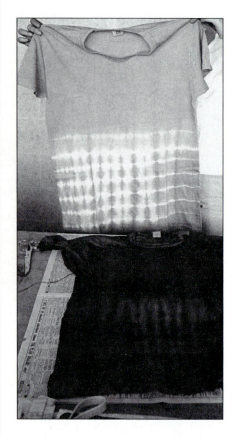

3

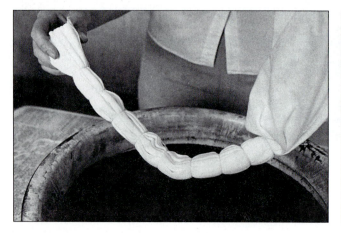

1

2

Melted crayon batik and print

Before beginning, it is important to discuss and show pictures of the chosen subject and also to give a brief demonstration.

procedure

1. Fasten cloth to board with masking tape, stretching the cloth as tightly as possible.
2. Draw the design on the cloth using a soft pencil.
3. Hold the end of the crayon briefly over the flame of the candle until the crayon softens.
4. Press, drag, or drip softened crayon on the drawing.
5. A number of different colors can be used to complete the design.
6. Don't let the crayon get too short. Take every precaution.
7. When finished with the melted crayon, the cloth may be painted with various colored dyes rather than dipping the cloth. The crayon will resist the dye.
8. The decision may be to dip the cloth in a bucket with dye so that all of the unwaxed areas of the cloth will be the color of the dye. If that is the case, remove the cloth from the board, dip it in cold water (crumple if a crackle effect is desired), and place it in the glue solution, stirring constantly with a stick. Remember to wear gloves when handling dye.
9. Remove the cloth from the dye, rinse it in cold water, and allow it to drip dry. If the dye is painted on the cloth, it should also be rinsed out and allowed to dry.
10. To make the print of the crayon portion of the batik, place the dried cloth on a pad of newspaper and cover the design with a piece of paper. Cover with newspaper and iron until the crayon has transferred to the paper. Only one print can be made.
11. Store the dye in an airtight container.

 CAUTION: Baking soda should be kept nearby whenever hot wax is used in case of fire. Every precaution should be observed. Rubber gloves should always be used when handling dyes.

supplies

1. Wax crayons, with paper wrapping removed
2. Newsprint
3. Candle
4. Cloth (cotton muslin or any natural material that will absorb the dye easily. Avoid permanent press fabrics)
5. Dye and wooden sticks for stirring
6. Large glass or plastic jars for storing dye
7. Wax paper
8. Masking tape
9. Heavy cardboard
10. Soft pencil
11. Brush
12. Rubber gloves
13. Newspaper
14. Iron

Batik

1. Fabric. Unbleached muslin works very well. Natural fibers absorb dyes easily

2. Electric skillet and an old pan or a double boiler for melting the wax

3. Small crock-pot keeps wax molten

4. Brushes. Use old brushes because they can only be used for wax

5. Paraffin and beeswax

6. Newspapers

7. Newsprint paper and pencil

8. Frame or board with tape, tacks, or staples that can be used to stretch material

9. Large jars or buckets to hold dye

10. Stir sticks for dye baths

11. Iron

12. Cold water dye

13. Rubber gloves, always used in handling dye

14. Wax paper to put under the cloth. The lids from plastic containers are very handy to block the drips

It is important to discuss and show pictures of the subject before beginning the design for a batik. A demonstration and a brief history of the resist techniques on fabric should be included in the introduction to this craft.

Resist techniques, such as batik, may have originated somewhere in Asia. It is known that the use of a starch paste preceded the use of hot wax as a resist tool. With trade, the technique spread throughout Asia. Pieces have been found in Egypt, Persia, India, and China. In about 300 A.D., Indian traders brought the knowledge of resist dyeing to Java in Indonesia. From that time to the present day, the technique has flourished in Indonesia.

procedure

1. Develop a design on a piece of newsprint the same size as the fabric.
2. Transfer the design to the fabric with a light pencil line.
3. Smooth the material as much as possible. The fabric can be stretched on a frame or board with tacks, staples, or tape or keep it straight.
4. Melt equal parts of paraffin and beeswax in a double boiler or an old pan floating in water in an electric skillet. Use only enough heat to render the wax liquid. Pour wax carefully into a crock-pot if one is available. **Only the teacher should pour hot wax.**
5. With newspaper under the fabric, paint the wax on the areas that are to remain the natural color of the material.
6. Check the underside of the material to make sure the wax is penetrating the cloth.
7. Mix the dye as directed on the package. Cold water dye is a necessity.
8. Remove the cloth from the board and dip in cool, clean water. Crumple the cloth if a crackle effect is desired, and then place it in a dye bath, stirring constantly with a stick.
9. Remove the cloth from the dye, rinse it in cold water, and allow it to drip dry.
10. Smooth the fabric when it is dry or place it on the frame and fasten in place.
11. Paint the melted wax over the areas just dyed to retain this color. Remove the cloth from frame, and dye it in a second color. This operation can be repeated several times. As you can see, lighter colors of dye should be used first with darker colors coming later in the sequence. Remember the colors will mix in the second bath with the color of the first bath creating a different color on the material.

12. Remove the wax from the material by ironing it between newspapers or paper towels. Change the paper often because the paper absorbs the wax.

VARIATION: Stamps can be dipped in the molten wax and printed on the fabric. There are metal stamps available commercially, but simple stamps can be made from pipe cleaners bent into shapes. Make sure there is an end left for a handle. Clothespins can be used as handles for objects dipped in wax and printed. Tjanting tools, made of metal, are small cups with a spout that trails the hot wax in lines on the fabric. Wax paper is very helpful in masking areas so that wax doesn't accidentally drip in an unwanted place on the fabric.

 CAUTION: Baking soda should be kept nearby whenever hot wax is used in case of fire.

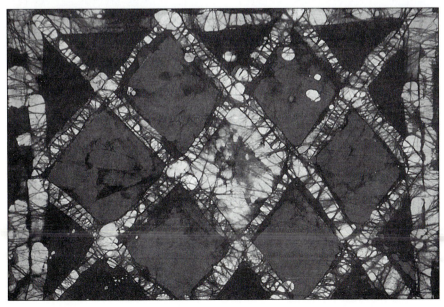

 NOTE: It is very important to discuss and show pictures of the subject before beginning. A demonstration and brief history of batik should also be included.

Resist techniques used with fiber may have originated somewhere in Asia. It is known that starch preceded the use of hot wax as a resist tool. With trade, the technique spread throughout Asia. Pieces have been found in Egypt, Persia, India, and China. In about 300 A.D., Indian traders brought the knowledge of resist dyeing to Java in Indonesia. From that time to present day, the technique has flourished in Indonesia.

 Coyote and the Laughing Butterflies by Harriet Peck Taylor, Simon & Schuster, New York, N.Y., 1995

Ulaq and the Northern Lights by Harriet Peck Taylor, Farrar Straus & Giroux, New York, N.Y., 1998

Secrets of the Stone by Harriet Peck Taylor, Farrar Straus & Giroux, New York, N.Y., 2000

 NOTE: Nigeria adire is a paste resist used on cloth. It can be made by mixing 1 c. flour, 1 c. water, and 1 tsp. alum. It can be applied with a squeeze bottle or by using the traditional method of applying the paste with a feather.

Silk painting

Silk painting was once only done in the Orient, but has become popular with fabric designers and artists. Paints are now available that are water-based, non-toxic, and will heat set with an iron. They can be applied by brush, dropper, cotton ball, cotton swab, spray bottle, or airbrush. They are light, fast, and can be intermixed. They can be diluted by simply adding water. Resists are available that are used to contain the paint in a particular area. These resists may be clear and may be removed at the end of the process, or the resists may also have color to become part of the design.

procedure

1. Wash fabric to remove any sizing. Press.
2. Stretch fabric on frame or in embroidery hoop.
3. If resist is used, a squeeze bottle with a fine nozzle or a fine brush works well for application. Don't let resist build up. Allow resist to dry completely.
4. Check the resist for any holes before proceeding.
5. Apply paint, not with strokes but by beginning in the middle of an area and guiding the paint toward the resist lines. Allow paint to dry several days before heat setting with an iron.
6. Soak piece in lukewarm water to remove clear resist. Colored resists stay in the fabric as part of the design.
7. To heat set, use a pressing cloth and iron the painting on the wrong side for 3 minutes at the temperature suited to the fabric. The cloth may also be wrapped in aluminum foil and put in a preheated 300° F oven for 10 minutes.

1. Silk paints in a variety of colors
2. Resists, may be clear or colored
3. Silk material, fine color or synthetic. No permanent press
4. Fine brushes, cotton balls, squeeze bottles
5. Newsprint to plan
6. Pencil
7. Frame with fine tacks or embroidery hoop

NOTE: Art salt may be sprinkled on wet paint. It should stay on the fabric for at least 10 minutes. It will absorb paint from the fabric, and lighter areas will appear around the salt crystals. One dark spot will appear directly beneath the salt.

Another possibility is to apply a mixture of 70 percent rubbing alcohol and 30 percent water to make fine details on a dried painting. This will create fine black lines where the dye is moved around.

masks and puppets

16

NOTE: There are activities in other parts of this book that would lend themselves to making masks. Such activities including paper sculpture, torn paper, geometric cut paper, painting, drawing, oil pastels or crayons, chalk, and clay can all be used in the creation of masks.

Masks

The paintings in the caves of France, dating between 30,000–13,000 B.C., show humans wearing animal masks. Masks have been used by humans for one reason or another in almost all parts of the world. There seem to be three main ideas that masks represent: Ancestors and Tradition, Spirit Helpers, and Theater.

African masks are used as a bond between a group of people and their ancestors, and become a guarantee of continuity. The death masks found on the mummies in central America, northern China, Egyptian and Mycenaean civilizations, and ancient Africa were all crafted to help the spirit continue in the afterlife.

The masks of Native Americans often took the form of animals or a totemic symbol. The totem pole of the tribes of North America is an example of the use of the bird, fish, and animal symbols as special spirits to protect and provide for their people. The mask in the hands of a shaman or medicine man acted as a *spirit helper* and had the magic quality not only to represent an animal or character but to change the wearer into that character.

Theater masks were used in classical Europe and are still used extensively in Indonesia and Japan. Some of the most beautiful masks come from Japan where theater masks were developed to a very high level.

Many of the masks seen today (Carnival or Halloween) are used as a disguise and can be classified as funny or scary folk art.

Masks may be held in front of the face, worn over the face, or on the head like a helmet or hat. They may include coverings for some or all of the body, or additions may be well above the head. They may have a lot of color or very little color, and they can be made from almost any material that can be manipulated and decorated.

Kwakiutl Indian Mask. One example of masks made by cultures throughout the world. Courtesy Department of Library Services, American Museum of Natural History (#2A 21548).

Masks have been used by many cultures for many reasons. This one is quite complex. Areogun, African, Nigeria, Yoruba Ekiti People, Epa Society Mask, 1930s, wood with polychrome painted decoration, Ht. 49½ in. (125.7 cm) (1977.22) The Toledo Museum of Art, purchased with funds from the Libbey Endowment, gift of Edward Drummond Libbey.

Materials and tools
for masks and puppets

1. Material—Felt works well since it does not fray and can be glued. Fleece material hides stitches, and soft material gives the puppet more movement
2. Yarn, string, thread
3. Feathers including marabou and boas
4. Cardboard, tagboard, paper
5. Pipe cleaners, lightweight wire
6. Buttons, beads, costume jewelry
7. Trim of any sort
8. Plastic that can be cut
9. Styrofoam
10. Polyurethane carpet padding or thick foam, such as used in upholstery
11. Pins and pin cushion
12. Needles
13. Tacky Glue or Thick Tacky Glue. Foamtastic™ Glue works on foam
14. Poster chalk
15. Acrylic or tempera paint, Acrylic medium to seal tempera
16. Latex paint
17. Brush
18. Fun or fake fur
19. Eyes of all kinds, including ping pong balls and Leggs containers
20. Polyester stuffing
21. Pom poms
22. Any material is fair game to use for puppets or masks

One of the most helpful tools to use when making masks and puppets is a low-heat glue gun. This glue gun does not get as hot as other hot glue guns, but the nozzle and the glue itself gets quite hot. There must be very close supervision and safety rules. The instructor could use one to help with some difficult-to-glue areas. The glue pot for the low-heat glue sticks is a good tool to use and may be safer. The glue is applied with popsicle sticks.

Cardboard build-up mask

A brief discussion of masks and their history would be appropriate before beginning this activity. It would also be valuable to have a demonstration of the possibilities available.

1. Corrugated cardboard. Cut up boxes or collect packing cardboard
2. Thick white glue
3. Heavy-duty scissors
4. **Utility knife or mat knife would be valuable and should be used by the instructor**
5. Paint, acrylic, latex, tempera
6. Shoe polish rubbed over cardboard produces a finish that looks like wood.

procedure

1. Cut a main cardboard shape that will be large enough to add additional features in layers on top of it. $12'' \times 18''$ is a good size.
2. Cut smaller pieces of cardboard to use for features. Since a mask usually is symmetrical, it is advisable to cut at the same time those features that need to match.
3. Some shapes that are to protrude may be glued in groups with their edges glued to the base piece. This would allow the shape to be more three-dimensional.
4. Move the parts of the mask around and experiment with placement until acceptable.
5. Glue features of the mask in place. Allow the mask to dry. It may be necessary to place weights, such as books, on the flatter parts of the mask so that the mask will be straight.
6. Decorate with paint or by applying shoe polish.

NOTE: This mask is not to be worn, but is for display. When finished with shoe polish, it resembles a wooden mask.

connections
African masks
Native American masks

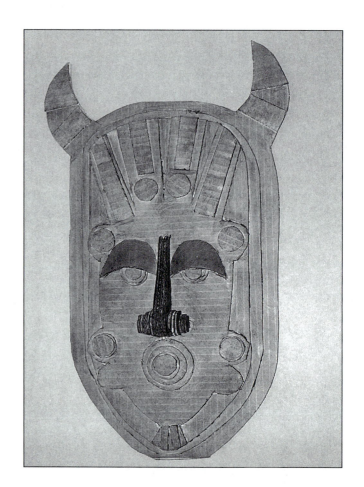

Paper bag mask

It is important that the students know some of the history of masks and their use before beginning the activity. It is important to show the bag, where the eyes will go, and where the shoulders will be cut. It is also good to show the many possibilities available in the design of their masks.

procedure

1. Slip the bag over the child's head. The *bottom* of the bag will be the *top* of the mask. You may need to cut out sections at the sides of the bag so that it will fit more comfortably over the shoulders. **Use safety scissors if available.**

2. Locate the peek holes by gently marking them with a blunt crayon. These holes are 4″ from the top of the head and 1½″ apart. They should be about ¾″ in diameter. Remember that the eyes of the mask character do not necessarily need to be at the peek holes.

3. Cut the peek holes after removing the bag. The bag may be painted or decorated at this point. A method that works well is to slide the bag over a straight chair back, taking care to protect the chair and floor. Begin to paint the mask. If oil pastels or crayons are used, the mask may be put on a table to decorate. The nose, beak, mouth, ears, and other features should be added.

4. Remember that the mask is three-dimensional and should be finished on all sides to be effective.

supplies

supplies

1. Paper bag large enough to slip over child's head

2. Scissors

3. Ruler

4. Pencil

5. Paste, thick white glue, and a stapler, if one is available

6. Watercolor, oil pastels or crayons, acrylics, or tempera. Mix a little white glue with the tempera for a better bond

7. Materials for decorating the mask, such as felt, colored construction paper, cloth, buttons, yarn, pipe cleaners, ribbons, etc.

8. Paint brush and container for water, if paint is used

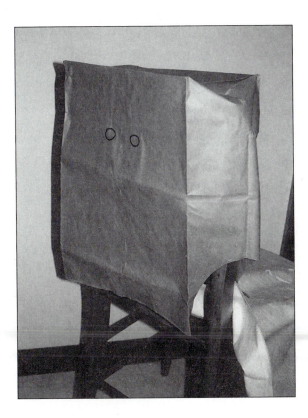

1. Clothes hanger
2. Knee-high nylon hose are perfect, but regular nylon hose would work
3. Duct tape
4. Thick white glue or low-heat glue gun
5. Felt, pom poms, pipe cleaners, fun foam, etc.

Stocking handheld mask

This is a simple handheld mask that can be used while speaking or singing. A discussion of masks and their history would be appropriate. It would also be valuable to talk about the features on the face of the characters to be created.

procedure

1. Bend the hook of a clothes hanger so that it becomes a handle.
2. Bend the main part of the hanger into a triangle shape.
3. Pull the opening of one hose over the triangle so that it covers the triangle and so that the opening is pulled down to the handle.
4. Tape both the top of the hose and the handle together and cover them neatly.
5. Use the felt, pom poms, pipe cleaners, and so forth, to make the important features of the character.
6. Glue everything in place.

connections

Festival masks of Native Americans

Paper plate mask

It would be appropriate to have a discussion of masks and their history before beginning the activity. Examples of some of the possibilities would be valuable. **There are at least three different kinds of masks that could be made from paper plates.**

1. One mask fits over the face, with eye holes and a nose flap, and has string or a strip of poster board or tagboard fastened to the back to hold it on. This mask may also be a half mask, covering the eyes and cheeks but allowing the mouth to be uncovered.
2. Another mask that could be made is one that is held in front of the face of the person by an attached short stick. It should have eye holes, but doesn't need the nose flap.
3. The third type of mask uses two finished paper plates fastened back to back with a long stick supporting the two faces. Cloth can be attached to the bottom of the faces so that it appears to have a body. Hands, with controls or rods, can be attached to the edges of the fabric so that it becomes a large rod puppet.

Mask with peek holes and nose flap

1. Heavy-duty paper plate
2. Safety scissors or X-acto knife
3. Cardboard
4. Markers, watercolors, tempera, acrylic, and oil pastels
5. Scrap construction paper, string, yarn, feathers, and any other material
6. String or yarn, 1″ strip of tagboard or poster board, short stick for handheld mask or long stick or dowel for two-faced mask

connections

Mardi Gras
Ancient Greeks, theater masks

procedure

1. Measure down from the top of the mask 4″. Draw a light horizontal line across the underside of the paper plate at 4″. Draw a vertical line in the middle so that it crosses the horizontal line. This will be the center of the nose flap.
2. The peek holes should be at least ¾″ in diameter and should be positioned 1½″ apart. The center vertical line should be midway between the two peek holes. Carefully cut out the peek holes with scissors or an X-acto knife. **Take care with the use of the X-acto knife.** The peek holes do not have to be the designed "eyes" of the mask. The bottom of the nose flap should be 1½″ from the horizontal peek hole line, and the flap should be 1″ across. Cut like a letter U, with the top of the U still attached to the plate. This will allow room for the nose and make the mask more comfortable to wear.
3. Draw other features as needed for the mask. Scrap construction paper may be used, and any other kind of material can be used to make features or decorate the mask.
4. Other materials may be added to the edge of the mask to build it out and away from the face.
5. A hole may be punched into each side of the mask and a piece of yarn or string inserted and tied in place. A more stable method for wearing the mask would be to attach a strip of tagboard or poster board to one side of the mask, measure for size, and staple to the other side. An additional strip with one end fastened to the top of the mask and down to the other holding strip will form a cap. This also allows other materials to be added to these other strips if desired.

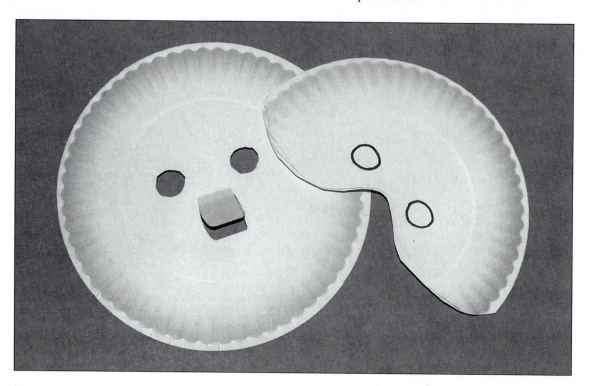

Handheld paper plate mask

procedure

1. Measure for peek holes as seen in previous instructions.
2. It is not necessary to have a nose flap.
3. Cut out peek holes with scissors or X-acto knife. **Use extreme care** [when?] **cutting with the X-acto knife.**
4. Draw any features needed for the mask. Construction paper may be [used?] and any kind of material can be used to make features or decora[te the?] mask.
5. Other materials may be added to the edge of the mask to build it [out?] away from the face.
6. Attach a short flat stick (tongue depressors, screen molding) t[o the bot-?]tom of the mask.

Two-faced mask or puppet

procedure

1. Make two different faces on two plates or a face on one paper plate and the back of the head on the other paper plate.
2. Sandwich a long flat stick, a dowel, or a broom stick between the two plates. It may be necessary to cut a bit of the bottom of the plates to allow room for the stick. Fasten the end of the stick securely and then staple the two plates together.
3. Fabric may be attached to the bottom of the paper plates for a body, and at the edges of the fabric, hands can be attached with wires or rods to control them.

Papier-mâché or plaster wrap mask

1. Papier-mâché materials (p. 000)

2. Plaster wrap, cut into appropriate strips

3. Water container for paste mixture for papier-mâché or for warm water if using plaster wrap

4. Newspaper

5. Armature

6. Anything to build up the surface where protrusions are desired (cut-up egg cartons, paper tubes, small plastic containers, lids, pieces of Styrofoam, or tagboard, cut and made into shapes)

7. Masking tape

8. Paint, latex, acrylic, or tempera

9. Brush and water container

10. Thick white glue or low-heat glue gun. **If a fixative spray is used, make sure that there is optimal ventilation.**

A discussion with pictures of masks and the history of masks would be of great value before beginning this activity. The mask has been used by almost every culture and could be connected very easily to those cultures.

The papier-mâché or plaster wrap mask may be done over a variety of armatures or forms. Each one of these armatures has its own special qualities that may or may not suit the needs of the student designing the mask. The selection of the armature is the first decision to be made and may be determined by the instructor. The procedure is very similar in all cases except when using the human face as an armature.

armatures

1. One-gallon plastic jug (cider, water, or milk) cut in half
2. 2-liter soft drink plastic container cut in half

3. Balloon, may be cut in half after it is covered with papier-mâché or plaster wrap to make two masks
4. Blow up a large plastic storage bag
5. Wadded newspaper that is taped in shape
6. Plastic face form
7. Existing plastic face mask
8. Cardboard box or a part of a box made by cutting off one corner along with part of the three sides
9. Styrofoam shape covered with clear plastic wrap

procedure

1. If necessary, cut the armature in half. **If a knife is used, the instructor should do the cutting.**
2. Experiment with tubes, cutting and taping to decide where to place them. If peek holes will be cut, the instructor should do the cutting.
3. Tape any of the shapes in place by putting tape on all four sides. Any really large shapes, such as ears or horns, may be added later. If a balloon or blown-up plastic bag is used, it might be advisable to add these shapes after the first layer of plaster wrap or papier-mâché is dry and more stable.
4. Papier-Mâché—Mix the paste and tear the newspaper strips with the grain of the paper. Dip the torn strips into the paste mixture, smooth excess paste between fingers, and lay over the form with the strips going in

NOTES: If papier-mâché is used, a coat of gesso or white latex paint covering the form would be advisable. The color applied over the white background is much brighter.

Polyurethane foam may be colored with acrylic paint if the foam is sprayed first with a little water. It does tend to make the foam brittle. Chalk fixed with hair spray works very well. A spray paint used for flowers called *Design Master* works well on foam. **In all cases, if a spray is used, it must be done with optimal ventilation.**

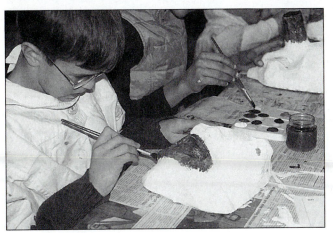

different directions. Use different colors of paper for each layer so that it is easy to see where the one layer ends and the next begins. Paper towels work well as an alternative layer. If the armature is to remain in the mask, fewer layers of mâché are necessary.

5. Plaster Wrap—Dip the strips into warm water, laying the strips in different directions and smoothing each strip before putting on the the next strip. Check for holes. It requires three layers of plaster wrap.

6. Allow the mask to dry. If the mask feels cool to the touch, it is not yet dry.

7. The student should draw several designs on paper in preparation for painting the mask. When satisfied, draw the design on the surface of the mask.

8. Decorate with paint. If it is necessary to use a spray or painted sealer, do it after painting and before any other additions.

9. Attach other materials, such as feathers, beads, pipe cleaners, pom-poms, fun fur, felt, scrap paper, seeds, polyurethane foam, and so forth. Foam is great to use to add large shapes to the basic mask form.

Direct body casting

It is important that a discussion of masks and their history precede the activity. **This activity is best done with older students, under close supervision.** The students must have a good working knowledge of the technique and what to expect. Not all students would be comfortable doing this activity.

procedure

1. Two students should work on this activity with one acting as the body to be cast and the other doing the plaster wrap. These roles can then be reversed. The one student should lay on a flat surface and be made comfortable.
2. Cover the body with a plastic drape and the hair with a plastic shower cap.
3. Lubricate the facial hair (eyebrows, eyelashes and other hair) using solid vegetable shortening or water-soluble lubricating jelly. Moisturizing lotion should be applied to the face.
4. Dip the strips of molding tape into warm water and lay them over the face going in different directions and overlapping them.
5. Leave the bottom of the nose open for breathing.
6. Eye pads placed over the eyes makes it more comfortable to the model. If younger students are the models, the eye areas may be left open with no covering wrap.
7. Make a few layers and make the edges of the mask a bit thicker and stronger by smoothing extra long strips around the edge (more layers may be added after it is removed from the face).
8. It is normal to feel heat because of the chemical reaction of the plaster.
9. Remove the mask by having the model wiggle his or her facial features and by working the fingers underneath the mask all around the edge.
10. The model should wash his or her face immediately and thoroughly.
11. Shapes of cardboard, tubes, etc., may be applied and covered with more plaster wrap.

supplies

1. Good-quality plaster wrap that is specifically used for direct body casting (Rappit™ modeling tape). Cut it into 2″ strips that are 6″ to 8″ long. Some smaller pieces would be helpful. Make sure there is enough cut before beginning
2. Water container
3. Solid vegetable shortening or water-soluble lubricating jelly
4. Eye pads, shower cap, plastic drape

NOTE: This mask may be constructed as a half mask or a talking mask.

connections

Ancient Greeks, theater masks

Commedia Del-l'Arte masks

Japanese No masks

Egyptian burial Masks

Cardboard and paper mask

procedure

Method a

1. Fold paper or tagboard in half.
2. Draw lightly, with a pencil, a shape that will cover the eyes and part of the face, reserving a place for the nose. The fold of the paper will go between the eyes.
3. Open the folded shape and check for eye position and mark it gently with a pencil.
4. Put the shape back in a folded position and cut the eye holes. X-acto knife works the best. **Use X-acto knives with extreme care and supervision.** Make sure there is cardboard under the knife while cutting.
5. Punch holes in the sides so that the mask can be worn over the face.
6. Decorate the mask.

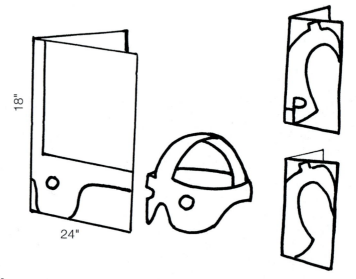

Method b

1. Fold the 12″ × 18″ paper in half vertically.
2. Draw the desired shape on the side of the open edges (the fold will be the center of the mask).
3. Find and gently mark the eye after opening the shape.
4. Fold down nose or beak shape.
5. Add pattern, color, and other things to finish the mask.

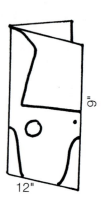

Helmet mask

A helmet mask is worn on the top of the head like a cap. It may cover part of the head or may have an open lightweight covering over the whole head. Most characterization portrays it on the top of the head. This type of mask also lends itself to the use of the voice, either speaking or singing.

Method a

procedure

1. Using the 1½″ wide strips, make a headband. Staple or glue in place.
2. Glue or staple another strip to the front of the headband. Bring it over the head and staple or glue it in place on the back of the headband. Add two more strips between the middle strip and the headband. This will form the base for the rest of the paper sculpture mask.
3. This structure can be covered with papier-mâché if desired.

supplies

1. Poster board
2. 1½″ wide strips of poster board
3. Stapler
4. Scissors
5. Materials of all kinds for decorating
6. Thick white glue or low-heat glue gun

connections Iroquois Indians

African masks

supplies

1. Polyurethane foam or polyfoam carpet padding. Use the smooth type, not the type with compressed pieces.

2. Chunks of foam, such as those used in upholstery or mattresses

3. Sharp scissors, such as Fiskars®. A utility or mat knife would be handy, but should always be handled by the instructor

4. Permanent markers

5. Low-heat glue gun or Foamtastic™, a thick white glue used with foam

6. Poster chalk, acrylic paint, or Design Master floral spray paint

7. Hair spray if chalk is used

8. Electric meat knife to cut chunk foam into basic shapes. **This knife should be used by the instructor only**

 NOTE: Acrylic paint makes the surface of the foam hard. Chalk color is much easier to use and the foam stays spongy.

Method b

procedure

1. Measure around the head of the wearer at the forehead or around the face, depending upon the type of mask desired; then add another inch.
2. Cut a piece of foam 1½″ wide and as long as the measurement.
3. Cut each end at a slant and glue the two ends together with a glue gun.
4. Round the edges of the foam ring with scissors.
5. Cut others parts to be added, such as ears, horns, and so on, from the foam scrap or chunks of foam.
6. Color all the parts with acrylic paint or chalk. If acrylic paint is used, mist the foam first with water so that the paint will spread. A scrap piece of foam can be used as a brush. If chalk is used, use the side of chalk and spray with hair spray when completed. **Use hair spray with optimal ventilation.** Allow all pieces to dry.
7. Put the pieces together using a low-heat glue gun. **Observe safety rules for the glue gun.**

VARIATION: A muzzle mask can be made by measuring around the head at the nose and cutting a strip of foam 2″ wide to cover the nose, cheeks, and ears of the wearer of the mask. It may be necessary to cut some of the foam out of the back side to make room for the nose. Other pieces are attached after they are colored.

Method c

procedure

1. Make a pattern in brown wrapping paper that is large enough to cover the ball cap and that will make the main shape of the head. The pattern can be a long rectangle the measurement of the ball cap with the addition of several inches. Darts should be cut to shape the one side of the rectangle. Darts are triangles that are cut out so that the edges can be glued together.

    Another method would be to use a strip foam that rings the ball cap and then other strips of foam that go over the top of the cap and connect to the foam ring. (As done in poster board in method a.)

2. Experiment with the sheet foam. Fold it and move it around. Often ideas will come with this kind of experimentation. When ready, make a pattern in brown wrapping paper.

3. Trace to sheet foam. A Sharpie marker works well.

4. Cut the foam carefully with Fiskar® scissors.

5. Glue the parts of the mask together with a low-heat glue gun or Foamtastic™ and clothespins.

6. It is better to add color to the individual parts before gluing. Depending on the design, it is sometimes better to cover with fabric before assembling the mask.

1. Ball cap. The visor may be cut off

2. Rug foam or polyurethane foam

3. Fiskar scissors

4. Brown wrapping paper for pattern

5. Pencil

6. Low-heat glue gun or Foam Glue (Foamtastic™)

7. Pinch type clothespins

8. Poster chalk, Design Master (floral spray paint)

9. Cloth that has a nap and a one-way stretch could be used to cover the basic foam form. Velour, stretch terry cloth, would work (use the same pattern as for the foam but allow more material for the seams)

10. Different supplies to make the features for the character. Might include pipe cleaners, felt, pom poms, fake fur, and so on

Puppets

A puppet is an object that appears to be alive when manipulated by the human hand. It can entertain, educate, and amaze. The puppet has been used extensively in almost all cultures, including Africa, India, China, Japan, Indonesia, throughout Eastern and Western Europe, and the Americas.

Puppets may have had their beginnings in religious ceremonies. The shaman or medicine man used the puppet as a means of communication to influence the people. Puppets may have begun as a mask with the jaw hinged so that it would move and seem to bring the ancestors spirits to life. Unfortunately, most of the ancient puppets were made out of perishable materials and thus have disappeared. A few figures were made of clay by the Egyptians and the people of India. Aristotle writes in 400 B.C. about the use of puppets in Greece.

Puppets are very diverse, ranging from found inanimate objects used as characters, to very complex and detailed characters. They may be as small as a finger or larger than life. Any material may be used to build the puppets. They may be moved by using the hand, rods, or strings attached to the body, head, and other parts. Puppets can now be controlled by computer for special movie effects.

Designing, sculpture, painting, sewing, directing, acting, writing, music, and choreography are all combined in puppetry. Perhaps this is why artists such as Paul Klee, Wassily Kandinsky, Jean Cocteau, and George Bernard Shaw were interested and involved in puppetry. Many fine puppeteers, such as Jim Henson, have passed on the traditions of puppetry and added contributions of their own.

The main types of puppets are **hand or glove puppets,** which may include **mouth puppets,** consisting of heads with mittentype bodies. They may also have legs and feet, although normally puppets only show above the hips. The puppeteer's wrist is the puppet's waist. The mouth puppet has a large head with a moving mouth that is attached to a tube body. The fingers of the puppeteer go on top of the mouth in the head with the thumb in the lower jaw. Rods may be attached to the hand or hands or the puppeteer's free hand may become the puppet's hand.

Rod puppets are built around a central rod secured to the head. The head may be able to nod, turn, or do both. The body may be a simple shoulder block with loose robes or it may be a complete costumed body with legs. A rod or rods may be attached to the hand or hands for additional expression.

Marionettes are fully movable. The head and neck may be made in one piece or they can be jointed. The body and limbs all have joints. Marionettes are manipulated from above by the use of strings attached to wooden controls. The number of strings and the kinds of controls vary depending on the action required of the puppet.

Shadow puppets are cut-out figures or shapes held between a light source and a translucent screen. The shapes may be solid silhouettes or may be decorated with cut-out details. Color may also be added. Usually the figure is done in an Egyptian arrangement, with the legs, head, and feet in profile and the body partially turned toward the audience with the arms hanging in front of or behind the puppet.

Designing and crafting the puppet is only one stage in the art of puppetry. Before the puppet can be made, thought must be given to the character of the puppet. Is the puppet human or animal? Is the puppet male or female? Is the puppet a particular character in a play or a story? Is the puppet a hero or a villain? Is the puppet going to sing or dance? All of these kinds of questions need to be answered before a puppet can be crafted because it will make a vast difference in the form of the puppet.

After designing and constructing the puppet, it is still only a doll, until the puppeteer gives it life through movement. Only after direction and a great deal of practice, will the puppet and puppeteer be ready to perform for an audience.

Working with puppets takes a commitment and a lot of work, but the rewards and benefits are tremendous. The student will discover and analyze, learn skills, make decisions, interact socially, role play, learn from others, work with different material, and make something worthwhile.

Paper finger puppet

procedure

Method a

1. Cut a strip of paper to form a tube that will fit the finger snugly. **Use safety scissors if available.** A small paper tube will also work.
2. It is possible to glue felt or cloth to the rectangle before gluing it into a tube shape.
3. Glue the tube together. Clothespins or paper clips could be used to hold it together long enough so that it will stick.
4. While the tube is drying, work on details that will be added.
5. Add details to make the characters.

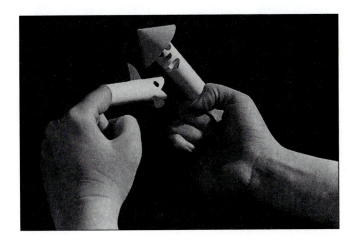

Method b

1. Cut off an old cloth glove finger or make a tubelike shape from pieces of felt.
2. Add details like ears, eyes, etc., to make the character.

supplies

1. Tagboard
2. Paste, glue, or glue stick
3. Scissors
4. Crayons, markers, scrap paper, and any other scrap materials

Method c

1. Cut a rectangle of tagboard wide enough so that the first two fingers will fit with space to spare.
2. Fold under one end of the rectangle. Draw two half circles on the fold and cut. Fit the first two fingers through the holes in the fold. If the holes are not big enough, refold and cut to fit. Make sure that there is space between the holes and on each side. The two fingers will be the puppet's legs.
3. Make the character's torso, arms, and head in the space above the holes.
4. Excess tagboard around the character may be cut away as long as the holes and lower torso are not disturbed.

Paper bag puppet

procedure

1. Put a hand in the bag, find the fold, and use the hand to open and close the fold. This is the moving part of the puppet, and the flat bottom of the bag will be an area of the face or the top of the head.
2. The face can be drawn or glued directly on this flat bottom, or another piece of paper can be shaped and glued onto the bottom. Don't forget to put color and details inside the fold. This could be either the mouth or the eyebrows.
3. Three-dimensional additions are excellent. Noses or beaks to stick out and Jacob's Ladders for the arms and legs may be used. Cut paper can be fringed or curled to make hair or feathers. Other materials can be added to enrich the puppet form.

supplies

1. Paper bag with a flat bottom, the size to be determined by the size of the hand (paper lunch bag works well)
2. Colored construction paper
3. Glue or glue stick
4. Markers
5. Scissors

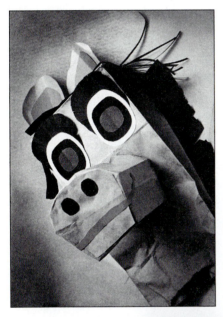

Jacob's Ladder

supplies

1. Strips of construction paper
2. Glue or glue stick

 NOTE: This form is very flexible and strong. It is like a spring and can be used in paper sculpture forms. It makes great arms and legs for puppets because of the movement. If the ends of the Jacob's Ladder are glued together, it will form a rosette and can also be used in many ways.

procedure

1. Glue two strips of paper together to form a corner, making sure they are square. For beginners, it is easier to use two different colors.
2. Fold one color straight across where the two colors are glued together. Fold the second color across at the same point. It is like weaving up, folding first one color and then another.
3. Fold the strips alternating the colors until the strips have been used. One may be used before the other, and the longer one will need to be trimmed.
4. Glue at the top between the two color ends.

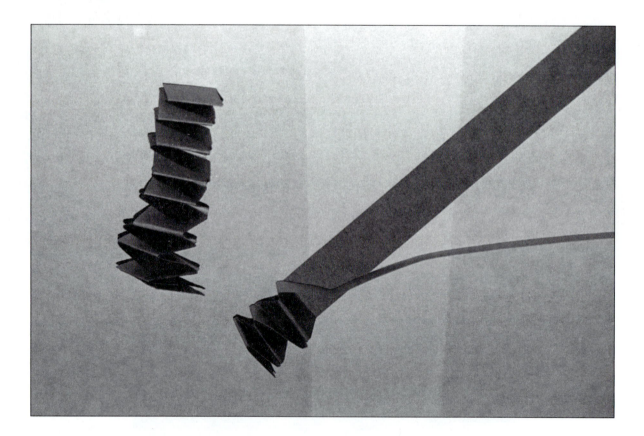

Paper bag puppet on a stick

procedure

1. Fill the bag with small pieces of torn or shredded newspaper.
2. The dowel or stick should be inserted in the open end of the bag until it touches the bottom of the bag. Gather the open end of the bag around the stick and tie the string tightly to form a neck. Make sure the stick extends far enough out of the bag to make a handle.
3. The features of the face can be added with paint, crayons, or with pieces of colored paper cut to shape.

 NOTE: Shapes of faces or animals can be cut from tagboard or paper and mounted on a stick.

supplies

1. Paper bag
2. Newspapers
3. Wooden stick or dowel
4. String, ribbon, or rubber band
5. Colored paper and scissors
6. Paints, oil pastels, or crayons
7. Glue or glue sticks

Felt hand puppet

1. Newsprint and pencils

2. Scissors

3. Variety of felt colors. Each puppet will need a 9″ × 36″ piece

4. Thick white glue, or a low-heat glue gun with compatible glue sticks

procedure

1. Place the hand on newsprint in the desired puppet position and draw around with at least one inch extra around the hand.

2. Cut out newsprint pattern and pin it on a folded-over piece of felt, with the head touching the fold. Draw around the pattern with chalk.

3. Turn the felt with the chalk line to the inside and sew or glue the edges of the felt pieces, making sure the bottom is open. An over and under or running stitch can be used. Low-heat glue guns are instant. **If glue guns are used, supervise to ensure that safety rules are followed.** Machine stitching is fine.

4. Using the scraps from the main bodies, cut a face or head from a contrasting color and glue it in place. Place all other features and details to make the puppet into the selected character.

Papier-mâché or plaster wrap puppet head

procedure

Method a—papier-mâché

1. Create a puppet head and neck with the plastic clay. The neck will eventually serve two purposes: first, a place to fasten clothing and secondly, a place for the middle finger to control the puppet. When forming the head, exaggerate the features, as the thickness of the applied paper strips tends to reduce feature recognition.
2. Tear the newspaper, brown paper bags, or paper toweling into ½″ wide strips.
3. Mix the paste in a bowl or pan to the consistency of cream.
4. Place a strip of paper into the paste until it is saturated. Remove the strip from the bowl, and wipe off the excess paste by pulling the strip between the fingers.
5. Apply the paste-saturated strip directly to the puppet head.
6. Continue to apply strips until the entire head is covered. Repeat until at least six layers of paper strips are applied. The number of layers can be readily counted if a different kind or color of paper is used for each layer. The strength of the finished puppet will be much greater if each strip is applied in a different direction. Make sure that all wrinkles and bubbles are smoothed out before adding a new strip.
7. Place the puppet head on a rack or accordion-folded paper to allow it to dry thoroughly.
8. When the puppet head is dry, cut it in half with a sharp knife or saw to remove the clay (Ill. 1 on the following page). **Use knives and saws with extreme care and supervision.**
9. Place the two halves together and fasten with additional strips. It may also be necessary to apply several strips over the bottom edge of the neck for strength.

supplies

1. Newspaper, brown paper bags, paper towels
2. Ross Art Paste or thinned white glue
3. Container for mixing glue or paste
4. Plastic clay
5. Sandpaper
6. Mat or utility knife, saw
7. Paint (tempera, latex, or acrylic)
8. Brush
9. Clear spray sealer or acrylic medium

10. When thoroughly dry, sandpaper until smooth and then decorate (Ill. 2).

11. If tempera paint is used for decoration, the surface should be sprayed with clear plastic, or painted with shellac or varnish for permanence. **Use sprays with optimum ventilation.**

12. Additional material such as yarn for hair, buttons for eyes, and so on, can be added to further enhance the finished product (Ill. 3).

1   2   3

supplies

Paris Craft and warm water in a plastic container replaces the paste and newspaper strips. All other supplies are the same.

VARIATION OF METHOD A: PARIS CRAFT

1. Cut the Paris Craft into appropriately sized strips and pieces.

2. Dip the strips into warm water and lay them in different directions over the base form. Smooth each strip before putting on the next strip. Three or four layers would be sufficient but always check for holes. Check edges to make sure they are smooth.

3. It is possible to crush a piece of wet Paris Craft and shape it to form some features but not large parts. Lay strips over the crushed piece to make sure it will not come off.

4. Finish the form as you would for papier-mâché.

Method b

Method b is the same as method a except the base form of the puppet head is a small 5″ balloon almost inflated with a tagboard or cardboard cylinder securely taped over the air intake to make a neck. Crushed tissue paper is taped in place on the balloon for noses, muzzles, and so on. Three layers of Paris Craft or six layers of papier-mâché are necessary to cover the entire form, including the neck. (The hole in the bottom stays open.)

Method c

A Styrofoam shape (oval, circle, and so on) is the base form for the puppet head with Styrofoam pieces attached by using Tacky Glue and broken pieces of toothpick to hold them in place. (Place toothpick pieces at an angle on each side of the piece to be attached, going through the piece and into the base.) If Paris Craft is used, wet pieces of Paris Craft can be wadded up and held in place with strips of wet Paris Craft put over the entire base form. The neck can be a cylinder of cardboard or a poster board made into the correct size. It will be necessary to make a hole first to insert the neck. Glue neck in place. Cover with two layers of papier-mâché or one layer of plaster wrap.

A quick and easy material that can be used with method c is torn tissue paper strips and diluted white glue. Brush the glue over the Styrofoam and lay strips of tissue on top, pushing the strips down with a brush full of the diluted glue. Cover everything including the neck. (Leave space to insert a finger in the neck.)

NOTE: Line the inside of the neck with felt for comfort.

The most famous hand puppets are Punch and Judy. Punch is portrayed with a hunchback, with a large nose and chin. *Louie* by Ezra Jack Keats, Scholastic, New York, N.Y., 1975.

Hand positions for puppets

Try out the finger positions to find the one that is the most comfortable and allows the most movement. Sometimes this needs to be decided before the puppet is crafted.

These puppet heads need to have a mitt or hand covering to help make them the chosen character. Make a pattern for the mitt by drawing around the hand in the chosen position to be used with the puppet. Allow at least 1″ additional all around. Lay the pattern on the material (felt works well) and draw around it with chalk. Cut out two pieces of the mitt and sew or glue the edges together, but leave the bottom open for the hand and the small top open to attach to the puppet neck. Glue the small top to the neck of the puppet. Many things can be added to this mitt, such as aprons, ties, pockets, belts, buckles, bows, collars, spots, and so on. If a tail is added, put it in the middle of the back halfway from the bottom so the audience will be able to see it.

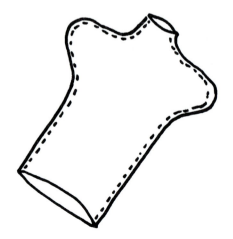

Jumping jacks

procedure

1. Draw the character's head and body on a rectangle of tagboard. It must be large enough to attach legs and arms.
2. Draw the upper arms and lower arms, including the hands, separately on another piece of tagboard.
3. Draw the upper and lower legs, including the feet, separately on a piece of tagboard.
4. The arms and the legs need to be wide enough to punch in the holes, especially the tops of the upper arms and legs.
5. Add color. Remember the features of the face and the details needed for the character.
6. Overlap the upper and lower legs, punch holes, and put in brass fasteners with the smooth side to the front. Connect the arms in the same way.
7. Turn the body piece face down and lay the legs and arms in position. Make sure to overlap them. Punch the holes close to the outside of the body, leaving room on the upper legs and upper arms for an additional hole that will be punched for the control string.
8. Put brass fasteners in place to connect the arms and legs with the body piece. Do not press the fasteners too tight, since they need to move.
9. Punch holes in the upper legs and arms slightly above and toward the center of the body.
10. Cut a string or piece of yarn about 18″ long. Tie one end in the control hole in the upper arm and the other end in the other upper arm.
11. Cut another string about 14″ long and tie each end in the control holes of the upper legs.
12. The puppet's arms and legs can move separately or the strings can be tied together and they can move at the same time.

supplies

1. Tagboard
2. Markers, crayons, oil pastels, or colored pencils
3. Scissors
4. Paper punch ¼ inch is good
5. Brass fasteners
6. String or yarn

 NOTE: A simple variation is to create any kind of bird and make only the wings move.

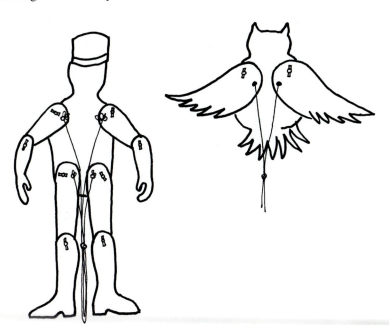

supplies

Shadow puppet

procedure

1. Make a pattern using a piece of newsprint. Make a silhouette that is recognizable, usually a side view of any character.
2. Make any moving parts larger so that there will be enough space to overlap and fasten. One or two parts may be made to move.
3. Using the pattern, draw the pattern on tagboard or cardboard and cut carefully. **If X-acto knives are used, all safety rules must be observed.**
4. Overlap the moving parts, punch holes, and put in brass fasteners so they can move.
5. Interior details can be added by cutting them in with an X-acto knife. Color can be added simply by covering the openings with colored tissue or cellophane.
6. If a shape is small, a large soda straw can be taped to the back of the main body and taped in place. Make sure the tape will not interfere with the movement. If the shape is large, use a lightweight clothes hanger wire and bend it so that it can be taped in place. A wire cutter is helpful, but use only with supervision.
7. Soda straws can be taped in place coming down from the moving parts. Some parts may not need control if fastened with a brass fastener and the puppet is moved so that there is a pendulum movement. For example, a human puppet is made with a stable body, head, and one leg. The other leg is attached with a fastener and will swing when the rest of the body is moved. Controls could be used on one arm or both.

supplies

1. Tagboard or cardboard
2. Wire (clothes hangers work well)
3. Soda straws, straight or bendable
4. Tape
5. Markers
6. Colored tissue or cellophane
7. Brass fasteners
8. Paper punch
9. Scissors (X-acto knives could be used to cut small designs within the silhouette)

connections

World of Shadow: Teaching with Shadow Puppetry by David Wisniewski and Donna Wisniewski, Teacher Idea Press, Englewood, Colorado

Shadows by Blaise Cendrars and Marcia Brown, Aladdin Paperbacks, New York, N.Y., 1995

China

India

Java

Middle East

Turkey

Greece

Europe

CAUTION: Extreme care and supervision must be given whenever X-acto knives are used. Safety instructions should be given before *every* use of the knives. X-acto knives are now sold with safety caps, but separate caps may be purchased for older knives. Heavy corrugated cardboard should always be placed under the paper or material being cut. The X-acto knife is held like a pencil, with the fingers holding the knife on the textured ring. The slanted, sharpened edge should be directly over the line to be cut, and the position of the knife or the paper should be changed if the line changes direction. Keep the fingers of the holding hand out of the way of the blade, above the cutting area. Remind students often to check themselves and the position of the knife and their hands. The safety cap should be on the knife at all times except when actually in use.

Simple marionette

A marionette can be anything that moves and is controlled by strings. The puppet may be as simple as a scarf or a gathered piece of cloth controlled by one string. It can be a very complex form controlled by as many strings as can be handled by the puppeteer.

procedure

Method a

1. If Styrofoam shapes are used, they should be sealed by brushing watered-down white glue and putting tissue paper scraps on top. Brush additional glue mixture on top of tissue to smooth it. Two layers should do. Allow to dry.
2. If polyurethane foam is used, smooth it with sharp scissors.
3. If cereal box is used, cover it with tissue papier-mâché or by covering it with construction paper or fabric. Allow to dry.
4. Color the body and head if they are not covered by material.
5. Color two triangles for the beak with markers, felt, or paper scraps. Reinforce with tagboard if necessary.
6. Cut out four feet for the creature (actually two layers for each foot). Put the weight between them and glue in place.
7. Wings can be added using construction paper, feathers, and so on.
8. Connect all parts.
9. Make main control by gluing two popsicle sticks or pieces of screen molding together in a crossed position. Holes can be drilled in the ends and in the middle of the cross. Saw slots near holes.
10. Glue the short pieces of bobby pins in the sides of the head and the sides of the body. If Styrofoam, push into shape and glue.
11. String puppet by starting with the body. (See diagram.) String head and finally string feet.
12. Put the strings through the holes from the bottom and through the slot. Adjust and make a knot in the string. If the puppet tangles it can be untangled simply by dropping the strings and restringing.

supplies

1. Styrofoam ball, individual cereal box, or chunk of polyurethane foam (used in upholstery or mattresses). Smaller Styrofoam ball or oval for head.

2. Flexible material for legs and neck (string of pom-poms, tubes of material, heavy cord, or strips of polyurethane)

3. Felt scraps, construction paper scraps, feathers, and any other scraps available

4. Markers or acrylic paint

5. Weights, for feet, such as washers, pennies, or fishing weights, for example

6. Buttonhole thread for stringing the marionette

7. Tongue depressors, popsicle sticks, or screen molding for the controls

8. Thick Tacky Glue, Foamtastic™, or low-heat glue gun

9. Cut bobby pins (four will be needed)

connections Marionettes performed in the great theater of Dionysus in Greece in the 5th Century B.C. The string puppets disappeared following the Roman period but reappeared during the Middle Ages. They were used to teach religious stories in the church until their undisciplined behavior led to them being forced out of the church and into the streets.

Method b

1. Cut the body into a rounded triangle shape. The wide part will be the shoulders and the more pointed end will be where the legs are attached.
2. Cut four pieces of foam that are long and thin and that can be rounded on the edges and narrowed on the ends. These pieces are the upper arms and upper legs.
3. Cut the lower legs to include the feet.
4. Cut two more long, narrow pieces for the lower arms.
5. Hands can be made from felt scraps, cutting them like mittens. Small pieces of rug foam can be used also and fingers may be cut if desired.
6. Color with chalk or acrylic paint all parts that will show. If acrylic is used, mist the foam before applying the paint. Use hair spray to protect chalk colors. **Provide for optimal ventilation.**
7. Position all the parts in relation to the body and make cuts in the body and the appendages where they will join. Use cut strips of material to join the pieces together. Glue them in place with a low-heat glue gun. **Observe safety rules for the glue gun.** Make sure the joints have free movement.
8. Cut a piece of the 2″ foam into a head by rounding with scissors. Pieces can be glued on for noses, chins, and so on.
9. Color the head and add anything necessary to make it into the selected character.
10. Cloth can be draped or glued in place to make a costume.
11. Cut small slits in the side of the head to insert either small loops of material or shortened bobby pins for the stringing.
12. Make small slits in the shoulders and put loops in place or if material has been used, string through the fabric.
13. String the puppet beginning with the shoulders. The string goes from one shoulder, up through the control from the bottom, down through the other hole, and fastened to the other shoulder.
14. The strings from each side of the head go to the holes at the end of the cross piece. The string goes through the hole from the bottom and through the slot. Adjust and tie a knot in the string and slide the string in the slot.
15. Tie the end of a string around one wrist. Pull the other end of the string up through the hole in the front of the control and down to the other wrist, where it is tied.
16. Fasten a string to each knee and up to the holes on the end of the added stick on the front of the control.
17. The final string goes from the lower back of the character to the hole in back of the control.

supplies

1. Polyurethane foam, 1″ thick for appendages and 2″ thick for body and head.
2. Material for joints and costume
3. Low-heat glue gun and glue sticks
4. Chalk and hair spray. Acrylic paint can be used
5. Permanent markers
6. Scrap materials, buttons, pipe cleaners, eyes, yarn, and so on.
7. Buttonhole thread
8. Control made with popsicle sticks, tongue depressors, or screen molding

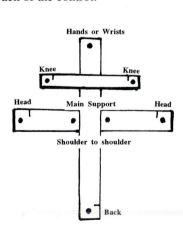

Labels on diagram: Hands or Wrists, Knee, Knee, Head, Main Support, Head, Shoulder to shoulder, Back

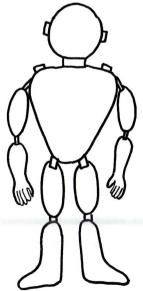

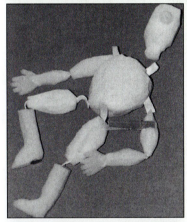

Cardboard cylinder rod puppet

supplies

supplies

1. Cardboard cylinder such as a toilet paper roll or a cylinder made from cardboard or tagboard.

2. Colored construction paper, markers, material, or felt to cover tube.

3. All kinds of scraps

4. Thick white glue, or a low-heat glue gun

5. Tongue depressors, chopsticks, or pieces of screen molding

6. Scissors

7. Skewers for hand controls

procedure

1. Cover cylinder with color or material, remember the face is on one end of the cylinder.
2. Add features for the character selected.
3. Add arms and costumes. Legs could be attached at the bottom of the cylinder.
4. Glue the main support stick inside the cylinder with the handle sticking out of the bottom of the cylinder. **If a glue gun is used, observe all safety rules.**
5. If desired, the arms can be made longer and skewers can be used as controls. **Care should be taken because the skewers are sharp on one end.** The point of the skewer can easily be clipped off with heavy-duty scissors.

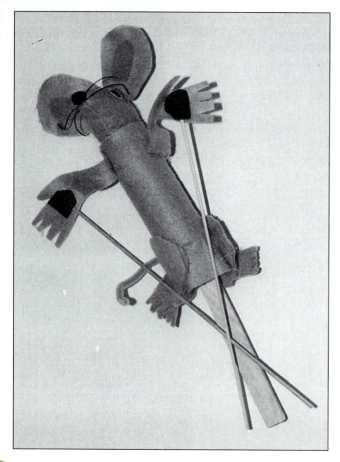

Simple rod puppet

Discuss the characters that will be needed before beginning the activity. A demonstration of how to craft the puppet is important. Simple drawings might be helpful to the students.

procedure

1. Remove the cardboard cylinder from the clothes hanger.
2. Bend the wires of the coat hanger in an upward position, and bend the hook to flatten it to make a handle. The wires will be attached to the hands and will be controlled by this handle.
3. Push the cardboard cylinder or a dowel stick into the center of the Styrofoam ball. Remove the cylinder or stick.
4. Fold the fabric circle in half, and stitch with a long running stitch (over and under) along the folded edge from the center to the edge on each side. This will be gathered later to fit it to the cord that will form the arms and shoulders.
5. Cover the end of the cardboard cylinder or stick with glue. Position the circle of fabric in the center of the cylinder, and push it into the glue to make a good bond.
6. Cover the center of the fabric with glue, and push the cylinder and fabric back into the hole in the Styrofoam.
7. Tie a length of clothesline or cord under the fabric on the stick. Try to center the amount of cord on each side. After it is positioned, glue to the stick. These cords will be the support of the arms.
8. If possible, allow the puppet to dry while forming the hands.
9. Cut four hands from felt so that the lightweight cord coming from the shoulders can be sandwiched between two pieces of felt. Glue the two pieces for hands together on each side, making sure that the cord is glued securely. Thumbs should be up.

supplies

1. Styrofoam ball
2. Clothes hanger with the cardboard at bottom
3. Circle of fabric
4. Felt to make hands
5. Clothesline or heavy cord
6. Other materials to make eyes, hair, and so forth

connections — Asian and Indian cultures

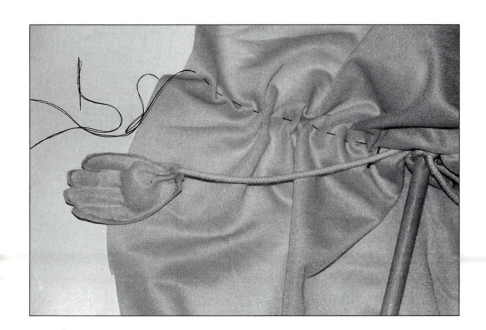

NOTES: The head, neck, and shoulders may be made in Styrofoam, attached to a 24″ dowel and covered with papier-mâché. When dry, the head should be painted and finished. The circle of fabric can be opened at the center and glued to the shoulders. Proceed as above except use longer hand controls. Old umbrella frames can be taken apart and used. Lightweight wooden dowels with drilled holes will also work.

10. Attach the wire loops to the hands between the thumb and first finger. Sew with needle and thread.

11. Finish the puppet by adding features and details with all kinds of materials.

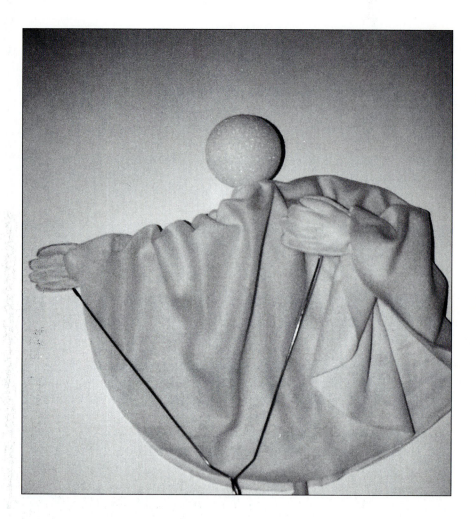

Simple mouth puppet

It is important to discuss the characters needed and the possibilities for crafting the puppets to make those characters. Demonstrating the basic construction is necessary.

procedure

1. Fold one of the paper plates in half.
2. Color inside of plate for inside of mouth. The inside may also be covered with felt.
3. Cut the other paper plate in half. Shape the curved edge for the top of the head.
4. Fold ½″ of the straight edge to make a glue tab.
5. Apply color to the top of the head and the top of the mouth plate where it will show.
6. Glue top of head to the mouth plate on the top. Cut into the glue tab from the edge so that it will curve. Allow enough room in the back so that the puppeteer's fingers will fit.
7. Put on features such as eyes, eyelids, eyebrows, ears, and so forth, after experimenting with placement.
8. Put on any finishing touches to make the character.
9. Fold a 1″ wide strip of tagboard twice on each end; the first fold will make a glue tab, the other fold will allow enough room for the fingers of the puppeteer's hand. This strip should be glued behind the head, on top of the mouth plate.
10. Fold a shorter strip of tab board and glue to bottom of mouth plate to accept thumb of the puppeteer.

supplies

1. Two paper plates
2. Tagboard
3. Markers, oil pastels, crayons
4. Scissors
5. Other materials such as felt, pipe cleaners, feathers, yarn, construction paper, and so on.
6. Thick white glue

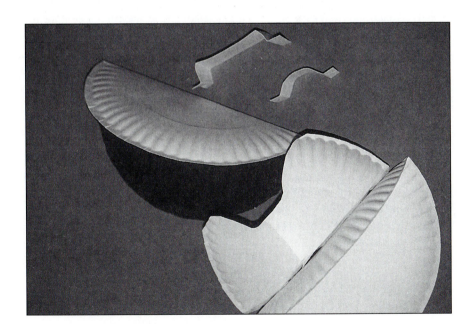

1. Mat board, illustration board, corrugated cardboard for the mouth. Cut to shape for the character

2. Mat or utility knife. **Used by instructor only**

3. Sheet rug foam. Polyurethane. (Do not use the pad made up of chunks of foam)

4. Fiskar® scissors for foam or material

5. Sharpie permanent marker

6. Brown wrapping paper for patterns

7. Low-heat glue gun or glue pot. Thick white glue and Foamtastic™

8. Clothespins

9. Lightweight foam sheet (available at fabric stores)

continued

Foam mouth puppet

It is important to discuss the characters and the possibilities for crafting the puppets to make those characters. Demonstrating the basic construction is necessary.

procedure

1. Cut out mouth shape or beak from mat board, illustration board, or cardboard. Draw a line to one side of the center point and score the board. Fold at the scoring line. Use duct tape on top and bottom at the fold to reinforce and make a hinge.
2. Check to make sure the mouth will fit back into the hand rather than on the fingertips. Cover the inside of the mouth with felt, using thick white glue. Do not trim around the edges until it is dry.
3. Measure the curved edge of the mouth to get the length of the straight edge of the sheet foam that will form the head. This measurement will be the same for the straight edge of the chin also.
4. Make a pattern for the top of the head and the chin with brown wrapping paper. The front of the head and the back of the head will be the same pattern. Remember to draw triangle indentations on the curved edge of the pattern. These are for the darts, so that the foam can be formed into a rounded shape.
5. Use a Sharpie marker to draw around the patterns on the sheet foam.
6. Cut out the foam shapes and darts carefully.
7. Glue the edges of the darts together. Do all the darts on all three pieces of foam. If Foamtastic™ is used, use clothespins to hold the edges together. Line them up carefully. Low-heat glue guns or the low-heat glue pot could also be used.
8. Attach the front of the face with the flat edge to the curved edge of the top of the cardboard mouth. Attach the straight edge of the chin to the other part of the mouth.
9. Make three circles of thin foam that fit the fingers of the puppeteer. Glue them in place on the top of the cardboard mouth just behind the front of the face. Glue another circle on the lower cardboard mouth to use for the thumb. This circle should be placed in a position that will be comfortable.
10. Attach the back of the head to the front of the head.
11. Apply color to the head with poster chalk or Design Master floral spray paint. It is best to test on scrap foam before fixing the head. Poster chalk should be fixed with hair spray. **All spraying must be done with optimal ventilation.**
12. When head is dry, experiment with placement, and glue on features for the character.
13. Ping pong balls cut in half make good eyes. Sharpie Marker can be used to make circles on the balls. Other eyes are also possible, such as colored marbles or buttons. Make sure to fill the half circle of ball with chunk foam before gluing to the head.
14. Cut the nose from chunk foam with Fiskar® scissors.

15. Attach ears and hair if desired.
16. The fabric for the body should be long enough to cover the puppeteer's arm and wide enough to be made into a tube that can be attached to the open back of the chin piece and the opening of the back of the head. With stretch fabric, make the stretch go across rather than up and down.
17. Make a pattern from brown wrapping paper for the hands and arms (they can be made in one piece). Cut them from the same material as the body, again with the horizontal stretch. Allow extra material for seams.
18. Sew the arms and then stuff. Pipe cleaners can be inserted in the fingers first if desired.
19. Attach one arm to each side of the body, a little below the mouth. Make sure they are even. Hand sew them after pinning in place.
20. Costume. Humans can be dressed in children's clothes with modifications (use size 2 or 3).

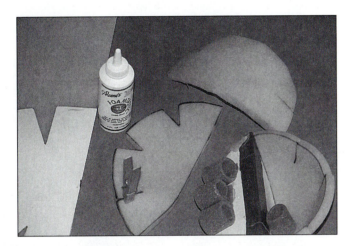

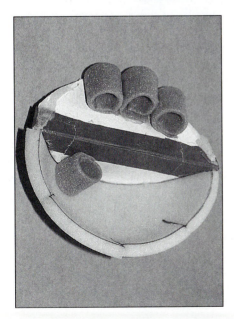

NOTE: If making a bird with a beak or an animal with a muzzle, the top of the head should be make first. The mouth or beak will need to be made separately with a top and bottom. Cut a hole into the head at the bottom to glue the top of the muzzle or beak in place on the front of the head. Finger controls will need to be inserted or polyester can be stuffed into the beak or muzzle to help control it.

One mouth shape.
Variations are possible.

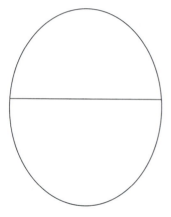

Score and bend.
Tape to make hinge.

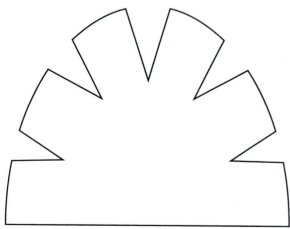

Front and Back of Head (cut two)

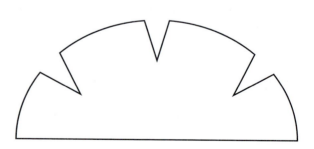

Chin (cut one)

Puppet stages

Hand or rod puppet stages

- Table turned on its side
- Card table or a piece of cloth fastened across a doorway
- Pressure curtain rod and curtain used across a doorway
- Broomstick or a dowel placed between the backs of two chairs with a blanket or cloth over it
- Tabletop
- Cardboard box with a hole cut in it
- Folding screen

Marionette stages

- Box with a hole cut into it at the bottom
- Screen made of corrugated cardboard
- Tabletop
- Table laid on its side behind a doorway with scenery, with a cloth covering the top of the front of the doorway
- Dowels or broomstick tied to the front legs of an overturned table and a cloth or paper attached to the sticks. Another cloth for the scenery can be attached between the back two legs of the table
- Marionettes often perform without curtains

Shadow puppet stages

- Frame made from a big box with enough space below for the puppeteer to work without obstructing the light
- Picture frame with muslin. Use tape or staples to pull and secure material with no sags or wrinkles

Light sources

- Daylight. Put the screen with its back to a window
- Fluorescent tube placed behind the screen
- Gooseneck lamp to the side of the screen
- Overhead projector or a slide projector allows scenery to be added easily

Keep the puppets close to the screen if you want the shadow to be the same size as the puppet and in sharp focus. If you want the puppet to appear bigger, move the puppet away from the screen and closer to the light source. The shadow form will also be more diffused.

Scenery

- Keep it very simple and make sure that it adds to the illusion. If it gets in the way, it will not serve the purpose
- Several change-of-scene backdrops would work well and other things can be added if needed

matting and framing

17

Mat proportions

The matting of display material is an additional cost, but it makes displays more effective and is a practical method of retaining and storing outstanding material. It should be pointed out that display material of similar size is interchangeable, enabling the mat to be used more than once.

For effective and proper matting of creative artwork and other display material, the following rules generally apply:

1. In matting a square illustration, the top and sides of the mat should be equal, with the bottom margin wider (Ill. 1).
2. In matting a vertical rectangular illustration, the bottom margin is the widest, and the top margin wider than the sides (Ill. 2).
3. In matting a horizontal rectangular illustration, the bottom margin is the widest and the top margin should be smaller than the sides (Ill. 3).

The optical center of a picture area is always a certain distance above the measured center. Measured centering of a work in a mat therefore creates a top-heavy appearance, whereas optical centering creates greater frontality and balance and more comfortable viewing. Precut mats are often available.

1

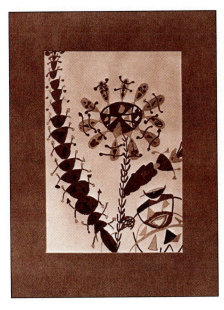

2

3

Cutting a mat

1. Mat board (pebbled or smooth, colored or white)

2. Cardboard (which should be of the same rigidity as the mat board)

3. Pencil

4. Ruler

5. Mat knife or utility knife

6. Gummed tape

NOTE: Acid-free mat board should be used for any picture that is to be preserved for any length of time.

procedure

1. Cut the mat board large enough to accommodate the picture to be matted, including a generous margin (Ill. 1).
2. Cut a piece of cardboard of equal dimensions. This piece will be the backing for the finished mat (Ill. 2).
3. Using the suggestions for square, horizontal, or vertical pictures mentioned earlier, measure and draw a light line the size of the opening to be cut on the face of the mat board (Ill. 3). Be sure that these lines are drawn at least ½″ smaller than both the length and width of the actual picture to be mounted. This will allow the mat to overlap the picture on all sides.
4. Place a piece of heavy scrap cardboard under the line to be cut. Cut carefully along the pencil lines with a sharp mat knife or single-edged razor blade. Apply enough pressure on the tool to cut through the mat with one cut if possible. A ruler held firmly will serve as a guide while cutting. If the cutting tool is held at a 45° angle, a beveled edge can be cut—but only after considerable practice (Ill. 4).
5. Turn the mat over and butt the top edges of the mat and the cardboard backing. Hinge the two pieces together with gummed tape (Ill. 5).
6. Close the mat on the cardboard with the window opening facing up. Mark the four corners of the opening on the cardboard backing with a sharp pencil. This will help in locating the picture directly behind the window (Ill. 6).
7. Open the mat again and center the picture behind the window, making sure that the closed mat overlaps the picture on all four sides (Ill. 7).
8. Fasten the picture to the cardboard along the top edge with gummed tape (Ill. 8), making sure that the tape does not overlap the work far enough to be seen when the mat is closed. A picture fastened this way is easily removed and replaced with another without harm to the mat.
9. Finished matted picture (Ill. 9).

CAUTION: Young students should not do any of the cutting. The instructor should cut the mat.

1

2

3

4

5

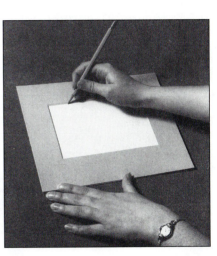

6

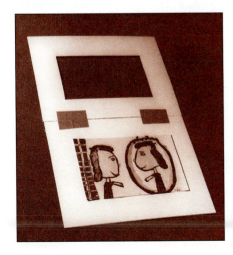

7

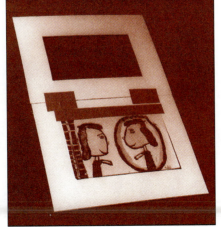

8

9

Covered mat

supplies

1. Mat board or corrugated cardboard
2. Pencil
3. Ruler
4. Mat knife or utility knife
5. Thick white glue
6. Cloth, wrapping paper, or wallpaper
7. Steam iron

procedure

1. Cut the mat as instructed on pages 382 and 383 (Ill. 1).
2. Select a piece of material that is larger than the mat (Ill. 2).
3. Cut the material so it exceeds the measurements of the mat by about 1″ or less (Ill. 3).
4. Cut the corners of the material diagonally up to the corners of the mat (Ill. 3).
5. With the mat face down on the material, cut the inside corners of the material diagonally from the corners of the mat (Ill. 3). Leave about ½″ of material around the window.
6. With the finger, smooth white glue over the entire one side of the mat. Allow the glue to dry.
7. Place the material on top of the mat with the backside toward the glue side of the mat.
8. With a steam iron, carefully iron the material to the mat. The glue reactivates and bonds the material to the mat.
9. Turn the mat face down. Smooth glue in a 1″ band around the window and allow it to dry. Fold the edges of the material tight over the window edge and iron in place. Do all edges (Ill. 4).

NOTE: Decorative trim, cord, or strips of paper may be added to the front of the mat around the window as desired to make it more decorative (Ill. 5).

CAUTION: The instructor should cut the mat for younger students.

1   2   3   4

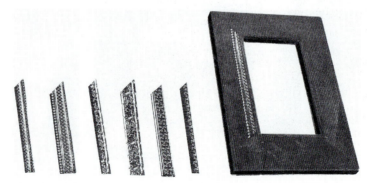

5

Mounted picture mat

procedure

1. Choose a picture to be mounted, and cut it to the desired size.
2. Cut the material to be used as a mat large enough to accommodate the picture to be mounted, including a generous margin. Use matting proportions for square, horizontal, or vertical pictures on page 381 as a guide.
3. Place the cut picture on the mounting material, and use a ruler to make sure the border proportions are correct.
4. Draw around the picture with a light pencil line.
5. Remove the picture, and apply rubber cement to the pencil-enclosed area. Allow to dry.
6. Apply rubber cement to the back of the picture. Allow it to dry.
7. Carefully replace the picture in the penciled shape. Lay a clean piece of paper over the illustration, and smooth it with the hand.

 CAUTION: The instructor should cut the mat for younger students.

1. Picture to be matted
2. Mat board or colored cardboard
3. Rubber cement
4. Scissors, mat or utility knife
5. Pencil
6. Ruler

Shadow box frame

supplies

1. Shallow cardboard box, slightly larger than picture to be framed (Ill. 1)

2. Picture or print to be framed (Ill. 2)

3. White or colored cardboard for mounting picture (Ill. 3)

4. Colored cardboard for framing strips (Ill. 4)

5. Glue

6. Rubber cement for mounting picture

7. Decorative trim (Ill. 6)

8. Scissors

procedure

1. Select a box larger than the picture to be framed (Ill. 1).
2. Mount the picture or print (Ill. 2) to be framed on a piece of cardboard the size of the interior of the box. The cardboard left exposed will form a mat around the picture (Ill. 3).
3. Cut four cardboard strips with a 45° angle at each end (Ill. 4). The shortest dimension of each strip should be slightly shorter than the box.
4. Glue these four strips at the corners to form a flat frame (Ill. 5).
5. Glue the decorative trim (Ill. 6) to the flat frame (Ill. 7).
6. Glue the mounted picture in the bottom of the box (Ill. 8).
7. Glue the decorative flat frame (Ill. 7) to the top edge of the box (Ill. 9).
8. Glue a picture hanger or cardboard support (Ill. 10) to the back of the box.

CAUTION: Care should be taken while cutting.

1

2

3

4

5

6

7

8

9

10

Three-dimensional picture frame

procedure

1. Choose the picture to be framed, and mount it with rubber cement on a piece of cardboard, allowing at least 1½″ of cardboard on all sides (Ill. 1).
2. Score around the edge of the mounted picture deep enough so it can be bent forward (Ill. 1).
3. Cut out four V-shaped corners. The larger the V, the deeper the frame (Ill. 2).
4. Turn up all sides until corners meet.
5. Hold corners together and tape on back (Ill. 3).
6. To hang, place a piece of tape across two ends of a loop of string, fastening them toward the top of the back.

CAUTION: Care should be taken while cutting.

supplies

1. Cardboard
2. Ruler
3. Scissors
4. Pencil
5. Rubber cement

resources

part three

formulas and hints

Acrylic medium and varnish

This material can be used as a nonremovable gloss varnish. It is nontoxic.

Antique plaster finish

Soak the plaster in linseed oil. Remove and dust with dry umber or yellow ochre while still wet. Wipe off excess with a cloth until antique finish is obtained.

Art tool holder

Paper, folded several times, will make a holder that keeps tools from rolling.

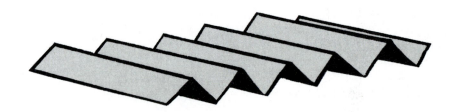

Bench hook

This tool is used to secure linoleum or wood blocks for cutting. Purchased bench hooks may be made of metal or wood. When building a bench hook, 3/4″ wood is usually used.

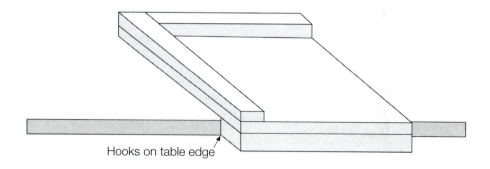

Hooks on table edge

Blown eggs

Raw, whole eggs can be emptied, and the shells, when kept intact, can be decorated and used in many attractive ways. If eggs are blown, exercise caution; salmonella is a possibility.

With a needle, gently pierce a hole about the size of a grain of rice into both ends of a fresh raw egg at room temperature. Make sure the yolk is broken.
Blow hard into one end of the egg, which is held over a bowl, and the contents will leave the other end.
Let water run inside the eggshell, and rinse well until all of the contents of the egg are removed. Allow it to dry before decorating.
The holes at each end can be covered with melted paraffin or candle wax applied with an old brush.
Proceed to decorate the eggshell with dye, ribbon, decorative braid, crepe paper, colored tissue paper, paint, beads, and so on.

Candle wax

Wax from an old candle is best.
Paraffin alone is good but melts rapidly.
Beeswax alone is excellent but expensive.

Carving gesso

Mix whiting and shellac to the consistency of thick cream. Add powdered tempera as needed to color.

Carving material

1 part modeling plaster
1 part sawdust

Mix ingredients. Pour into a cardboard box, and allow to harden. Soak the block in water if it becomes too hard to carve.

Carving paste

5 parts whiting
1 part liquid glue

Mix with water, thinning to the consistency of cream, and add powdered tempera for color.

Casting cement

3 parts sand
1 part portland cement
Mix with water to a smooth consistency.

Clothesline

Hang finished work on a clothesline with clothespins for drying. When there is little space, hang a clothesline close to the wall. This can be hung as a *wall hugger* in a hallway or further up on a wall. Wet batiks and tye dye can also be hung on cork tack strips if plastic is fastened on the cork first.

NOTE: Wax crayon, drawn or melted, painted on the surface of the egg will resist colored dye for interesting effects.

Dye the light colors first, then add more wax and dye darker colors.

A larger opening may be made in the front of the egg by first coating the area to be cut away with colorless nail polish. The opening then may be cut with sharp nail scissors. If the egg cracks around the opening, the cracks can be covered with beads, braid, and so on.

A scene or decoration may then be glued in place inside the egg. Such decorative eggs are especially nice on the Christmas tree or Easter tree.

Development delayed student

Be consistent with the use of terms such as *turning hand* or *holding hand,* which would be the left hand for those students that are right-handed and the right hand for those that are left-handed.

The seating should be close to the instructor.

Check often to make sure the student is keeping up. Don't go on until they have caught up.

Hints for cutting
1. Learn to put on scissors correctly with thumb in small hole, three fingers in bottom hole or larger hole.
2. Thumbs should be up for correct cutting position.
3. Put cutting line in marker, preferably colored.
4. Right-handed students should cut to the left, left-handed should cut to the right.

Use Fun Tack to tack paper down to help stabilize it.

"Grade it." Pare down the lesson so that the student will to be able to do a part of the lesson.

Limit choices. When there is a choice of color, it helps to pick up a handful of colors so that there are fewer to choose from.

When gluing, use a plunger dispenser to apply glue. Apply dots of glue rather than a bead of glue.

Drying rack

Drying racks for wet artwork are ideal if space is at a premium. A number of uniform wooden sticks tacked or stapled to uniform pieces of corrugated cardboard will make a drying rack. If pieces of wood are not available, substitute two, three, or four pieces of corrugated cardboard and tape together, then tape to the base cardboard.

Another method for making drying racks is to use spools or drilled dowel sticks that are 1″ in diameter and cut approximately 1½″ long as spacers on each corner between sheets of sealed corrugated cardboard or sealed Peg-Board. Dowel sticks go through the spools and holes in the corners of the cardboard and are anchored in a 1″ dowel cut 1½″ long and drilled half way through with the hole the same size as the corner dowel stick. The 1″ anchor dowels are glued to the Peg-Board, and a plastic foot can be fastened to the bottom of the Peg-Board in each corner. This drying rack can be taken apart easily.

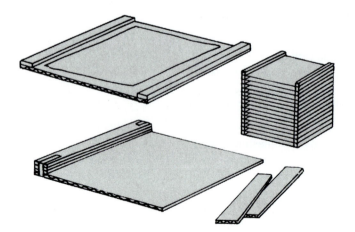

Encaustic paint

1 oz. beeswax
2 teaspoons dry pigment or dry tempera for each color

Heat the beeswax and stir in the color with a stick. Transfer hot encaustic color to picture with brush or palette knife. Wipe wax from brushes while still warm. Turpentine or mineral spirits will act as a solvent.

Felt applicator

A piece of felt held to a stick by a rubber band will ease application of chalk dust to a picture, and keep it permanent.

Finger paint

1. 1 cup liquid starch
   6 cups water
   ½ cup soap chips (nondetergent)
   Dissolve the soap chips in the water until no lumps remain; then mix well with the starch and remaining water. Color with dry or wet tempera or food coloring.
2. Mix wheat paste (wallpaper paste), that does not contain insecticide, into cold or lukewarm water. Stir until smooth. Pour into containers, one for each color, and stir in color pigment.
3. Small pieces of colored chalk finely ground and added to paste of a smooth consistency makes an inexpensive finger paint.
4. Finger paint can be made from toothpaste or thick hand lotion and food coloring.
5. Mix nondetergent soap flakes, food coloring, or dry tempera paint and water to a creamy consistency for an ideal finger paint.
6. Liquid starch mixed with tempera paint to a creamy consistency is also a suitable finger paint.

A piece of notched cardboard, when pulled and/or twisted through the finger paint, will produce interesting patterns.

Fiskars® scissors

This company produces a wide variety of different types of scissors. Scissors for kids come with either pointed or blunt tips and will fit left- or right-handed students. Fiskars® also make paper edgers.

Gesso

Gesso is a primer to make a surface receptive to numerous media. It dries bright white. White latex paint is less expensive and works well.

Glossy plaster finish

Dissolve white soap flakes in a pan or bowl to the consistency of thin cream. Soak the plaster cast or carving thoroughly in the solution for at least 30 minutes. Remove and polish with a dry cloth.

Glues

1. Aleene's Tacky Glue™—Nontoxic, all-purpose craft glue. Dries clear, easy cleanup. Can be thinned with water or made thicker by freezing.
2. Aleene's Designer Tacky Glue™—Nontoxic, super thick, and super tacky, that is an alternative to the glue gun. Fast tack.
3. Aleene's No-Sew Fabric Glue™—Nontoxic. For decorative fabric crafting. Can be used for natural and synthetic fabrics. Holds tight.
4. Aleene's "Ok to Wash-It™" Fabric Glue—Permanent fabric bond. Dries clear and flexible. Will not stain most fabrics. Glues almost every fabric and forms a permanent bond that will withstand repeated washings. Nontoxic.
5. Aleene's Foamtastic™—Ideal for foam and foam rubber. Nontoxic. Soap and water cleanup.
6. Elmer's® Craft Bond Tacky Glue—Nontoxic. Fast-setting, strong, flexible, and bleed-through resistant. Dries clear. Thick no-run formula.
7. Tri-Tix™ Rubber Cream Glue—Nontoxic, nonflammable, nonstaining, nonwrinkling. Dries flexible. Permanent bond on porous surfaces, temporary on nonporous. Easy cleanup. Makes an excellent, inexpensive Frisket (seals out water and color).

Glitter glue

1. Colorations—Will not crack, peel, spoil, or separate. Nontoxic. Applies to almost any surface. Can be applied with brushes or fingers.
2. Elmer's® Fun Dimensions™—No-run gel formula has easy to open and close caps.
3. Magic Glitter Glue—Nontoxic, washable. Makes fine or thick lines. Use for all kinds of decorating.
4. Crayola® Washable Glitter Glue—Nontoxic. Squeeze tubes. Designed to wash from skin and most clothing. Dries in 30 minutes.

Hyplar modeling paste

(M. Grumbacher, Inc., New York)—This is a water-based paste that dries and hardens quickly. It can be used for papier-mâché or can be modeled, shaped, carved, chiseled, or sawed when dry. The paste can be colored with acrylic watercolors that will dry to be waterproof.

Liquitex

(Permanent Pigments, Inc., Cincinnati, Ohio)—A modeling paste with a water base, this is quick drying and can be modeled, carved, tooled, textured, and tinted with acrylic watercolor paint that dries to be waterproof. Thinned with water, it can be used for papier-mâché.

Low-heat glue gun

This glue gun has a lower melting temperature (225° F). Magic Melt™ glue gun is trigger fed and can bond a broad range of materials. Glue sticks are oval in shape and can be purchased separately. Magic Melt™ Glitter Glue Sticks can also be purchased to use in the glue gun and are good to use to make jewelry, decorate fabric, etc.

Mat or utility knife

Mat knives can be used to cut heavy cardboard, mat board, or illustration board. Make sure that the knife has a retractable blade.

Matte medium

This medium can be mixed with colors to maintain a matte or flat, dull finish. Should never be used as a varnish. Nontoxic.

Matte varnish

Used as a finish coat, it will give a nonglare, satin finish. Nontoxic.

Modeling cement

1 part portland cement
1 part asbestos cement
1 part powdered clay that has been sieved

Mix with water to consistency of putty.

Nonsmearing chalk

Add 6 to 8 tablespoons of sugar to an inch of water in a pan. Mix well until all of the sugar is dissolved. Soak chalk in the solution for 10 to 15 minutes. Draw with the chalk.

Paint container

Paper milk containers stapled together with tops removed and with a cardboard handle make an ideal container for colored paint and water.

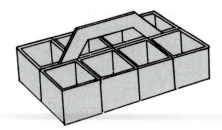

Paint dispensing

Plastic mustard or ketchup containers make good paint dispensers. An aluminum nail in the top of each will keep the paint fresh. In some cases the plastic containers can be used for painting. Syrup pitchers make good paint dispensers and are ideal for storing paint.

Papier-mâché

1 box Knox Gelatin
3 oz. white glue
2 oz. water

Mix ingredients and stir until mixture is smooth and creamy. Tissue paper or paper toweling strips, saturated with water, are placed over the object to the desired thickness. Papier-mâché will dry translucent and with a shiny surface.

Parchment paper

Brush the surface of a piece of cream-colored manila paper with burnt linseed oil; brush the back of the paper with turpentine, and allow to dry.

Plastic spoon

Keep plastic spoons in cans of powdered tempera for easy paint dispensing.

Prang media mixer

(American Crayon Company, Sandusky, Ohio)—This water-based mixer is a colorless, odorless, gelatinlike formula for converting liquid or dry tempera into colored finger paint. Used in a clear form, it will act as a binder for papier-mâché and as an adhesive for paper collage.

Printing gimmicks

Glue heavy string or scraps of felt to a cardboard tube. Slip this tube over a painting roller so that it fits snugly. Roll it in paint and then over a piece of paper, possibly in various directions, to produce a design.

Soft foam rollers can be used for special effects in printmaking, stencil work, cutouts, and other water-based painting and printing techniques.

Ross® art paste

This paste dissolves in cold water to make a colorless, odorless paste. Stays fresh indefinitely and will not ferment or turn sour. Nontoxic.

Salt and cornstarch modeling mixture

1 cup salt
½ cup cornstarch
¾ cup water

Cook in an old double boiler for two minutes; mixture will form a glob or mass. Place the mass on wax paper until it is cool enough to handle, then knead (as bread dough) for three minutes. The material can be wrapped in foil until time for use. It will keep several days, but must be kneaded again before using. It works well around wire or armatures.

Salt and flour beads

2 parts table salt
1 part flour

Mix the salt and flour and water to a doughlike consistency. If color is desired, add dry pigment or food coloring. Break off small pieces and form into beads. Pierce each with a toothpick, and allow to dry, then string.

Salt and flour gesso

2 cups flour
1 cup salt
1½ to 2 cups water

Mix until it is smooth and does not stick to the fingers.

Salt and flour modeling mixture

1 cup salt
1 cup flour
1 tablespoon powdered alum

Mix with water to the consistency of putty.

Salt and flour relief mixture

3 parts salt
1 part flour

Mix with water for the desired consistency.

Sawdust and wheat paste for modeling

2 parts sawdust
1 part wheat paste

Add paste to cold water to form a smooth and creamy mixture. Add sawdust and more water, if necessary, until paste becomes like putty.

Silk screen paint

Combine liquid or powdered tempera mixed with a stiff mixture of nondetergent soap flakes and warm water, or with Prang Media Mixer (mentioned earlier in this section).

Simulated marble

1 part Vermiculite
1 part modeling plaster

Mix ingredients and add water, stirring constantly until the mixture becomes creamy. Pour into a cardboard box and allow to harden. Model with knife, rasp, sandpaper, or any similar tool.

Simulated stone

Formula a
1 part sand
1 part cement
4 parts Zonalite
1 part modeling plaster

Mix ingredients, then add water to form a thick paste. Pour into a cardboard box and allow to harden.

Formula b
2 parts sand
2 parts cement
4 parts Zonalite

Mix ingredients, then add water to form a thick paste. Pour into a cardboard box and allow to harden.

Soda and cornstarch modeling mixture

1 cup cornstarch
2 cups baking soda
1¼ cups water
Food coloring
Aluminum foil or plastic bag

Combine the first three ingredients in a saucepan and cook over medium heat, stirring constantly. When the mixture is thickened to doughlike consistency, turn out on a piece of aluminum foil or on a breadboard. Food coloring may be worked into the clay when it has cooled slightly.

Keep the clay in a refrigerator covered with aluminum foil or in a plastic bag to keep it pliable when not in use.

Clay may be rolled and cut into shapes or may be modeled into small shapes.

Stencil paper

Typing paper pulled through melted paraffin in a flat pan makes an ideal stencil paper. Melt paraffin in a large, shallow pan over a *very low* fire. Holding the end of the typing paper with tweezers, run the paper through the melted paraffin. Allow the paraffin to set by holding the paper over the pan for just a short time. Recoat the paper in the same manner and allow to dry. The stencil paper is now ready to be used.

Synthetic oil paint

Add dry color to regular wheat paste that has been mixed to a thin, smooth consistency. Apply with a stiff brush.

Tempera paint for glossy surfaces

Liquid detergent, or a few drops of glycerine mixed with tempera paint, enables the paint to adhere to shiny or oily surfaces, such as aluminum foil, glass, and so on.

Translucent paper

2 parts turpentine
1 part linseed oil

Brush or wipe the mixture on the paper, and allow it to dry.

Transparent paper

Two parts linseed oil and one part turpentine applied to the back of a drawing with a brush or rag will cause the illustration to become transparent.

Zonalite sculpture cement

1 part cement
5 parts Zonalite

Mix cement and Zonalite with water until smooth. Pour into a cardboard box or mold to harden. Zonalite cement is lightweight and can be cut with a saw or carved with any metal tool.

appendix: art resources

The material listed in this section should be helpful in achieving an improved level of art understanding. The listing is, of course, by no means exhaustive. Those books indicated by an asterisk (*) are out of print: it is recommended that libraries be searched for them.

Books and journal articles

Art appreciation

Arnason, H. *History of Modern Art: Painting, Sculpture, Architecture and Photography,* 4th ed. New York: Harry Abrams, 1997.

Cahan, S., and Kocur, Z. (ed.). *Contemporary Art in Multicultural Education.* New York: Routledge, 1995.

Canaday, J. *What is Art?* New York: Alfred A. Knopf, 1989.

Carr, D. *Looking at Paintings: A Guide to Technical Terms.* New York: Oxford University Press, 1992.

Chicago Children's Press. *Getting to Know the World's Artists Series,* 1988.

Erlande-Braneburg, A. *Cathedrals and Castles.* New York: Abrams, 1995.

Goldman, P. *Looking at Prints, Drawings and Watercolors.* Los Angeles: J. Paul Getty Museum, 1988.

Gombrich, E. *The Story of Art,* 6th ed. New York: Phaidon Press, 1995.

Greenberg, J. *The American Eye: Eleven Artists of the Twentieth Century.* New York: Delacorte, 1995. Grades 6–12.

Greenberg, J., and Jordan, S. *The Painter's Eye.* New York: Delacorte, 1991.

Janson, H., and Janson, A. *History of Art.* New York: Harry Abrams, 1991.

Little, C. *Winslow Homer and the Sea.* Beverly Hills, CA; Pomengranate, 1995. Grades 5–12.

Looking at Paintings Series. New York: Hyperion Books, 1993.

LRN Company. *Art for Children Series.* New York, 1988.

Mayer, R. *The Harper Collins Dictionary of Arts, Terms and Techniques.* New York: Harperperennial Library, 1992.

Millard, A. *Pyramids.* New York: Kingfisher LKC, 1996. Grades 3–9.

Muhlberger, R. *What Makes a . . . Artist Series.* New York: Metropolitan Museum of Art, 1993.

Thomas, J. *Masterpieces of the Month: An Art Appreciation Program for Grades K–5. Teacher Created Materials,* 1997.

Understanding the Masters Series. London: Trewin Copplestone, Ltd., 1976.

Art education

Abhau, M.. *Architecture in Education.* Foundation for Architecture, 1990. Grades K–12.

Alexander, K (ed.), and Day, M. *Discipline-Based Art Education: A Curriculum Sampler.* J. Paul Getty Museum, Los Angeles, 1992.

Anderson, F. *Art for All the Children.* Springfield, IL: Charles C. Thomas, 1992.

Barret, T. *Talking About Student Art.* Worcester, MA: Davis, 1997.

Battock, G. *New Ideas in Art Education.* New York: E.P. Dutton, 1973.

Beattie, D. *Assessment in Art Education.* Worcester, MA: Davis, 1998.

Blandy, D., and Congdon, K. *Art in a Democracy.* New York: Teachers College Press, 1987.

Brittain, W. *Creativity: Art and the Young Child.* New York: Macmillan, 1979.

Brouch, V. *Art Education: A Matrix System for Writing Behavioral Objectives.* Phoenix: Arbo Publishing, 1973.

Cane, F. *The Artist in Each of Us.* New York: Art Therapy Publications, Basic Books, 1983.

Carle, E. *Hello Red Fox.* New York: Simon & Schuster, 1998.

Capek, M. *Murals: Cave, Cathedral to Street.* Flushing, NY: Lerner Publications 1996.

Chapman, L. *Approaches to Art in Education.* New York: Harcourt Brace Jovanovich, 1978.

Churchill, A. *Art for Pre-adolescents.* New York: McGraw-Hill, 1971.

Colter, L. *Junior Art Museum.* New York: J.A.M. Printing, 1977.

Defrancesco, I. *Art Education.* New York: Harper & Row, 1958.

Diehn, G. *Making Books That Fly, Fold, Wrap, Hide, Pop Up, Twist and Turn.* New York: Random House, 1998.

Dimondstein, G. *Exploring Art with Children.* New York: Macmillan, 1971.

Edwards, B. *Drawing on the Right Side of the Brain.* Los Angeles: Jeremy P. Tarcher, 1979.

Eisner, E. *Educating Artistic Vision.* New York: Macmillan, 1972.

Erdt, M. *Teaching Art in the Public School.* New York: Holt, Rinehart & Winston, 1962.

Fukurai, S. *How Can I Make What I Cannot See?* New York: Van Nostrand Reinhold, 1974.

Gaitskell, C, and Hurwitz, A. *Children and Their Art,* 4th ed. New York: Harcourt Brace & Jovanovich, 1982.

Gardner, H. *Artful Scribbles.* New York: Basic Books, 1980.

Gentle, K. *Children and Art Teaching.* London: Croom Helm, 1985, *My Name is Georgia.* Silver Whistle: Harcourt Brace, 1998.

Greene, R. *When a Line Bends . . . A Shape Begins.* New York: Houghton Mifflin, 1997.

Greer, D. "Discipline-Based Art Education: Approaching Art as a Subject of Study." *Studies in Art Education* 25 (1984) 212–18.

Greh, D. *Computers in the Art Room.* Worcester, MA: Davis, 1990.

Herberholtz, B., and Hanson, L. *Early Childhood Art,* 4th ed. Dubuque, IA: Wm. C. Brown, 1990.

Herberholtz, D., and Alexander, K. *Artworks for Elementary Teachers,* 6th ed. Dubuque, IA: William C. Brown, 1990.

Henley, D. *Exceptional Children, Exceptional Art.* Worcester, MA: Davis, 1992.

Hoover, F. *Art Activities for the Very Young.* Worcester, MA: Davis Publications, 1961.

Hoyt-Goldsmith. *Day of the Dead.* New York: Holiday House, 1995.

Hurwitz, A. *The Gifted and Talented in Art.* Worcester, MA: Davis, 1983.

Jefferson, B. *Teaching Art to Children.* Boston: Allyn & Bacon, 1963.

Laliberte, N. *The Reinhold Book of Art Ideas.* New York: Van Nostrand Reinhold, 1976.

Laliberte, N., and Kehl, R. *100 Ways to Have Fun with an Alligator.* Blauvelt, NY: Art Education, Inc., 1964.

Lanier, V. "To Have Your Cake and Eat it Too: A Response to Beyond Creating." *Studies in Art Education* 25 (1986), 152–53.

Lauer, D. *Design Basics.* New York: Harcourt Brace Jovanovich, 1997.

Levete, G. *The Creative Tree: Active Participation in the Arts for People Who Are Disadvantaged.* Great Britain: Michael Russell, 1987.

Linderman, E., and Linderman, M. *Crafts in the Classroom.* New York: Macmillan, 1977.

Linderman, M. *Art in the Elementary School.* Dubuque, IA: William C. Brown, 1990.

Linstrom, M. *Children's Art.* Berkeley: University of California Press, 1957.

Loughram, B. *Art Experiences.* New York: Harcourt, Brace & World, 1963.

Lowenfeld, V, and Brittain, W. *Creative and Mental Growth,* 7th ed. New York: Macmillan, 1982.

Matearis, A. *Too Much Talk.* London: Candlewick, 1997.

Mattil, E. *Meaning in Crafts,* 3rd ed. Englewood Cliffs, NJ: Prentice Hall, 1971.

Presilla, M., and Soto, S. *Life Around the Lake.* Austin, TX: Henry Holt, 1996.

Proctor, R. *Principles of Pattern Design.* Mineola, NY: Dover, 1990

Qualley, C. *Safety in the Classroom.* Worcester, MA: Davis, 1986.

Read, H. *Education Through Art.* New York: Pantheon, 1984.

Saccardi, M. M. *Art in Story: Teaching Art to Elementary School Children.* North Haven, CT: Linnet Professional, 1997.

Schuman, M. *Art from Many Hands.* Englewood Cliffs, NJ: Prentice-Hall, 1981.

Sprintzen, A. *Crafts.* Worcester, MA: Davis, 1986.

Stewart, M. *Thinking Through Aesthetics.* Worcester, MA: Davis, 1997.

Taylor, J. *Learning to Look: A Handbook of the Visual Arts.* Chicago: University of Chicago Press, 1983.

Thorne-Thomsen. *Frank Lloyd Wright for Kids.* Chicago: Chicago Review, 1994.

Topal, C. *Children and Painting.* Worcester, MA: Davis, 1992.

Uhlin, D., and DeChiara, E. *Art for Exceptional Children,* 3rd ed. Dubuque, IA: William C. Brown, 1984.

Winters, N. *Architecture Is Elementary.* Layton, UT: Gibbs Smith, 1985.

Wolf, D., and Perry, M. "From Endpoints to Repertoirs: Some New Conclusions About Drawing Development." *Journal of Aesthetic Education* 22, no. 1 (1988), 17–34.

Yenawine, P. *How to Look at Modern Art,* New York: Harry Abrams, 1997.

Lettering and calligraphy

Allen, L. *Clever Letters: Fun Ways to Wiggle Your Words.* Middleton, WI: Pleasant Company, 1997.

Angel, M. *The Art of Calligraphy.* New York: Charles Scribner's Sons, 1978.

Ballinger, R. A. *Lettering Art in Modern Use.* New York: Van Nostrand Reinhold, 1979 (student edition).

D'Ancona, P. and Aeschlimann, E. *The Art of Illustration.* New York: Phaidon, 1969.

Douglass, Ralph. *Calligraphic Lettering with Wide Pen and Brush.* New York: Watson-Guptill, 1975.

Ecke, T. Y. *Chinese Calligraphy.* Philadelphia: Philadelphia Museum of Art and Boston Books and Art, 1971.

Fairbank, S. A. *Handwriting Manual.* New York: Watson-Guptill, 1976.

Gaitskell, C. D.; Hurwitz, A.; and Day, M. *Children and Their Art,* 4th ed. New York: Harcourt Brace Jovanovich, 1983.

Goines, D. L. *A Basic Formal Hand,* 3rd ed. New York: St. Hieronymus Press, 1976.

Gourdie, T. *Calligraphy for the Beginner.* New York: Taplinger, 1979.

Harris, D. *Art of Calligraphy.* New York: DK Publishers 1995.

Harthan, J. *The Book of Hours.* New York: Thomas Y. Crowell, 1977.

Harvey, M. *Lettering Design.* Barre, MA: Barre Publishing, 1976.

Hassall, W. O., and Hassall, G. *Treasures from the Bodleian Library.* New York: Columbia University, 1976.

Khibati, A., and Sivelmassi, M. *The Splendor of Islamic Calligraphy.* New York: Rizzoli International Publications, 1976.

Kuiseko, R. *Brush Writing.* New York: Kodansha International, 1988.

Lancaster, J. *Lettering Techniques.* New York: Arco, 1983.

Lehman, C. *Italic Handwriting and Calligraphy for the Beginner.* New York: Taplinger, 1982.

McDonald, B. J. *Calligraphy: The Art of Lettering with the Broad Pen.* New York: Taplinger, 1966.

Rinner, J. *Creative Lettering.* Pleasant Grove, UT: Red Point Publishing, 1998.

Svaren, J. *33 Alphabets for Calligraphers.* New York: Taplinger, 1986.

Switkin, A. *Hand Lettering Today.* New York: Harper and Row, 1976.

Whalley, J. I. *The Student's Guide to Western Calligraphy: An Illustrated Survey.* Boulder, CO: Shambala Publications, 1984.

Wotzkow, H. *The Art of Hand Lettering.* Mineola, NY: Dover Publications, 1952.

Color

Birren, F. *Creative Color.* New York: Van Nostrand Reinhold, 1961.

Itten, J. *The Art of Color.* New York: Van Nostrand Reinhold, 1973.

Renner, P. *Color, Order and Harmony.* New York: Van Nostrand Reinhold, 1965.

Zelanski, P. *Color.* Paramus, NJ: Prentice Hall, 1998.

Design

Bethers, R. *Creative Color. Composition in Pictures,* 2nd ed. Belmont, CA: Pitman, 1964.

Bevlin, M. E. *Design Through Discovery,* 4th ed. New York: Holt, Rinehart & Winston, 1984.

Lauer, D. A. *Design Basics,* 2nd ed. New York: Holt, Rinehart and Winston, 1985.

Ocvirk, O. G.; Stinson, R. E.; Wigg, P. R; and Cayton, D. *Art Fundamentals,* 8th ed. New York: McGraw-Hill, 1998.

Paper and cardboard

Grater, M. *Paper Faces.* New York: Taplinger Publishing Co, 1968.

Grater, M. *Make It in Paper.* Mineola, NY: Dover, 1983.

Grater, M. *Paper Projects with One Piece of Paper.* Mineola, NY: Dover, 1987.

Hiner, M. *Paper Engineering for Pop-Up Books and Cards.* Eatontown, NJ: Parkwest, 1986.

Irvine, J. *How to Make Pop-ups.* New York: Beech Tree Books, 1991.

Irvin, J. I. *How to Make Super Pop-ups.* New York: William Morrow, 1992.

Irvin, J. I. *How to Make Holiday Pop-ups.* New York: William Morrow, 1996.

Jackson, P., and Frank, V. *Origami and Papercraft.* New York: Crescent Publishers, Inc., 1973.

Johnson, P. *Creating with Paper.* Seattle: University of Washington Press, 1958.

Newman, T.; Newman, J.; and Newman, L. *Paper as Art and Craft.* New York: Crown Publishers, Inc., 1973.

Temko, F. *Paper: Folded, Cut, Sculpted.* New York: Collier Books, 1974.

Ziegler, K. *Paper Sculpture: A Step by Step Guide.* Cincinnati, Ohio: North Light Books, 1997.

A number of books on printmaking have information on papermaking.

Clay

Ball, F., and Lovoos, J. *Making Pottery Without a Wheel.* New York: Van Nostrand Reinhold Co., 1965.

Chaiarri, J. *Hand Building Techniques.* New York: Watson-Guptill, 1999.

Giorgini, F. *Handmade Tiles: Designing, Making, Decorating.* Asheville, NC: Lark Books, 1994.

Kong, E. *The Great Clay Adventure.* Worcester, MA: Davis, 1986.

Mattison, S. *Two Books in One Ceramics.* New York: Sterling Publications, 1998.

Nelson, G. *Ceramics.* Austin, TX: Rinehart & Winston, 1984.

Priolo, J., and Priolo, A. *Ceramics by Coil.* New York: Sterling Publishing Co., Inc., 1976.

———. *Ceramics by Slab.* New York: Sterling Publishing Co., 1977.

Speight, C. F., and Toki, J. *Hands in Clay.* White Plains, NY: Mayfield Publishing Co., 1999.

Tiplett, K. *Hand Built Ceramics.* Asheville, NC: Lark Books, 1997.

Topal, C. *Children, Clay and Sculpture.* Worcester, MA: Davis, 1983.

Zakin, R. R. *Hand-Formed Ceramics.* Radnor, PA: Chilton Book Co., 1995.

Fibers

Bawden, J. *Applique.* NJ: Chronicle Books, 1991.

Belfer, N. *Batik and Tie Dye Techniques.* Mineola, NY: Dover Publications, Inc., 1992.

Guild, V. *Painting with Stitches.* Worcester, MA: Davis Pubs., 1976.

Held, S. E. *Weaving, A Handbook of the Fiber Arts.* New York: Holt, Rinehart and Winston, 1978.

Held, S. E. *Weaving.* New York: Harcourt Brace Jovanovich, 1998.

Meilach, D. *Basketry with Fibers and Grasses.* New York: Crown Publishers, 1976.

Meilach, D., and Snow, L. *Weaving Off-Loom.* Chicago: Contemporary Books, 1973.

Noble, E. *Dyes and Paints: A Hands-On Guide to Coloring Fabric.* Middleton, WI: Martingale & Co., 1998.

Proctor, R., and Surface, L. J. *Design for Fabric.* Seattle: University of Washington Press, 1995.

Rainey, S. *Wall Hangings, Designing with Fabric and Thread.* Worcester, MA: Davis Publications, 1973.

Rainey, S. *Weaving Without a Loom.* Worcester, MA: Davis Publications, 1966.

Soboit, M. *Pictures in Patchwork.* New York: Sterling Publishing Co., 1977.

Sommer, E., and Sommer, M. *A New Look at Felt.* New York: Crown Publishers, 1975.

Zegart, T. *Quilts, An American Heritage.* Louisville Kentucky: Kent Quilt Pub. 1993.

Masks

Finley, C. *Art of African Masks.* Minneapolis, MN: Lemer Pub., 1999.

Frand, V., and Jaffe, D. *Masking Masks.* Atlanta, GA: Chartwell Books, Inc., 1992.

Grater M. *Paper Maskmaking.* Minneola, NY: Dover Publications, 1984.

Lindahl, C. *Cajun Mardi Gras Masks.* Jackson, MS: University Press of Mississippi, 1997

MacNair, P. *Down from the Shimmering Sky; Masks of the Northwest Coast.* Seattle: University of Washington Press, 1998.

Sivin, C. *Maskmaking.* Worcester, MA: Davis, 1986.

Tommel, A. *Masks, Their Meaning and Function.* New York: McGraw-Hill Book Co., 1972.

Puppetry

Baird, B. *The Art of the Puppet.* New York: Bonanza Books, 1966.

Currel, D. *Introduction to Puppets and Puppet-Making.* New York: Book Sales, 1996.

Engler, L., and Fijan, C. *Making Puppets Come Alive.* New York: Taplinger Publishing Co., Inc., 1980.

Fijan, C., and Ballard, F. *Directing Puppet Theatre.* San Jose, CA: Resources Publications, Inc., 1989.

Fling, H. *Marionettes: How to Make and Work Them.* Mineola, NY: Dover Publishing, 1973.

Flower, C. *Puppets: Methods and Materials.* Worcester, MA: Davis Publications, 1983.

Grater, M. *Puppets, Jumping Jacks and Other Paper People.* Mineola, NY: Dover Publications, Inc., 1994.

Henson, C. *The Muppets Make Puppets.* New York: Workman Publishing, 1994.

Hodges, D. *Marionettes and String Puppets.* New York: Antique Trader, 1998.

Latshaw, G. *The Complete Book of Puppetry.* Mineola, NY: Dover, 2000.

Long, T. *Make Your Own Performing Puppets.* New York: Tamos Books, 1995

Reininger, L. *Shadow Puppets, Shadow Theatres and Shadow Films.* Boston: Publishers Plays, Inc., 1975.

Renfro, N., and Armstrong, B. *Make Amazing Puppets.* Santa Barbara, CA: The Learning Works, 1979.

Ross, L. *Hand Puppets: How to Make and Use Them.* Mineola, NY: Dover, 1990.

Taylor, B. *Marionette Magic.* Blue Ridge Summit, PA: Tab Books, 1989.

Printmaking

Brommer, G. *Relief Printmaking.* Worcester, MA: Davis Publications, Inc., 1970.

D'Alleva, A. *Native American Arts and Cultures.* Worcester, MA: Davis Publications, 1993.

Herald, J. *World Crafts.* Asheville, NC: Lark Books, 1993.

Ross, J., and Romano, C. *The Complete Collagraph.* New York: The Free Press, 1980.

———. *The Complete Intaglio Print.* New York: The Free Press, 1974.

———. *The Complete Printmaker.* New York: New York Free Press, 1974.

———. *The Complete Relief.* New York: The Free Press, 1974.

———. *The Complete Screenprint and Lithograph.* New York: The Free Press, 1974.

Saff, D. *Printmaking.* New York: Harcourt Brace Jovanovich, 1998.

Saff, D., and Sacilotto, D. *Printmaking.* New York: Holt, Rinehart & Winston, 1978.

Toale, B. *Printmaking Techniques.* Worcester, MA: Davis, 1992.

Sculpture

Bridgewater, A. *Carving Totem Poles and Masks.* New York: Sterling Publishers, 1991.

Coleman, R. *Sculpture: A Basic Handbook for Students.* Dubuque, IA: William C. Brown, 1980.

Hoyt-Goldsmith, D. *Totem Pole.* New York: Holiday, 1994.

Roukes, N. *Sculpture in Paper.* Worcester, MA: Davis, 1993.

Stewart, H. *Looking at Indian Art of the Northwest.* Seattle: University of Washington Publishers, 1979.

Stewart, H. *Looking at Totem Poles.* Seattle: University of Washington Press, 1993.

Wolfe, G. *3-D Wizardry.* Worcester, MA: Davis, 1995.

Other resources

Bahti, M. *Pueblo Stories & Storytellers.* New York: Treat Chest Books, 1995. Grades K–12.

Barbash, S. *Oaxacan Woodcarving: The Magic in the Trees.* San Francisco, CA: Chronicle Books, 1993.

Blier, S. *Royal Arts of Africa.* New York: Harry Abrams, 1993.

Braun, B. *Arts of the Amazon.* New York: Thames Hudson, 1995.

Chanda, J. *Discovering African Art.* Worcester, MA: Davis, 1996.

Cockcroft, J. *Diego Rivera.* Broomall, PA: Chelsea House Pub., 1992. Grades 4–8.

D'Alleva, A. *Native American Arts & Cultures.* Worcester, MA: Davis, 1993.

———. *Arts of the Pacific Islands.* Worcester, MA: Davis, 1998.

Doherty, C., and Doherty, K. *The Zunis.* Culver City, CA: Blackbirch 1993. Grades 3–8.

Duggleby, J. *The Life of Jacob Lawrence.* New York: Chronicle Books, 1998. Grades 4–12.

Essary, L. *Art of the Hopi.* Cadillac, MI: Northland, 1998.

Fisher, J. *The Gods and Goddesses of Ancient Egypt.* New York: Holiday, 1997. Grades 2–6.

Harruch, *Discovering Oceanic Art.* Worcester, MA: Davis, 1996.

Herbert, J. *Leonardo Da Vinci for Kids.* Chicago, IL: Chicago Review Press, 1998.

Holt-Goldsmith, D. *Celebrating Chinese New Year.* New York: Holiday House, 1999.

———. *Day of the Dead.* New York: Holiday House, 1995. Grades 3–6.

Johnston, T. *Day of the Dead.* San Diego, CA: Harcourt Brace, 1997. Grades 3–6.

Klum, M., and Odoo, H. *Exploring the Rain Forest.* New York: Sterling, 1997. Grades 4–7.

Lelooska, C. *Stories and Paintings of; Spirit of the Cedar People* (includes book and audio CD). New York: DK Publishing, 1998. Grades 1–6.

Lewis, S. *African American Art for Young People.* New York: Utility Works, 1991.

Littlechild, G. *This Land Is My Land.* San Francisco, CA: Children's Books, 1993. Grades 3–8.

MacDonald, F. *How Would You Survive as an Aztec?* Culver City, CA: Watts, 1995. Grades 3–6.

Max, J. *Spider Spins a Story.* Flagstaff, AZ: Rising Moon, 1997. Grades 2–6.

Osofsky, A. *Dreamcatcher.* Chicago, IL: Orchard Books, 1992. Grades K–3.

Patton, S. *African-American Art.* New York: Oxford University Press, 1998.

Perl, L. *Mummies, Tombs and Treasures.* Chicago, IL: Clarion Books, 1990 Grades 3–8.

Presilla, M., and Soto, S. *Life Around the Lake.* Austin, TX: Henry Holt, 1966. All grades.

Remer, A. *Discovering Native American Art.* Worcester, MA: Davis, 1996.

Ringgold, F. *Talking with Faigh Ringgold, Linda Freeman and Nancy Roucher.* New York: Crown Publishers, 1996. Grades K–4.

———. *Tar Beach.* Albuquerque, NM: Dragonfly, 1996. Grades 1–6.

Ruddell, N. *Mystery of the Maya.* Seattle: Chelsea House, 1991. Grades 3–12.

Sekakuku, A. *Following the Sun and Moon: Hopi Kachina.* Cadillac, MI: Northland, 1995.

Trout, L. *The Maya.* Broomall, PA: Chelsea House, 1991. Grades 3–12.

Wood, M. *Going Back Home: An Artist Returns to the South.* Minneapolis, MN: Children's Press, 1996. Grades 1–5.

Book series

Art for Children Series. New York: Chelsea House, 1994. Set of 8.

Art for Young People. New York: Sterling Publishing, 1996.

Famous Artist Series. New York: Barrons Juvenile, 1994.

Famous Artist Series. Lakewood, NJ: Watson-Guptill Publishers, 1988.

Getting to Know the World's Greatest Artists Series. Chicago: Children's Press, 1993. Set of 25.

Knapp and Lehmber, Off the Wall Museum Guides for Kids. New York: Sterling Publishers, 1998. Includes Egyptian, impressionist, and American art.

Roaf, Peggy, and Lowe, Jacques. Looking at Paintings. New York: Hyperion Books for Children, 1993. Titles include *Cats, Landscapes, Seascapes,* and *Dancers* (all titles 1992), and *Musicians, Children, Circus, Self-Portraits, Flowers,* and *Horses* (all titles 1993).

Also, Eyewitness Books publishes many subjects.

Video series

The Big A. A 10-part Video Series. Art for Grades 1–3.
GPN, P. O. Box 80669, Lincoln, NE 68501-0669   15 minute programs.

Behind the Scenes. 5 Visual Arts Programs, 40 minutes each. Intermediate grades.

1. Illusion of Depth with David Hockney
2. Color with Robert Gil DeMontes
3. Balance with Nancy Graves
4. Framing with Carrie Mae Weemes
5. Line with Wayne Thiebaud

GPN, P. O. Box 80669, Lincoln, NE 68501-0669

Supplies

A.R.T. Studio Clay Co.
1555 Louis Avenue
Elk Grove Village, IL 60007

Bailey Ceramic Supply
P. O. Box 1577
Kingston, NY 12401

Chaselle
9645 Gerwig Lane
Columbia, MD 21046

Dick Blick
P. O. Box 1267
Galesburg, IL 61402

Graphic Chemical and Ink Co.
P. O. Box 7027
Villa Park, IL 60181

Minnesota Clay
8001 Grand Ave. South
Bloomington, MN 55420

Nosco Arts and Crafts
901 Janesville Ave.
Ft. Atkinson, WI 53538

Ohio Ceramic Supply, Inc.
2861 St. Rt. 59
P. O. Box 630
Kent, OH 44240

R. B. Walter Art and Crafts
Dept. SA/P. O. Box 6231
Arlington, TX 76005

Sax Arts and Crafts
2405 S. Calhown Rd.
New Berlin, WI 53151

Triaco Arts and Crafts
14650 28th Avenue North
Plymouth, MN 55447

United Art and Education Supply Co., Inc.
P. O. Box 9219
Fort Wayne, IN 46899

Audiovisual resources

Crizmac
Art and Cultural Education Materials
P. O. Box 65928
Tucson, AZ 85728-5928

Crystal Productions
1812 Johns Drive
P. O. Box 2159
Glenview, IL 60025-6159

Dale Seymour Publications
P. O. Box 10888
Palo Alto, CA 94303

Davis Publications, Inc.
50 Portland St.
Worcester, MA 01608

Dover Publications
31 East 2nd Street
Mineola, NY 11501

Sax Visual Art Resources
P. O. Box 51710
New Berlin, WI 53151-0710

Shorewood Fine Art Reproductions
27 Glen Road
Sandy Hook, CT 06482

Magazines

Arts and Activities
591 Camina de la Reina
Suite 200
San Diego, CA 92108

School Arts
50 Portland St.
Worcester, MA 01615-9959

Children's magazines

Children's magazines sometimes feature children's art. Check the school or public library for issues of the following magazines and others that may have features including art work, poems, or stories created by children.

1. *Cobblestone Publishing, Inc.* has several magazines that include student work. Write to Cobblestone Publishing, Inc.7 School St., Petersborough, NH 03458
2. *Crayola Kids* is a bi-monthly magazine that has a particular theme for each issue. Write to Crayola Kids, 1912 Grand Ave., Des Moines, IA 50309-3379
3. *Cricket Publishing Group* has several publications that include the arts. Contact The Cricket Publishing Group, 315 Fifth St. Peru, Ill 61354
4. *Creative Kids* is composed of work by students. Write to Creative Kids, P. O. Box 8813, Waco, TX 76714
5. *National Geographic World* has a regular monthly feature of a particular theme named in the previous issue. Write to National Geographic World, Art Mail Bag, P.O. Box 98002, Washington, D.C. 20090
6. *Shoe Tree* will take student work. Contact Shoe Tree Press, Betterway Publications, Inc., P.O. Box 219, Crozet, VA 22932
7. *Stone Soup* includes students' work up to age 13. Write to Stone Soup, P.O. Box 83, Santa Cruz, CA 95063

internet resources

1. http://www.artsednet.getty.edu
   The Getty Education Institute for the Arts
2. http://library.advanced.org/50072/
   Artful Minds
3. http://education.crayola.com
   Crayola
4. http://www.bemiss-jason.com/projects
   Bemiss-Jason
5. http://www.boston.com/mfa/mfahome.htm
   Museum of Fine Arts, Boston
6. http://pma.libertynet.org
   Philadelphia Museum of Art
7. http:www.umich.edu/~umma
   University of Michigan Museum of Art
8. http://www.thinker.org
   The Fine Arts Museum of San Francisco
9. http://www.acs.ucalgary.ca/~dkbrown/index.html
   Children's Literature Web Guide
10. http://www.carolhurst.com
    Carol Hurst's Children's Literature Site
11. http://www.amazon.com/childrens
    Amazon.com Children's and Young Adult
12. http://janbrett.com
    Jan Brett's Home Page
13. http://www.eric-carle.com
    Eric Carle Web Site
14. http://guardians.net/egypt
    Guardian's Egypt
15. http://www.clemusart.com/archive/pharaoh
    The Cleveland Museum of Art-Pharaohs
16. http://www.memphis.edu/egypt/main.html
    Institute of Eyptian Art and Archeology
17. http://www.sagecraft.com/puppetry
    Puppetry
18. http://www.geocities.com/Athens/Delphi/9096/drawing.html
    Tedd Arnold Illustration
19. http://metalab.unc.edu/wm/
    WebMuseum, Paris
20. http://www.nccil.org/children/index.html
    National Center for Children's Illustrated Literature
21. http://www.artmuseum.net
    Art Museum.Net
22. http://metmuseum.org/
    The Metropolitan Museum of Art
23. http://www.moma.org/
    The Museum of Modern Art, New York
24. http://www.nmaa.si.edu/
    National Museum of American Art
25. http://www.artchive.com/core.html
    The Artchive
26. http://www.nga.gov/
    National Gallery of Art, Washington, D.C.
27. http://mistral.culture.fr/louvre/louvrea.htm
    The Louvre
28. http://www.arca.net/uffizi/index.htm
    The Virtual Uffizi
29. http://www.christusrex.org/www1/sistine/0-Tour.html
    The Sistine Chapel
30. http://www.artic.edu/aic/index.html
    The Art Institute of Chicago
31. http://www.vangoghmuseum.nl
    Van Gogh Museum, Amsterdam
32. http://www.legendsandlore.com/puppet-resource.html

class levels suggested for the activities

The following are merely suggestions; we believe that the classroom teacher is the best judge of student capabilities. In some instances, when classroom size is small or maturity level of the students warrants, activities may be selected which are more challenging. Conversely, the activities may be changed to make them more interesting and challenging to the older or more mature student.

chapter 4

Lettering and calligraphy

1. Felt Pen Lettering—Intermediate
2. Cut Letters—Intermediate
3. 3-D Letters—Intermediate
4. ABC Book—Primary
5. Poster Art—Intermediate
6. Primary Poster Art—Primary
7. Lettering as Part of a Composition—Intermediate
8. Different Typeface Used as Texture and Value—Intermediate
9. Calligraphy—Intermediate
10. Illumination—Intermediate

chapter 5

Clay

1. Clay Modeling—Primary
2. Clay Castles—Intermediate
3. Dragons and Gargoyles—Primary
4. Clay Decoration—Primary
5. Pinch Pot—Primary
6. Clay Animal Bells—Primary
7. Connected Pinch Pots—Intermediate
8. Bottle—Intermediate
9. Coil Pot (method a)—Primary
10. Coil Pot (method b)—Intermediate
11. Container Coil Pot—Intermediate
12. Trivet—Primary
13. Clay Tiles—Intermediate
14. Mirror Frame—Intermediate
15. Coasters—Primary
16. Cylinder Seal—Intermediate
17. Slab Pot—Intermediate
18. Pocket Pot—Primary
19. Wind Chimes—Intermediate
20. Slab Clay Mask—Primary
21. Bells and Beads—Intermediate
22. Nonfiring Clay—Primary

chapter 6

Chalk/Oil pastels

1. Drawing with Chalk or Pastel—Primary
2. Charcoal with Pastel—Primary
3. Chalk or Pastel Textures—Primary
4. Wet Paper Chalk or Pastel Drawing—Primary
5. Chalk or Pastel Painting—Primary
6. Chalk/Pastel and Tempera Print—Primary

chapter 11

Paper and cardboard

1. Paper Textures
   (method a)—Intermediate
   (method b)—Primary
   (method c)—Primary
   (method d)—Primary
   (method e)—Intermediate
2. Matt Board—Cut and Peel—Intermediate
3. Cardboard Relief—Intermediate
4. Three-Dimensional Picture or Poster—Primary
5. Stabile—Intermediate
6. Colored Tissue Paper—Primary
7. Pierced Paper—Intermediate
8. Colored Tissue Transparent Discs—Intermediate
9. Geometric Design—Primary
10. Corrugated Cardboard
    (method a)—Primary
    (method b)—Intermediate
    (method c)—Primary
11. Cut Paper Design—Intermediate
12. Paper Quilling
    (method a)—Intermediate
    (method b)—Intermediate
    (method c)—Primary
13. Paper Mosaic—Intermediate
14. Distance Silhouette—Intermediate
15. Cut Paper Rubbings—Primary
16. Torn Paper Picture—Primary
17. Paper Script Design—Intermediate
18. Positive and Negative Design
    (method a)—Primary
    (method b)—Intermediate
19. Paper Mola—Intermediate
20. Swirl Paper—Intermediate

chapter 12

Papier-mâché

1. Papier-Mâché Bowl—Intermediate
2. Papier-Mâché Jewelry—Intermediate
3. Papier-Mâché over Balloon—Primary
4. Piñata—Primary
5. Papier-Mâché over Bottle—Primary
6. Papier-Mâché Pulp Objects—Primary
7. Papier-Mâché over a Frame—Primary

chapter 13

Prints and stencils

1. Blottos—Primary
2. Pulled String Design—Primary
   Alternative—Primary
3. Finger Paint Monoprint—Primary
4. Paint Monoprint—Primary
5. Sandpaper Print—Primary
6. Stick Print—Primary
7. Insulation Print—Primary
8. Potato Print—Primary
9. Paraffin or Soap Block Print—Intermediate
10. Collagraph—Primary
11. Collagraph using Cardboard or Rubber Block Print—Primary
12. Litho-Sketch Printing—Primary
13. Ink Pad Print—Primary
14. Styrofoam Stamp—Primary
15. String Stamp—Primary
16. Eraser Stamp—Intermediate
17. Glue Print—Primary
18. Styrofoam Prints—Primary
19. Printing Blocks—Intermediate
20. Wood Block Print—Intermediate
21. Reduction Blocks—Intermediate
22. Screen Print—Primary
23. Crayon or Oil Pastel Stencil—Primary
24. Stencil with Chalk—Primary
25. Spattered Stencil Design—Primary
26. Sprayed Stencil Design—Primary
27. Sponged Stencil Design—Primary
28. Stencil with Tempera—Primary
29. Textile Painting with Stencils—Intermediate

chapter 14

Sculpture

1. Paper Sculpture—Primary
2. Foil Sculpture—Primary
3. Paper Sculpture with Foil Sculpture—Primary
4. Stuffed Newspaper Sculpture—Primary
5. Kachina Dolls
   (method a)—Primary
   (method b)—Primary
6. Totem Poles
   (method a)—Primary
   (method b)—Primary

7. Shallow Shadow Box—Intermediate
8. Shadow and Peep Boxes—Shadow—Primary Peep—Intermediate
9. Folded Three-Dimensional Animals—Primary
10. Wooden Block People—Primary
11. Container Sculpture—Intermediate
12. Box Sculpture—Intermediate
13. Plaster Space Forms—Intermediate
14. Natural Object Sculpture—Primary
15. Salt and Flour Sculpture—Primary
16. Sawdust Sculpture—Primary
17. Soda and Cornstarch Structure—Primary
18. Sand Casting—Intermediate
19. Slotted Cardboard Structure—Intermediate
20. Folded Cube Design—Primary
21. Paper Cube Design—Intermediate
22. Triangular Room—Intermediate
23. Wire Sculpture—Primary
24. Soda Straw Construction—Intermediate
25. Toothpick Sculpture—Intermediate
26. Wood Scrap Sculpture—Primary
27. Mobiles—Primary
28. Plaster Wrap Figures—Primary
29. Plaster Wrap with an Armature—Intermediate
30. Plaster Block Carving—Intermediate
31. Cast Plaster Bas-Relief—Primary
32. Carved Plaster Bas-Relief—Intermediate
33. Bas-Relief with Cardboard—Intermediate
34. Bas-Relief with Plaster Wrap—Intermediate
35. Bas-Relief with Crayola Model Magic®—Primary

chapter 15

Fibers

1. Paper Weaving—Primary
2. Straw Weaving—Primary
3. Backstrap Loom Weaving—Intermediate
4. Cardboard Loom Weaving—Primary Round Cardboard Loom—Intermediate
5. Tapestry—Primary
6. God's Eye—Ojo de Dios—Primary
7. Coiling—Intermediate
8. Cotton Roving—Primary
9. Stitchery
    (method a)—Intermediate
    (method b)—Intermediate
10. Appliqué—Intermediate
11. Appliqué with Glue—Primary

12. Felt Picture—Primary
13. Felt Mola—Intermediate
14. Tie and Dye—Intermediate
15. Melted Crayon Batik and Print—Intermediate
16. Batik—Intermediate
17. Silk Painting—Intermediate

chapter 16

Masks and puppets

1. Cardboard Build-Up Mask—Intermediate
2. Paper Bag Mask—Primary
3. Stocking Handheld Mask—Primary
4. Paper Plate Mask
    Mask with Peek Holes and Nose Flap—Primary
    Handheld Paper Mask—Primary
    Two-Faced Mask or Puppet—Primary
5. Papier-Mâché or Plaster Wrap Mask—Intermediate
6. Direct Body Casting—Intermediate
7. Cardboard and Paper Mask
    (method a)—Primary
    (method b)—Primary
8. Helmet Mask
    (method a)—Intermediate
    (method b)—Intermediate
    (method c)—Intermediate
9. Paper and Cloth Finger Puppet
    (method a)—Primary
    (method b)—Primary
    (method c)—Primary
10. Paper Bag Puppet—Primary
11. Jacob's Ladder—Primary
12. Paper Bag Puppet on a Stick—Primary
13. Felt Hand Puppet—Primary
14. Papier-Mâché or Plaster Wrap Puppet Head
    (method a)—Primary
    (method b)—Primary
    (method c)—Primary
15. Jumping Jacks—Primary
16. Shadow Puppet—Primary
17. Simple Marionette
    (method a)—Primary
    (method b)—Primary
18. Cardboard Cylinder Rod Puppet—Primary
19. Simple Rod Puppet—Primary
20. Simple Mouth Puppet—Primary
21. Foam Mouth Puppet—Intermediate

glossary

abstract art   Art that departs from appearances to varying degrees; involves simplification or rearrangement.

acrylic   Polymers used to produce synthetic rubbers and lightweight plastics. It has been applied to the art field in developing a quick-drying medium for painting.

aerial perspective   The illusion of deep space made by lightening values, softening details and textures, reducing contrasts, and neutralizing colors in objects as they recede.

aesthetics   Critiquing the nature of pleasing qualities in art. The study of sensitivity to art forms.

appliqué   Work applied to, or laid on, another material.

ascender   The vertical trunk of a lowercase (noncapital) letter that rises above its body.

balance, formal   Similar or identical images and/or art elements given similar or identical placement on either side of the axis of the artwork.

balance informal   Dissimilar elements or images given dissimilar placement so that an effect of balance is felt.

beater   Tool to push the weft tight.

block print   A print made by lifting off (usually with paper) the ink applied to the uncut areas of a surface (such as wood or linoleum block); a relief print.

blotto   Am image that is duplicated by repeating itself in a symmetrical manner; one side of a sheet of paper is painted and the paper is folded while the paint is wet.

brayer   A roller used to spread ink over a printing surface.

calligraphy   Beautiful and/or decorative writing.

casting   The cast is the product that is freed from the mold. *See Mold.*

ceramics   Usually, though not always, pottery vessels originally made of clay, then fired for permanence.

chain stitch   An ornamental stitch in which each stitch forms a loop through the forward end of which the next stitch is taken.

clay   Viscous Earth which, when combined with water, forms a sticky paste that may be modeled and allowed to harden. Used by ceramists and sculptors. When combined with oil, is used as plastilene.

coiling   A fiber wrap technique arranging rings that lie side by side.

collage   An arrangement of objects and materials adhered to a surface (usually a canvas), sometimes as a supplement to drawn or painted surfaces.

collagraphic   Derives from collage. Usually a work printed on a press from a plate constructed from adhered elements.

collé   An image created by pieces of paper that are adhered to a surface, often abetted by drawn or painted passages.

color   Our response to wavelengths of light, such as red green, blue, and so on.

complementary colors   Hues opposite each other on the color wheel.

composition   Arrangements of the art elements and their resultant images.

cone   An elongated pyramidal object made of a substance that will cause it to droop at a prearranged temperature. Used in kilns for firing ceramic objects.

contour   The edge of a drawn or painted object as defined by a line or the outline of a painted area.

crackle effect   Created when a paper or cloth coated with wax and crumpled is dipped in a darker dye or painted with a darker color. The dye or paint will soak into the cracks and show as dark lines with wax removal.

descender   The vertical trunk of a lowercase (noncapital) letter that sinks below its body.

design   A framework or scheme of pictorial composition. The arrangement and handling of the art elements.

Egyptian knot   The weft encircles each warp. It passes over the warp and loops behind it and over itself in front.

element   In art, a line, a shape, an area of light or dark texture, or a color.

emboss The producing of protuberances in a planar surface, usually by pressing down the portions between those areas to create a relieflike appearance. *See Relief.*

encaustic A painting medium using colored pigments mixed with molten wax and applied to the painting surface.

engobe A white or colored coating of clay used to cover pottery, usually for decoration or to aid adhesion of glaze or enamel to the surface of the pottery.

etching Printmaking by eating into portions of a plate with acid. Creating an image by scratching through an acid-resistant ground exposing it to the acid. An intaglio process.

expression The manner in which artists try to say something about themselves, their time, a situation, and/or their environment. They are said to be "expressing" themselves.

fixative (Fixatif) A clear, fast-drying liquid substance that is sprayed on delicate artworks to protect them. May use a pressurized can or atomizer. Hair spray is sometimes used.

form The total appearance and organization of the visual elements.

fringing Ornamental bordering having projecting lengths of thread or cord, loosely or variously arranged or combined.

geometric Shapes deriving from geometry, such as squares, circles, triangles, and so forth.

gesso Plaster or gypsum mixed with water and applied to a surface to serve as a ground for painting.

Ghiordes knots Made with cut pieces of yarn. Creates a raised pile.

glaze A substance that becomes vitreous at a certain temperature and provides a watertight glossy (usually) and colorful (often) coating for ceramic articles.

God's eye A craft from Mexico in which yarn is wrapped around crossed sticks or metal arms to make a decoration.

Gothic An artistic style of the Middle Ages, or a style of typography and calligraphy.

gouache A type of opaque watercolor. A pliable adhesive is sometimes added for softness and slower drying.

harmony Related elements; the repetition of similar characteristics. A sense of belonging together.

heddle Parallel wires, string or stick that compose the harness to raise and lower the warp threads in a loom.

horizontal Movement from right to left or left to right; straight across.

hue The common name for color.

illumination Most often associated with the artwork on the pages of books of the Middle Ages. These served to clarify and embellish the text.

impressionism A style of somewhat realistic artwork, largely based on the varying effects of light.

incise Cutting into a surface, usually in a linear manner. Clay may be incised as a decorative or definite effect.

inlay The imbedding of a substance in a material of a different character.

intaglio A printing process. (See Chapter on printing.)

kachina Figures created by Native Americans of the Southwest to represent ancestral spirits.

kiln A furnace serviced with various fuels, most often used in ceramics to fire clay or other substances to make them long lasting.

lamination The adhering of relatively flat, thin materials and ordinarily employing several thicknesses.

latex A semirubberized, water-soluble, and relatively quick-drying paint.

line The path of a moving point.

linear perspective A system, developed in the Renaissance, that suggests space by directing parallel lines or edges toward a common point.

loom A weaving device through which yarn or thread is made into fabric by crossing the strands known as *warp* and *weft.*

lowercase Those letters of the alphabet that are noncapitals; also called *miniscules.*

manipulate Handling of objects for a particular purpose, such as to gain acquaintance with them or to use them in the mastery of some problem or technique.

maraca Latin American noisemaker used in rhythm sections of musical groups; gourds are often used.

marionette A puppet moved by strings.

mat A piece of cardboard or paper surrounding and setting off a work of art or document; often inside a frame.

mobile A sculpture piece made by suspending pieces from supporting arms so that they can move with currents of air. Popularized by Alexander Calder.

mola   A reverse appliqué.

mold (mould)   A hollow form into which a liquid or plastic material is poured or pressed and allowed to harden, taking the reverse shape of the interior surface. Duplicate casts can be made from certain types of molds. *See Casts.*

monoprint   A print in which the image is created on a smooth surface with liquid media. Paper is pressed over this, duplicating the image. Means *one of a kind,* hence the term *monoprint.*

mosaic   A technique in which small (usually colored) stones (tesserae) are pressed into cement to form an image.

mottle   Producing a patterned appearance with spots or blemishes.

naturalistic art   Art which attempts to reproduce the exnature of things seen.

nearikas   Yarn paintings made by the Huichol people of Mexico.

neoclassicism   A style strongly influenced by the works of ancient Greece and Rome.

oxidize   Oxides on metal will form on the exposure to the atmosphere, resulting in a darkened appearance; may be artificially induced by chemicals.

papier-mâché   Paper ground up or cut into strips and mixed with a gelatinous material such as glue or paste so that it can be molded into desired shapes that are retained as it dries.

Paris craft   Gauze impregnated with plaster of Paris. Plastr' craft or plaster fabric are names for the same material.

piñata   A papier-mâché form filled with candy and covered with tissue or crepe. Common in Mexico and Central America.

plaster   Sulphate of lime and gypsum. Used in a powdered form and mixed with water. After mixing, the plaster dries and hardens. Used by ceramicists, sculptors, dentists, and contractors. Comes in various grades.

plastilene   Oil-based modeling clay.

pointillism   A technique of paint application in dots or small swatches. The colors often produce a visual blending.

polymer   A natural or synthetic chemical compound or mixture of compounds formed by polymerization. This compound is used in the manufacture of a number of art products, such as polymer, tempera, and modeling paste.

polyurethane foam   A type of flexible foam used in upholstery and as carpet padding.

positive-negative   An art image, usually made with paper and scissors, in which the void, or cutout shapes, are joined to the positive, or shapes that have been removed, to create a symmetrical design.

postimpressionism   A style of art following impressionism that tries to restore a more expressive meaning to art.

pot   A vessel, usually made of clay, allowed to dry or fired in a kiln.

   Pinch pot   A vessel constructed by the pinching together of clay particles.

   Slab pot   A vessel constructed by adhering slabs of clay to form its side and base.

   Coil pot   A vessel built up from coils (rounded strips) of clay.

print   A multiple original artwork on paper that comes into direct contact with an image-bearing surface in such a way that the image is transferred to the paper. Prints are produced by the intaglio, relief, lithographic, or serigraphic processes.

quilling   A ribbon, strip of lace, and so on, pleated into small cylindrical folds resembling a row of quills.

realism   A form of artistic expression, or style, that retains the basic impression of visual observance, but often also attempts to relate and interpret the meanings that lie beneath surface appearances. Approximates camera vision (pure camera vision is naturalism).

reed   The tall straight stem of a weed.

relief   1. The elevation or projection of a design from a flat surface to create the effect of volumes in space. 2. Relief printing is a print made by drawing ink from a raised surface (such as a wood block).

repoussé   The art of ornamenting metal by making a pattern in relief.

resist   A material that protects against a chemical or physical action, or fails to be dissolved or penetrated by another material. Used as a *block-out* by artists who protect the original or subsequent color of a surface from a newly applied one.

romanticism   An art style which includes experiment, spontaneity, intuition, and picturesque work.

rya knot   The weft passes over a stick as it passes over and between the warps. The length of the loop depends on the stick used. Raised pile.

shape   An area with defined or implied boundaries.

shuttle   A device used in weaving to pass the thread of the weft.

Soumak knot   The weft encircles each warp. It passes under the warp and loops over the front and crosses itself behind the warp.

space (in art)   1. The illusion of distance between elements or images in two-dimensional work. 2. The area surrounding a three-dimensional work of art.

spectrum   Hues (colors) produced when light is broken into different wavelengths as in a prism or rainbow.

stabile   A sculpture that is often similar to the mobiles invented by Alexander Calcer, except that they are stationary rather than in movement.

stencil   A surface or material that prohibits the passage of ink or paint except where areas are left open. Used widely in screen printing or serigraphy.

stippling   Creating images by means of dots rather than lines.

subject   1. Persons or things portrayed in artwork. 2. The theme of an artwork. 3. Visual signs employed by the artist.

symbolic stage   Representing a quality, situation, or object with another object, emblem, or sign.

tapestry   Handweaving that has pictorial designs.

tempera   A painting medium in which pigments are combined with casein or skin glue. It is nonreflective as opposed to oil paint.

texture   The characteristics of a surface, such as degree of roughness or smoothness.

tonal   The appearance of lightness or darkness (value).

tortillon   Wrapped paper blending stick for art media. Also called *stump.*

totem pole   A column of cedar wood carved with totemic symbols.

translucent   Limited transparency through which things can be seen, but indistinctly.

unity   A compatible balance between harmony and variety.

uppercase   Capital letters of the alphabet, also called *majuscules.*

value   Degrees of lightness or darkness.

variety   Differences achieved by opposing, contrasting, and changing elements to create interest.

vermiculite   A free-flowing material normally used for insulation and as a landscaping material.

vertical   In art, the element that moves from bottom to top or top to bottom.

warp   A strand or filament moving in a certain direction that is usually at right angles to another (the weft).

wash   A highly diluted, liquid application of color, usually over a broad area. Often thought of in watercolor.

watercolor   A painting medium for which water is the vehicle; most watercolor paintings are characterized by their transparency.

wedge   As a verb, wedging is the act of using a taut wire for slicing chunks of clay which are later reassembled. This is done in order to render the clay more homogenous and to eliminate air bubbles that could cause the clay to shatter if fired.

weft   A strand or strands of fabric moving in a certain direction, usually at right angles to the warp. *See Warp.*

whiting   A finely powdered chalk that has been ground, washed, and refined. It is widely used in the arts for painting, printmaking, and sculpture.

chronologies

A chronology of Western art (beginning with Greece)

750 B.C.	**Greece**	Archaic age. Sculpture, pottery
470 B.C.		Classical age. Architecture, painting, sculpture
330 B.C.		Ptolemaic age (Egypt)
320 B.C.		Hellenistic age
280 B.C.	**Rome**	Sculpture, architecture, painting, minor arts
140 B.C.		Graeco-Roman art
30 B.C.-A.D.146		Imperial Rome
100 A.D.		Late imperial Rome and early Christian
300 A.D.	**Medieval Art**	Middle East, *Early Byzantine art;* Egypt, *Coptic art.*
330		*Early Christian art* in western Europe, decline of Rome.
400		Migratory, barbarian arts (Celts, Saxons, Vikings, Huns, Goths).
550		*Muslim* or *Islamic art,* northern Africa, southern Spain (*Moorish art*).
768		*Carolingian art,* France, Germany, northern Italy.
800		*Developed Byzantine art,* Middle East, Greece, Russia, parts of Italy (Venice, Ravenna, Rome, Sicily).
900		*Ottonian art*—mostly in Germany.
1000		*Romanesque art* (Roman-like or modified Roman art in France, England, northern Spain, Italy, and Germany).
1150		*Gothic art* in Europe.
1300	**Renaissance Art**	*Proto-Renaissance,* Italy: Giotto, Duccio, Nicolo Pisano (sculpture).
1400		*Early Renaissance,* Italy: Masaccio, Donatello, Francesca, Leonardo, and so on. Renaissance in West modified by vestiges of Medievalism: van Eyck, Weyden, van der Goes, etc.
1500		*High Renaissance:* Michelangelo, Raphael, Titian, Tintoretto; western Europe influenced by Italy.
1520		*Mannerism and Early Baroque,* Italy: Caravaggio.
1600	**Baroque Art**	*Baroque art* in Europe: Rubens, Van Dyck, Rembrandt, Hals (Netherlands); Velásquez, Ribera (Spain); Poussin, Lorrain (France); Bernini (sculpture, Italy).*Early Colonial art,* Americas,
1700		*Rococo art,* primarily French: Watteau, Boucher, Fragonard, Chardin; but spreads to other European countries: Canaletto, Guardi, Tiepolo (Italy); Hogarth, Gainsborough, Reynolds (England). *Colonial art,* Americas.

1800	**Nineteenth-century Art**	*Neoclassicism:* David, Ingres (France); Canova (sculpture, Italy).
1820		*Romanticism:* Gericault, Delacroix (France); Goya (Spain); Turner (England); Ryder (United States); Barye (sculpture, France).
1850		*Realism* and *Naturalism:* Daumier, Courbet, Manet (France); Homer, Eakins (United States); Constable (England)
1870		*Impressionism:* Monet, Pissarro, Renoir, Degas (France); Sisley (England); Hassam, Twachtman (United States); Medardo-Rosso (sculpture, Italy); Rodin (sculpture, France).
1880		*Postimpressionism:* Cézanne, Seurat, Gauguin, Van Gogh, Toulouse-Lautrec (France).
1900	**Twentieth-century Art**	Sculptors working in a *Postimpressionist* manner: Maillol (France); Lachaise (United States); Lehmbruck, Marcks, Kolbe (Germany).
1901		*Expressionism:* Picasso* (Blue, Rose, and Negro periods).
		Les Fauves: Matisse, Rouault, Vlaminck, Modigliani, Dufy, Utrillo (France).
		Recent *French Expressionists:* (1930) Soutine, Buffet, Balthus.
		German Expressionists: Nolde, Kirchner, Kokoschka, Schmidt-Rotluff, Marc, Jawlensky, Macke, Beckmann, Grosz, Dix; Munch (Norway).
		American Expressionists: Weber, Shahn, Levine, Avery, Baskin; Orozoco (Mexico).
		Sculpture: Marini (Italy); Epstein (England); Zorach (United States).
1906	**Abstract Art (early phase)**	*Cubism:* Picasso*, Braque, Léger, Gris (France); Laurens (sculpture, France).
		Futurism: Balla, Boccioni (sculpture and painting), Carra, Severini (Italy).
1910–50		*Developed Abstract and Nonobjective art:*
		Kandinsky, Albers (Germany); Moholy-Nagy (Hungary); *Constructivism:* Larionov, Malevich, Tatlin (Russia); Delaunay (France); Nicholson (England); *DeStijl:* Mondrian, Van Doesburg, Van Tongerloo (Holland); Dove, Marin, Feininger, Frank Stella, O'Keeffe, MacDonald-Wright, Stuart Davis, Demuth, Hartley, Knaths, Diller, Pereira, MacIver, Tomlin, Rothko (United States).
		Sculpture: Brancusi, Archipenko, Arp (France); Epstein, Passmore (England); de Rivera, Nevelson, Hajdu, Noguchi (United States); Gabo, Pevsner (Russian-Constructivists, United States).
ca. 1910	**Fantasy in Art**	*Individual fantasists:* Henri Rousseau (French primitive); de Chirico (Italy); Chagall (France); Klee (Switzerland/Germany).
1914		*Dada:* Tzara, Duchamp, Picabia, Arp (France); Ernst, Schwitters (Germany).
1924		*Surrealism:* Ernst (Germany); Delvaux, Masson (France); Dali (Spain, United States); Magritte (Belgium); Bacon (England).
1925		*Sculpture:* Giacometti (Switzerland); González (Spain); Arp (France).
		Surrealistic Abstraction: Picasso* (France); Miró (Spain); Tamayo (Mexico); Matta (Chile, United States); Baziotes, Tobey, Gorky, Rothko, Hofmann, DeKooning (United States).
		Sculpture: Moore, Hepworth (England); Lipchitz (Lithuania, United States, France); Calder (United States).

*Artists frequently change their styles, thus some names may appear under more than one category of form-style. Most notable in this respect is Pablo Ruiz Picasso.

1930–40	**Traditional Realism**	*Regionalists:* John Sloan, Grant Wood, Thomas Hart Benton (United States); Andrew Wyeth (independent realist, United States).
1945	**Post-World War II Trends**	*Abstract Expressionism* and *Action painting.* Pollock, Motherwell, Kline, Still, Reinhardt, Frankenthaler, Tworkov, Holty, Rothko (United States); Mathieu, Soulages, Manessier (France); Vieira da Silva (Portugal); de Stael, Appel (Holland); Okada (Japan): Tapies (Spain). *Sculpture;* Roszak, David Smith, Lipton, Lassaw, Lippold, Nakian (United States); Richier (France).
1950	**Post-Painterly Abstraction**	*Color Field* and *Hard-Edge* painters (all United States): Louis, Newman, Kelly Noland, Stella, Poons, Ron Davis. *Minimalists:* Olitsky Reinhardt (United States); Yves Klein (France). *Sculpture:* Judd, Tony Smith, Rosenthal, Andre (United States). *Primary-Structurists* (some called *Neo-Constructivists* and/or *Environmentalists*): Bontecou, Di Suvero, Nevelson, Bell, Stone, de Witt, Meadmore, Kipp, Katzen, Snelson, Rickey (United States): Paolozzi, King (England); Bill (Switzerland).
1955		*Neo-Dada* and *Funk art* (collage-assemblage): Johns, Rauschenberg (United States); Dubuffet (France). *Sculpture:* Kienholz, Stankiewicz, Mallary, Chamberlain (United States); César (France). *Pop art* and *Happenings:* Warhol, Lichtenstein, Dine, Indiana, Kaprow, Oldenburg, Segal, Grooms, Marisol, Wesselman, Rosenquist (United States); Hamilton, Kitaj, Smith (England). *Op art:* Vasarely (France); Anuskiewicz, Ortmann, Stanczak (United States); Agam (Israel); Riley, Denny (England).
1965–80		*New Realism:* Pearlstein, Ramos, Katz, Theibaud, Lindner, Close, Cottingham, Estes (United States). *Sculpture:* Gallo, de Andrea, Hanson (United States). *Technological art* (kinetics, neon, sound): Wolfert (color organ, 1930–63); Tinguely (Switzerland, United States); Chryssa (Greece); Samaris, Sonnier, Riegack, Flavin, Rickey (United States); Hess (Germany, United States); Soto (Venezuela); Castro-Cid (Chile); Le Parc (Argentina); Takis (Greece). *Environments, Land art,* or *Earthworks; Process and Conceptual art:* Lansman, Andre, Christo, Smithson, Serra, Lewitt, Heizer, Oldenburg, Kipp, Di Suvero; Katzen, Snelson, Rickey, Woody, Nauman (United States): Beuys, Kiefer (Germany).
1980–96		*Neo-Expressionism;* Schnabel (United States); Cucchi, Chia (Italy); Penck, Kiefer, Baselitz (Germany).
1980—		*Other artists, irrespective of style, who have created significant artworks since 1980 (some may be repeats):* Chuck Close, Duane Hanson, John De Andrea, Philip Pearlstein, Janet Fish, Miriam Schapiro, Joyce Kozloff, Pat Steir, Georg Baselitz, A. R. Penck, David Salle, Eric Fischl, Leon Golub, Richard Long.

A chronology of non-Western art

This section is included as diversion from geographically familiar art and to mark the breadth and depth of the creative spark. An attempt to be exhaustive would be suicidal for the authors; only truly significant art forms are noted and all regions are not covered. Dates are very general (c. for "circa"—approximate). The earliest dates indicate that art products have been found from periods when human beings first found refuge and the security and time to produce those works.

Schoolroom displays of exotic works from ancient and distant cultures may replace a provincial outlook with a worldview.

c. 500,000–12,000 B.C. c. 12,000 B.C.–circa	**Paleolithic Period**	Crude fetishes, utility instruments, cave paintings
7,000 B.C.	**Neolithic Period**	Tombs, sculpture, pottery
	Egypt	Pyramids, architecture, painting, sculpture, pottery, minor arts
3000 B.C.	Old Kingdom	
1500 B.C.	New Kingdom	
	Mesopotamia	Primarily architecture, sculpture
2850–1900 B.C.	Sumerian	
1600–1143 B.C.	Babylonian	
883–c. 745 B.C.	Assyria	
550–336 B.C.	Persia (Iran)	
	Aegean or Minoan	Architecture, fresco paintings, pottery
3000–1100 B.C.	**India**	Sculpture, painting, pottery, minor arts
3300–1500 B.C.	Dravidian	
1500–660 B.C.	Aryan	
650–300 B.C.	Saisumega/Nanda	
300–200 B.C.	Mauryan	
200 B.C.–A.D. 1	Sunga	
A.D. 1–300	Kushana, later Andra	
A.D. 1–400	Gandara	
A.D. 300–600	Gupta	
	China	Architecture, sculpture, painting, pottery, fabrics
3000–2205 B.C.	Patriarchal	
2205–1766 B.C.	Hsia dynasty	
1766–1122 B.C.	Shang	
1122–255 B.C.	Chou	
255–206 B.C.	Ch'in	
206 B.C.–221 A.D.	Han	
A.D. 221–265	3 states	
265–618	6 dynasties	
618–907	T'ang	
13th–14th centuries	Yuan	
14th–17th centuries	Ming	
17th–20th centuries	Ch'ing	

	Japan	Architecture, painting, fabrics, sculpture, minor arts
A.D. 645–710	Mahayana Buddhism	
710–794	Nara	
794–897	Jogan	
897–1192	Yamato Ye	
1336–1603	Zen (Ashikaga)	
1603–1868	Tokugawa (Ukiyoye)	
	Mohammedan/Muslim	(Saracenic) Architecture, calligraphy, nonfigurative painting, textiles, ceramics, mosaics
A.D. 700–present	**Egypt, Constantinople, Asia Minor, Persia, India, Spain**	
	Africa	
3900 B.C.–A.D.	1500 Nubia (Egyptian influence)	
	"A" Group	Minor arts
2300 B.C.	**"B" Group**	Sculpture, painting, minor arts
11th–12th centuries B.C.		Kush Architecture, sculpture
1500 B.C.–A.D. 1500	**West Africa**	Sierra Leone, Dahomey, Senegal, Mali, Ghana, Benin, Ife Bronze, copper, brass sculpture, minor arts
A.D. 100–1500	Bantu, Congo, East coast, Zimbabwe, and Swahili	Swahili and Zimbabwe—iron, copper, brass casting, architecture, sculpture
	Oceanian	(Pacific) Assembled and painted masks, pottery Migrations from South East Asia began about A.D. 400 Nearer islands (Indonesia), then New Guinea, Australia (Melanesian), Micronesia, and Polynesia
	Native American	Art varies with sites
A.D. 1–1600	Mayan and Aztec art of Yucatan, Honduras, Mexico	Inca art of Peru Prehistoric and historic art of the Southwest, the Plains, Pacific coast, and Eskimos

index